Socialists, Socialites, and Sociopaths

Socialists, Socialites, and Sociopaths

Plays and Screenplays
by Frank Tuttle

Edited,
with an Introduction,
by John Franceschina

BearManorMedia.com

Copyright © 2007 by The Frank Tuttle Estate
Introduction copyright © 2007 by John Franceschina
All rights reserved.

Published by:

Bear Manor Media
PO Box 71426
Albany GA 31707

www.bearmanormedia.com

Book Design by Leila Joiner

Printed in the United States of America on acid-free paper

ISBN 978-1-59393-079-0
ISBN 1-59393-079-8

Contents

Introduction 7

The Merry Ha Ha 17

Bet Your Life 83

Head over Heels 157

Falling Star 255

Introduction

Socialists, Socialites, and Sociopaths is a quartet of plays and screenplays written by Frank Tuttle between film directing assignments during the last twenty-five years of his life. Even more than his autobiography, *They Started Talking*, Tuttle's original plays reveal the wit and imagination that made him one of Hollywood's most sought after (if often underrated) directors of the 1920s and 30s.[1] In addition the plays and screenplays provide vibrant behind-the-scenes views of the many facets of the entertainment industry as well as an honest portrayal of how politics and show business intersect, with Tuttle's pacifist and socialist political views emerging loud and clear from the plays, though more subtly from the screenplays.

THE MERRY HA HA

The Merry Ha Ha was registered for copyright on 20 March 1939, in between the release of two major directing assignments: a Bing Crosby musical for Paramount Pictures, *Paris Honeymoon*,[2] on 27 January, and a George Raft crime melodrama for Universal, *I Stole a Million*, on 21 July.[3] By the end of the year, Tuttle would add another film to his résumé, a comedy whodunit for Universal, *Charlie McCarthy, Detective*, for which production began late in November with a scheduled release date of 22 December. The play evokes the spirit of Tuttle's 1939 films, borrowing the

---

[1] Although the FBI rated Tuttle in the 1920s as a film director in the same class as Cecil B. De Mille, Richard Koszarski in *Hollywood Directors 1914-1940* echoes the typical critical appraisal when he introduces Tuttle as "a director of some skill who showed occasional flashes of talent, but for the greater part of his career he buried himself in irredeemable studio assignments." Although he "still maintained hopes of creating something not merely artistic, but 'meaningful,' ... Tuttle had neither the talent nor the clout to achieve his aims." In *The Parade's Gone By*, however, Kevin Brownlow names Tuttle along with Chaplin, Lubitsch, and Mal St. Clair as directors whose light touch managed to diffuse the overbearing "curse" of melodrama in the movies (304).
[2] In his autobiography, *They Started Talking*, Tuttle notes that the completion of *Paris Honeymoon* coincided with the end of his Paramount contract. Because of his desire not to be associated only with musical films, Tuttle decided not to renew his contract with the studio.
[3] Two weeks after the copyright registration, the *New York Times* (4 April 1939) announced that Frank Tuttle had replaced Edward Ludwig on the project which began as a film treatment of the life of the historical mail bandit Roy Gardner. Production began six weeks later on 24 May.

sophisticated lifestyle and comedy of *Paris Honeymoon*, a noir-ish potential for violence and melodramatic heroism from *I Stole a Million*, and a reference to a ventriloquist's dummy on radio (Smarty Kelly in the play), an open allusion to *The Charlie McCarthy Show*, a weekly variety series that aired on NBC beginning in 1937. In addition, *The Merry Ha Ha* reflects the anti-Fascist attitude Tuttle described in an article published by *TAC* in June, 1939:

> Hollywood has suffered many a foul gust from Kaiser Adolf and his gang of cut-throats, but the wind has changed ... it blows from Hollywood now, and the first hurricane to strike Berlin and Rome and even Tokyo is going to be *School for Barbarians*.[4] That old wind might even blow down a few of those little Brown Houses that are messing up our American landscape just now.[5]

Most interesting is how the play anticipates Tuttle's own experience with the leadership of the American Communist Party. The plot of *The Merry Ha Ha* turns on the attempts of politicians and businessmen to strong-arm a film and radio personality into making the "right" decision politically, even though he may have to perjure himself in the process. On 24 May 1951, Tuttle appeared before the House Committee on Un-American Activities and gave testimony to his experience:

> When I was in New York ... my present wife answered the telephone one day and a functionary of the New York branch [of the Arts, Sciences, and Professions organization] was asking me to sign a telegram of protest to the American State Department

---

[4] *School for Barbarians* was a film based on the 1938 book by Erika Mann about education in Nazi Germany and scheduled for production in the summer of 1939.
[5] Tuttle's sentiments are echoed in Michael Elkins's essay, "Some Shocking Facts about Hollywood" published in the November 1939 issue of *TAC*. Elkins, a special investigator for the Hollywood Anti-Nazi League, reported on the 12 October 1939 "emergency meeting" of the organization called by Virginia Bruce, Edward Chodorov, H.S. Kraft, Wells Root, J. Walter Ruben, and Jo Swerling, and attended by Harold Arlen, John Carradine, Eric Korngold, Dudley Nichols, Robert Rossen, Harlan Thompson, Erika Mann, Ira Gershwin, and Frank Tuttle (among others).

for refusing to allow certain people to enter this country who were supposed to participate in a peace conference.

I asked my wife to ask the functionary who was talking on the telephone please to give me the history of some of these people who had been refused, because I didn't know if I agreed or did not agree that permission should be refused.

The functionary was very nasty and said I should accept the explanation of the committee at its face value and not question it, and should automatically lend my name. I was very angry and refused to lend my name, . . . and I shall not forget my reaction at the time I hung up. I remember thinking, very, very definitely, "Well, I have reassumed a very sacred right of Americans to think for themselves," and I realized I had lost that right while I had been a Communist.[6]

Bet Your Life

In 1940, while Tuttle was on the lookout for another film project (the one that would become one of his most famous films, *This Gun for Hire*), he completed work on *Bet Your Life*, a play about Hollywood stunt men, a group of performers of whom he was especially fond. Not surprisingly, several of the stunt sequences in the play were inspired by Tuttle's own experiences: the train stunt in act one evoked a particularly hair-raising experience during the filming of *Dude Ranch* in which an oncoming express train smashes a wagon—but just in time for the hero to be knocked out and land safely. Although the stunt man, Billy Jones, had been warned not to delay his dive from the wagon since the train would be running at 35 miles per hour, he chose to add an extra element of danger to the stunt. In his autobiography, Tuttle recalled:

> Billy was wearing black sneakers instead of shoes to give himself a surer takeoff. When the train was about thirty-five feet away, he decided to give his watching friends an extra thrill. Out of camera range, he bent over and tied his right shoelace. Then he

---

[6] *Communist Infiltration of Hollywood Motion-Picture Industry—Part 3: Hearings before the Committee on Un-American Activities, House of Representatives, Eighty-Second Congress, First Session.* 24 May 1951, 643-644.

dived. I have a still picture of the locomotive smashing into the wagon. *Billy's body is still in the air!*[7]

The scene in which a temporarily blinded stunt man performs a dangerous fight sequence was inspired by the story of Jack Holbrook, who was hired to do a fight on a bridge, even though his vision had been impaired temporarily due to blows to the head taken in performing a stunt weeks before. Because Holbrook needed the money to pay off a loan, he took the job and talked his friends into standing around him so that his blindness would not be noticed by the director and cameramen. As Tuttle suggests in the stage directions to a similar sequence in the play, Holbrook's friends whispered instructions to him on the platform to guide him from one mark to another. The stunt man threw punches, got hit, and fell off the bridge into a net—every action perfectly timed so that no one knew he was blind at the time.

The camaraderie among stunt men in the play is based on Tuttle's personal observations of the group at a party he threw at his home in the summer of 1931.

> I remember watching one of them conversing casually with his closest friend in a loveseat near the fireplace. To emphasize a point he picked up a poker and tapped his buddy on the shin. Pal Joey told him to quit. He kept right on tapping. The tappee extended his hand and shoved the lighted end of his cigarette into the poker-wielding fist. The tapping stopped.
>
> One of the stunt men was their patsy. He would risk his neck for a hundred bucks but he was not exactly the intellectual type. His playmates slipped a fistful of my best silver into his pocket. Later someone asked him for a cigarette. He reached into his pocket and came up with two spoons and a butter knife. They shook reproving fingers at him. How could he be such a miserable thief—and in the home of their amigo? He blushed and stammered. I just couldn't play straight, but even when I told him he'd been framed, he kept on apologizing. It took several minutes to snap him out of it.

---

[7] *They Started Talking* 80–81.

To break up the embarrassing moment, I urged everyone to wander out to the swimming pool and the lawn. What ensued was a series of nip-ups, pratfalls, collapsing human pyramids, and hundred and eights—stunt man slang for a somersault through the air. By the time the party was over, my sides ached from laughing.[8]

The anti-war tone of Tuttle's *Bet Your Life* echoes the spirit of many members of the entertainment community in 1940. A pictorial article, "Actors and War 1917–1939," published in *TAC* (November 1939) argued that, in 1917, show business personalities were betrayed by jingoism and dishonest propaganda into using their talents to recruit soldiers and raise money, becoming unwitting "accessories to the most murderous swindle of modern times." In 1939, however, the situation in the entertainment community is seen to be vastly different:

Midnight rallies, backstage parties, hurried plane trips to Washington before curtain call, voices for the millions over the radio, a reception for a leading member of the Negro race—this has provided the background for today's political independence by the American professional and artist. Actors have learned to speak their own lines; they have educated themselves to analyze carefully all issues, to look behind the propaganda in the controlled press and radio, to be willing to fight for honest democratic principles—even at the sacrifice of glamour and personal vanity. And they will not so easily be pawns for political and economic profiteers, who at this moment are again attempting to whip them into line for selling an old war (under new disguise) to the American people.[9]

On a lighter note, the malapropisms written into the character of Sol Herzog, the President of Phoenix Pictures, are not so subtle pokes at the "Goldwynisms" of Sam Goldwyn,[10] for whom Tuttle directed *Roman Scandals*. Unhappy with his working relationship with Goldwyn, Tuttle wrote: "For weeks after my job was finished, I avoided driving past the Goldwyn studio, because when I did drive by I was seized with an acute

---

[8] *They Started Talking* 81.
[9] *TAC*, November 1939, 12–13.
[10] Among the more notorious sayings attributed to Goldwyn are "Include me out," and "A verbal contract isn't worth the paper it's written on."

attack of nausea. If he remembers me at all, I am sure that Mr. Goldwyn will be delighted to hear this."[11]

HEAD OVER HEELS

Following the January 1947 release of *Swell Guy*, a post-war melodrama that Tuttle neglected to chronicle in his autobiography, he was in New York City working on *Head over Heels*, a "*Ball of Fire* meets *The Secret Life of Walter Mitty*" screenplay based on an original story by film and television actor Walter Brooke. In a letter dated 24 September 1948, Tuttle expressed an almost desperate need for the screenplay to be produced, suggesting that "[his] whole future may depend on this sale." A sense of desperation is not surprising. On 20 October 1947, the first day of the hearings before the House Committee on Un-American Activities, independent producer Sam Wood testified that John Cromwell, Irving Pichel, Edward Dmytryk, and Frank Tuttle had attempted to steer the Screen Directors Guild "into the red river" of Communism. A few months later, in the spring of 1948, Tuttle had married actress-model Carla Boehm and it was not a good time for the well of a steady income to suddenly run dry.[12] As Frank described in the September letter:

> The real problem at the moment is my lack of personal funds. My agent friends here are looking for directing and play-doctoring jobs in New York. I don't believe it will be possible to complete my financing and six weeks preparation [for *Head over Heels*] before some time in November. I would therefore take any quick job out [in Los Angeles] as long as it did not affect my status. So, if [you] see any flowers in the desert, pluck one for me.

The screenplay for *Head over Heels* was completed in August 1948 and immediately sent to Maurice King of King Bros. Productions.[13] In a

---

[11] *They Started Talking* 97. Goldwynisms are found throughout *The Merry Ha Ha* as well.

[12] In addition to fulfilling his financial obligations to two former wives and three children, Tuttle was faced with a new wife who was a confirmed alcoholic. Carla Henrietta Boehm had appeared, uncredited, in a handful of films in the early 1940s, one of which, *Hostages* (1943), had been directed by Frank Tuttle.

[13] It is clear that Tuttle was in a hurry to get the King Brothers onboard since he did not take the time to have the original script copied before he mailed it out. In

letter dated 23 August, Tuttle attempted to sell the producer on the project by dropping the names of the artists he hoped to hire: Joan Caulfield (then free from her contract with Paramount) was cast as the female lead, Dandy Lyon, Dennis O'Keefe and Barry Sullivan were in line for Larry, Roland Young was earmarked for Briggs, and John Carradine would be "an ideal Marko." In addition, Floyd Crosby, who had been the second unit cameraman on Tuttle's film *Dr. Rhythm* in 1938 and who had won the Academy Award for his work on Murnau's film *Tabu*, had agreed to film the movie.

On 26 August, Maurice King replied that the script had possibilities, "though of course it will need some revisions and additional work." He offered to produce the film and obtain a release through Allied Artists so long as there were "definite assurances . . . that the entire financing for the picture has been lined up." He went on to define "definite assurances" as "written commitments from a bank and/or other money source to show exactly how the picture is to be financed." Tuttle's response two days later indicated that he was on the trail of "bank and second money people," and noted that Vitalis ("Hi") Chalif, a lawyer and spokesman for United Artists was trying to convince Tuttle to release the film through United Artists. Chalif had suggested that many of the studios that are also releasing companies supply the completion money[14] for outside pictures and Tuttle inquired whether the same deal could be struck with Allied Artists.

In an attempt to cover his bases, Tuttle had also contacted James Nasser Productions about utilizing studio space for *Head over Heels* and the issue of completion money. On 1 September, James Nasser replied: "I would be very much interested in working out a deal with you for studio space at our studio. We do furnish completion bond under certain conditions and also defer part of the studio charges. However, the deferments and the furnishing of bonds are all dependent on the amount of cash advanced in the picture." The following day, Tuttle received a reply from Maurice King:

---

a later communication (2 September 1948), Maurice King makes a special note of the fact that "Under separate cover I am returning the screenplay—since it is the original I don't want it to become lost."

[14] Completion money guarantees that a motion picture will be completed, delivered on time, and within budget. If the film is not made, the completion money repays all of the money invested in the film by banks or individual investors.

> [P]lease understand that a deal with Allied Artists must be wholly financed, which means that Allied Artists will not supply the completion money or bond. Normally here, however, where a picture is shot on an independent lot (that is, a lot other than the one of the company releasing the picture), the studio at which the picture is shot in some cases supplies the completion bond.
>
> As to our deal with you, it would be on a 50–50 basis, that is, we would divide the producer's share of the net profits equally, you retaining your director's fee and we retaining our producer's fee.

Evidently Tuttle was dissatisfied with the proposed arrangement with Allied Artists, for on 3 September he signed an agreement with Hi Chalif authorizing him (and the law firm of Leon, Weill, and Mahony) to act as counsel for *Head over Heels* and to assist in the acquiring of the financing necessary for the production budgeted between $325,000 and $500,000. Chalif convinced Tuttle to produce the film on his own rather than split the profits with an established production company or studio and thus began a long walk uphill in search of money. None of the investors[15] approached came through with anything but interest in the project (it appears that there was genuine interest in the script), and *Head over Heels* was shelved while Tuttle left for Paris to direct *Time Running Out*.

Falling Star

The romantic comedy-melodrama, *Falling Star*, dates from 1957 when Frank Tuttle was in the employment of Alan Ladd's Jaguar Productions for which, the previous year, he had directed *A Cry in the Night* starring Natalie Wood, Edmond O'Brien, and Raymond Burr.[16] The allusion to the

---

[15] Among the investors approached were William Miesegaes, a millionaire Hollander who had initially approached Tuttle about producing *Head over Heels*. He ran out of money producing a non-commercial feature for Transfilm and was unable to fund the Tuttle project. Other private individuals who declined participation were Harold Lifton, the furniture magnate, Benjamin Cone (of Cohama Woolens), Jack Seidman, a theatrical producer, and Louis Heyman (of Schenley Distillers). It is likely, though difficult to discern with certainty, that Tuttle's being named in the HUAC hearings had a profound impact on his ability to raise money to produce the film.

[16] Much of Tuttle's work in the 1950s was associated with Alan Ladd: in 1954-1955, he directed Ladd in *Committed* and *Farewell to Kennedy*, two episodes of

Eisenhower Doctrine in shot 122 of *Falling Star* places the fictive time after January 1957 when the United States announced its policy of helping Middle Eastern countries combat the influence of Communism.

While working on *Falling Star*, Tuttle was involved in the preparation of several television projects for Jaguar, some details of which would be integrated into the new screenplay. The "Young Hopefuls" was a series idea designed for William Demarest who had appeared as Alan Ladd's detective sidekick in *Hell on Frisco Bay*. In the series Demarest was to play a retired actor and widower who had an old frame house in Hollywood and enough money to help talented young people get a start in show business. Chuck, the hero of the "Juvenile Delinquent" episode in the television series bears more than a casual resemblance to Johnny of the screenplay in the things he does and how he does them. Another television project, "Taxi," depicted a taxi driver who, in spite of his hard-boiled exterior, was an intellectual genius able to quote from Marcus Aurelius, Confucius, Spinoza, et al. (much like Johnny's ability to quote poetry in *Falling Star*). Like Jimmy Aquilina of *Bet Your Life*, the hero of this series would take rich drunks across the country in his taxicab and help them solve their problems.[17]

Unable to find the capital to produce *Falling Star*, Tuttle returned to directing the work of other authors, Jaguar Productions' *Island of Lost Women*, released April 1959, and Tuttle's final film. Almost exactly two years later, Tuttle directed a production of *The Floor of Heaven*, a play he co-authored with Allan Gruener, at the new Valley Theatre in Woodland Hills, California. Opening on 21 March 1961, the production, advertised as "prior to Broadway," boasted that Academy Award winner Edith Head was on board as "costume consultant." Even so, the play did not make it to New York City and, although Frank Tuttle continued to seek support for his original projects, he died on 6 January 1963 without seeing a production of any of the plays published in this collection.

---

the television series "General Electric Theatre," in addition to *Hell on Frisco Bay*, another film for Jaguar Productions that co-starred Edward G. Robinson.

[17] Although the television series were never made, Tuttle's ideas were not without merit. "Taxi" would become a popular series in the late 1970s and another of Tuttle's speculations, "The Lady is a Cop" would become "Police Woman" starring Angie Dickinson. A third idea, "The Magician," about a professional magician traveling all over the world who gets involved in all kinds of intrigues became "The Magician" starring Bill Bixby in 1973.

Although the texts of the plays and screenplays are presented here the way Tuttle wrote them with minor grammatical corrections (mostly for clarity) and punctuation regularized, the format (Tuttle's practice of centering the speaker's name above the text) has been adapted to accommodate spatial considerations.

The Merry Ha Ha

A Play in Three Acts

Characters

Phil Merry, the radio star
Esther Merry, his wife
Judith Gordon, Merry's secretary
Abe Kliegel, Merry's agent
Chatfield Martin, Merry's sponsor
Ruxton, Merry's butler
Togo, Merry's Japanese chauffeur
Sol Mintz,
Jack Farrell,
Al Hartman,
Harry Durkis,
George Petty, Merry's five writers
Larry Schultz, a make-up man
Jerry Mayo, an assistant director
Governor William Apperson Goodfellow
Frank Mace, union organizer
Harry Donovan, Mace's attorney
The Man (Mr. Smith)
Telegraph boy
Police detective
Deputy District Attorney
Court Judge
Clerk of the court
Court reporter
The Shadow of a man
Bailiffs
Policemen
Six chorines

Act One

Phil Merry's dressing room at World Wide Pictures. There are two windows at the right and an entrance door leading out to the lot. A door left center in the back wall leads to a smaller room and bath. The main room is vaguely modern in character. There is a poster on one of the walls advertising a World Wide picture starring Phil Merry, the radio star.

When the curtain rises, Judith Gordon, Merry's secretary, is taking dictation from one of five writers, Sol Mintz. A second writer, Jack Farrell, is picking pieces of paper out of the scrap basket, looking at them and throwing them back. A third, Al Hartman, is lying on his back on the couch. He has taken off his shoes and is juggling a pillow in the approved Japanese fashion. A fourth, Harry Durkis, is walking the carpet, following the design on it like a tightrope walker. Occasionally he loses his balance, but he always recovers himself and continues his cautious way. The fifth writer, George Petty, is sprawled out in a big armchair. He wears a hat over his eyes, and if it were not for the fact that he occasionally speaks, he would seem to be asleep. A make-up man, Larry Schultz, is arranging his stuff on a table.

Mintz (*Dictating*). The Dickey Moore sings—er—whatever he sings.
Judith. "Aren't You the Cute Little Feller?"
Mintz (*Startled*). Huh?
Judith. That's what Dickey Moore sings.
Mintz (*Relieved*). Oh. Thanks. (*The telephone rings.*)
Judith (*Answering it*). Pardon me. Mr. Merry's dressing-room. Oh, thank you, Helen. Will you send it over here? No. He's not on the set, he's here. He's inside shaving—he's going to work on his radio program with his writers till they call him over on Stage 5. That's right. Thanks. (*To the group.*) It's a telegram.
Petty. Phil's got to cut out this picture work. It breaks my train of thought.
Farrell. Break! Break! Break! What've we got, Sol?
Durkis. Yeah, read it, Sol.
Hartman. He can't read.
Mintz (*Angrily*). Certainly I—oh, yeah! Listen. "Signature—our theme song, *Peaches and Cream*."
Hartman. I been lied to.
Petty. Sure. Sol's been going to night school.

Mintz. Shut up! "While the theme song is playing, Dillon is announcing. Dillon: This is the Merry Ha Ha—(*The other four writers instantly start to harmonize the theme song, interrupting themselves to speak but hopping right back into the harmony.*)—featuring Phil Merry and his Merry-makers, coming to you—"
Farrell. "—Through the courtesy of Tubby's Yum Yum Peaches—"
Hartman. "—The perfect peach in the pop-open can—"
Petty. "No jagged edges to cut your fingers—no cranky can opener to slip and slither. Just press the little pusher and pop! Out comes the perfect peach!"
Durkis. "Yum! Yum! Yum!" (*He gives a Bronx cheer.*) We know all that. Get to the gags.
Mintz. Okay—okay—here we go. "Introducing the pit of the peach, the Yum Yum Yogi, the Hey Hey Herald of Health and Happiness—your own—Phil Merry! Ha! Ha! Ha!" Now Phil says, "Good evening, everybody, good evening. Before we plunge into tonight's Merry Ha Ha, I'd like to read you a telegram from Washington. Dopey Dora: You can't do that! Phil: Oh, good evening, Dora. What do you mean, I can't do that? Dopey Dora: You can't read a telegram from Washington. Phil: Why not? Dopey Dora: He's dead. Phil: Dora! Control yourself. This is from Washington D.C. Dopey Dora: Oh, him! Phil: Quiet! This wire is from my senator. Dopey Dora: Oh, I know what that is. Phil: Well, I should hope so. Dopey Dora: Sure. A senator is half a man and half a horse."
Hartman. Hey, wait a minute. That gag was in a play.
Petty. I told you he could read.
Mintz. I didn't read it. It's original. It came to me in a dream.
Durkis. You shouldn't sleep in the theater, Sol. It annoys the actors.
Mintz. Aw-w-w! (*Jerry Mayo, an assistant director, comes in.*)
Jerry. Hi, boys.
All. Hi, Jerry.
Jerry (*To Larry Shultz*). You can take your time on Phil's make-up, Larry. We've got two tough set-ups before we get to him.
Larry (*Slight German accent*). Okay, Jerry. He's still shaving.
Jerry (*To Judith*). Did you leave the lunch passes for Mr. Martin and Governor Goodfellow, Judith?
Judith. Uh-huh. They're at the front gate.
Jerry. Thanks. Mr. Martin telephoned me on the set. They're on their way. I'll check at the restaurant about the table. I told 'em twenty people.
Judith. Better make it twenty-five.

Jerry. Mrs. Merry coming?
Judith. Yes. She called.
Jerry. Okay. I'll buzz you when we're ready for Phil. (*He leaves.*)
Durkis. Say—are we invited to this lunch, or is it exclusive?
Judith. Mr. Martin asked the whole staff.
Farrell. Well, boys. Looks like our sponsor is digging up votes for Goodfellow. I wonder what the Governor has promised to do for American Food Products.
Hartman. Maybe he's going to have his picture taken eating Yum Yums.
Farrell. That'll be pretty. Smiling Bill Goodfellow—the old peach. Yummy!
Durkis. Hey, listen, Jack. Goodfellow's all right. He may not be so bright, but he's solid, and he knows the ropes. Believe me, we could do a lot worse.
Farrell. How?
Durkis. With *your* little candidate, Mr. Paul Davis, that's how. That guy is crazy. He's positively dangerous. If you ask me, he's a goddamn red.
Farrell. Oh, fuff!
Durkis. The reds are backing him, aren't they?
Farrell. What reds?
Durkis. Frank Mace. That CIO son of a bitch.
Judith. Mr. *Durkis!*
Durkis. Oh, excuse me.
Judith. I should think so! Saying "CIO" in front of a lady! Where was you brung up?
Durkis. I'm sorry.
Judith. You ought to be. And let me tell you something else—while my mouth is still open. The next time you call Mr. Frank Mace a son of a bitch, you'd better smile—because I don't like it.
Durkis. Oh, you don't?
Judith. No, I don't. Did you read his speech last Tuesday?
Durkis. Me? I should say not!
Judith. Well, I did. As a matter of fact, I went downtown and heard him—and he's swell.
Mintz. Aha! A Shirley Temple in the midst of our bosoms!
Hartman. Sure. Didn't you know? Judith's the secretary of the Office Workers Guild. *Ver*-ry suspicious!

Judith. Oh, puhdoodle! The place was jammed with people who wanted to find out what he's like. You should have been there. A guy who's got nearly ten thousand people behind him must have something on the ball.
Durkis. Why must he? Those fruit packers are all reds too. Did you see what they're asking?
Farrell. Ten cents more an hour.
Durkis. And *overtime!* They'll ruin business.
Judith. It's just the opposite. No kidding. Mace explained it perfectly. (*She digs up a paper.*) He said that if people don't get decent pay they can't buy the things that keep business going—food and clothes—even the radios that pay your salaries. (*Looks at paper.*) Where is that? Oh, yes, here it is. There was one thing he said—a quotation he ended up with. Here—listen. "Capital is only the fruit of Labor and could not have existed if Labor had not first existed. Labor is the superior of Capital and deserves much the higher consideration."
Durkis. Well, what more do you want? Of course, he's a red. Imagine a guy being allowed to say stuff like that.
Judith. He didn't say that. He was quoting from somebody else.
Durkis. Yeah? From Joe Stalin, I suppose.
Judith. No. From Abe Lincoln.
Durkis. Huh? Hey—who're you kiddin'?
Judith. I'm not kidding. And I looked it up. He said it in 1860—it's in his message to Congress.
Farrell. Never mind, Harry. You could still be right. I mean, after all, any guy who wears a beard and talks like that you've got to keep an eye on. (*A boy comes in with a telegram and some mail.*)
Boy. Here's that telegram for Mr. Merry.
Judith. Thanks. (*She starts to open it.*)
Boy. Sure. (*He looks around at the gang.*) Like to hear a good joke?
Petty. Is it clean?
Boy. Sure it's clean. You can have it for the program.
Farrell. That's mighty white of you, stranger. What do you say, men? Can we take it?
Durkis. I can hardly wait.
Farrell. Shoot, son. Fire when ready.
Boy. What is it that's half a man and half a horse? (*There is a moment's silence.*)
Hartman. It came to him in a dream! (*Petty rises and urges the boy toward his chair.*)

Petty. You sit right here.
Boy. Wait a minute. I haven't told you the answer.
Durkis. The answer is, "Outside!" (*He urges the boy toward the door.*)
Hartman. While you're still young and pure.
Farrell. Don't touch him, Al, you're contagious.
Hartman. Shoo! (*The boy backs out. Hartman closes the door.*)
Petty (*To Mintz*). Isn't anything sacred?
Mintz. Aw-w-w! (*He moves close to Judith's desk. She finishes reading the telegram. He sneaks a look at it. She quietly hands it to him with a magnifying glass.*)
Judith. Want any help? (*He accepts the wire and reads it. Suddenly he whistles.*)
Durkis. What's the matter?
Mintz. Hey, listen. This is from a fan. He heard the program last night. He says, "Congratulations on signing Joe Miller to your writing staff. One more assortment of broken down gags like last night and your public will move in a body to listen in on the Javelin Car Hour. That ventriloquist's dummy, Smarty Kelly, is getting all the laughs these days. Why not fire your writers and hire Kelly?" Well, what do you think of that?
Judith. I think he's got something. (*The door to the dressing room opens. Phil Merry steps into the room. He is about forty-four, and attractive, despite a certain tired, over-sophisticated quality that comes from years of joke-making. Mintz crumples the telegram and drops it in the scrap basket. Merry sees the move.*)
Merry. Uh-uh! Mustn't do that. (*He fishes out the telegram and starts smoothing it out.*) You've probably thrown away the best gag you've thought of in a month. Let's see. (*He reads the wire, then turns to the others.*) You boys read this?
Hartman. Sol read it. Of course, that's only one guy's opinion, Phil.
Merry. Yeah? Well, if you ask me, he's the one guy who's right. We've been heading for this for weeks. (*A silence.*)
Mintz. I don't think that dummy's so funny!
Merry. That's not the point. The trouble is we've been trying to beat him at his own game. When he started to smart crack, we smart cracked, and that's no good. Boys, we've got to get back to fundamentals. We've got to get back to character—to character and situations that people will recognize. Smarty Kelly can pull those nifties because he's not human. He's a dummy. Well, I'm not. And from now on, I'm going to quit trying to

get laughs by acting like one. (*He sits in the make-up chair.*) All right, Larry. (*There is a moment's silence as the make-up man goes to work.*)
Petty. Phil's right, boys. He's as right as a trivet.
Mintz. What's that?
Petty. Don't ask. You're too young. (*To Phil.*) What kind of a character did you think you should be?
Merry. I don't know—except he's got to be human—a terrible coward, for instance. The kind of a guy that gets a swelled head over nothing—that boasts and brags and is full of his own importance. The kind of a guy that every wife will recognize because he'll be just like her husband.
Hartman. Boys, I'm telling you, this can be terrific. I can see this bird at a family picnic—with his arms full of beer bottles that he can't open because he forgot to bring an opener—
Durkis. Or getting all balled up with a time table—
Farrell. Or in politics.
Merry. No. Politics is out. It's dangerous. If you rib the Republicans, then you've got to rib the Democrats. When there's two sides to a question, a good rule is lay off it. Entertainment should be for everybody.
Farrell. Going to tell that to the Governor?
Merry. If he asks me—sure. Why not?
Farrell. I just happened to think that maybe this lunch is a come-on.
Merry. How do you mean?
Farrell. I mean maybe Martin is going to ask you to stooge for Goodfellow.
Merry. I wouldn't do it, and he knows it. I told Abe Kliegel that yesterday.
Farrell. Who gave Abie the idea?
Merry. I don't know. I guess he thought of it himself. After all, he's my agent.
Farrell. No. He was talking for Martin.
Merry. Well, what if he was? What's the difference? The point is I'm not going to do it.
Durkis. Well, I think you're crazy. Jeez, Phil, it would be a hell of a spot. Nobody's touched politics since Will Rogers. Talk about a character! Say—you'd leave that dummy so far behind, he'd look like a clothespin. And think what those big shots behind Goodfellow would do for you. Why don't you do it?
Merry. I've told you why.
Durkis. Yeah—but I'm not sold.
Merry. What do you mean by that?

Durkis. I mean it don't make sense. You know what I think? I think the real reason you won't do it is because you want the other guy to win. I think you're for Davis. (*During the last speech, Esther Merry enters and stands in the doorway. She is over-dressed and flighty. At the moment she is carrying a tiny dog in her arms. She swoops into the room.*)
Esther. Of course he is, and it's perfectly terrible.
Merry. Oh, hello, Esther. You know the gang. Mrs. Merry.
Esther. Yes, *indeed*. Sit down, boys. I'm leaving immediately—if not sooner. I just dropped in to get the seating list for the luncheon. Good morning, Judith. Have you got the place cards?
Judith. I sent them over to the restaurant, Mrs. Merry.
Esther. Oh, that was very intelligent. Aren't you wonderful! I'll zip right over. Oh! But first—Phil, you haven't met my angel-pie! I just bought him. Isn't he darling! He's a Maltese hairless. They're practically extinct.
Merry. They certainly do.
Esther. Oh, you! You should see his pedigree. I'm having it framed. I've christened him Smiling Bill. We're going to give him to the Governor. I just found out it's his birthday. He's sixty-one.
Mintz. My God! What stunted him?
Esther. What? Oh, no. Not precious—the Governor. Smile for the gentlemen, presh. There! I'd like to see Roosevelt beat that! Tell your father Philip that he mustn't vote for Mr. Davis—no, he mustn't. Mr. Davis wants to tax everybody and give the money to the WPA. He's a bad, bad man. M-m-my precious! (*She kisses the dog. Abe Kliegel, Merry's agent, sleek, fattish and unctuous, rushes into the room, waving an "Extra" edition of the newspaper.*)
Kliegel. Hello, Esther. (*To Judith.*) Morning, Beautiful. Hey, boys, look at this!
Farrell (*Reading*). Some fun!
Durkis. What is it?
Farrell (*Reading aloud*). Vice Crusader Faraday Shot by Gangsters. Office Rifled. Underworld check-up demanded by Mayor Smith and Governor Goodfellow.
Petty. Well, what do you know!
Esther. Who in the world is Faraday?
Farrell. The chief investigator for Paul Davis, wasn't he?
Durkis. That's right. Four years ago—when Davis was screaming about that oil grab.

Esther. I'm all mixed up. I mean—should we be sorry that he was shot, or glad? (*This stops everyone for several seconds. At last Farrell clears his throat.*)
Farrell. Err—suppose I read the rest of this—
Merry. Yes. Darling, you just relax.
Esther. I can't, Angel. I've simply got to see about those place cards. You can tell me all about the shooting at lunch. I hope it hasn't spoiled the Governor's appetite. We're having shrimp surprise. (*She goes.*)
Durkis. What else, Jack? Davis say anything?
Farrell. Plenty. He says Smiling Bill staged the whole thing. He says those gangsters are a myth.
Mintz. What?
Farrell. A myth.
Merry. That's a female moth.
Mintz. Oh.
Farrell. Mmmm. Davis says whoever did it was after the stuff that was in Faraday's safe. Proof that the Governor was in on the oil grab.
Durkis. Aw. That's a lot of marmalade.
Kliegel. Sure it is. Somebody's got to muzzle that Davis. Phil, I'm telling you, you've got to help Goodfellow.
Merry. I won't do it. I tell you, entertainment and politics don't mix.
Kliegel. But, Phil—this isn't politics, it's self-defense. Ask Mr. Martin. If Davis gets in he'll tax the pants off us. We've got to stick together. If we don't, you know what we'll get? Taxation without recommendation, and that's un-American. It's absolutely unconstitutional—it's lousy. We got to stick to the side our bread is buttered on.
Farrell. Sure we do. Only don't kid yourself, Abie. Our bread is buttered on the bottom. Where do you think Martin gets the dough to pay our salaries? Why, from the millions of little guys who buy his peaches—and they're the guys that a fat hunk of that tax money is going to give jobs to.
Kliegel. You're crazy. What you're saying is just a vicious circuit. Goodfellow's the guy for us.
Farrell. What do you mean—"us"? Look, you don't really kid yourself that Phil and us and you flesh peddlers who get yours out of ours are in the same class with the guys we work for, do you?
Kliegel. Certainly I do.
Farrell. Well, you can include me out—because that just doesn't make sense.

Kliegel. Certainly it makes sense. I'm telling you—what is good for Goodfellow—

Farrell. Is good for Goodfellow. Abie—he's terrible. He's crooked as hell—and he's got brain fever.

Merry. Now, wait a minute. He can't have that.

Farrell. Why not?

Merry. Well, I mean—can a worm have water on the knee?

Farrell. Boy! Is that wonderful.

Durkis. What's wonderful about it?

Farrell. Oh, baby, just wait till that gets around. They'll laugh Goodfellow into the dump heap.

Kliegel. You see what I mean, Phil? Jeez! You mustn't say things like that. People will think you mean 'em. Hey! Wait a minute. You could have said that about Davis.

Merry. You're nuts.

Kliegel. Listen. It's perfect. And it could fit Davis like a glove. Just ask Martin. He'll tell you. Why don't you spring it at lunch.

Judith. Excuse me, Mr. Merry. Mr. Martin and the Governor are on their way over here.

Kliegel. Holy Christmas! Jeez, boys, snap out of it! Brush up! Look intelligent. I'll stall 'em off a minute. Okay, Phil, you stick with the money. We're counting on you. (*He pauses at Judith's desk.*) Goo'bye, Beautiful. (*He hurries out. There is terrific confusion and ad lib as the boys dust themselves off and get organized. Merry is alone for a moment near Judith's desk.*)

Judith. What are you going to do?

Merry. I don't know. You heard that last crack of Abie's. They're counting on me.

Judith. I'm counting on you. (*Abie appears at the door with Martin and Goodfellow. The former is handsome and suave. The Governor is large and a stuffed shirt.*)

Kliegel. Come in, Mr. Martin. Come in, Governor. I'll let you do the honors, Mr. Martin. You know everybody.

Martin. Yes, of course. How are you, gentlemen—Miss Gordon? The Governor of California. Good morning, Phil. Governor Goodfellow—this is Phil Merry.

Merry. How d'y'do, Governor?

Goodfellow. I'm well, thank you—very well. And this is a pleasure—a real pleasure. Yes, sir. Mrs. Goodfellow and I are great fans of yours, Mr. Merry.

Yes, sir. Never miss a broadcast. No, sir. I believe in laughter. It's good for the soul. "A little nonsense now and then—." You know the saying.
Merry. I think I remember it.
Goodfellow. Of course you do. Of course. Ha, ha. You know all the answers.
Merry. Well—not quite all.
Goodfellow. Oh, yes, you do. Tell me, Mr. Merry, how's your young friend?
Merry. My friend?
Goodfellow. Your buddy. The little fellow.
Merry. You mean Sol Mintz?
Goodfellow. No, no. I mean your little boy-friend—the dummy—Smarty Kelly. (*There is a moment's pause.*)
Merry. I'm afraid you've got the wrong number.
Kliegel. Smarty Kelly is on the Javelin Car Hour. Mr. Merry's program is the Merry Ha Ha—peaches. Peaches and cream. (*Petty and Hartman hum the refrain.*)
Goodfellow. Of course. Of course. How stupid of me! I don't know what I could have been thinking of. Why, I don't even like that ventriloquist. He's common—he's vulgar. I never listen to him.
Merry. You're missing a lot of laughs.
Goodfellow. No, no. He's very cheap. That joke last week about the night nurse. Pretty risqué, if you ask me. Er—my wife told me about it. We're sending out a protest. Not funny at all.
Merry. Got a belly out of me.
Goodfellow. Well—of course, among professionals—in private—that's different. But in principle, I'm right. Yes, sir. Take your own program, for instance. Clean as a whistle. That's what we want. Good, clean, American fun. (*Mintz starts to applaud. Petty shushes him.*)
Martin. And that's what Phil Merry is going right on giving you—and for a long time. He doesn't know it yet, but I've been talking to Abe Kliegel, and we've decided to tear up his old contract and give him a brand new one—if he'll accept it—with quite a little boost, too—and for five more years.
The writers. Say, that's swell, Phil. Good boy, Phil.
Merry. Well, thank you.
Martin. Not at all, Phil. It's only what you deserve. American Food Products simply appreciates what you've done for our peaches. It's really

astonishing, Governor, the way the Merry Ha Ha program has made this country Yum Yum conscious.

Goodfellow. I'm not a bit astonished. It's the logical result of intelligent, up-to-date business methods applied to psychology. (*A new character strolls into the doorway. He wears his hat cocked on the back of his head. A newspaper is stuffed into one pocket. He takes it out and, as Goodfellow goes on, jots down a note or two.*) Naturally you've got to have the product to sell it. That's fundamental. But you've got to tell the people about it, too. That's basic. It's a great age we're living in, Mr. Martin. When you think of modern miracles like the radio and what's being done with them, I tell you, gentlemen, you really wonder how people lived at all before progress and civilization began to brighten their lives and brought them the key to happiness. (*The Governor's audience lets this sink in. The man in the doorway looks up from his paper.*)

Mace. Can I quote that, Governor?

Goodfellow. Certainly you can quote it—er—what? Who asked that?

Mace (*Steps forward*). Excuse me. I'm here to ask a couple of questions, Mr. Goodfellow.

Goodfellow. Oh. Well, what was it about?

Mace. I just wanted to ask you a few things about the Faraday shooting.

Goodfellow. I gave out a statement on that this morning.

Mace. Yes, I know. Very interesting. But there are one or two points—

Goodfellow. I see. Hmmm. What did you want to know?

Mace. I've just come from the District Attorney's office. They're holding five men there on suspicion in connection with the shooting.

Goodfellow. That's right. Five gangsters—all with police records. All connected with the gambling interests. If the guilty man's among them, I hope he gets exactly what's coming to him.

Mace. Oh, you know about them?

Goodfellow. Certainly. I saw the District Attorney this morning.

Mace. And you talked to him about these gangsters?

Goodfellow. Yes—in a general way.

Mace. Did you say anything to him about the sixth man?

Goodfellow. What? What sixth man?

Mace. Early this morning they were holding six men. After you left they let one go.

Goodfellow. If they did, I don't know anything about it. If they let anyone go, I suppose it was because they made a mistake.

Mace. You're right about that, all right. It was a hell of a mistake. The cop who made the pinch on a telephone tip found that out when you and the D.A. called him in on the carpet.
Goodfellow. I don't know what you're talking about.
Mace. Okay. Let me ask you something else. Did you ever hear of Benny Dirk?
Goodfellow. No.
Mace. That's funny. He's been on the Richland Oil Company's payroll for ten years—as a hired strong man and a strikebreaker.
Goodfellow. Well, what if he has?
Mace. Benny Dirk was the sixth man. We've got witnesses who saw him leave the D.A.'s office. We want him booked on the charge of murdering Jim Faraday. And we want to know if you'll use your influence to see that he's brought to trial.
Goodfellow. It's not in my jurisdiction. The case is in the hands of the District Attorney.
Mace. Who *you* talked into springing Dirk.
Goodfellow. That's a lie! Now, look here—who is this man? Who do you represent?
Mace. A few thousand guys who work here in California. My name is Frank Mace.
Goodfellow. This is a frame-up. Get this man out of here! He's a red. He's the paid organizer of the United Fruit and Vegetable Packers. He's been sent here to embarrass me.
Mace. That's right. How 'm I doin'?
Goodfellow. Get out of here! Will someone please *do something*!
Mace. Don't bother, boys. I'm leaving. I'm all set—unless you'd like to add something, Governor.
Goodfellow. Yes, I would. You can tell those subversive red bastards who sent you here they can think any goddamn thing they please. No decent, God-fearing American believes what they say anyway. Yes—and let me tell you something, Mr. Frank Mace. You'd better watch your step or else!
Mace. Or else what?
Goodfellow. Or else you're finished. Yes, sir! We've had just about enough of you and that red union of yours. We're going to send you right back where you came from.
Mace. Please, Governor—not to New Jersey.

Goodfellow. Don't try to be funny. As a matter of fact, deportation is too good for you. You ought to be whipped within an inch of your life. You ought to be strung up to the nearest lamp post.
Mace. Is that a threat?
Goodfellow. It's anything you want to make out of it!
Mace. Thank you. I hope you gentlemen all heard that. If anything should happen to me, I might ask you to be my witnesses. Don't look so worried, Mr. Merry, nothing *is* going to happen. Mr. Goodfellow knows now that he bungled the Faraday killing. He won't make the same mistake twice. He's not quite that stupid. And he's really through. That's not a threat, Mr. Goodfellow—that's just a plain statement of what the people of California are going to do to you in November. They're not going to whip you within an inch of your life—except at the polls. They're not going to string you up to a lamp post, because lamp posts have lights on them, and they're tired of even looking at you. They're not going to send you back where you came from either, because they wouldn't even like to wish you on the Richland Oil Company—it's oily enough as it is. No. All they're going to do is turn you loose and kiss you goodbye, because what's good for California is goodbye for Goodfellow. So, goodbye, Mr. Governor. We'll see you in the ash can. (*He goes out. The Governor stands a moment in the silence that follows, then strides to the door and shouts after the vanished Mace.*)
Goodfellow. Is that so! (*He walks back into the room.*) I guess that's telling him. Can you imagine such a thing. It's unbelievable. I—I—has somebody got a drink? (*Mintz, Hartman, Durkis, and Petty instantly produce pints and flasks. The Governor accepts one. He takes a quick but healthy swig.*) Thank you. I think I'd like a breath of air.
Kliegel. Maybe you'd like to look around the studio, Governor?
Goodfellow. Yes, yes, thank you. I can't breathe—that man! A human stink bomb!
Kliegel. Come on, boys. What's on tap?
Mintz. They got a swell set on Stage 5. Something brand new. It's a cabaret.
Kliegel. Yeah, that'll be fine. Huh, Governor?
Goodfellow. Yes, splendid. Thank you.
Kliegel. Okay, boys. Here we go. (*They hurry out, leaving Martin, Merry, Judith, and Larry Shultz, the make-up man, alone. Martin picks up the telephone.*)

Martin. This is Mr. Chatfield Martin in Mr. Merry's dressing room. I'd like to talk to the studio police. (*To Merry.*) I'm going to make sure that man gets out of here.
Larry. He's headin' for the front gate right now, Mr. Martin. I'll run over and check up for you.
Martin. Oh, thank you. (*Into the phone.*) Never mind. (*He hangs up.*)
Larry. Goddamn foreigners! (*He exits.*)
Martin. I wonder how he got in here. Don't they check people at the gates?
Judith. He must have had somebody's time card.
Martin. They should watch those things. Once you let people like that get started, there's no stopping them. They've got the nerve of the devil.
Merry. That one certainly didn't look as if he'd scare very easily.
Martin. No. A definitely dangerous character, Phil. He's got a lot of force and magnetism. You can see just how those packers are taken in by him. A typical dictator—drunk with his own power. And those fools would follow him to hell.
Merry. Yeah, I can imagine.
Martin. That's always the way with a personality. What he says can be drivel, but the way he says it—that's everything.
Merry. He's pretty good, all right.
Martin. Yes, there's no getting away from it. You can't beat a man like that with logic. You've got to fight personality with personality.
Merry. Mmmmm.
Martin. As a matter of fact, this whole campaign has been a little short on showmanship. Goodfellow's been a fine governor. He has a great record. But frankly—from a showman's angle—
Merry. I think I know what you mean.
Martin. Precisely. (*The telephone rings. Judith answers it.*)
Judith. Hello. Oh, hello. Okay, just a minute. (*To Martin.*) It's Larry Shultz—that make-up man. He says that Mace just drove off with two other men in a Ford.
Martin. That's fine. Thank him, will you? Oh—and I wonder if you'd ask him to wait about fifteen minutes before he comes back. There's something I want to talk to Mr. Merry about.
Judith. Surely. Hello. Look, Larry, Mr. Martin wants to know if you could mess around with your grease paint for about fifteen minutes. He's going into conference with Mr. Merry. Right. (*To Martin.*) He's on his way to the make-up department. He'll toy with a toupee until I call him.

Martin. Thank you very much.
Judith. I'll be over in the restaurant if you need me, Mr. Merry.
Merry. Oh, all right. No—wait a minute, Judith. I'll tell you what. (*Indicating the other room.*) You park in there by the extension until we're through. There might be some messages.
Judith. Right. (*She pauses in the doorway.*) If you need me for anything—
Merry. I'll holler for help. Thanks. (*Judith closes the door.*)
Martin. Sit down, Phil. Cigar?
Merry. Thanks. (*He takes the cigar. Martin uses his lighter.*)
Martin. Abe Kliegel was telling me that joke you made about Davis.
Merry. About who?
Martin. About Davis—about his having brain fever.
Merry. Oh. Oh, yes.
Martin. Very funny, too. I've been thinking what a shame it is that more people couldn't hear you say it.
Merry. I'm afraid Abie has been letting his imagination run away with him.
Martin. I don't understand.
Merry. Well, you see, I made the crack, all right, but I didn't make it about Davis.
Martin. No? Well, that's not important. The point is you could say it about him.
Merry. You mean on the program?
Martin. Yes.
Merry. I'm sorry, Mr. Martin, but I'm afraid I couldn't.
Martin. Why not?
Merry. We-ell—I've got a sort of theory that politics is a good subject for a radio comic to steer clear of. You see, half the people would go for a slap at Davis, and the other half would dial you right off the air.
Martin. Not if *you* said it, Phil.
Merry. Oh yes, they would. I remember once when I was new at this racket. I made a joke about Mr. Hoover. Now you would've thought that would have been okay with anyone, but quite a few Republicans raised hell about it. I guess they thought it was bad taste to crack jokes about the dead.
Martin (*Attempting a laugh*). Hmmm. Yes, I—I see what you mean. But times have changed. Nowadays the air is full of politics.
Merry. Still I think you'd lose a lot of Yum Yum addicts. It wouldn't be very smart business.

Martin. I'd take a chance on that. If we help beat Davis, we'd get back a lot more than we'd lose.
Merry. I still think it's a bad idea.
Martin. What are you afraid of? We could be as subtle as you like. In fact, that's where you'd be particularly valuable.
Merry. No, I'm afraid from my angle it's no good.
Martin. I think I can show you that from your angle it would be very good.
Merry. Really?
Martin. Yes, really. As I told you, this new contract we're offering you is the direct result of what you've done for our product; and I can assure you that if you help us defeat this crazy gang of radicals that Davis represents, we'd be even more grateful, and we'd be willing to show our gratitude in a very substantial way.
Merry. It's as important to you as all that, huh?
Martin. It's important to everyone. Do you realize what your taxes will be if those madmen are elected?
Merry. Well, I sort of had a hunch that they'd be pretty big no matter who gets in. The Republicans talk a lot about Federal spending, but haven't we got to do something like that? I mean, the money to buy peaches has got to come from somewhere, hasn't it?
Martin. But if they'll leave business alone, there'll be plenty of money. Business will pick up. Unemployment will be cut to nothing. We'll have recovery—normal recovery—instead of this half-baked, jacked-up variety we've just been through. Give us a real hands-off-business administration and we'll have prosperity again.
Merry. Like in '28.
Martin. Exactly.
Merry. I guess that's what people are afraid of.
Martin. What do you mean?
Merry. The exactly part. You know—whatever goes up must come down. (*He gestures up and down.*) '28—'29. Boom. Boom!
Martin. Not this time. We've learned something. We wouldn't let it come down.
Merry. Oh.
Martin. It's a fact. Do you know what's holding business back? Fear. They could start the wheels turning full tilt right now if they wanted to; but they won't do it—and you can't blame them. They won't invest, they won't build, and they won't employ, till they know that government meddling is

through with, once and for all—that this country is back where it belongs—in the hands of the only people who are wise enough and strong enough to keep it running. I tell you, Phil, the time has come when you can't stay out of these things. You've got to take sides, because if you don't, the wrong side will take you and your property and divide you up like so much gangster's loot.

Merry. Maybe you're right. You certainly know a lot more about it than I do, but I've still got a funny hunch that says, "Take it easy, kid. It's not your racket. Keep out of it."

Martin. Well, that's that. If you feel that way, there's nothing more I can say. I'm sorry, but I'm certainly not going to argue with you—and naturally what's in that new contract still goes—one hundred percent.

Merry. Thank you.

Martin. Not a bit. Oh, there is one thing I think you should know about. There is a group on our board of directors—fortunately, it's a minority group at present—who have been agitating the idea that we shouldn't be satisfied with having the second most popular program on the air—that we should have the first.

Merry. They want Smarty Kelly.

Martin. Yes.

Merry. Well, maybe they're right.

Martin. They're not right, and you can count on me to keep on telling them that.

Merry. I'm certainly grateful for that.

Martin. That's all right. Naturally, I don't know what effect your decision may have on the present majority—none, I hope. I don't even know what Smarty Kelly's political convictions are.

Merry. Oh, I think the dummy's a Republican. That's not a crack.

Martin. No, of course not. I understand. Well, if you're right, of course that's a point which our minority might use in an argument. I just wanted you to understand how the thing stood.

Merry. I think I get the idea.

Martin. Well, I guess that's all. I'll see how the Governor's getting along. If you should change your mind—?

Merry. I'll let you know.

Martin. Thank you. You're an important person, Phil. *The Merry Ha Ha* is a great program. I can't imagine how either you or it could be bigger, unless it came about through your devoting yourself to the great task of molding public opinion in the cause of liberty and right. I'll see you at

lunch. (*He goes out. Merry looks after him a moment and throws his cigar into the gas log fireplace. Judith comes in from the other room.*)
Judith. May I be the first to congratulate you?
Merry (*After a keen look*). How much did you hear?
Judith (*Opens her notebook and finds a page*). Quote: I'm afraid Abie has been letting his imagination run away with him. Unquote. That's where I started.
Merry. Now is that nice?
Judith. I thought it was swell.
Merry. Judith, you're wonderful. You know, if you could cook—
Judith. I can.
Merry. That settles it. It's an offer. What do you say?
Judith. What are you proposing?
Merry. Er—bigamy—in the first degree.
Judith. No, I'm sorry.
Merry. That's final?
Judith, Uh-huh.
Merry. Well, there you are. You make a girl an honest, straightforward proposition, and what do you get? (*Judith shrugs.*) A shrug. Fine thing. I can't understand women nowadays. They want the moon.
Judith. That's right.
Merry. Not half the moon, mind you, but the whole moon—all of it—with starlight.
Judith. Pretty crazy, aren't we?
Merry. Absolutely nuts.
Judith. That's right.
Merry (*Regards her for a moment*). Oh! What did you think about that last crack of Martin's—about his board of directors?
Judith. What did you think about the Governor's last crack about Mace?
Merry. You mean it was a threat?
Judith. What else?
Merry. I was afraid of that. Sit down a minute, Judith. I want to talk to myself—out loud. If you don't mind, it's easier with you listening. (*Judith sits down.*) I'm going to tell you a secret. About me. I'm a coward.
Judith (*Smiles and indicates her notebook*). The record says different.
Merry. That was only the first round. If what you just said is true, they won't stop.
Judith. No, they won't.

Merry. Well, then what? How long can I stall them? I mean if they really start taking a sock at my pocketbook?
Judith. As long as they need you.
Merry. And how long ill that be? Not so long, maybe, unless that program picks up. Oh, that reminds me. I got an idea while Martin was talking to me. Make a note, will you? I was thinking it might be funny if we did one program where the orchestra told the jokes and we gave out with the music. What do you think?
Judith. Sounds swell.
Merry. Dora could sing. I'd play the piccolo.
Judith. Be very funny.
Merry. Yeah. It might be all right. You know—one of those numbers—(*He whistles, then sings a coloratura falsetto response. When he finishes he becomes intensely serious and stares ahead of him, lost in thought. Judith watches him. He looks up suddenly and sees her.*) What's the matter?
Judith. Nothing. You just had that look.
Merry. What look?
Judith. I call it "the joke-smith's stare." You remember—
Under the spreading chestnut tree
The village joke-smith stands.
The smith, a morbid man is he—
Merry. With joke-infested hands.
Judith. And the nifties from his bulging brain—
Merry. Are fatal to his "frands." (*They both laugh.*)
Judith. You see. You've really got it. It's a disease.
Merry. I guess it must be.
Judith. No fooling. When the program doesn't suit you I've seen you go around hollow-eyed for days. You look as if a little leprosy would be a pleasure.
Merry. Bad as that, huh?
Judith. Yes, sometimes I've looked at you and thought, "There he goes—America's ace comedian—top of the heap—top salary—best in the business. Jokes! Laughs! Gags! Sure. His life's so full of them he hasn't room for five minutes' fun."
Merry (*Thinks for a moment*). Maybe I should take a rest.
Judith. Of course you should.
Merry. When we finish this series, maybe.
Judith. What would you like to do?
Merry. Travel, I guess—except—

Judith. Except what?

Merry. Well, the way I'd want to do it wouldn't suit Esther, I'm afraid. I'm a sneaker-around-er, and she likes the brass bands and the ballyhoo. She's always been like that, and she's always been able to travel that way—even on our honeymoon when all my assets were gilt-edged liabilities. Boy! All I had was my health and a million dollars worth of stale gags which nobody laughed at but Esther. She used to roll in the aisle. The day we eloped her old man raised the roof. He was Jacob Hirsh, you know, of Hirsh Brothers, the big department store. First he was going to cut her loose without a dime, but Esther stopped that in its tracks. She told him we'd spend our honeymoon in the worst hotels in the country and broadcast whose daughter she was. That did it. But the next thing you know we were scrapping ourselves, because I wouldn't travel on Hirsh's dough. That almost split us up right there. Esther wouldn't travel the hard way and I wouldn't travel on the old man's transfer.

Judith. What happened?

Merry. Moving picture finish. I had sixty beautiful bucks, so I eased myself into a crap game and made twenty-seven straight passes. That settled it. We went Esther's way but on my dough.

Judith. And since then?

Merry. Oh—Esther took the high road and I took the low road—and that's the way it's been—not a fight in fifteen years—practically. What are you smiling at?

Judith. Nothing.

Merry. No kidding. We never fight.

Judith. I'm sure you don't.

Merry. Mmm—what was I talking about?

Judith. You were talking about going places. Why couldn't you go alone?

Merry. Who'd listen to my jokes?

Judith. You wouldn't make any. You'd go on the wagon. You'd swear off.

Merry. I wonder how long that would last. It's a pretty old habit.

Judith. How did you start, anyway?

Merry. Playing piano—on the Tenderloin. My old man was screwy about music. He went in hock to pay for piano lessons for young Philip Mirkovitch, the boy wonder—which was me. I wasn't bad, either—only I wouldn't practice—except when the old man played percussion on me with the family knout—an eight-foot trunk strap. Boy! I can still feel that buckle. He used to lock me in the front room and set my kid sister to snitch on me if I played ragtime. But I foxed him. There was a big sissy upstairs who had a crush on me. He could really play. He used to sneak down the fire-escape and bang out scales while I cut jokes out of the Sunday paper and pasted them in a scrap book. I was working up a vaudeville act. A big novelty. I played piano and told jokes to a talking parrot. The parrot was a fake. It was a real bird, all right, but it couldn't talk. I dug up a cross-eyed little Jewish girl named Hester, with a voice like a Scotch bag-pipe, and hid her behind a screen. The night we tried out the act at the Dutch Village Rathskellar, a drunk knocked the screen over. You should have seen Hester. She took off for the front door like a cockeyed Donald Duck. When I got home the old man was sitting up waiting with the trunk strap. Yeah, man! As soon as I could walk I powdered out of there for Coney Island. For six weeks I loaded guns in a shooting gallery till my pals from Ludlow Street found me. We hatched a plot. The next night they kidnapped Hester and we had a real tryout. The act wowed 'em. Phil Merry and his human parrot. The boy wonder was off to the races. Gosh! That was just after they shot Lincoln.

Judith. What then?

Merry. Vaudeville. Eight-six-two a day. Different backdrops, but the same routine. Then came the dawn—the miracle age the Governor was drooling about. Radio and pictures—carbon copy comedy—Merry by Mimeograph! The Big Dough! Phil Merry the capitalist. Funny. When I was a punk I voted Socialist.

Judith. Bribery and corruption, hmm?

Merry. That's it. Did I ever tell you the "Monumental Merry Method for Stopping Socialism"?

Judith. No. What is it?

Merry. Very simple. Just give everybody a fistful of blue chips.

Judith. I see. You mean the way to stop it is to have it.

Merry. You know what I mean. A rich radical is a contradiction in terms. He's either a saint or a sucker. You can't worry much about humanity when you've got swollen knuckles from clipping coupons. You know, I think Shakespeare was on the wrong track when he said it was conscience that makes us into cowards. It isn't that at all. It's that big bag of clinkers in the savings bank. Look at me. Right now. I'm scared to death to run away and catch my breath, even, because they might get another boy if I don't stick around and keep the jokes up to scratch. And I'm scared of my boss and that lousy Goodfellow ballyhoo of his. Terrible, isn't it?

Judith. It's awful. Man's full of stuff, and he just won't give out with it. What am I going to do with you?

Merry. Give up, I guess. Fine job you've got anyway. You have to laugh at my jokes, listen to the story of my life, and do a little spine-stiffening on the side. Next thing I know, you'll holler for overtime and picket me.
Judith. If you listen to Martin, I'll do worse than that.
Merry. You wouldn't quit?
Judith. I might.
Merry. Oh, now wait a minute. You wouldn't do that. How long have you been with me, Judith?
Judith. Five years, two months, and—(*She figures a moment.*) four days.
Merry. What did you do before that?
Judith. Worked.
Merry. All your life?
Judith. Since I was fourteen. My father lost his job when I was ten.
Merry. What did he do?
Judith. He taught Economics back East. They fired him during the big Palmer Red Scare in 1920. He had a copy of Marx's *Capital* in his study. Some of the rich students saw it and got up a petition. As a matter of fact, he wasn't even a Socialist—that is, until after they fired him. I remember the day I went out to look for a job. He was a little guy, but his eyes were as big as saucers. He kissed me, and then he said, "Good luck, Judy. You're going to work for a living. That's fine—but there's a funny thing about it. Some girls who work like to feel that because they look neat and pretty and keep their hands clean they're just a little bit superior to the rest of the working people. They're even ashamed to call themselves workers at all. I can't understand that. The people who work are the people who made this country. They built its cities and its factories—they tilled its soil. They're the ones who produced its wealth. You ought to be proud to be one of them." I've never forgotten that.
Merry. I can imagine. He must be a grand guy.
Judith. He is.
Merry. And Tillie the Toiler. She's okay too. A real working stiff. And don't think I'm kidding. (*He looks pointedly at her hands.*) In spite of the lily white hands.
Judith. They're not so lily. (*She holds up her right forefinger. It has a smudge on it.*) That damn machine. (*She starts to open the desk drawer. Merry pulls out his handkerchief.*)
Merry. Here. Hey. Where do you suppose Mace got that time card?
Judith. I don't suppose.

Merry. That's what I thought. (*He takes the finger, makes a wad of his handkerchief and holds it up to her.*) Spit. (*She does so. He goes to work on the finger. Suddenly his eyes fasten on the top of her head.*) Hey! What have you done to your hair?
Judith. What? What do you mean?
Merry. It's got red in it.
Judith. Well?
Merry. It never used to have.
Judith. Oh, didn't it?
Merry. Well, did it?
Judith. Of course.
Merry. Since when?
Judith. Since always.
Merry (*Takes a long look that finally includes more than the hair*). Well, I'll be damned! (*They stand for several seconds, Merry still holding Judith's finger. Abe Kliegel bursts in upon them.*)
Kliegel. Oh, excuse me—but Jesus, Phil, Jake Darrenberg is on the lot.
Merry. Who?
Kliegel. Darrenberg. Smarty Kelly's agent. He's got a letter to Martin from a guy on his board of directors.
Merry. Round two! Here we go again.
Kliegel. Luckily for me, Martin was inside on Stage 5, so I told Darrenberg he'd left. But he'll get to him tonight sure at his hotel. I tell you, Phil, you've got to do something.
Merry. Or else—as the Governor said to Mr. Mace.
Kliegel. What?
Merry. Nothing.
Kliegel. Well, what about it?
Merry. Into a clinch and stall.
Judith. Or let him have it—right on the button. (*Merry stares at her. Jerry, the assistant director, comes in.*)
Jerry. You won't work till after lunch, Phil.
Merry. Oh, all right. Thanks.
Jerry. And the Governor's on his way back here. Mrs. Merry told me to tell you not to start to lunch till she got here. She's got a surprise for him.
Merry. That'll be fun.
Jerry. Here he comes now. (*The Governor, Martin, and the writers barge into the room. The Governor is talking excitedly. He turns to Merry.*)

Goodfellow. This is a wonderful industry, Mr. Merry. It's really astounding. Why, I hadn't the slightest idea that making movies was such hard work. They took the scene we were watching five times. I understand that with some of the more difficult actors they sometimes have to take it as many as eight or nine times.
Merry. Thirteen is my favorite number.
Goodfellow. You don't say so.
Merry. Oh, yes—yes, indeed. (*Esther Merry appears in the doorway. She gives directions to someone offstage, then trips forward, holding her little dog aloft.*)
Esther. Mr. Goodfellow—
Goodfellow (*Turns quickly to her*). I refuse to answer!
Merry. Er—this is Mrs. Merry, Governor.
Goodfellow. Oh, how are you?
Esther. Well, thank you. Governor Goodfellow, I just wanted you to know that we know.
Goodfellow. What's that?
Esther. Umm-hmm. We know that this is a very special day for you. Yes, *indeed*. It's your birthday.
All. Well, congratulations. (*Other ad libs follow.*)
Goodfellow. Thank you. Thank you.
Esther. And so, on behalf of all of us—and I'm sure I *can* speak for all of us—I want to present you with a little living token of our good wishes and esteem. Here he is, and he's all yours—Smiling Bill, the Second.
Goodfellow. Thank you, thank you very much indeed. Thank you, Mrs. Merry—and Mr. Merry.
Merry. No, really, Governor, I'm afraid that Mrs. Merry gets all the credit for Weasel-puss.
Martin. You see, Mr. Merry's birthday present comes a little later.
Esther. Oh, Phil—what is it?
Martin. Well, it's not quite decided yet, but I think I can promise you that before much longer it will be.
Durkis. But what is it?
Martin. Well, how would you all feel if I told you that Phil has practically decided to devote a good share of the Merry Ha Ha program to keeping good government in California—in short, to the great cause of returning William Apperson Goodfellow as the Governor of our Golden State?
(*With the exception of Farrell and Judith, everyone in the room applauds loudly. Esther signals offstage again. Six chorines enter in scanty costumes*

bearing a huge birthday cake. As they give forth with "For He's a Jolly Good Fellow!" a generous attack of handshaking seizes everyone in the room. The curtain descends on Act One.)

Act Two: Scene One

Judith's living room in Hollywood. The house is one of those tiny places at the foot of the Hollywoodland hills. There is a door, right, leading to the bedroom, and one in the back wall to the left of center leading to the street. There is an alcove in the back wall which is used as a breakfast room. The door in the left wall leads to the kitchen. The living room is simply furnished. The walls are decorated with three or four modern drawings. The most conspicuous article of furniture is a small combination phonograph and radio which was a present from Phil Merry.

When the curtain rises, Merry is walking nervously up and down. He pauses once to straighten a picture and again to look out the window. When he leaves the window he pulls down the shade. His next move is to wander to the bookcase and start reading the titles. One interests him. As he starts to take the book from the shelf, the telephone rings. He replaces the book and answers the telephone, pausing just a few seconds before he finally picks up the receiver.

Merry (*Falsetto*). Hello. No. Miss Gordon isn't home. No. She didn't say. Can I take a message? Yes, Mr. Kliegel. I'll tell her. Goodbye. (*He hangs up. The strain of talking in falsetto causes him to cough. He pours himself a drink of water from a table carafe, drinks it and clears his throat. He peeks out the window again, then goes to the phonograph, picks out a record, reads the title that is printed by hand on the white central disc, and puts it on the machine. The telephone rings again. Merry crosses and picks it up. He speaks in falsetto again.*) Hello. (*Natural voice.*) Oh, hello, Judith. What happened? Well, you tell your damn committee meeting to break up. So, is this important, hmmm? No—no—not a chance. No, I absolutely will not start talking to myself unless you're here to listen to me. No! Okay. Then hurry it up. Oh, and listen. What do I do if the doorbell rings? Yeah, but what about my reputation? Certainly—just think it over. Here I am, alone in a beautiful woman's boudoir. What? Well, I'm practically in it. Sure, I'm lying around here in a drunken stupor—in my cerise lounging pajamas. Your roommate's away on location—my wife's in Palm Springs—I tell you it's a hell of a thing. Hmm? Okay. You hurry. That's right—oh, Abe Kliegel called you. I don't know. I gave him the boy soprano. (*Falsetto.*) Hello, kid. (*Natural voice.*) Mmm-hmm. I told him you'd gone to the dentist. Hmm? No. I told him you were out. Yeah. Now listen to me, lady. You tell that committee of yours to adjourn immediately. All right. You step on it. 'Bye. (*He hangs up and goes back to the phonograph. He makes a final adjustment and starts the machine. The record plays the following dialogue.*)

Announcer's voice. Introducing your own, Phil Merry.

Merry's voice. Good evening, everybody, good evening. Before we start tonight's Merry Ha Ha, I have an announcement to make. Little Dora can't be with us tonight. No. She's gone into politics. She's up in San Francisco speaking on the same platform with Mr. Paul Davis.

Dora's voice. Yoo-hoo! No, I'm not!

Merry's voice. Why, Dora—what happened?

Dora's voice. They called the meeting off.

Merry's voice. Dear, dear—what was the trouble?

Dora's voice. Mr. Davis couldn't come. He has brain fever.

Merry's voice. What? Why, that's impossible.

Dora's voice. Why?

Merry's voice. Well, I mean—can a worm have water on the knee? (*Laughter.*)

Dora's voice. Oh, you!

Merry's voice. Tell me, Dora, what kind of a speech were you going to make?

Dora's voice. Would you like me to show you?

Merry's voice. Dora! How can you ask?

Dora's voice. Well, all right—if you insist—here we go. (*Silence.*)

Merry's voice. Well, I'm waiting.

Dora's voice. Quiet! Don't interrupt me.

Merry's voice. Interrupt! You haven't said a word.

Dora's voice. Oh, no? What do you think goes on with my fingers?

Merry's voice. Well, what *does* go on? What is all that? A finger wave?

Dora's voice. Don't be ridic! It's sign language.

Merry's voice. Sign language? I thought this speech was for a crowd of Davis fans. Sign language is what you use to talk to dumb people.

Dora's voice. Huh! You're telling me! (*Long laughter.*)

(*The doorbell rings. Merry hesitates, then turns down the record and starts toward the door. En route, he picks up his hat and pulls it over his eyes. Then at the last minute he fishes out a pair of dark glasses from his pocket and slips them on. Thus, semi-disguised, he opens the door. Frank Mace is standing on the threshold.*)

Mace (*After a long pause*). Oh, hello, Mr. Merry. Remember me?

Merry. It's Frank Mace, isn't it?
Mace. That's right. I—(*Merry takes off the glasses.*) Eye-burns?
Merry. What?
Mace. Studio lights hurt your eyes?
Merry. Oh—oh, yeah. (*He puts the glasses on again.*)
Mace. Funny your being here.
Merry (*Self-conscious*). What do you mean?
Mace. Well—you see—I dropped by to ask Judith to read you the riot act about something.
Merry. Oh. Oh, by the way, how's Paul Davis's campaign fund doing?
Mace. Fine. We've got almost half what Goodfellow's gang has collected. In other words, we've got 'em licked about four to one.
Merry (*Nods*). They're not turning down any donations, are they?
Mace. That depends on where they come from.
Merry. Mmmm—this one would be anonymous.
Mace (*Grins*). I get it—a little hush money for your conscience, huh? (*Merry says nothing.*) Look. Could I pinch-hit for Judith? I'd like to raise a little hell with you on my own account. Got a minute?
Merry. Sure. I—I'm waiting for Judith myself. She's bringing me some stuff she's been typing. Sit down. I'll turn that off. (*He goes to the phonograph and turns it off.*)
Mace. Your last week's program, isn't it?
Merry. Mmm-hmm—a transcription.
Mace. I thought I recognized it. As a matter of fact, I've heard nearly all your programs. (*Right at him.*) I used to be a fan of yours. (*There is a pause of several seconds. Finally Mace blurts it out.*) What in the hell made you do it? (*Merry is silent.*) You think it's none of my business. Well, it is my business. This election is everybody's business.
Merry. If you don't mind, let's not discuss it.
Mace. Okay—at least that's some encouragement.
Merry. Hmmm?
Mace. Look. I'm going to speak my piece and get out of here. You're not going to like this—not any of it—so I might just as well talk turkey. It's encouraging that you don't want to discuss your sellout to Martin and Goodfellow because that means your conscience is bothering you. It means you're not quite as much of a louse as that thing you were just playing makes you sound like.
Merry. That's a lot of gags and wisecracks. So what?
Mace. You know damn well what. Whose idea was it? Not yours, I'll bet.

Merry. Why not?

Mace. Because it wasn't. No, you can kid your pals, maybe—you might even kid yourself. But you can't kid me. I've talked to too many people. I get to feel 'em. I know when they're for me and when they hate my guts. I felt you that day I heckled Goodfellow in your dressing room. All the time I was riding him I could feel you listening—and you're okay. Yep. You may try your damnedest to be a heel, but you'll never quite make it, because deep down in your heart you're for us a hundred percent. That's what burns me up.

Merry. I still say those gags don't mean a thing.

Mace. Oh, they don't? How many people do you think listen to you every week—just in California, I mean?

Merry. Oh—

Mace. Plenty. And you don't think it means anything when you tell that mob that Paul Davis is a dope and that that oil-drip Goodfellow is the white-haired friend of the people? Say, why do you suppose Martin boosted your pay check? You know damn well. It's because those pretty little lousy peaches you're ballyhooing were selling under ten thousand cans a month when you went on the air for them, and one year later they were selling over thirty thousand. If you did that for Yum Yum Peaches, you can certainly do it for Goo Goo Goodfellow. No kidding, if you go on with that anti-Davis junk you'll wake up the morning after election day and read in the papers that Mr. Goodfellow is in again—that he's won by a nose—by just that little "oomph" that your build-up has given him. I said I was going to be tough, but the more I talk to you the harder it is for me to pour it on, because I sit here and I look at you and I say to myself, "What's it all about? He knows you're right. He's all sold." I mean it's just nuts. You *can't* keep on being the Smarty Kelly for those big time ventriloquists. You're too much of a guy. You see, way down inside you there's something that keeps on saying, "I'm for them." I mean the millions and millions of little guys who haven't got what it takes—big dough—or some special trick they can sell for big dough. You know they're what really count, and once you buy that idea, nothing can kill it. It's a Joe Hill.

Merry. A what?

Mace. Don't you know about Joe Hill?

Merry. No.

Mace. Well, he was one of the millions who had a talent. Only he didn't sell it. Instead, he used it to write songs that they still sing on the picket lines. "There is Power, There is Power in a Band of Working Men," and a lot more. Wait a minute. (*He starts looking through Judith's records.*) In 1915 Joe Hill was framed on a phony murder charge and shot. He left a flock of songs and a slogan, "Don't mourn for me—organize!" Here! Here's what I was looking for. (*He holds up a record and puts it on the machine as he talks.*) A couple of guys named Hayes and Robinson wrote this song about him. Listen a minute. (*He plays the first three verses of "Joe Hill," which will comprise the first side of the record.*)

> I dreamed I saw Joe Hill last night
> Alive as you and me.
> Says I, "But Joe, you're ten years dead."
> "I never died," says he.
> "In Salt Lake, Joe, by God," says I,
> Him standing on my bed,
> "They framed you on a murder charge."
> Says Joe, "But I ain't dead."
> "The copper bosses killed you, Joe.
> They shot you, Joe," says I.
> "Takes more than guns to kill a man,"
> Says Joe, "I didn't die."

(*At the end of the three verses, Mace stops the machine and takes off the record. There is a moment's silence.*)

Mace. Like it?

Merry. Swell.

Mace. Hell of a song, isn't it? The rest is on the other side if you want an encore. Well, I'll blow. Thanks for listening. Good night.

Merry. Good night.

Mace (*Pauses at the door*). Next Wednesday night I'll be listening to you, and so will a million more. Just think that over. So long. (*He goes. Thinking, Merry wanders over to the phonograph and puts on the other side of "Joe Hill." While he is doing this, he notices that the mantel clock says 7:15. When the record starts, he goes over and, checking with his wristwatch, winds the clock and sets it at 8:43. Then he settles down to enjoy the record. He is so lost in listening that he doesn't hear the key in the lock. Judith comes in and listens with him as the last verse is finishing.*)

> And standing there as big as life,
> And smiling with his eyes,

> Joe says, "What they forgot to kill
> Went on to organize."
> "Joe Hill ain't dead," he says to me.
> "Joe Hill ain't never died.
> Where workingmen are out on strike
> Joe Hill is at their side."
> "From San Diego up to Maine,
> In every mine and mill,
> Where workers strike and organize,"
> Says he, "You'll find Joe Hill."

Judith. Going to put that on the program?
Merry. Oh, hello. That's an idea. I'll talk to Martin about it. How was the meeting?
Judith (*Taking off her hat*). All right. How're you doing?
Merry. Not so good. I'm on my seesaw.
Judith. How do you mean?
Merry. Oh, they get me down. Then I think up is the place to be, so up it is for a couple of minutes—then I begin to think about all the big-shot comedians who've died in the Actors' Home and down I go again. I guess that once you've been in the money you're kind of corrupted. (*Suddenly.*) You think I was a louse to give in to Martin, don't you?
Judith. What do you think?
Merry. I'm all balled up. You know what that gang could do to me, don't you?
Judith. What?
Merry. They can kick me the hell right out of the business.
Judith. I don't believe it. But suppose they did. Suppose you never worked again in your life. You'd always eat, wouldn't you?
Merry. Yeah, I guess so.
Judith. Well—what more do you want?
Merry. I hate to take a licking. I hate to think of people saying, "Get him. That's Phil Merry—he used to be the tops, but he couldn't stay there—he's a has-been. He's a bum."
Judith. I know. But how do you like it the other way? A first-class sellout. Goodfellow's gigolo. Do you want to live with that for the rest of your life?
Merry. Lady! The tactful way you put things! I'm beginning to wonder why you still speak to me. Why *do* you?

Judith. Oh, I don't know—why does a nice girl put up with a five-star stew-bum?
Merry. I suppose she thinks she can snap him out of it.
Judith. You know—you're just a human Quiz—carry your own answers around in the back of the book.
Merry. Yeah. (*He sits thinking. After a few seconds he makes a decision and stands up.*) Take a letter. (*Judith gets her notebook and pencil.*) Mr. Chatfield Martin—know the address? (*Judith nods.*) Okay. Dear Mr. Martin: The reaction from our first program in which the political situation was touched on has convinced me that my original objections to the idea were correct, and that it will be a mistake for us to continue this feature in our future programs. I am sure you will appreciate that I have come to this conclusion only after a most careful consideration of all the reactions to last week's broadcast. I am also sure that you will understand that as far as I am concerned this decision is final. With warm personal regards, I am—yours sincerely—any suggestions?
Judith (*Shakes her head*). It's perfect.
Merry. Got a typewriter?
Judith. Over there.
Merry. Some letterhead?
Judith. Behind you—on the desk.
Merry. Let's go then—right now—before I get cold feet. (*Judith moves to get set. Merry rises.*)
Judith. Coming up.
Merry. Here. I'll help you with that. (*They move the typewriter into position and continue talking as Judith types.*)
Judith. God, this is marvelous. And all on your own. From now on, I suppose, no help wanted.
Merry. Who said so? Listen, I'm scared stiff. I need you more than ever.
Judith. Okay. I'll be around.
Merry. You'd better be. (*He pauses.*) What do you suppose Martin's going to do when he reads that?
Judith. Holler his head off.
Merry. He'll do more than that. They'll sign that dummy.
Judith. There you go again. What if they do? You'll sign a better deal with somebody else.
Merry. Yeah—maybe. Oh. I told you Abe Kliegel called?
Judith, Mmm-hmm. Was he sober?
Merry. He sounded okay. Why?

Judith. Oh, nothing—except sometimes when he's high he has hallucinations that I'm Hedy Lamarr.
Merry. No kidding.
Judith. No kidding. He thinks I've got woof.
Merry. Well, well.
Judith. "Yours sincerely"—There you are. Change the date on that to the fourth of July and you could sign it Thomas Jefferson.
Merry (*Signing*). Life, liberty, and the pursuit of happiness. Sincerely yours, Phil Merry. There. Give me a stamp. I'm going to mail this while I'm still in the mood. (*Judith gives him a stamp.*) Thanks.
Judith. The mail box is down there—two blocks—in front of the drug store.
Merry. I know—that's where I parked my car. Okay, I'll be back before you can say "Bill Robinson." (*He goes hurriedly out the door without even bothering to put on his hat. Judith smiles and starts straightening up the papers and the typewriter. The doorbell rings. Judith crosses and opens the door, revealing Abe Kliegel who has a nice little bun [he has been drinking]. He holds up two tickets.*)
Kliegel. Hi'ya, Beautiful? Look, I've got seats for a preview. How's about it?
Judith. Oh, thank you, Abie, but I've got a date. I'm sorry.
Kliegel. Oh. Well, that's okay. The hell with it. (*He tears up the tickets as a magnanimous gesture.*) There's a poker game at Sol Mintz's. I'll crash that. Gee, you look swell. Who's the lucky guy?
Judith. You don't know him.
Kliegel. Somebody new, huh?
Judith. Brand new.
Kliegel (*Slowly*). Well, I don't want to be a drug on the manger. I'll hop along. (*He moves toward the door, then turns back.*) Oh, say, Judith, who is that dame that answered your phone when I called?
Judith. I suppose it was Sally.
Kliegel. I thought she was on location.
Judith. She is. But she said something about coming back with the cutter to check up on some film that got lost. I guess they dropped by to pick up an extra set of Sally's red flannels.
Kliegel. Yeah. Funny, though, it didn't sound a bit like Sally. Her voice must be changing.
Judith. Well, it's about time. Sally's getting to be a big girl.
Kliegel. Yeah. Well, bye-bye, blackbird. Have yourself a time.
Judith. Thank you, Abie.

Kliegel. Not at all. (*He weaves once more toward the door and once more back, bringing a bent cigarette out of his coat pocket.*) You haven't got a match, have you?
Judith. For you, Abie, I've got matches to burn. (*She turns to the desk to get a box of matches. Abie's eye falls on Phil's hat. He picks it up.*)
Kliegel. Hey, why didn't you tell me the boy friend was here already?
Judith. What?
Kliegel. Well, you're not gonna tell me this is your hat, are you?
Judith. Why, for heaven's sake! That must belong to Sally's cutter.
Kliegel. Oh, yeah. I guess so. (*He suddenly looks inside the hat.*) What's his name?
Judith. Mmm—I haven't the faintest idea.. Why?
Kliegel. Never mind. (*Very foxy.*) Say, would you mind if I washed my hands?
Judith. What?
Kliegel. Not necessary, if you have any objections.
Judith. Why should I? Go right ahead.
Kliegel (*With great dignity*). Thank you. (*Indicating.*) Through there?
Judith. That's right.
Kliegel. Pardon me. (*He weaves his way into the bedroom. Judith goes quickly to the front door, opens it and looks out. Then she crosses quickly and closes the door to the bedroom. As she turns back to the front door, Merry appears.*)
Judith (*Breathless*). Don't come in. Abie!
Merry. What?
Judith. Abe Kliegel. (*She points.*)
Merry. My God! (*He steps quickly out of the room again. Judith closes the door just as Abie enters from the bedroom.*)
Kliegel. I'd like to beg your pardon.
Judith. Why, Abie, what for?
Kliegel (*Still mysterious*). Never mind. I'm just begging your pardon. (*He starts toward the door.*) Ho-hum. The mystery of the cutter's hat. The nigger in the woodshed. Well, such is life. Goodbye, Judith. My regards to the boy friend. (*He pauses a moment in the door.*) P.M. Maybe it wasn't a cutter at all. Maybe it was Paul Muni. (*He disappears. Judith closes the door and goes to the window. A car is heard driving away. She turns to the door, opens it and admits Merry.*)
Merry. What was all that about?
Judith. He found your hat.

Merry. Oh.
Judith. I told him it belonged to a friend of Sally's. I don't know whether he believed me or not. When he left he was playing anagrams with the initials.
Merry. Oh, well, the hell with him. I feel much too good to be annoyed by Abie the Agent.
Judith. I feel pretty good myself.
Merry. I think I'd like a drink.
Judith. That's practically a coincidence. (*She goes to the breakfast alcove and starts to get out glasses.*)
Merry. How do I help?
Judith. Just relax.
Merry. I can't—I'm all steamed up—Fourth of July! *E Pluribus Unum*!
Judith. Okay, then, you can do things about ice and Shasta water. (*Indicating the whereabouts of both.*)
Merry. Swell. (*He exits, whistling "Yankee Doodle." Judith goes on setting things up. She takes out two bottles, holds one up to the light, shakes it and puts it down. The second bottle seems to satisfy her.*)
Judith (*Calling*). Scotch all right?
Merry (*Offstage*). Scotch is great.
Judith. That's a break.
Merry (*Offstage*). What?
Judith. I said that's a break. On account of we're fresh out of Bourbon, Rye, vanilla, raspberry, and points west. (*Judith puts a stack of records on the phonograph. Merry returns with a bowl of ice and a bottle of Shasta. They mix two drinks.*)
Merry. Well, here's to what?
Judith. You name it.
Merry (*Deliberating*). To the new man—to freedom—that all sounds pretty corny. Let's make it simple.
Judith. Okay.
Merry. Then here's to us. Long may we wave. Never may we waver. (*They drink. Both sit down.*) This is sensational. I mean the way I feel. You know something—I almost wish Martin would fire me. I could really use that layoff we were talking about last month. Maybe I can powder off for a few days when Esther gets back from Palm Springs. No, that's no good. I need much more than that. I've got to make tracks for some place where I can look at people as people and not as a collection of He's and She's in a joke book. Yep, and I want to find out some things about myself too. God! It's

just beginning to dawn on me what a total stranger to the rest of the world a comic can get to be. I've always prided myself on being up-to-the-minute Merry, but this Goodfellow thing has knocked some sense into me. You know what I am? A sausage machine. For fluff that's flying around on the surface—headlines—movies—other people's gags—they all squish in and come out again a week later—a long, luscious link of Merry Ha Ha baloney. But anything that's really real—I mean the kind of things *you* get excited about—no soap. Honest, it's a riot. I'm always screaming about being human. As a matter of fact, I guess the last human being I really looked at was twenty years ago on Ludlow Street. Life was tough then, but it was salty. You could taste it, and you really saw things. Everything since has been warmed-over hash. (*He pauses, then goes on.*) You know everything, Judith. What about it? What about the old dog and the new tricks? Can he learn a couple? Or is that out?

Judith. Why not—if he wants to?

Merry. Let's drink to that. (*He rises.*) To new tricks and a whole new dog.

Judith. Skoal! (*They drink. He sits down beside her on the couch. They are quiet for a moment. Merry listens to the music.*)

Merry. What is that?

Judith. It's a song about New Russia.

Merry. Hmmm. It's got a lot of—you know.

Judith. It's a peasant song—about a collective farm. A boy, a girl, and a tractor.

Merry. You're kidding.

Judith. No—in this song the tractor's practically the hero.

Merry. You mean all that steam and stuff is about a bunch of machinery?

Judith. Sounds funny, doesn't it? But you see, their machines are different. They don't belong to Joe Doakes, Incorporated. They belong to everybody. The more they turn out, the more everybody gets. A good tractor is sort of a local Santa Claus. So they sing about it.

Merry. That must be kind of tough on the boys in the lyric local. I mean—no "moon in June," no "love above." Is that fair to organized song writers?

Judith. Oh, they do all right. There's a spot in this song where the boy goes to town. He tells the girl her hair is like the harvest grain in the wind.

Merry. Say, that's all right. I like that. (*They sit for several seconds in silence. Merry takes her hand. Silence again.*) Boy, it's really funny.

Judith. What is?

Merry. Me. I've been dead. I've been dead for twenty years. As dead as last week's funny story, and I didn't even know it.
Judith. You weren't dead. You were just asleep.
Merry. Rip Van Winkle instead of Lazarus, hmmm? Okay. Anyway—now I'm alive again.
Judith. And you're going to stay that way.
Merry (*Nods*). Like this. (*His fingers tighten on hers.*) New dog—new tricks. (*He turns to her.*) Only this isn't a trick, Judith. There's magic in it, but it's not a trick. (*He takes her in his arms.*) I feel like that Russian kid—sure—any minute now I'll be singing songs about your hair.
Judith. Look out. It's got red in it.
Merry. I'll take a chance. (*Kisses her. Blackout.*)

Act Two: Scene Two

The living room of Phil Merry's Beverly Hills house. If possible, this should be a rearrangement of the elements used for Judith's living room so that the scene change can be made as quickly as possible. The main features of the room are a large stairway and a door on the left leading into a den. A piano has a prominent place among the furniture. The entrance door is on the right in the back center wall. Before the lights come up, a clock starts striking 6:00 A.M. When it finishes striking, the lights come up. The early morning light filters through the Venetian blinds. For a few seconds there is silence, then the doorbell rings. Silence again. And again the doorbell, followed by a violent rat-tatting on the door knocker. Finally an English butler, tousle-haired and very sleepy, comes from the back of the house in his bathrobe. He opens the door, revealing Esther Merry.

Ruxton. Oh, good morning, Mrs. Merry.
Esther. Good morning, Ruxton. Didn't you get my wire?
Ruxton. No, Mrs. Merry, nothing since you said you'd be back next Thursday.
Esther. Well, that's very funny. (*Togo, the Japanese chauffeur comes in with two bags, puts them down and starts out for more.*) I certainly sent, didn't I, Togo?
Togo. Excuse me, please?
Esther. I said I certainly sent Ruxton a wire, didn't I?
Togo. No, Mrs. Merry.
Esther. I didn't?
Togo. No, Mrs. Merry.
Esther. Oh, well, that's why you didn't get it.
Ruxton. Yes, Mrs. Merry.
Esther. Dear me! Well, there's no harm done. I can tell you exactly what it would have said. I won a thousand dollars at the Dunes and I want breakfast in my room in fifteen minutes. That's why I came home. If I'd stayed five minutes longer I'd have lost every single penny. And I've thought up the most wonderful story for Mr. Merry—for his next picture. (*Togo comes in with more bags.*) I told it to Togo on the way home and he's mad about it, aren't you, Togo?
Togo. Excuse me, please?

Esther. Never mind, Togo. Take the bags upstairs. I'm going to dictate it. Oh, yes, Ruxton, that reminds me. When does Miss Gordon usually get here?

Ruxton. About 9:30, I believe.

Esther. Oh, I'll never remember it that long. Call her up and tell her to come right over this minute.

Ruxton. Yes, Mrs. Merry.

Esther. And tell Helma I'd like three wee wee little pieces of toast with my eggs—I'm simply famished.

Ruxton. Yes, Mrs. Merry.

Esther. The whole thing happens in a radio station on Mars. Isn't that original? And I want a wee bitty bit of that new strawberry jam that good-looking boy sold us. His mother makes it. I'll have it all written down by the time Mr. Merry wakes up. Was he out for the evening?

Ruxton. Yes. He was playing poker. He telephoned about midnight and told me to leave his key under the mat—he'd forgotten it.

Esther. Oh, then I'll have plenty of time. You call Miss Gordon. Tell her I'll expect her for breakfast in fifteen minutes. (*Togo comes downstairs, having got rid of the bags.*) You can go to bed, Togo. (*To Ruxton.*) And tell Helma to coddle the eggs. It activizes the albumen.

Ruxton. Yes, Mrs. Merry. (*Mrs. Merry goes up the stairs. Ruxton goes to the telephone and dials a number.*) Hello, Miss Gordon. This is Ruxton at Mr. Merry's. Mrs. Merry just came home. No, *Mrs.* Merry. Yes. She wishes you to come right over, please. She wishes you to have breakfast here. Yes. Thank you, Miss Gordon. No. Mr. Merry is asleep. Thank you. (*He hangs up. As he turns to go to back of the house, a key sounds in the lock. He pauses. The door opens. It is Merry. He stares at Ruxton, surprised. Ruxton, equally surprised, stares back.*)

Merry. Oh. Good morning, Ruxton. What got you up so early?

Ruxton. Mrs. Merry just arrived, sir. I thought you were home, sir. I told her that you'd been playing poker and that you were sleeping.

Merry. Oh. Well, that's my story then. As a matter fact, you're right. I have been sleeping.

Ruxton. Yes, sir.

Merry. For twenty years.

Esther (*Offstage*). Ruxton! (*Merry goes quickly into the study, pantomiming to Ruxton as he exits. Esther appears and comes down the stairs.*) Something horrible has happened, Ruxton. Mr. Merry's bed hasn't even been slept in.

Ruxton (*Quite loud*). Perhaps he fell asleep in the study. He sometimes reads there when he comes in late.

Esther. Oh. Yes. I suppose that's possible. It certainly is very peculiar. (*She crosses and opens the door. What she sees apparently satisfies her. She sighs deeply.*) What a relief! You'd better put something over him, Ruxton. We had a friend who went to sleep like that once and he never woke up at all. I've forgotten what was the matter with him. Good heavens! I left the water running in the bathtub. (*She rushes upstairs. The doorbell rings.*) Answer that. It's probably Miss Gordon. (*Esther disappears. Ruxton starts for the door. Merry opens the study door and pssts to him.*)

Merry. If that's Miss Gordon, knock on this door.

Ruxton. Yes, sir. (*He goes to the door and admits Abe Kliegel. The latter is a little the worse for wear, but he is sober.*)

Kliegel. 'Morning, Ruxton. Mr. Merry up?

Ruxton. No, sir. He was out quite late—at a poker game.

Kliegel. Oh, yeah? Where?

Ruxton. He didn't say, sir.

Kliegel. Well—you'd better stir him up, Ruxton. It's important.

Ruxton. Yes, sir.

Esther (*Offstage. Almost sing-song and quite cheerful*). Ruxton. Bring a mop. I've done it. We've got a little flood.

Ruxton. Yes, Mrs. Merry. (*He starts for the back of the house.*)

Kliegel. I thought she was in Palm Springs.

Ruxton. She got back this morning. Excuse me, sir. (*He exits. Kliegel reaches in his pocket and takes out a pipe. As he looks for a tobacco humidor, he finds Phil's hat. He picks it up and examines it carefully. With the hat still in his hand, he goes over and sits down near the study door. He reaches over and knocks the ashes out of his pipe. At the rapping, Merry appears in the study door. Kliegel sees him. Merry sees that he has the hat.*)

Merry. Oh, hello, Abe.

Kliegel. 'Morning, Phil. Well. How'd you make out last night?

Merry. All right.

Kliegel. Big game?

Merry. Not very.

Kliegel. Table stakes?

Merry. Mmm-hmm.

Kliegel. *That's* the game.

Merry. Yeah. Stop stalling around, Abe—what is it?

Kliegel (*Holding up hat*). Well, to put it tactically, Phil, don't worry about this. There *was* a poker party last night at Sol Mintz's. They were all there except Jack Farrell. I can fix it with them that you were there too—see? What Esther don't know won't hurt her.
Merry. But suppose she does know?
Kliegel. But, my God, she can't. Who'd tell her?
Merry. I might.
Kliegel. Are you crazy?
Merry. No.
Kliegel. Phil, listen. You can't do that!
Merry. Why not?
Kliegel. Why not? Do you realize what Esther could hook you for if she wanted to get tough?
Merry. I can imagine.
Kliegel. And it isn't only that, Phil. A scandal just now would be terrible. Mr. Martin wouldn't like it at all. Listen, I'm telling you, at this minute he is very strong for you—so for God's sake don't let him get thinking about getting somebody who is absolutely scandal-proof—like that goddamn dummy.
Merry. The hell with Martin!
Kliegel. How can you talk like that? About your biggest booster in the whole business. Are you going positively to bite in the pants the hand that's feeding you?
Merry. I'll do what I feel like.
Kliegel. Now listen, Phil, take it easy. Don't burn your bridges before you come to them. Think the whole thing over at least for a couple of days. Talk to your lawyer.
Esther (*Offstage*). Ruxton!
Kliegel. Psst! Phil. Let me tell you something. (*He drags Merry into the study as Esther appears at the stairs.*)
Esther. Ruxton. (*The butler appears.*) Oh, Ruxton. Please bring my breakfast down here. The plumber just came and I can't hear myself chew.
Ruxton. Yes, Mrs. Merry. (*The doorbell rings.*)
Esther. See who it is.
Ruxton. Yes, Mrs. Merry. (*He opens the door. It is Judith.*)
Esther. Oh, Judith, come right in. You'll never guess why I've sent for you. Bring Miss Gordon's breakfast down, too, Ruxton.
Ruxton. Certainly, Mrs. Merry.

Esther. At first, of course, I was simply astounded. I'd never dreamed such a thing could happen.
Judith. I suppose not—I—
Esther. I mean I'd never had the slightest suspicion.
Judith. Mrs. Merry—
Esther. But then I suppose one never knows. It didn't happen to Conrad until he was over forty, you know.
Judith. Who?
Esther. Joseph Conrad—yes—he never wrote one word until he was forty—and of course, he was writing in a foreign language which makes it even harder, I suppose. Really, it was simply wonderful. Here I've been going along for years—just a little helpmate—a little house-mouse. People must have said, "Esther Merry! Why, I'll bet she hasn't a brain in her head." And in a way I'd have to agree with them. Then, all of a sudden, it happened this morning. Pop! A whole story! Just in a flash. I don't even know where it came from—but I suppose that's what inspiration is like. Did you bring your notebook?
Judith. It's in my bag.
Esther. Then let's get right at it. We can nibble while I'm thinking. It's a moving picture story for Phil—or did I tell you?
Judith. No, you didn't.
Esther. Oh! And wait! Wait till you hear the title: *A Love Nest on Mars*. Isn't that cute?
Judith. Mmmm—
Esther. Well—here we go then. *A Love Nest on Mars* by Esther Merry. Whirligig! Whirligig! Whirligig! A whirl of music coming from a radio station. Oh, I should have said, "Fade in"—you'll remember to put that in, won't you? They always start with "Fade in." I don't know why. Whirligig! Whirligig! Whirligig!
Judith. I've got that. (*Ruxton appears with the breakfast.*)
Esther. Oh, yes—where was I—?
Judith. A whirl of music coming from a radio station.
Esther. That's right. The music sweeps up and up, right through a cloud. They can do that in pictures, you know. It's called a transparency or something. Just pour the coffee, Ruxton. Then it sweeps up to the moon. The man in the moon starts to sing and then—the stars—and then Mars. Tiptoe, Ruxton, tiptoe! I don't mean that Mars sings, of course. I mean the music whirligigs right up to it—and then it goes—(*Someone bangs on the*

door knocker.) Good heavens! What on earth is that? Will you see, Ruxton?

Ruxton. Yes, Mrs. Merry. (*He opens the door. A police detective and two cops are in the doorway.*)

Detective. Is Mr. Merry home?

Ruxton. He's asleep, sir.

Detective. Well—I'm afraid you'll have to wake him up. It's important.

Ruxton. Yes, sir. (*He crosses to the study.*)

Esther. I'm Mrs. Merry. Will you please explain—

Detective. Now don't you be worried, Ma'am. It's all right, I'm sure. We just have to ask Mr. Merry a couple of questions. (*Merry and Kliegel come out of the study.*)

Merry. Did you want to see me?

Detective. Yes, Mr. Merry—I'm just checking on a story someone's been telling us. You see a time bomb exploded in the Governor's car in front of Mr. Chatfield Martin's house at about 8:30 last night.

Merry. God! Was he badly hurt?

Detective. No. Luckily he was inside having dinner and his driver was in the kitchen, so nobody was touched. Now here's what I wanted to see you about. We picked up what was left of a pocketbook on Mr. Martin's lawn, and we've got the guy it belongs to.

Merry. Yes?

Detective. Yeah, his name's Frank Mace. Know him?

Merry. Yes, I know him.

Detective. He's out there. Could I bring him inside a minute?

Merry. Yes, certainly.

Detective. All right, boys. (*The cops leave. The detective turns to Mrs. Merry.*) The reason I asked is he don't look very pretty. The boys kind of had to put him down a bit—if you know what I mean.

Esther. Oh, yes, of course. Of course.

Detective. Okay, then. (*They bring Mace in. He has been badly beaten up and practically has to be carried.*) Come in, Mr. Mace. Here's Mr. Merry. I just wanted him to hear what you said about him. (*One of the cops lifts up Mace's head which has been hanging limply on his chest.*) Mr. Mace says he's innocent, Mr. Merry. He says he was with you last night.

Esther. Why, that's ridiculous. Mr. Merry was playing poker all evening.

Kliegel. Absolutely, officer. I was with him. At Sol Mintz's.

Detective. Well, that's fine. All right, boys, you can take Mr. Mace downtown. (*They start to take Mace out. He tries to speak. Judith makes an involuntary gesture toward him.*)
Mace. Mr. Merry—will you—(*The speech ends in a mumble.*)
Merry. What is it, Mace?
Kliegel. For goodness' sake, Phil, don't say a word till you see your lawyer. Even you might make him delirious. Let the chief handle this. He knows what to do with him. Go ahead, boys. (*The policemen start out.*)
Detective. Sorry we had to bother you, Mr. Merry. We'll call you later for a statement. Good morning, Mr. Merry. Good morning, Miss. (*He leaves. Kliegel jumps quickly into the silence.*)
Kliegel. 8:30! A fine story! Why, that was just when you took that first big pot with those three little deuces, for heaven's sake.
Esther (*Regards the two men*). I'm going to call Sol Mintz. (*She starts for the telephone.*)
Kliegel. Please! Let me get him for you—you won't understand a word he's saying. When Sol's been losing, his accent is terrible. (*He joins Esther at the table. Merry exchanges looks with Judith, then starts for the door. Kliegel turns, runs after Merry and swings him around.*) Where are you going?
Merry. I want to talk to him.
Kliegel. You talk to nobody till I get ahold of Sol Mintz. Esther! (*Esther joins them.*)
Esther. That's right, Phil. (*Merry turns from the door. Kliegel starts back toward the telephone.*) What do you suppose they did to his face?
Merry. "Or else," they told him. "Watch your step—or else." (*Kliegel moves from the telephone toward the study.*)
Kliegel (*Muttering*). I'll get him on the extension. (*He goes into the study.*)
Merry. Or else—(*The curtain descends on Act Two.*)

Act Three: Scene One

Merry's living room, several hours later. Kliegel has apparently been talking for some time to Petty, Durkis, Hartman, and Mintz, who are disposed about the room in characteristic attitudes. At the moment, Kliegel is concentrating on Mintz.

Kliegel. Sol, I've explained it fourteen times already. My God, it ought to be as plain as the nose on your face.
Mintz. Don't get personal.
Kliegel. Oh, for God's sake, be reasonable. That's only a figment of speech.
Mintz. I still don't like it.
Kliegel. All right, then—the nose on George Petty's face.
Mintz. Which is not so plain, if you ask me, and neither is what you're saying.
Kliegel. Why not?
Mintz. Well, lookit. If Phil Merry was someplace else when this Mace guy says he was with him, why do we have to say he was playing poker with us? Why can't he say where he really was?
Kliegel. I told you why. In the first place, his butler here, Ruxton, told Mrs. Merry Phil was playing poker, so that's what he's stuck with. In the second place, where he really was is Phil Merry's own personal business.
Petty. Sure, Abie, but what about that hearing on Tuesday? Anybody who testifies there is under oath. You gotta speak the truth, the whole truth, and nothing else but. What about that?
Kliegel. George, please. Nobody's going to have to testify at that hearing except me. I just talked to Eli Brodkin, Phil's lawyer, and that's all set. The only thing is that talking around Hollywood I want you to tell people what a lousy frame-up this is when Phil Merry was positively playing poker at Sol Mintz's from eight o'clock on. That's all.
Hartman. Well, that's okay—if you're sure about the hearing.
Kliegel. Listen, boys, I told you I talked to Eli Brodkin, who knows more about the law than you ever forgot, and what's more important, I talked to Mr. Martin. Yes, for twenty-three minutes I talked to him—and believe me, if we don't squash that phony alibi of Mr. Mace's, the jobs around here in the writing department are going to be scarcer than hen's feet. There won't maybe be any Merry Ha Ha even. And don't think I'm kidding.
Durkis. Sure, you're not. And I don't blame Martin. No, and I don't believe anybody here wants to stick his nose into Phil Merry's private business.

But I do feel personally that if I knew what Phil was really doing last night I'd be a lot happier about going to bat for him.

Mintz. Sure. That's just what I been trying to say.

Hartman. That's right, Abie. Harry's right.

Kliegel. Well—okay, then. You're all good pals of Phil's. I'll spill the dirt. He was with a dame.

Petty. Well, why didn't you say so?

Hartman. Sure, Abie—what the hell!

Kliegel. You see what I mean, Sol?

Mintz. Well, certainly.

Kliegel. Fine. That's all fixed then—(*Merry appears on the stairs. He has shaved and changed. He hesitates.*) What do you say? Can I count on you?

Durkis (*Rising*). You can on me.

The rest (*ad libs*). Sure. Okay, Abie.

Kliegel. All right, now. Get around. Circulate. Spread the news.

Petty. Right. We'll do that, Abie.

Kliegel. Thank you, boys, and so long. Phil will certainly appreciate this, and so will Mr. Martin. (*Merry starts down the stairs. Mintz sees him.*)

Mintz. Psst!

Durkis (*Catching the signal and laughing heartily*). Yes, boys, I'm telling you, it's perfect. The whole thing could be a fishing party—Dopey Dora could be rowing the boat and Phil could be doing the fishing. (*He pretends to see Merry for the first time.*) Oh, good morning, Phil.

Merry. 'Morning.

Durkis. Look, we've got a swell idea for the next program—a fishing party. It would start off with you telling Dora she has to whisper so as not to scare the fish and we'd end up with you yelling your head off. What do you say?

Merry. That's up to you, boys—I always give 'em whatever you write, don't I?

Hartman. No—no kidding, Phil, it's a hot idea, isn't it?

Petty. Fishing, Phil—you can't miss. Remember that old vaudeville act of Harry Tate's? Used to murder people—absolutely assassinate 'em!

Merry. Look, boys—if you like it, write it. Only don't tell me about it. I'm on a diet. Doctor's orders. Yep, I've got comedian's heart—in the last stages—wheezing and gagging. Doctor says if I hear even one joke it might be fatal. You wouldn't want to have that on your conscience, would you?

Petty. Yeah, but suppose we write it and you don't like it?

Merry. Listen, George, I'll like it. As long as I don't have to listen to it, I'll love it.
Durkis. Well—
Merry. Okay, boys, hop to it. Leave me with Abe—he's just what the doctor ordered. He's going to read me the gossip column from the Undertakers' Journal. (*The writers look at one another and start to laugh.*)
Hartman. I guess you're still all right, all right. Come on, boys. Good luck, Phil—good luck with everything.
Merry. Thanks. (*The writers depart with a chorus of goodbyes in which Kliegel joins. As soon as the door is closed, Kliegel turns to Merry.*)
Kliegel. Listen—I fixed everything. The boys are all set. You played poker with us till twelve o'clock. There's nothing to it. Now you got nothing to worry about.
Merry. Nope, not a thing.
Kliegel. On the level, I'm telling you, it's a cinch. Oh—Mr. Martin called. He's coming over later. He wants to talk to you. Where's Judith?
Merry. Upstairs. She's taking dictation from Esther.
Kliegel. Ha! That's life. Er—now look here, Phil—about her—
Merry. About her, the less you say the better I'll like it.
Kliegel. Now, please—(*The telephone rings. Kliegel answers it.*) Hello. Okay, put him on. Eli Brodkin, Phil. (*Into telephone.*) Just a minute. (*He hands the receiver to Merry.*)
Merry. Hello. Oh, hello, Eli. Yeah, I guess so. What time? All right. Mmm-hmm. Okay, Eli. Three o'clock. I'll be there. So long. (*He hangs up.*) He wants me to come down to his office after lunch—he wants to talk over the whole thing—get me set for the hearing.
Kliegel. Sure. You just leave the whole thing to Eli. He'll tell you exactly what to say.
Merry. Yeah. Sure. He'll tell me. They'll all tell me—Eli, Martin, all of 'em. But how can I do it? What kind of a guy do they think I am?
Kliegel. Phil.
Merry. Yeah?
Kliegel. Was Frank Mace with you last night?
Merry. Yes—he was.
Kliegel. At Judith's?
Merry. That's right.
Kliegel. God! Well, what if he was? He was just trying to plant an alibi. He set the bomb in Goodfellow's car—his pocketbook proves that—and then

he came to talk to Judith—so's he'd be with somebody when the thing went off. What time was he there?

Merry. He left at about 8:40. I remember because Judith's clock had stopped at 7:15. I set it by my wrist watch to 8:43.

Kliegel. Did you tell Judith you'd seen Mace?

Merry. No. No, I didn't.

Kliegel. Well, you mustn't—or anybody else. Look, Phil—think what it would do to Judith if this ever came out. Think of the dirt people would put on her. A nice mess. She'd be a scarlet woman, Phil—absolutely gone with the wind. And what for? I tell you, Mace did it, and you know he did. So what's all the shooting for? Mace is playing you for a sucker. Don't stand for it. Stick by your poker story—keep Judith out of it. If you don't, Phil, this will be the end of you both—the absolute end.

Merry. You're a fool, Abie. Judith knows the poker story is a lie—and she's going to believe Mace.

Kliegel. Not ahead of you she isn't.

Merry. But I'm not going to lie to her.

Kliegel. Okay, don't—tell her the truth.

Merry. I'm going to.

Kliegel. Sure, you are. You're going to tell her that Mr. Mace was there all right—but that it won't do him one bit of good for you to say so—because he left the joint at 7:15—7:15. That's the truth, Phil, and that's one whole hour before that bomb went off. You tell her that and see what she says.

Esther (*Offstage*). Phil darling—Phil-*lup*!

Merry. Yes. Yes, Esther. (*Esther appears carrying a newspaper with violent headlines.*)

Esther. Have you seen the papers? They're simply terrible. That man Mace's name is in the headlines as big as yours. I had to stop dictating. I simply couldn't keep my mind on it. I've told Judith to finish typing what I dictated and then go home—unless you want her—do you? (*Merry is silent.*) Phil! Do you want Judith?

Merry. What? Oh—er—no—except—well, I suppose I'd better give her a few notes on the stuff I'll be taking down to Eli Brodkin. I've got to see him after lunch.

Esther. Yes—well, tell him I said hello to Mrs. Brodkin. The bombing is absolutely all over the paper. You simply can't find a word of news anywhere—not a word. Oh, yes. There is one little thing way back here near the sports section. Daisy Kirkland is suing Henry for divorce. Mental cruelty! Humph! I can't understand girls like Daisy. What's she being so nice about? Everybody knows it's that little red-headed extra girl. Why doesn't she say so? Why doesn't she show her up for the gold-digging little tart that she is? The trouble with Daisy is she's still in love with Henry, and she thinks if she's nice he might come back to her some day. Well—she's a fool. I'd like to see some cheap little bitch try to make a monkey out of me like that. When I got through with her, nobody would marry her—they wouldn't touch her with a ten-foot pole! (*Judith comes down the stairs.*) Oh, Judith—Mr. Merry wants you to take some notes. He'll explain. Did you finish what I gave you?

Judith. It's all on the card table in your dressing-room.

Esther. Oh, thank you, darling. I'll look it over. (*She starts up.*) What are you saying to the reporters when they call up, Phil?

Kliegel. He's not saying anything. You're both out. If it's important, Ruxton turns 'em over to me and I talk 'em black and blue in the face.

Esther. Oh, good. I wouldn't have the least idea what to say.

Kliegel. You just leave it to me. (*Esther is gone. Kliegel looks at Judith and Merry.*) I'll be in here if you need me. (*He goes into the study. Judith and Merry face each other in silence for a few seconds. Then Judith speaks quietly.*)

Judith. Have you told them yet?

Merry. I haven't told anybody anything.

Judith. Why not?

Merry. There's a hearing downtown on Tuesday. That's official. Not much use talking till then, is there?

Judith. No, I suppose not.

Merry. You seem to take it for granted that your friend, Mr. Mace, did see me last night.

Judith. He says he saw you.

Merry. Which settles it, huh?

Judith. Well, of course.

Merry. But suppose he—oh, Christ! What a mess. What a nice lousy hunk of flypaper I've stuck my foot into.

Judith. I know—and I'm sorry it had to be you. I know how you hate it. Yet in a way, I'm glad. If it was anyone else I'd be afraid they might get to him with their money and their power. But with you holding our case ace, I feel safe—I know we'll win.

Merry. Aren't you afraid that pocketbook will fix him—no matter what I say?

Judith. No, I'm not. That was a pretty obvious plant. Even the kind of anti-labor judge we'll probably get must see that. Besides, look what that police expert said about the bomb.
Merry. What did he say? I didn't read that.
Judith. He says the thing was timed to go off fifteen minutes after it was left in the car.
Merry. He did, huh—God!
Judith. What is it?
Merry. I guess you'd better know. Mace is wrong about the time.
Judith. What?
Merry. It wasn't 8:30 when he left me. It was quarter past seven.
Judith. But he couldn't be that wrong.
Merry. Why? I've done it. I've done exactly that.
Judith. Then perhaps you're wrong this time.
Merry. No. I'm positive. 7:15. That's what your clock said, Judith. I looked at it just after he left. I'll swear to that on a stack of Bibles. Judith, listen. What do you think I should do? Judith, I'm going to get a divorce and marry you—if we use our heads, we can do it quietly—with no yaw-yaw and mud slinging. It looks as if this alibi of mine is no good. So what's the use? What's the use of trying it at all, if all it's going to do is give them a chance to smear you with filth? Why can't I just keep my mouth shut and keep you out of it? (*He takes her by the shoulders.*)
Judith. You're a sweet guy—but you're an awful dope.
Merry. What are you getting at?
Judith. You're all balled up—about us. If you want it to happen, then it will, no matter how tough people make it for you. But you mustn't kid yourself it will ever happen "quietly," because it won't. No matter how it's done, there'll be lots about it that won't be pretty.
Merry. But it won't be like this. Those ghouls at the hearing will really crucify us.
Judith. Well, let them—if it's going to help Frank Mace, let them!
Merry. Sure—if—IF!
Judith. But it will help him, even if all you say is that he was with you—at least you'll prove he was telling the truth about that. Why, you might not even have to mention the time.
Merry. Don't worry. Those weasels will dig it out of me—then we'll have waded through all that muck for nothing.
Judith. Not for nothing. Can't you see—?

Merry. No. Right now I can't see anything except that I want you and that I don't want any part of this mess. I'd give everything I own this minute to grab you and run like hell from the whole damn business. Why can't they leave me alone? I didn't ask to get mixed up in this, goddamn it! I've got nothing to do with it!

Judith. Everybody's got something to do with it. You see, this isn't just a one-man frame-up. We're all being framed—every mother's son of us in the State of California. This whole phony bombing is a last desperate gag to keep Man Mountain Monopoly in the saddle. And if it works, what a laugh! What a grand and glorious guffaw! From Sacramento to San Diego they'll give us all the Merry Ha Ha. "So what?" you say. "After all, so what?" So I'll tell you what. There's a Frankenstein factory in the world today, and the monster it's making is a Fascist monster—a thing of war and horror that spits death and destruction on the little lonely people who get in its way. The forces of democracy and progress stand in its path—but their strength is isolated, and their will to resist is feeble and confused. Whenever the people are beaten the monster moves on and its appetite grows sharper. But when the people win, the monster trembles and hesitates. I guess that sounds kinda fancy, but the damn thing is so fantastic, I don't know how else to describe it. The point is this. If reaction wins in California, the Fascist monster is one step closer to America. So if you can help stop that, if you even think you can help stop it, you've got to do it and forget what'll happen to you or me or anyone else.

Merry. If I could only see it that way—

Judith. You've got to see it. (*Someone bangs on the front-door knocker. Kliegel appears instantly in the study doorway, like the bird in a cuckoo clock.*)

Kliegel. Hello? (*Merry indicates the front door.*)

Merry. See who it is, will you?

Kliegel. Sure. (*He starts across as Ruxton appears.*) Never mind, Ruxton. (*Ruxton bows and exists. Kliegel opens the door. Martin and Goodfellow are standing there.*) Well, hello, Governor. Hello, Mr. Martin.

Martin. Good morning. Good morning, Phil.

Merry. How'r'you, Mr. Martin—Governor?

Goodfellow. I'm as well as could be expected—

Martin. A terrible shock, as you can imagine. Er—could we—?

Judith (*To Abie*). I'll take any messages. (*To the rest.*) If you'll excuse me.

Martin. Oh—good morning, Miss Gordon. Yes, thank you—certainly. (*Judith goes into the study. Kliegel locks the door. Martin turns to Merry.*)

There are one or two things—first of all, I got your letter this morning. Frankly, it came as quite a shock. However, I imagine that what's happened must have shown you how wrong you were.
Merry. In what way?
Martin. I mean you must realize now what kind of people are fighting against Governor Goodfellow and how important it is to beat them.
Merry. Don't you think it would be a good idea to wait until after the hearing before we argue about that?
Martin (*After a moment's silence*). Perhaps it would—that is, if there's any doubt in your mind as to what will happen at the hearing—
Kliegel. Lookit, Phil. I took the liberty a few minutes ago of calling Mr. Martin while you were talking to Judith. He knows everything that I do.
Merry. I see.
Martin. I think we all understand perfectly that the fact that Mace actually was with you for a few minutes last night is completely worthless as an alibi.
Merry. Really?
Martin. Naturally—in the face of the other evidence against him. However—it would certainly simplify things if his story could be contradicted.
Merry. You mean if I lied about it?
Martin. That's a very crude interpretation of what I'm getting at.
Merry. I'm sorry. I apologize. Maybe you'd better say it over again with flowers.
Kliegel. For God's sake, don't be like that, Phil. You're only making Mr. Martin mad.
Martin. No—I'm not angry—not at all. I'm only beginning to wonder about certain things I've heard.
Kliegel. What things—for heaven's sakes indeed?
Martin. Oh, things that have been written to certain members of our Board of Directors—accusations that Phil Merry is a radical sympathizer, and that he ought to be blacklisted in every radio station in the country.
Kliegel. I couldn't believe such a thing. My God!
Martin. I dropped a hint of this to you some time ago, Phil. I told you then I'd been standing up for you. I hope—with a clean conscience—I can go on defending you now.
Merry. That's up to you, Mr. Martin.
Martin. No—I'm sorry. It's definitely up to you.
Goodfellow. May I say something?

Martin. Please.

Goodfellow. I'm sure Phil's heart is in the right place. He knows which side is the right side. But I don't think he realizes the fundamental American principle that's at stake in this case—

Merry. I'm beginning to find out.

Goodfellow. Of course you are. The issue is Americanism. Americanism against Communism and all the other isms. What difference does it really make whether a man named Frank Mace put that bomb in my car—or some other red?

Merry. It might make a difference to Mace.

Goodfellow. All right, then—I'll pardon him. Yes, sir. If there's one reasonable doubt of his guilt in anybody's mind, I'll pardon him. On my word of honor—that is, of course, if I'm elected. In the meantime, someone's got to pay for this outrage and pay now. In my opinion, it doesn't matter whether it's Frank Mace or Earl Browder. They're all guilty if you take a long view look at the thing—all of them. So don't let's confuse the issue with personalities. The thing that will be on trial at that hearing will be the liberty and the constitutional Americanism of the State of California. So I'm asking you a simple, straightforward question, Mr. Merry. Are you going to act for Americanism or against it?

Merry. If you're talking about the hearing, Mr. Goodfellow, I'm afraid I'll have to tell the truth. If that's un-American, I'm sorry, and I guess I'll just have to take the consequences.

Kliegel. Listen, Phil, for God's sake—

Martin. Never mind, Kliegel. (*He turns to Merry.*) I'm sorry things have turned out this way—I really like you, Phil. You could have had a brilliant future. It's really too bad. Well—Governor?

Goodfellow. Yes—yes. (*Martin and Goodfellow go to the door and out.*)

Kliegel. For the love of God! Phil, it's still not too late. Let me go talk to 'em. I can tell 'em you didn't know what you were saying.

Merry. Oh, quiet!

Kliegel. They'll blacklist you.

Merry. Fine. I'm sick of it all, anyway.

Kliegel. Ten thousand a week and you're throwing it in the garbage can.

Merry. Shut up, will you?

Kliegel. And not only Martin you give phooey to—but the Governor. Just wait till some of those Sacramento tough boys hear what you did to him. What happened to Mister Faraday will be mere horseplay.

Merry. Will you get out of here! And stay out!

Kliegel. A pleasure. (*He goes to the door, then pauses.*) This is like you were socking my heart in the stomach, Phil. And let me tell you something. It'll be a long time before you find somebody else who'll be like your own flesh and blood to you—for ten percent. (*He goes. Judith tries the study door from the inside and finds it locked. Phil hears her, crosses, and opens the door.*)
Merry (*After a moment*). Hear the whole thing?
Judith. I heard enough.
Merry (*He takes her in his arms*). I need you so badly. When that seesaw of mine starts going down—I need you like hell to hop on the other side and send me up again.
Judith. Okay. As long as you want me, I'll be there to hop.
Merry. And if I decided I didn't want to go up—?
Judith. You won't.
Merry. Don't duck my question.
Judith. You mean could I keep on loving you if you went the way Martin and Goodfellow want you to?
Merry. Mmm-hmm.
Judith. I don't know, Phil. I can't even imagine such a thing.
Merry. It could happen.
Judith. I don't believe it—but if it did—well, I guess after awhile something would happen. Because to me—together means together—hearts and heads and where you're going. Anything else and you'll end up strangers and a million miles apart.
Merry. Then you think that "Love Conquers All" stuff is a lot of sentimental marmalade?
Judith. I think that if love is so little that there's no room for the world in it—it's going to sizzle for a minute and then blow up like a penny firecracker.
Merry. Hmm—well, I guess that's telling me.
Esther (*Offstage*). Judith! I'm in the mood again. (*Merry and Judith look at each other uncomfortably for a second, then Judith starts up the stairs.*) Are you coming, Judith?
Judith. Yes, Mrs. Merry.
Esther (*Offstage*). Hurry up, darling. Get me while I'm hot. (*Merry stands thinking a moment, then he moves over to the piano and sits down. His fingers pick out the melody of "Joe Hill." He hums a moment and speaks the refrain.*)

Merry. "Says Joe, 'I didn't die.' Says Joe, 'I didn't die.'" (*His fingers continue to improvise. Suddenly the study door opens and a man steps into the room. He wears a black suit, a black shirt, and an orange tie, and is completely bald. A black Fedora is over his right hand; his right elbow is crooked. He moves quietly over to the table that holds the telephone. When he is behind the table, his left hand takes the hat; his right hand drops behind the table. Merry turns and sees him. There is a moment's pause.*)
The Man. Hi'ya, Mr. Merry.
Merry (*Rings the servant's bell*). How did you get in here?
The Man (*Jerks his head toward the study*). Your window's open. Have a seat.
Merry. What do you want?
The Man. Just a coupla right answers. Sit down.
Merry. Get out of here!
The Man. Now look. Don't make me nervous. Just relax. When I'm nervous I don't act nice. I'm telling you. Sit down. (*Ruxton comes in from the back of the house.*)
Merry. Show this man out, Ruxton.
Ruxton. Yes, sir. This way, please. (*The man replaces the hat on his right hand and walks over to Ruxton in front of whom he pauses.*)
The Man. Get me a drink. (*Ruxton pauses.*) You heard what I said. Get me a drink. (*Ruxton pauses a moment, looks at Merry. Then he starts out.*) Plain water. (*Ruxton continues out. Merry has crossed to the table. He picks up the telephone and dials the zero.*) Look, I wish you'd relax. (*He removes the hat and shows a pair of wire cutters. Merry picks up the telephone from the table. The wire dangles free.*)
Merry. What do you want?
The Man. Now that's the way to be. Now we're going places. All I want is a coupla plain yes and no-ses.
Merry. What about?
The Man. Don't rush me. Take it easy. I don't like people that get excited. (*Merry sits on the edge of the table.*) That's it. (*He sits down.*) Now. I been readin' this morning's papers, and they all say you wasn't with Mr. Mace at all like he says—but I didn't read nothin' about what you said on the subject.
Merry. I haven't said anything.
The Man. Oh. Savin' your jaw for the hearing, huh?
Merry. That's right.

The Man. Well, that's fine—I'm gonna do a little song and dance at that hearing myself.
Merry. Really?
The Man. Yeah. I kinda think I saw somebody who looked just like Mr. Mace pokin' around the Governor's car at quarter past eight last night, and I'm going to kind of tell the judge about it. What do you think of that?
Merry. I don't think anything. Tell him whatever you like.
The Man. Thanks—I wish I could say the same to you.
Merry. What do you mean by that?
The Man. What do you think I mean? (*Merry studies the man's face a moment, then swallows. His fingers involuntarily move to the knot of his tie. The man grins.*)
The Man. That's right. That's what I mean. (*He pauses.*) Don't stick your neck out, Mr. Merry. I mean there's people that don't like it. They don't like no trouble. It's like I'm telling you—it makes 'em nervous. (*He takes out a match.*) I mean, what's the idea a dope like Faraday poking his nose into other people's business. (*He lights the match with his thumbnail.*) What'd it get him? What happened to him? (*He blows out the match.*) That's bad. Don't be like that, Mr. Merry. Don't make no trouble on Tuesday. You understand what I mean? (*He pauses, then smiles.*) Sure, that's right. Take it easy. (*Ruxton comes in with the drink on a tray. The man takes the drink.*) Thanks. Well, here's to our side. (*He drinks and replaces the glass on the tray.*) So long, Mr. Merry. See you Tuesday. (*He goes out the front door. Merry stands looking after him. Blackout.*)

Act Three: Scene Two

The scene is Division I, on the seventh floor in the Hall of Justice, Los Angeles. The back wall is not quite parallel to the rear wall of the theatre. The stage-right extremity of it is considerably further downstage than the stage-left corner. From the stage-left corner, a second wall goes off downstage at right angles to the rear wall. This second wall has a large window in it. There is a platform set against the rear wall. On it is the judge's stand and a witness chair. To one side of the judge's stand on the rear wall is a large blackboard on which a diagram of a street has been drawn in chalk. The drawing shows a ground plan of the sidewalk in front of a house with a limousine indicated as standing at the curb. There is a lamp post indicated about ten feet behind the car. In front of the platform and parallel to it is a long council table, or perhaps two tables put together. On the stage-right side are the Deputy District Attorney and his entourage, and on the stage-left end the defendant's attorneys. The witnesses are distributed around the table. The clerk of the court, bailiffs, and policemen are in their correct positions. Present are Judith, Merry, Mace, Esther, Kliegel, Farrell, Mintz, and Durkis, and a Mr. Smith who is on the witness stand. Mr. Smith turns out to be the gentleman who visited Merry at the end of the last scene. The Deputy District Attorney is finishing his examination of Smith. He indicates the blackboard with a pointer.

Deputy D.A. Please look carefully at this diagram, Mr. Smith. Here is Mr. Martin's house where Governor Goodfellow was dining on the evening of September 21st. This is the Governor's car which we have shown had been left there by the chauffeur when he went into the kitchen. Now, as I understand it, you were on your way to Mr. Martin's house with a letter at about 8:15 when you stopped under this lamp post.
Smith. That's right.
Deputy D.A. Why did you stop there?
Smith. I wanted to check the address on my letter to be sure that was the house.
Deputy D.A. The letter you refer to was the one which we have marked as People's Exhibit E, addressed to the Governor and recommending you as a bodyguard during the remainder of his stay in Los Angeles—is that right?
Smith. That's it.

Court Judge. Just a minute, gentlemen. My calendar is crowded. I should like to know how much longer it will take to present the People's case.
Deputy D.A. This is my last witness, your honor. We should be through very shortly.
Court Judge. Very well. Proceed.
Deputy D.A. Thank you. Mr. Smith, will you please tell the court what happened while you were looking at the address on the letter?
Smith. A guy comes down the street from the direction of the car—
Deputy D.A. You mean the Governor's car—that is, from here? (*Pointing to the diagram.*)
Smith. Uh-huh. When he got about fifteen or twenty feet away from me he started to cross the street.
Deputy D.A. (*At the blackboard*). Like this?
Smith. About like that. I hollered at him, "Hey, Buddy, come here a minute."
Deputy D.A. What did he answer?
Smith. He didn't answer. He kept right on walking.
Deputy D.A. What did you do?
Smith. I hollered, "Hey *you*, come here!"
Deputy D.A. What did he do then?
Smith. He stopped walking and come a little closer.
Deputy D.A. How close?
Smith. Oh, he was about ten feet away when he stopped.
Deputy D.A. You mean ten feet away from where you were?
Smith. Yeah.
Deputy D.A. Was he within the range of the light from the lamp post?
Smith. Yeah, sure.
Deputy D.A. Very well. What happened then?
Smith. Well, I says, "Which house is number 219?"—and he says, "I don't know," and walked away—so I went up to the house and asked if the Governor was there, and the guy said, "Yes," and I give him the letter and he says, "Wait," so I waited, and then the guy come back and took me inside.
Deputy D.A. When the man stopped under the light, were you able to see him quite plainly?
Smith. As plain as I see you.
Deputy D.A. Is he present in the courtroom?
Smith. Sure—that's him over there.
Deputy D.A. You mean the defendant, Frank Mace?

Smith. That's right.
Deputy D.A. You're absolutely positive?
Smith. Certainly I'm positive.
Deputy D.A. Thank you. That's all. People rest.
Court Judge. Proceed with the defense. (*Mace's attorney, Harry Donovan, now rises.*)
Donovan. Mr. Smith, I infer that your application for the position of bodyguard to Governor Goodfellow implies previous experience in this field.
Smith. Will you gimme that again?
Donovan. In your career, you've been a private bodyguard more than once?
Smith. Yeah, sure.
Donovan. For whom?
Smith. Their names wouldn't mean nothin'.
Donovan. You worked for Legs Moran, didn't you?
Deputy D.A.. I object to that question as immaterial and irrelevant.
Court Judge. Objection sustained.
Donovan. If the court pleases, I am trying to show that the witness has been employed by political and underworld characters whose records have a direct bearing on the validity of his testimony.
Court Judge. Objection sustained.
Donovan. I have evidence to show that the witness has also acted as a strikebreaker and a labor spy.
Deputy D.A. I object on the same grounds and ask that Mr. Donovan's remarks be stricken from the record.
Court Judge. Granted. Proceed.
Donovan. You say that the man you saw under the street light was the defendant?
Smith. That's right.
Donovan. How was he dressed?
Smith. Dark suit. No hat.
Donovan. Was he wearing a necktie?
Smith. Mmmm—yeah, that's right.
Donovan. What kind of a tie?
Smith. I don't know—it was a dark tie. Oh, yeah—I remember—it had little white dots on it.
Donovan. Did you see the papers the morning after the explosion?
Smith. Yeah.

Donovan. Which one did you read?
Smith. The *Examiner.*
Donovan (*Pointing at paper*). Like this one?
Smith. That's right.
Donovan. Then naturally you saw this picture of the defendant taken after his arrest—is that correct?
Smith. I don't remember.
Donovan. Very well. I now offer this newspaper into evidence as the defense's exhibit next in order and call the attention of the court to the fact that every detail of the defendant's appearance is plainly evident in the picture that accompanies the story. That's all. (*Smith rises and leaves the platform. As he comes down he mutters almost to himself.*)
Smith. It's hot in here. (*He starts toward the window. The bailiff anticipates the movement and starts to open the window for him.*) Thanks. I got it. (*Smith opens the window.*)
Donovan. Mr. Phil Merry. (*Merry rises after a brief exchange of looks with Judith. He meets Smith just as the latter leaves the window. Smith has fished into his pocket and produced a match. Without looking at Merry he lights it with his thumbnail and blows it out, then continues to his own chair which is drawn back, a little apart from those of the other People's witnesses. He sits on the arm of the chair. Meanwhile, Merry has taken the witness stand, his eye on Smith.*)
Clerk. Hold up your right hand. (*Merry does so.*) Do you swear to tell the truth, the whole truth, and nothing but the truth so help you God?
Merry. I do.
Donovan. Please state your name.
Merry. Phil Merry.
Donovan. What is your occupation?
Court Judge. I believe I can take judicial notice of the witness's business. I imagine it is a matter of common knowledge. (*The shadow of a man appears on the upstage vertical sash of the window. The courtroom's attention is on Merry so that the shadow is unobserved by anyone except Smith.*)
Donovan. Very well, your honor. Mr. Merry, will you please describe to the court exactly what you did on the evening of September 21st, starting at seven o'clock.
Merry. I had dinner alone about quarter of seven and left the house about twenty minutes past.
Donovan. Where did you go from your house?

Merry. I got in my car and drove to a poker game. (*Donovan, Mace, and Judith are completely flabbergasted by Merry's statement. Smith smiles quietly to himself.*)
Donovan (*Stunned*). Do you understand the question I just asked you?
Merry. Yes.
Donovan. Mr. Reporter, will you please read the question back to the witness?
Deputy D.A. I object, your honor. The witness has already stated that he understood the question.
Court Judge. I know, but no harm can come from our permitting the Reporter to read the question back. Will you please do so?
Reporter. Where did you go from your house?
Merry. I got in my car and drove to a poker game. (*The shadow disappears.*)
Donovan. That's all. You may cross-examine.
Deputy D.A. Mr. Merry—at whose house did this poker game take place?
Merry. At Mr. Sol Mintz's.
Deputy DA. What time did you arrive there?
Merry. At about twenty-five minutes of eight.
Deputy D.A. Who was present at the game?
Merry. Besides Mr. Mintz there were three other writers—Mr. Harry Durkis, Mr. George Petty, and Mr. Al Hartman—and my agent was there—Mr. Abe Kliegel.
Deputy D.A. How long did the game last? (*No answer.*) How long did the game last?
Merry. Until a little past midnight.
Deputy D.A. Then you went home?
Merry. Yes.
Deputy D.A. From the time you arrived at Mr. Mintz's until you left after midnight, did you ever leave the house for any reason?
Merry. No.
Deputy D.A. That's all. (*Merry returns to his place. Donovan and Judith lean toward him and whisper. He merely shakes his head and refuses to speak. Donovan gives up and rises.*)
Donovan. Mr. Frank Mace. (*Mace takes the stand.*)
Clerk. Hold up your right hand. (*Mace does so.*) Do you swear to tell the truth, the whole truth, and nothing but the truth so help you God?
Mace. I do.
Donovan. Please state your name.

Mace. Frank Mace.

Donovan. You are the defendant in this action, Mr. Mace?

Mace. I am.

Donovan. You are the secretary of the Pacific Coast branch of the United Fruit and Vegetable Packers, are you not?

Mace. That's right.

Donovan. Mr. Mace, will you please describe to the court exactly what you did on the night of September 21st, starting at 7:30 in the evening.

Mace. At 7:30 I was eating dinner alone at Martini's Cafeteria on Hollywood Boulevard. I finished some time after eight and drove my jalopy up to Miss Gordon's house on Beachwood Drive, which is about five or six minutes away from there.

Donovan. You mean Miss Judith Gordon, Mr. Phil Merry's secretary?

Mace. Yes. I wanted to get a list of people from her—people connected with the radio show who might be interested in getting copies of our campaign literature, and I wanted to tell her to talk to Mr. Merry about the anti-Davis broadcast he'd made the week before.

Donovan. Let's be quite clear about this. What time did you arrive at Miss Gordon's?

Mace. About half past eight. I looked at my watch while I was waiting for someone to answer the bell.

Donovan. Did Miss Gordon let you in?

Mace. No, she wasn't there. Mr. Phil Merry answered the door. I told him about wanting to talk to him and we discussed his radio broadcast for about fifteen minutes. Then I left and drove on home.

Donovan. In other words, it was close to a quarter of nine when you left Mr. Merry?

Mace. Yes, it couldn't have been more than five or six minutes different from that, one way or the other.

Donovan. You may cross-examine.

Deputy D.A. Mr. Mace, are you in the habit of eating at Martini's Cafeteria?

Mace. Oh, I suppose I've eaten there half a dozen times in the last two years.

Deputy D.A. Do you think the proprietor or the cashier or any of the employees would know you if they saw you?

Mace. I don't believe so.

Deputy D.A. Don't you think someone in that cafeteria would recognize a well known figure like yourself?

Mace. No—not in Hollywood.
Deputy D.A. Just one more question. As I understand it, in the face of Mr. Merry's testimony, you want the court to believe that you were alone with him at Miss Gordon's house from approximately 8:30 to quarter of nine?
Mace. That's correct.
Deputy D.A. Your honor, the brazen effrontery of this witness is so extraordinary that I cannot allow it to pass without comment.
Donovan. I object. This is improper and argumentative. The credibility of witnesses will be argued at the conclusion of the case.
Court Judge. Overruled. Proceed.
Deputy D.A. Thank you, your honor. The attempted murder of the Chief Executive of the State of California calls for the most drastic punishment, and I am confident that the fullest penalty which the law provides will eventually be exacted. But when this crime is obviously part and parcel of a subversive conspiracy to destroy the basic institutions of our country—when it attempts with perjured testimony to hide behind the integrity and honesty of a man whose name is loved and cherished by millions of Americans—then I believe that even the most rigorous penalties will seem lenient and ineffectual. The desperate and fantastic character of this attempt beggars description. It is not easy for the average warm-hearted American to condemn a fellow man to a lifetime of imprisonment, no matter how steeped in hatred that man may be, no matter how much he may envy those whose efforts have won for them the rewards which the American system of life provides for persons of outstanding talent and character. Apparently this racketeer, this revolutionary agitator and disruptionist, has pinned his hope of freedom on the kindness of a fellow human being—but he failed to understand that true Americans cannot be seduced from principle by an appeal to that weak-kneed and misguided charity which sets criminals at liberty and asks clemency for dangerous and vicious enemies of society. Fortunately the man he sought to involve was a man of character—a man to whom truth and honor came first—a man incapable of falsehood—a man who could not be hoodwinked into a lie!
Merry. Your honor!
Court Judge. Yes, Mr. Merry.
Merry. I want to say something—I—could I come up there again?
Deputy D.A. I object. The witness has already testified and if his counsel wishes to recall him, he may make proper application.
Donovan. I make that application, your honor.

Court Judge. Very well. Mr. Merry recalled. Take the stand, Mr. Merry. (*Mace steps down, comes to the corner of the table nearest the stand and sits down. Merry takes the stand. As he does so, the shadow reappears. This time the shadow of a gun can be seen quite clearly.*) If there is anything in your testimony which you wish to explain, please proceed with that explanation.

Merry. It's about that poker game, your honor. When I said I drove to Mr. Mintz's house, that wasn't true.

Court Judge. Mr. Merry, are you aware that you were under oath?

Merry. I know, your honor—I'll explain that in a minute. Just let me tell you what really happened. (*The shadow raises the gun. Mace sees it. He springs up and moves quickly toward the window.*)

Mace. Merry!

Merry. When I left my house I drove straight to Hollywood—

Mace. Look out! (*Mace reaches the window. There is a fusillade of shots. Mace crumples to the floor. There is a moment's horrified silence, then Merry springs up and runs to Mace. Judith follows him. Smith leaps to his feet and crosses as if to join them. As several of the spectators surge forward, Smith slips through the window and disappears. Two policemen who were on the other side of the room were also on their way to see where the shots came from. They see Smith's exit and follow him out the window, drawing their guns as they go. Merry, Donovan, and Judith bring Mace forward and place him gently in Donovan's chair. More shots are heard offstage. Among the lad lib remarks of the crowd, someone says, "Get a doctor," and the clerk rushes off right. The crowd quiets down. Mace looks up at Merry who is on his right. He tries to grin. His lips move.*) You tell 'em.

Merry. Don't worry. (*Mace closes his eyes for a brief instant, then opens them again.*)

Mace. Takes—takes more than guns—(*His face contorts with pain, drops down, his chin on his chest for a second or two. He grips the arms of the chair and lifts his eyes again to Merry. Merry sees that he is trying to speak and bends close to him. He whispers something, shudders, and collapses limply in the chair. Merry looks at Judith. Their faces tell you that Mace is dead.*)

Judith. What did he say?

Merry. He said, "I didn't die." (*Merry looks at Mace, then once again his eyes find Judith's. The curtain falls.*)

Bet Your Life

A Play in Three Acts

Characters

Jimmy Aquilina, a young taxi driver
Walter Deming, the director
Vernon Jones, an assistant director
Art, the 2nd assistant director
Otto, the first cameraman
Billy, 2nd Cameraman
Assistant cameraman
Billy, 2nd assistant cameraman
Georgie, the head grip
Eddie, the second grip
Harry, the sound man
Edie, the script girl
Joe, the prop man
Motorcycle cop
Chuck Burden, stunt man
Babe Harvey, stunt man
Flabby Jordan, stunt man
Jig Smith, their friend
Peewee, another stunt man
Jack Trent, leading man
Carmen Sherry, the "Woof Girl"
Mimi, her maid
Two hospital interns
Doctor Evans
Nurse Harris
Nurse Horton
Sol Herzog, the president of Phoenix Pictures, Inc.
James Tillinghast, the president of the Hapwood Aircraft Company
Gladys, an overblown blonde
Reverend David Ely, of the First Methodist Church
Henry McGowan, a veteran of World War I

Mrs. Barney, secretary of the Women's Peace League
Bill Daggett, a representative of the Studio Painters Union
Tom, a male nurse
Eddie, a sound man
Another sound man
A policeman
A telegraph boy
Harry, a reporter
Jack, a reporter
Stunt men
Photographers
Reporters
Stagehands
Delegates
Voice of a radio announcer

ACT ONE: SCENE ONE

The brow of a hill in Southern California. A young man, about twenty-seven years old, is eating his breakfast, which he has cooked himself. His coat is off and he is wearing a sweater which is frayed at the elbow. As he finishes his beans and starts swabbing his tin plate with a piece of bread, the sound of several trucks, apparently pulling up the hill off right, grows gradually louder. The young man becomes conscious of the sound. He jumps up and goes to a point where he can look down at the road below. He returns immediately, dumps water on the coals of his fire, stamps on the remnant, and begins to gather up his few belongings. The first truck stops offstage and voices are heard giving directions for unloading. The young man finishes tying up his small bundle. Meanwhile, other cars are heard stopping off and the voices grow louder. The young man has his coat on now and decides to stay and see who is coming. He sits down on a rock upstage and to the left of center. Vernon Jones, an assistant director, comes on from the right, followed by a first and second cameraman, a sound man, a head grip, a property-man, a motorcycle cop, and one or two other assorted employees of Phoenix Pictures, Inc.

Jones (*To the first cameraman*). Mr. Deming marked the setup Sunday, Otto. It's right here on this hill. Here. This is it. (*He indicates a stake that has been driven into the ground downstage center. Jones stands over the stake and makes the gesture with his hands that directors use to frame on the suppositions angle the camera will see.*) Right here. The car comes along the road down there, right to left. You pan with it—(*He moves his head and his hands from right to left as he speaks.*) till it crashes into the fence—there. Two cameras. Second one of a four foot right behind you, Otto.
Otto (*Slight German accent*). Okay. Get the stuff up, Georgie, will you?
Head Grip. Sure. (*To his assistant.*) Better bring a six foot parallel too, Eddie. I don't think a four's gonna be high enough. Silent cameras, Otto?
Otto. That's right. Barney Googles. (*To the sound man.*) You can get a wild track, huh, Harry? We'll undercrank it.
Harry. Sure. You can put some blankets on the Barneys. (*The second grip leaves.*)
Jones. Make a nice shot, Otto. (*He starts to pan with his hands again. He is looking over the heads of the theatre audience. Suddenly, he drops his hands.*) Jeezus! Hey, you! (*He shouts down to the road below—beyond the*

audience.) Keep comin', will you! You're in the shot! Why do they do that? The whole San Fernando Valley to park in an' that prop truck has to stop there. Go on! Get out of there! (*He turns to the motorcycle cop.*) Hey, buddy, will you go down there with your motorcycle and keep 'em moving.
Cop. Okay, Vern.
Jones. How many boys you got with you?
Cop. Three.
Jones. All right. Put 'em at both ends of that road and stop traffic when I give you the whistle. I'll give you two to start it again.
Cop. Okay, Vern.
Jones. If you see that stunt man, send him up here, will you? He'll be in a yellow roadster.
Cop. Chuck Burden, huh?
Jones. Damn right. Phoenix Pictures uses nothin' but the best.
Cop. That Chuck's a lulu all right. Babe and Flabby ain't bad though.
Jones. Yeah. Well—they'll probably be around to look things over. When one of 'em works, the other two always turn up sooner or later.
Cop. That Babe murders me on a motorcycle. Jeez!
Jones. Someday he's gonna murder himself. He's gettin' brittle. (*Yelling.*) Hey! Go on! (*To cop.*) You better scram down there. (*The cop goes.*)
Otto. Where's Joe with that coffee?
2ⁿᵈ Cameraman. He'll be along, Otto.
Otto. It's cold up here.
2ⁿᵈ Cameraman. Gonna be hot as hell in two hours. How much stuff we got to shoot, Vern?
Jones. If Deming's hot, we'll be wrapped up by three o'clock.
2ⁿᵈ Cameraman. Hmm. Here's Joe, Otto. (*A prop man appears with a coffee container. A second assistant comes up to Jones.*)
Assistant. Hey, Vern—listen. Do you hear that?
Jones. What?
Assistant. Down there. Sounds like they were repairing the road. Yeah—look! Look at those tractors.
Jones. Jeezus! What breaks! Yesterday it was airplanes. Wait till Deming hears that. Look, Art, go on down and see if you can bribe 'em to lay off while we're shooting, will you? Better take your coat off. You look too good. You look like you worked for David Selznick. Tell 'em it's a quickie company.
Assistant. Okay. What's it worth?

Jones. You gotta stop 'em. We can't shoot sound with that going on. (*The Young Man steps forward.*)
Young man. I'll go down and stop 'em for you. What do you want me to pay 'em?
Jones. Are you with the company?
Young man. No. I was here when you came. I slept here last night. I'll get 'em to stop for whatever you say. You can pay me a buck if I get your price.
Jones. That's fair enough. See if he'll settle for ten. If he says "yes," gimme that (*He waves his arm.*) and I'll send Art down with the dough.
Young man. Okay. Any chance of a real job with this outfit?
Jones. Afraid not, buddy—not unless you got a union card.
Young man. I got a card all right, but—
Jones. But what?
Young man. It's no good, I guess. I mean, my local's a long ways from here.
Jones. Where—for instance?
Young man. New York—for instance.
Jones. Holy Jeezus. You *are* off base. What's your racket?
Young man. I wheel a hack.
Jones. How the hell did you get out here?
Young man. Happened three weeks ago Tuesday. I picked up a lush in a fur overcoat outside the Club Morocco about four in the morning. I says, "Where to?" and he says, "Los Angeles," and passed out. So I started.
Jones. Took an awful chance, didn't you?
Young man. The way I figure it, everything's a chance. You got born. That's a chance. A nine-to-one shot you starve to death. You fall for some dame. A buck'll get you a hundred she kicks your teeth in. So, what the hell? Besides, I liked the looks of this guy.
Jones. What happened?
Young man. Everything was fine till we got to Albuquerque. Harold paid for everything. Harold Featherbottom—some tag, huh? In Albuquerque, Harold borrowed the hack to peddle rugs for a Navajo Indian—romantic fella, Harold. He ran my cab off a cliff.
Jones. Kill him?
Young man. I wouldn't know. I hopped a rattler for California when that Navajo's squaw started looking for Jimmy Aquilina with her tomahawk.
Assistant. Who is Jimmy Aquilina?
Young man. That's me. Well—I'll go down and talk to that guy. If I wigwag it's okay. See if you can figure out a real job for me, will you, Mister?

Jones. I'm afraid there's not much chance. (*To the assistant—pointing over the heads of the audience.*) Here comes Chuck.
Jimmy. Okay. Can I come back and watch?
Jones. Sure, help yourself.
Jimmy. Thanks. (*He goes. Meanwhile, the grips have dragged in a parallel and are setting it up. The cameramen are placing their cameras, the sound man his boom and sound panel. A script girl has joined the group. She comes up to Jones.*)
Script girl. Morning, Vern. What's the first shot?
Jones. Hello, Edie. We'll do the smack first. Chuck is doubling for Jack Trent. He'll drive up that road—right to left—and skid into the fence there. Two cameras.
Script girl. Mm-hmm. (*To assistant cameraman.*) That'll be Scene 106. (*To Billy, 2nd assistant cameraman.*) You take an "A" on it, Billy.
2nd Assistant cameraman. All right, Edie. (*He adjusts his slate. Three men walk into the scene from the right. They are all in their mid-forties and though their personalities are dissimilar, they possess in common a nervous reckless quality that manifests itself chiefly in their eyes. The first is Chuck Burden. He is of medium height and the most sober seeming of the three. He is dressed—to match the actor he is doubling—in a topcoat, white scarf, and top hat. The second is Babe Harvey. He is much smaller than the other two and projects an impish restlessness. Flabby Jordan is the third member of the trio. He is over six feet tall and not very quick-witted. The property man has just given the script girl a small backless camp stool. She unfolds it and bends over to place it beside the camera. As she does this, she speaks to Jones.*)
Scrip girl. Where's Chuck? I ought to check up on his clothes. (*Chuck steps up behind the script girl, reaches out and "burns" her on the fanny. This consists in snapping the two first fingers loosely, but with enough force to hurt, against the protruding "canetta."*) Ow! (*She straightens up in pain and turns on her assailant.*) Oh, you!
Chuck. Morning, Edie. Want me?
Script girl. Yes—I do! (*She lunges at Chuck. He jumps behind Babe. Flabby grabs the outraged Edie. She continues to lunge at Chuck.*)
Script girl. Strike a woman, you coward!
Chuck. Whoa, now! Hold her, Flabby! I'll give you a free burn—how's that?
Script girl. Sure—with that coat on—you big sissy!

Chuck. Oh, yeah? Well, here! (*He takes off the topcoat, revealing the fact that he has on only the scarf, trousers, and his undershirt underneath. He bends over, his rear toward Edie, Babe holding him. Flabby moves Edie into position to swing.*) Okay, Edie. Let her go! (*Babe pushes Chuck's head down so that he can't see and signals Flabby. The latter quickly replaces Edie and lets go with a terrific burn—a bull's eye. Chuck straightens up in pain. Flabby shoves Edie back into position so that when Chuck turns, it looks to him as though Edie has been the aggressor. He speaks, in pain.*) Oo-oo-oooh! Boy! (*He faces Edie.*) What a woman! (*He catches the grin on Flabby's face.*) Flabby! (*He starts forward. Flabby ducks behind Edie. Babe holds on to Chuck.*)
Flabby. No, Honest, Chuck. It was her. Swear to God, Chuck. I hope to die!
Chuck. You dirty double-crosser! (*Walter Deming, the director, walks on from the right. He is about forty-eight years old and is wearing grey flannels and a polo shirt with an initialed pocket. He is carrying his script, a Morning Examiner, and a polo coat. Joe, the head prop man comes up to him. Deming tosses him the coat.*)
Prop man. Morning, Mr. Deming.
Deming. Morning, Joe. Hey! What goes on! (*He moves over to the struggling group and bops Chuck on the head with his script.*) Come on, Chuck, lay off my woman.
Chuck. Oh, hello, Mr. Deming. (*It is evident from Chuck's attitude that he likes Deming. They have made a lot of pictures together and are on a free and easy basis which has not, however, destroyed their mutual respect.*) They're pickin' on me.
Deming. Now Edie! You leave Chuck alone till we've got the shot. You know how easy he bruises. He's getting old.
Script girl. He started it.
Deming. Oh, he did, huh—and brought his gang too. Hi, Babe—hello, Flabby.
Babe and Flabby. Morning, Mr. Deming.
Babe. We just stopped off on our way to work. We're going to Chatsworth.
Flabby. In case Chuck flops—you can send for us.
Deming. Okay. I'll do that. Who's shooting at Chatsworth?
Babe. Some "hoss" opera. We're Indians. Woo-hoo! (*He gestures hand to mouth.*)
Deming. Well, keep out of the hospital. I can use you both next week if you're still alive. Got a big fight sequence—about Wednesday, isn't it Vern?

Jones. It's Friday, Mr. Deming. We're two days behind schedule.
Deming. Never mind now, Vern. (*To Chuck.*) He's beginning to talk like a front-office spy. (*Vern's assistant has been watching Jimmy Aquilina down the hill. He comes forward and joins Vern.*)
Jones. Well, you asked me.
Assistant. That taxi driver just gave me the high sign, Vern. It's all set.
Jones. Swell. Here's ten bucks for the guy with the tractor and a buck for what's-his-name.
Assistant. Jimmy Aquilina.
Jones. Yeah.
Assistant. Okay, Vern. (*He takes the money and goes.*)
Jones (*To Deming*). There's a noisy tractor down below. They'll stop it for eleven bucks.
Deming. Oh, fine. Well, Chuck, let's go. How does it look? Morning, Otto—let's take a peek. (*Deming steps behind the camera, looks through the finder and pans the camera as he talks. Otto stands by to watch. This gives Flabby the chance he has been waiting for—to give Otto a "hot foot." This operation consists in shoving a paper match between the sole and toe leather of a shoe and lighting the match which eventually burns down to the leather with delightful results. Flabby gets the match into place and lights it, then stands back to watch the effect, calling the attention of the bystanders to Otto's foot. As he is watching, Babe slips up and inserts a match into Flabby's shoe. Flabby moves and Babe has to wait a couple of seconds before lighting the match.*)
Chuck (*Pointing*). Looks okay, Mr. Deming. I'll come along that road about forty and skid around the curve. That'll just take me into the fence nice—unless you want me to turn over.
Deming. No—forty's fine. We'll goose it up with the camera—about 18, Otto, huh?
Otto. Eighteen is good. (*To second cameraman.*) Billy, you take sixteen.
Deming. Just figure to take most of the fence with you, Chuck. It's all breakaway. I don't want you to take any chances. Save yourself. We've got to do that train gag today, too.
Chuck. Okay. (*Otto looks down and sees the match. He eyes the spectators suspiciously as he steps on the flame. Flabby's eyes innocently seek the sky. At this moment, the match in Flabby's shoe that Babe has finally lighted burns down to Flabby's foot. Flabby leaps into the air with a howl of pain.*)
Flabby. Ow! Who did that? (*The crowd roars with laughter. Flabby turns his eye on Babe.*)

Babe. Er—come on, Flabby. We've got to blow. Got to put on all that war paint.
Flabby. That was *you*!
Babe. Now don't start anything, Flabby, or Mr. Deming won't use you on Friday.
Flabby. I'll fix you—you little squirt.
Babe. 'Bye, Mr. Deming. Thanks for the Friday call. Vern's got our number. (*To Chuck.*) So long, brittle-bones. I'll give that fence the once over when we pass it—just in case it isn't break-away.
Chuck. It's okay. I checked it Sunday when they put it up. Look, why don't you and Flabby give Mr. Deming a free rehearsal on your way down. Just drive along up to the fence about forty. It'll give the boys a chance to judge the speed.
Babe. Good idea. We'll do that. Come on, lunk! (*They start to go. Babe notices that Deming's newspaper has dropped to the ground. He picks it up.*) You dropped your paper.
Deming (*Taking it*). Thanks. Did you see those headlines? Looks like we'd be in it in six months.
Babe. Yeah. (*Reading.*) "Congress Votes Neutrality Revision." Jeez, that's bad, all right.
Jones. What's bad about it? We ought to be in it. Somebody's got to lick those guys, or there just won't be any democracy.
Babe. Okay, kid, you lick 'em. Come on, Flabby. So long, Chuck. 'Bye, Mr. Deming. (*They go, almost running into Jimmy Aquilina who comes on as they leave.*)
Jones. What's the matter with Babe?
Deming. Nothing. You just reminded him of something he's been twenty-two years trying to forget—am I right, Chuck?
Chuck (*Ducking the subject*). Maybe.
Deming. Sure. Save democracy! Shades of Woodrow Wilson! That's where we came n.
Chuck. Can we make the shot?
Deming. All set, Chuck. Let's go.
Chuck (*To Jones*). I'll give you the horn when I'm ready. There go Babe and Flabby. Look 'em over. (*The cameramen follow the car. Chuck goes.*)
Jones. I didn't know Babe was in the war.
Deming. They all were. Their whole company was wiped out in the Argonne, except Chuck and Babe and Flabby, and a guy named Jig Smith.
Jones. What happened to him?

Deming. He's in the Soldiers' Home at Brentwood—what's left of him. (*Jack Trent, the actor for whom Chuck is doubling, enters from the right. Like Chuck, he is dressed in topper, scarf, and topcoat. He signals to Jones.*)
Trent. Hey, Vern.
Jones (*Walking over*). Morning, Jack.
Trent. Listen, what's the idea of giving me an 8:30 call? I'm not in this shot. I won't work for an hour, for Christ's sake.
Jones. Sure you will. This shot'll be in the bag in ten minutes. Anyway, Mr. Deming wants you to watch Chuck—so you can match up the action in the close-up. (*He blows his whistle and waves down to the motorcycle cop. Jimmy Aquilina has recognized Trent and is all eyes.*)
Trent. Edie could check the action. That's what you have script girls for, isn't it? Jesus, Vern, I've been in the first shot every morning for a week. Got a cigarette? (*Jones reaches into his pocket. A prop man beats him to it.*) Thanks, Joe. (*Jimmy Aquilina hops in with a match.*) Oh, thanks.
Jimmy. I saw your last picture, Mr. Trent.
Trent (*Surprised*). Oh, yes?
Jimmy. Yeah. I thought you were swell.
Trent (*Pleased*). Well, thanks.
Jimmy. Yeah. That was some fall you took off that fire escape. Boy! You've really got what it takes.
Trent. Hmm. Glad you liked it. (*To the prop man, who is holding a folding chair with "Jack Trent" printed on the back.*) I'll sit over by the camera, Joe.
Prop man. Okay. (*He places the chair by the camera. Trent goes over and sits down with a "Morning" to Deming. Edie looks him over and pushes his breast pocket handkerchief a few inches down into the pocket.*)
Jimmy (*To Jones*). Did I say something?
Jones (*Grinning*). No-o-o. Not a thing! Except—that fall you liked was strictly Chuck Burden.
Jimmy. Huh? Oh, my God! (*He looks over toward Trent, then down the hill at Chuck. The motor of Chuck's car can be heard racing. The horn sounds. At the sound of the horn, Jones moves forward and looks down the hill.*)
Jones. Chuck's all ready, Mr. Deming. Shall we go?
Deming. Right now. Ready, Otto?
Otto. All set.
Deming. Turn 'em over.
Jones. QUIET! QUIET! Roll 'em, Harry.
Sound man (*At the sound panel*). We're turning.
Script girl. What lens are you using, Otto?

Otto. A forty. Billy's got a thirty-five.
Script girl. (*Making a note*). Thank you.
Jones. Quiet, everybody, PLEASE!
Sound man. Speed!
Sound grip. Scene 106—Deming. Sync—wild sound track.
Jones. Quiet! (*He waves his handkerchief and shouts at the top of his lungs.*) COME AHEAD, CHUCK!! CAMERA!! (*The cameras hold in position as the car is heard starting off right, behind the audience. Then, as it shifts into high, they start slowly panning right to left. The sound of the car goes behind the audience until it is offstage left, when the cameras stop panning and there is the sound of a terrific crash. Everyone holds quiet for a count of about three. Deming is the first to move.*)
Deming. Cut! Boy, what a pip! He was doing sixty. Are you okay, Chuck? (*He exits quickly left. Jones, followed by the second assistant, the prop man, and several others, go with him. The cameramen turn to the cameras.*)
Otto. How was it for you, Billy?
2nd Cameraman. Perfect.
Jimmy (*To Trent*). Baby, look at that fence! He really smacked it. Jeezus, what a guy!
Trent. Yes, Chuck's *all* right. (*Trent takes out a mirror and a powder puff and goes to work. Jimmy shoots him a look. The prop man returns and goes to his prop case, getting out iodine and bandages.*)
Jimmy. Is he okay?
Prop man. He's got a cut over one eye. A piece of that breakaway fence hit him. He'll be all right, I guess. (*Chuck comes on with Vern and Deming. He is holding a blood-stained handkerchief over his right eye. Deming is guiding him.*)
Deming. Here, Chuck, sit down. (*He reaches out with his foot and signals Trent to get out of his chair. The latter rises and Deming helps Chuck into the chair. He sits with his back to the audience.*) Let's have a look. (*He whistles.*) Hi-yi! Another inch and you'd be minus an eye, young feller. Go ahead, Joe. (*The prop man goes to work on the eye.*) How does it feel?
Chuck. It's okay. (*As the iodine hits, he snaps the fingers of one hand.*) I'll be all set to go again in ten minutes.
Deming. The hell you will. We got it, didn't we, Otto?
Otto. Sure. Both cameras.
Deming. There you are, Chuck.
Chuck. It wasn't too fast for you?
Otto. It was perfect.

Trent (*Calling*). Make-up! (*A make-up man comes up to him.*) Better match up that eye. (*The make-up man nods, sits Trent down and goes to work on his right eye with carmine and glycerin. Jimmy Aquilina observes this.*)

Jones (*To Assistant*). Hey, Art. Go on down to a telephone. Call the studio. Tell 'em to send out an ambulance and another stunt man—Frankie Baker, if he's not working.

Chuck. Hey, what's the idea?

Jones. We still got that train shot to do, Chuck.

Chuck. So I'll do it. I'm okay. By the time you get the close-ups, I'll be all set. Listen, baby, nobody's going to gyp me out of that extra stunt check.

Jones. Well—I'll get the doctor out, anyway.

Chuck. I tell you, I'm okay.

Jones. All right, Chuck. (*He signals Art to go ahead. Art leaves.*) Can we set up for the close-up, Mr. Deming?

Deming. Yeah—sure—go ahead.

Trent. Edie!

Script girl. Coming! (*She crosses to Trent.*)

Jones. Down by the car, Otto. One camera.

Otto. Take it away, boys! (*The grips start moving Otto's camera off left.*)

Trent. What do I say, Edie?

Script girl. You don't say anything. It's silent. You just stagger out of the car toward the house.

Trent. This whole goddamn picture is silent. I haven't spoken a line in three weeks.

Script girl. What do you care? You're still the prettiest.

Trent. I'm going back on the stage.

Script girl. You're too late, beautiful. Vaudeville is dead.

Trent. Never mind, now.

Deming. I'll go down and give Otto the set-up, Chuck. Need anything?

Chuck. Not a thing. I'm fine. Unless Joe's got some hair oil in that case of his.

Joe. I got a broken down pint of Old Crow.

Chuck. Well, what are we waiting for?

Deming. Sure, Joe. Have a heart. Okay, Chuck. (*He leaves.*)

Jones (*To Trent*). Down in the car when you're ready, Jack.

Trent. Isn't my stand-in around?

Jones. Sure. He's down there now. But Otto'll be ready for you in five minutes.

Trent. I'll be there. Got some Fuller's earth, Joe?
Joe. Coming up. (*He hands Chuck a pint of whisky. Chuck takes a hefty pull. Joe gets a bag of Fuller's earth out of his case and starts dusting Trent's topcoat to give the effect of dirt.*)
Jimmy (*Taking Vern aside*). What's that stunt with the train you were talking about?
Jones. Chuck's going to drive a car in front of a freight train. Why?
Jimmy. He's hurt pretty bad. What does it pay?
Jones (*Lowering his voice and looking Jimmy over*). Mm—well, that depends.
Jimmy. I can do it. I done worse then that every day in New York. I'll make it as close as you want. What do you say?
Jones. Hmm—maybe—(*He holds up the fingers of both hands twice, then those of the right hand once more—indicating that the price is $25.00.*)
Jimmy. That's a deal. (*Jones nods and touches his finger to his lips. Carmen Sherry, the star of Deming's picture, comes in from the right. She is dressed in a revealing evening gown with a polo coat over it. Her hair is elaborately coiffed and is covered with an arrangement of tulle to keep it in place until she is ready to be photographed. She is followed by a maid who carries a make-up box and one or two other little bundles.*)
Carmen (*Calling*). Vern, darling!
Jones. Morning, Miss Sherry. You're early.
Jimmy (*Recognizing her*). It's the "Woof Girl"!
Jones. In person. 'Scuse me. (*He goes over to Carmen. Jimmy obviously impressed, slowly crosses after him.*)
Carmen (*To Jones*). Listen, my pet, I'll need a studio car to take me home tonight. I just fired that dreamy-eyed driver of mine—the son of a bitch.
Jones. Why, what happened? What did he do?
Carmen. He smacked into a laundry wagon. Right in the middle of Ventura Boulevard.
Jones. For God's sake! Was he drunk?
Carmen. No, darling. He was watching Mimi make up my "bos-oom" in the rear-vision mirror. Oh, well. Live and learn. Do you know any nice nances who can drive, Vern?
Jones. Let me work on it.
Trent (*Coming up*). That's what you get for not driving out with me, Carmen.
Carmen. Why, it's the Glamour Boy! My God, is that make-up, or did she bite back?

Trent. It's make-up. Chuck hurt his eye in the long shot.
Carmen. Chuck! Oh, my poor angel! (*She crosses to him.*) *Bay*-bee!
Chuck (*Rising*). Morning, Miss Sherry.
Carmen. Sit down, darling. Joe! (*Joe brings a chair with her name on the back. She sits next to Chuck.*) Let me look. How *awful*! How did you do it?
Chuck. Something blew in my eye.
Carmen. Why, it's *terrible*! Doesn't it hurt?
Chuck. Head aches a little. It's all right.
Carmen. Mimi. Give Chuck some aspirin. (*Mimi opens her bag and digs out a bottle.*) Have they sent for a doctor?
Chuck. What for? I'm fine.
Carmen. Yes. You look fine! Here. (*She takes two aspirins from Mimi and gives them to Chuck. Art, the assistant, appears from the left.*)
Assistant. We're all ready, Mr. Trent.
Trent. Okay. See you later, Carmen. (*He goes. Edie also leaves.*)
Carmen. That's what you think. (*To the prop man.*) Some water, Joe.
Chuck. I got something better. (*He washes down the aspirins with a slug of whisky. Jones follows Trent off. Jimmy Aquilina comes up.*)
Jimmy. You looking for a chauffeur, Miss Sherry?
Carmen. Hmm?
Jimmy. I'd like to apply for the job, Miss Sherry. I'm a good driver.
Carmen (*Eyeing him*). Hmm. No. No, thanks.
Jimmy. Give me a chance, Miss Sherry. You won't be sorry.
Carmen. I wouldn't bet on that. You look pretty virile.
Jimmy. I seen every picture you ever made, Miss Sherry. Even the bad ones.
Carmen. Oh—oh. Well, goodbye now. It's been nice knowing you.
Jimmy. I could even tell you the stories—from that first Gene Autry.
Carmen. Well, now. You must come around and do that some time. I'll invite Mr. Autry. He can bring his horse.
Jimmy. No kidding, Miss Sherry. I certainly would like to drive for you.
Carmen. I'm sorry, my lad, but you've got too much woof. I couldn't stand the competition.
Chuck. Screw, sonny. Scramola.
Jimmy. Okay. (*He walks away. Jones comes back.*)
Jones. You can get ready, Miss Sherry. It's just a drive up shot. You get out of your car and follow Mr. Trent into the farmhouse.
Carmen (*Brightly*). That'll be fun. I'll be right down, Vern. Come on, Mimi. Let's dust off the kisser. You relax now, Chuck. And keep out of the

sun. (*She goes off, followed by Mimi and Joe with her chair. Vern turns to Chuck. Chuck takes out a timetable.*)
Jones. How's that eye?
Chuck. It's all right. Say, Vern?
Jones. Yeah?
Chuck. When is your special train coming out?
Jones. They're standing by for a call after lunch. Why?
Chuck. I was just figuring. (*He holds up the timetable.*) There's a regular train goes by here in about ten minutes. If you set up the cameras over there, I could shoot across in front of it and you could steal the shot. You could cancel that special.
Jones. Hey, listen! That regular train'll be doing sixty.
Chuck. That's fine. Make a better shot. I'll keep right on going and drop off at the hospital.
Jones. That eye hurts, huh?
Chuck. Naw. Got a little headache, that's all. But I was thinking—if you call off the special, maybe you could afford to bump my ante. Be a hell of a shot.
Jones (*Whispering*). We're paying you a hundred now.
Chuck. I could use two hundred.
Jones. What's the matter? Been drawing to those inside straights again? Or is it an oil well?
Chuck. That's my business.
Jones. It's too risky, Chuck.
Chuck. Ask Deming, will you.
Jones. What's the use? You know what he'll say.
Chuck. You ask him.
Jones (*After a moment*). Okay. (*He goes. Jimmy Aquilina comes over to Chuck. They are alone.*)
Jimmy. You ain't gonna drive with that eye.
Chuck. Oh, no? You just stick around, sonny.
Jimmy. I'm going to. And *I'm* going to drive that car.
Chuck. Oh, yeah? Who put that idea in your head?
Jimmy. It's all set. I talked to that assistant. He gave me a price—and everything.
Chuck (*Suddenly looking at Jimmy*). How much did he say he'd pay you?
Jimmy. Twenty-five bucks.

Chuck (*After a pause*). Now listen to me, sonny. That gag's worth a hundred dollars to any stunt man in the business. And no fink is gonna cut the price on it, understand?
Jimmy. Don't give me that dog in the manger stuff. I gotta eat.
Chuck. Oh. Okay, kid. Here. (*He offers Jimmy a bill.*) There's groceries for the week. Now, run along and butt into somebody else's racket, but leave this one alone.
Jimmy (*Shaking his head*). I don't take dough unless I work for it.
Chuck (*Rising*). Yeah? Well, you don't take *my* dough—no matter what you do.
Jimmy. You've got yours. Now *I* want a break. I'm going to drive that car and you're not going to stop me.
Chuck. Now, look here—(*He puts out both hands, palm up and moves toward Jimmy. The minute his hands touch the latter's side, he jerks him around, pulls back his right, and clips Jimmy on the chin. Jimmy goes down like a log. Chuck rolls him over to the base of the camera parallel. Deming comes on, followed by Vern, Vern's assistant, and the camera men.*)
Deming. Hey, Chuck! Vern tells me you want to steal that train shot.
Chuck. Yeah, I'm getting bored sitting around.
Deming. A mile a minute, baby! Are you sure you can make it?
Chuck. I can't miss.
Deming. Okay. I'll take a chance if you will. Get the other box, boys. And we'll grind normal. (*The cameramen leave. Deming sees Jimmy.*) Hey! Who's this?
Chuck. I dunno. Some yokel who wanted to see how pictures were made, I guess. He climbed up on that parallel and fell off. He's okay.
Deming. See if anything's broken, Joe. (*The prop man bends over Jimmy. The train's whistle is heard some distance away.*) Here she comes! Hurry up with that camera!
Otto (*Entering*). On the fire. Right over here, Georgie. (*The grips start setting up the camera.*)
Chuck. I'll turn the car around. (*He starts to go. An ambulance siren is heard and the ambulance stops offstage. Chuck turns. Two interns run in with a stretcher.*)
Intern. Somebody want an ambulance up here?
Chuck. Yeah. (*Indicating Jimmy.*) Him! Hi, Doc. I'll beat you to the hospital. (*Trent and Carmen come on, passing Chuck as he runs off. The train whistle sounds again, closer. The interns are putting Jimmy on the stretcher.*)

Trent. Who's hurt now?
Carmen. My God—it's Curly Locks. (*To the interns.*) Hey, handle that with care—it's got possibilities.
Jones. Quiet, everybody! Quiet! (*He blows his whistle. The door of Chuck's car is heard slamming off left and a starter whirs.*) What about it, Otto?
Otto. Okey-dokey.
Jones. Turn 'em over!
Sound man. Turning.
Chuck (*Offstage*). Hold your hats, men—here I go! (*The car starts offstage. The train can be heard very plainly now. It whistles again.*)
Trent. My God—that's the real train.
Deming. You're goddamn right. And she's doin' seventy!
Carmen. Go on, Chuck. Step on it!
Trent. He'll never make it.
Carmen. Fifty'll get you a hundred that he does!
Trent (*Taking her hand*). It's a bet!
Sound man. Speed!
Jones. Camera! (*The sound of Chuck's car is lost in the sound of the train which whistles incessantly. The spectators hold their breath. The interns have paused to watch, holding the stretcher with Jimmy on it. Finally there is a gasp.*)
Deming. Son of a bitch! HE DID IT! (*The spectators react. The interns move off. The train noise continues. Blackout.*)

Act One: Scene Two

An enclosed porch in the Angel of Mercy Hospital in Los Angeles, about a week later.

The porch has two adjacent entrances at the right leading to a wing which is the Nurses' Dormitory. The left entrance leads from one of the main corridors of the hospital. The view that can be seen through the French windows in the background is similar to the view seen from the hilltop in the last scene. Flabby and Babe are seated in two chairs somewhat to the right of center. From their attitudes it is evident that they are waiting for someone. Both are nervously tossing their hats a short distance into the air and catching them. Eventually, the tosses begin to synchronize. They both notice this phenomenon in silence for a few seconds, then, as though upon a prearranged signal, both toss the hats a foot or two higher and at an angle so that each catches the hat of the other when it descends. After they have done this, for several catches, a nurse comes in from the left, pushing an empty wheelchair which she deposits in a corner, then exits through the door on the right nearer her. Both men miss their hats as they watch her. Babe picks his up, places it in the middle of the floor, then goes and gets into the wheelchair which he manipulates forward.

Babe. Come on, Flabby. Start over here and run me by the hat. I'll bet you a buck I can pick it up three out of five. (*Flabby calculates the distance of the proposed run.*)
Flabby. It's a sucker bet. There's nothing to it.
Babe. Not if you really step on it.
Flabby. Okay. (*He moves the chair with Babe in it to the right, turns it around and pauses.*) Set?
Babe. Shoot! (*Flabby rushes the chair across the stage at a good clip, keeping it far away from the hat so that Babe misses it.*)
Flabby. Once you didn't.
Babe. No! You gotta come somewhere near it!
Flabby. I can't get going.
Babe. Why not? You can start out in the hall.
Flabby. Well—(*Flabby pulls the chair back right, going offstage completely through the second entrance.*)
Babe (*Offstage*). Get set. Go! (*The nurse re-enters and starts across the room. The flying chair catches her from behind in the knees and deposits her*

on Babe's lap just as he picks up the hat.) Got it! (*Flabby slows down the chair so that it just upsets a doctor coming in from the left entrance, head first on top of the nurse. There is a considerable scramble as the doctor and nurse get to their feet.*) Oh, hello, Doc!
Doctor Evans. Why, it's Babe and Flabby.
Flabby. Hi'ya, Doc?
Doctor Evans. Hmm! Have you met these gentlemen, Miss Harris?
Nurse. Not socially.
Doctor Evans. Well—there they are. Babe and Flabby.
Flabby. M-m—how are you?
Nurse. I'm probably crippled for life. Put that chair back where you got it from! (*She goes out.*)
Flabby. Yes, ma'am. (*He returns the chair.*)
Babe. We were waiting for Chuck, Doc. How is he?
Doctor Evans. He's fine. I was just on my way to his room. Let's see, you went out of town for a week, didn't you?
Babe. That's right. On location. We haven't seen Chuck since last Thursday.
Flabby. They told us you were going to let him out today.
Doctor Evans. Yes, I am. I'm glad I had a chance to talk to you first, though. Maybe he'll listen to you. His eyes are coming along fine, but he's got to take it easy for a couple of weeks. Stay indoors and not use them. Understand?
Babe. Sure. We'll hold him down. Did something happen to the other eye?
Doctor Evans. Yes. Apparently the injury affected them both. If he isn't extremely careful, there's a very good chance of his developing a sympathetic opthalmia.
Flabby. Jeez. Imagine that.
Babe (*Scornfully*). Imagine what?
Flabby. Why an oph—thing like that.
Babe. What's it mean, Doc?
Doctor Evans. Opthalmia is blindness.
Babe. Oh. Well, don't worry. We'll make him behave himself.
Doctor Evans. Yes, please. He was talking about working in a fight scene this Friday. Of course I told him that was utterly impossible. He said, "Fine," but I didn't like the way he said it.
Flabby. We'll hold him down.
Doctor Evans. You see, I was afraid that perhaps the expenses in connection with your friend—

Babe. What friend? What do you mean, Doc?
Doctor Evans. Oh, of course—I keep forgetting you've been away. Well, the day before yesterday, they called Chuck from the Soldiers' Home. It seems that your buddy there—er—what's his name?
Babe. Jig Smith.
Doctor Evans. M-m. It seems he'd been complaining recently of severe pains in the region of his right kidney.
Flabby. Jeez. That's the bad one.
Doctor Evans. Chuck told me. Apparently it was quite serious, so we hustled him right down and made an examination yesterday. I have the X-rays here. (*He starts to open an envelope. Chuck comes in from the corridor. He has his hat and coat on and is wearing dark glasses.*)
Chuck. Hello, boys.
Babe. Hi, fella.
Flabby. 'Lo, Chuck.
Babe. The Doc just told us about Jig.
Chuck. Yeah—he was pretty bad when he got here. All doubled up.
Flabby. Doubled up? Jig?
Chuck. You know what I mean—bent forward in the chair. What's the verdict, Doc?
Doctor Evans. We've stopped the pain, of course. He's in pretty good spirits. But what he's got is a renal calculus—a kidney stone. Here, look. You can see it very plainly. (*He holds up the X-rays.*) That's it, there.
Chuck. What's the prescription?
Doctor Evans. I talked to Dr. Strauss this morning. We both think he'd be a lot better off without that kidney.
Chuck. Could he stand an operation?
Doctor Evans. Yes, definitely. He's amazing, you know. You should have heard him kidding the nurse this morning. I never saw such a constitution!
Flabby. Jig's pretty tough all right.
Babe. Yeah—the frog surgeon who whittled him down in '17 said he was like a Ford truck. Parts practically replaceable.
Doctor Evans. It was Dr. Strauss's opinion—and I agree with him—that he'd be in pretty good condition for a good many years if we got rid of that stone.
Chuck. Wouldn't it be a big job?
Doctor Evans. Mm—yes—but Strauss could handle it beautifully.
Chuck. Is he expensive?

Doctor Evans. He'd be reasonable.
Chuck. How much?
Doctor Evans. Well—of course I can't speak for Dr. Strauss, but I imagine everything—operation—nurse—hospital—he'd have to stay here for several weeks of course—would be something under two thousand.
Chuck. Mm-hm. Well—(*He looks at the other two. They both nod.*) Okay. You better go ahead, then. Could we see him?
Doctor Evans. Why not. Wait right here. I'll see if I can't have the burse bring him down.
Chuck. That'll be fine.
Doctor Evans. All right. I'll see what I can do. (*He goes.*)
Chuck. Two thousand buckaroos. How much did you and Flabby bring back from location?
Babe (*After a moment*). Well—
Flabby. Er—yeah.
Babe. You see—there was a crap game the last night.
Chuck (*Nodding*). Mm-hmm.
Babe. Yeah.
Chuck. I see. Well, there's about three hundred in the kitty, I guess. Maybe that fight stuff on Friday will run a couple of days. If we can sell Deming something special, we ought to be able to build that up to a grand anyway. At least that would give us enough for a down payment.
Flabby. But the Doc said you can't work on Friday.
Chuck. He's an old woman.
Babe. Do you really think you ought to, Chuck?
Chuck (*Taking off the glasses*). Look. My eyes are fine. I haven't even had a headache for two days. Between shots I'll sit in a dark corner and relax, and while I'm working I'll just be careful not to look into any lights. There's nothing to it.
Flabby. I don't know, Chuck—
Chuck. Well, I do—so forget it. We'd better snoop around when we leave here and see what's doing at Paramount and R.K.O. If there's still time, we can check at Columbia and Universal. We've got to get some extra work.
Babe. Yeah. All right, Chuck. (*A nurse comes in, followed by Jimmy Aquilina.*)
Nurse. Oh, there you are, Mr. Burden.
Chuck. Hello, Miss Horton.
Jimmy. Thanks, sister.
Nurse. Not at all. (*The nurse goes, Jimmy crosses to Chuck.*)

Jimmy. I understand you paid my doctor's bill here. I also owe you one sock in the jaw. How's your eye?
Chuck. It's fine. And you don't owe me anything.
Jimmy. Here's ten bucks. The nurse gave me your address. When you get rid of those glasses I'll drop around and settle up the rest of the account.
Chuck. Now, listen, sonny. Forget it, will you? (*To the boys.*) This is that would-be daredevil I told you about. (*To Jimmy.*) The doctor's bill cancels the sock, see. As a matter of fact, I still owe you fifteen bucks. (*To the boys.*) That chiseller Vern Jones promised him $25 if he'd do my train gag. Can you imagine?
Babe. Those guys'll try anything.
Flabby. Look, buddy. You don't want to fight Chuck. In the first place, he don't fight fair. If you're bigger than he is, he'll hit you with a bottle or something. See that! (*He parts his hair to show a scar.*) Haig and Haig—1922. In the second place, suppose you was lucky and licked him, he'd holler for his gang, which is us, and we'd annihilate you. In the third place, he don't believe in fightin'. None of us do. It's stupid. So, just shake hands and forget it. (*Chuck puts out his hand. Jimmy takes it. The next minute he is on the floor. As he scrambles to his feet, Babe and Flabby grab him.*)
Flabby. See what I mean?
Chuck. Sure, Kid. Here. On the level. (*He grabs Jimmy's hand and really shakes it.*) Now, tell me. What you been doing with yourself?
Jimmy (*After a doubtful look at the three*). Oh, a couple odd jobs. I drove Miss Sherry for three days till she sobered up and found out it was me. She's got a complex about me having woof. She says I stimulate her hormones. Now what the hell is that?
Flabby. Don't ask. Believe me, it's nothing that a boy of twelve should know.
Jimmy. Well, anyway, she gave me the gate. Some Filipino boy is driving for her. So I'm looking for a job again. You don't know of anything, do you?
Babe. Look, Chuck. How about recruiting him for Friday? We could collect an agent's commission. Twenty percent.
Jimmy. What is it—what does it pay?
Flabby. Just taking some bumps. A fight scene. It's thirty-five a day, unless we do something special—then it's whatever we can get.
Jimmy. Sounds all right to me.

Babe. We need some quick cash, see. All we can collect. A pal of ours has to be operated on. If we ace you in, you'll have to kick in with twenty percent.
Jimmy. Okay.
Babe. What do you say, Chuck?
Chuck. I dunno. Deming's kind of choosy.
Jimmy. I can do it. I used to fight a little.
Chuck. This is different.
Jimmy. You could show me, couldn't you?
Chuck. M-m-m. Maybe.
Babe. Look. Could you do this? Left hook, Flabby. I'll duck. You miss. Zowie! You do a hundred and eight.
Flabby. Okay. Here I come! (*They square off. Flabby swings a wild haymaker with his left. Babe ducks, pretends to drive his right into Flabby's back. Flabby arches his back, Babe catches him on his hip and, exerting pressure with his left arm across Flabby's throat, throw him to the floor. Flabby lands in a sitting position, facing the corridor door through which at this instant a nurse propels Jig Smith in a wheelchair. Smith's chair is followed by Doctor Evans. Smith is in pajamas. The left sleeve is completely empty. The right is pinned up to the shoulder, revealing the fact that the arm is amputated at the elbow. There is a blanket over Smith from the waist down. Jig leans over the side of his chair, and waving his arm, begins to count.*)
Jig. Six, seven, eight, nine, ten! YOU'RE OUT!
Flabby (*Still seated*). Hi, Jig.
Jig. Hello, you big palooka. What's the matter? Having one of your dizzy spells?
Flabby (*Getting up*). No. We were just showin' this fella how to take a bump. This is Jig Smith, Mr.—er—
Jimmy. Aquilina—Jimmy Aquilina. Glad to know you. (*Jimmy starts to put out his hand, then realizes the faux pas and manages to convert the gesture into fumbling with his hat.*)
Jig. Hi-ya. (*The nurse moves the chair forward. The movement is just enough to cause the blanket to fall to the floor, revealing the fact that Jig is legless. The nurse replaces the blanket. Chuck steps forward and helps her. Jimmy reacts with an embarrassed gesture.*)
Babe (*Quickly, to Doctor Evans*). Mr. Aquilina is going to pinch-hit for Chuck on Friday.

Doctor Evans. Oh. That's a good idea. I've been telling Jig what we'd like to do, Chuck. He's quite agreeable.

Jig. Sure, why not? The sooner, the quicker. I've got a speaking date the middle of March, Doc. How about it?

Doctor Evans. Well. Yes. That's possible. If there are no complications.

Jig. Listen to him. What could be complicated about a fiddly little "kidley"?

Doctor Evans. Nothing, we hope. However—

Jig. However my asthma—and no alibis! March 15th—that's a date. Shrine Auditorium—Peace and Progress Program. Among those present—Jig Smith.

Doctor Evans. We'll do our damnedest.

Jig. You'll get me there.

Doctor Evans. I won't promise.

Jig. Sabotage, huh? (*To Chuck.*) I'll bet he's loaded with munition stocks.

Doctor Evans. Oh, no, I'm not. I hate war as much as you do, Jig. It's loathsome—horrible. There's no sense to it. But how in the hell are you ever going to stop it?

Jig (*After a moment's pause*). How do you feel about cancer, Doc?

Doctor Evans. What?

Jig. I said, "How do you feel about cancer?" Hopeless, isn't it?

Doctor Evans (*After a pause*). No. Of course, it isn't. We'll lick it—some day we'll find the cure.

Jig. Sure you will—but how?

Doctor Evans. Why, goddamn it, we've got to.

Jig. Now you're talking, Doc. The man of medicine, boys, and what's his answer? What's his scientific solution for kicking death in the nuts? "Goddamn it," says he, "we've got to!" Well, that's good enough for me, boys. That's a hell of an answer. Don't let's forget it. Pass the word around. Tell 'em to shout it out. Who says we've got to die in this war? Who says it? Quiet, profiteer! Shut up, louse. This time we ain't fightin' in your phony war. Do you hear that? We ain't going to fight! We're keeping out of it! Goddamn it, America, we've got to!

Chuck (*Quietly*). Take it easy, Jig.

Jig. Okay, Chuck. Excuse me, Doc. I got kind of wound up.

Nurse. I think you'd better go back to your room—

Jig. All right, nurse. (*To the others.*) See what happens to a poor peace agitator? Gets sent back where he came from. Well, so long, boys. Glad to have met you, Mr. Aquilina.

Jimmy. Thanks. I certainly got a kick out of what you said.
Jig. That's fine. Get a load of me next month. Shrine Auditorium. March 15th—right, Doc?
Doctor Evans. Right.
Jig. That's better. (*To the nurse.*) Come on, baby. I'll take you on at checkers. (*The nurse wheels him out.*)
Doctor Evans. I'll get ahold of Dr. Strauss, Chuck. If it's all right with you, we'll set the party for tomorrow morning.
Chuck. All right, Doc. Go to it.
Doctor Evans. Fine. Goodbye, Babe. 'Bye, Flabby.
Babe and Flabby. So long, Doc. (*Doctor Evans goes.*)
Jimmy. That's the guy, huh?
Chuck. That's him.
Babe. The one and only.
Flabby. Yeah.
Jimmy. Jeez. Look. I guess maybe we could up that twenty percent. Let's make it fifty.
Chuck. Okay, kid. And thanks.
Jimmy. A pleasure. Say, what about that trick you was showing me? Could I try it once?
Flabby. Sure. Just duck under my left and sock me in the back. Then gimme "hmmp"! I'll do the rest.
Jimmy. Okay. Come ahead.
Flabby. Here we go. One, two—SOCK! (*He swings his left. Jimmy ducks under it, whams Flabby in the back, heaves him to his hip and swings him to the floor.*)
Flabby. That's it. Not bad.
Chuck. Only look. You gotta get him up *higher*! Come on, Babe, we'll show him. Here I come. (*Babe and Chuck repeat the trick, Chuck taking Flabby's part. Jimmy watches, then goes again with Flabby. As he does so, the nurse who came on at the beginning of the scene, re-enters and stands a moment, spellbound.*)
Nurse. Doctor! Help! Doctor! (*As Babe and Chuck try to explain, Jimmy throws Flabby behind the other two, upsetting them and the nurse to the floor. Blackout.*)

Act One: Scene Three

A corner of Stage 9 at Phoenix Pictures, Inc. All that shows of Deming's set is the head of a stairway on the right, from which the stairs start down for about six steps. The remainder of the stairs is masked by an arch. There is a tall stepladder at the head of the steps. The character of the stairs suggests that the set below represents a warehouse. The rest of Stage 9 is empty, except for a few camera parallels and unused lights, a few people watching the action off right, and Carmen Sherry's portable dressing room which is on the left. When the lights come up, the sound of the fight scene that is being photographed off right can be heard. Carmen, dressed in a smart suit, hat, and veil, is seated outside her dressing room with Jack Trent, studying her script. They have trouble concentrating because of the noise and go inside the dressing room, slamming the door. The sound of the fight continues. Finally, Deming's voice cuts through the racket yelling, "Cut!" The noise subsides and the head electrician barks out, "Save 'em!" The brilliant offstage lighting is cut down to almost nothing, and the comparative quiet of preparing for the next setup replaces the bedlam of the fight.

Chuck, Babe, Flabby, Jimmy and three or four other stunt men who have been in the fight, come on from the set. Chuck, who is doubling again for Trent, is wearing a business suit, a light topcoat, and a brown hat. Babe is dressed in a replica of Carmen's modish suit, complete with wig, hat, and veil. The rest are all dressed like gangsters.

Stunt man (*To Babe*). Hey, lookit, Babe. I don't like the way you socked me in the back of the head with that bottle.
Babe. What's the matter? It was breakaway.
Stunt man. Your fist ain't breakaway. You come down right on the back of my neck. That's a rabbit punch. It's illegal!
Babe. Aw, don't get technical.
Stunt man. Well, don't do it again, see. Or I'll beat your ears down.
Babe. You and whose army?
Stunt man. Me and nobody's army!
Babe (*Whipping off the hat and wig*). Yeah?
Chuck. Hey, shut up, both of you. You give me a headache. Save that for the next scene!
Stunt man. Yeah, but— (*There is silence, then Babe breaks down.*)
Babe. Okay, Peewee—I'm sorry.

Stunt man. Well, watch it.
Babe. Okay.
Chuck. Look, boys—I've got an idea. (*He passes his hand across his eyes.*)
Flabby. You all right, Chuck?
Chuck. Yeah, sure—I guess I ran into somebody's elbow, that's all. Now, listen—(*Deming comes on, followed by Vern Jones and his assistant.*)
Deming. That was a honey, Chuck. That cleans us up, doesn't it?
Chuck. Well, I don't know. I got another one, if you'll go for it.
Deming. What is it?
Chuck. Over there. (*He points to the stairs.*) I could come up those stairs with Flabby after me and clunk him on the chin. He'd go down backwards and hit the gang comin' up. By the time they were ready to come up again, I could get up on that ladder, grab a hold of the wall and take off with the ladder right down the stairs on top of them. You could cheat the table with those boxes on it a little closer to the bottom of the stairs and I'd smack right into it.
Deming. That's all right. I'll buy that. (*To Vern's assistant.*) Look, Art. Take Chuck over to the production office, will you. Explain the shot, and tell 'em I okay it. You'll have to battle it out over there about the dough, Chuck.
Chuck. All right. I've done pretty good so far.
Deming. Swell. They'll scream bloody murder—but when the see it in the picture they'll know they got a bargain.
Chuck. Thanks. Well, let's go, Art.
Deming (*To Jones*). Tell Otto to set up over by the door, Vern. I'll take Jack Trent's entrance. After that I'll do the love scene with Jack and Carmen.
Jones. Okay. (*He goes out. The set telephone rings during the above exchange. On his way out with Chuck, Art picks it up.*)
Assistant. Hello—who? It's for you, Chuck. (*Chuck takes the receiver.*)
Chuck. Hello. Oh, hello, Doc. Who, me? No, I'm just here watching. What? Oh, that's swell. Thanks for calling. Yeah, I'll tell 'em. 'Bye. (*He hangs up, yells across to Babe and Flabby.*) That was the hospital. Jig just came out of the ether and he's okay. He came out cussin'.
Flabby. Jeez!
Babe. Hot damn. You talk that price up, Chuck.
Chuck. Don't worry. (*He and Art go. Vern knocks on Carmen's door.*)
Jones. You're in the next shot, Mr. Trent.
Trent (*Inside the dressing room*). I'll be right out.
Babe (*To the other stunt men*). Whose deal is it?

Stunt man. Flabby's.
Flabby. That's right—and I'll tell you what it is. Seven card stud with the deuces wild.
Stunt man. Have a heart, Flabby. That ain't poker. It's inflation.
Flabby. Well, it's what we're playing. (*They sit around a two-foot parallel on camera boxes and chairs. Meanwhile, Trent has come out of the dressing room and walked over to the set. Carmen appears. Jimmy Aquilina sees her.*)
Carmen (*Calling*). Edie! (*The script girl has been typing her notes. She rises and crosses.*)
Script girl. Yes, Carmen?
Jimmy. Deal me out. (*He leans against a six-foot parallel and watches Carmen.*)
Carmen (*To Edie*). Sit down, Edie, darling. I want to run over these lines.
Script girl. Sure, Carmen. What page is it?
Carmen. Middle of a hundred and eight—that love scene.
Script girl. Mm-hm. Just a minute. (*Jimmy wanders over where he can listen in. Carmen doesn't see him. Edie finds the place. Meanwhile, the poker game continues.*)
Carmen. Start with Jack's speech there.
Script girl. Right you are. (*Reading with no expression.*) "I suppose you're wondering why I followed you here."
Carmen (*Reading*). "Not particularly. I imagine you recognized me and decided to see what the wild Miss Warrington was doing in a place like this?"
Script girl. "Is that your name—Warrington?"
Carmen. "Oh, come now—you're not going to tell me you didn't know I was Diana Warrington?"
Script girl. "I don't even know who Diana Warrington is. All I know is that you were in the third row ringside the night I fought Mushy Donovan."
Carmen. "Good Lord! You're Tommy Britt!"
Script girl. "That's me."
Jones (*Appearing from the right*). Edie! Script please!
Script girl. Right away, Vern. What is it?
Jones. Mr. Deming wants you on the set.
Script girl. Will you excuse me, Carmen? I'll be right back.
Carmen. Go ahead, darling—I'll muddle through.
Script girl. I won't be a minute. (*She goes. Jimmy steps forward.*)

Jimmy. Could I help you with that, Miss Sherry?
Carmen (*Seeing him*). Oh, my God! Mimi! My vanishing cream!
Jimmy. Never mind—I'll blow.
Carmen. I thought I fired you.
Jimmy. You did. I'm working in your fight stuff with Chuck and the boys. I'm a stunt man.
Carmen. Well, isn't that ducky! Now you can find yourself a nice high building and fall off it.
Jimmy. I thought maybe you'd like someone to read those lines to you. I got nothing to do.
Carmen. Sit down. After all, who am I to struggle against fate.
Jimmy. That's right. What can you lose? I'll go back a coupla speeches. Here. "All I know is that you were in the third row ringside the night I fought mushy Donovan."
Carmen. "Good Lord! You're Tommy Britt!"
Jimmy. "That's me."
Carmen. "You really remember me from that night?"
Jimmy (*Warming up*). "You had on a red dress. It was right after Mushy connected with my chin in the seventh. The boys were working on me—hard. Things were still spinning. Then I saw you. You stood up and yelled right at me. 'Come on, Tommy! He's all through. Go get him!' When the bell rang, Mushy came out of his corner slugging—with both mitts—but he couldn't hurt me. I didn't even know he was there. All I could see was your face. And I could hear your voice, 'He's all through. Go get him!' Next thing I knew, somebody was lifting my hand, and inside my head something busted loose like they were feeding the lions in Central Park."
Carmen (*After a second*). Well, blow me down!
Jimmy. Huh? Where's that? That's not in here.
Carmen. No, baby—that was me. Hey, listen—are you an actor?
Jimmy. Ain't we all—as Shakespeare said?
Carmen. No, I mean—no kidding.
Jimmy. Oh, I done a coupla minstrel shows and stuff like that. Strictly amateur. (*He pronounces it "amachure."*)
Carmen. Well, I'll be goddamned! As Shakespeare said.
Jimmy (*Suddenly*). You know this is phony, don't you?
Carmen. What is?
Jimmy. This stuff we've been reading. It's from hunger.
Carmen. It didn't sound like it.

Jimmy. Well, it is. I mean, any fighter that would goo-goo at a dame during business hours is definitely a bum.
Carmen. If she was the Woof Girl?
Jimmy. If she was the Miss America of a Nudist Camp. Listen, I've done some fighting. And I've done some lookin', too. But not at the same time. They don't mix.
Carmen. You'd look at me.
Jimmy. I'm lookin' now.
Carmen. Well?
Jimmy. Mm-hm. (*Then, more decisively.*) Mmm-hmm. But if my meal ticket was waitin' in his corner to murder me, I'd *stop* lookin'! That's economic necessity.
Carmen. You know too much.
Jimmy. All I know is what I've seen. And believe me, Angel Puss, it ain't love that makes the world go 'round. It's empty stomachs.
Jones (*Offstage.*) Quiet! Quiet! We're turning.
Sound grip (*Offstage*). Scene eighty-two—Deming—sync. Silent camera—speed.
Carmen (*Lowering her voice*). Maybe you've seen too much.
Jimmy. Oh, no, I ain't, Only, you see, the way I figure it, the whole shebang's kind of a giant quiz. Millions and millions of questions—only they don't give you the answers. You got to dig 'em out yourself.
Carmen. You can pick your spot, can't you? Where the diggin's not so tough.
Jimmy. Sometimes. And sometimes, you can't. There's pay dirt, and there's rocks. And there's places where the dirt's soft and fresh, and you want to get right down like a kid and squush it in your fingers.
Carmen. That's for me.
Jimmy. Sure. For me, too. Only most of those places have got signs on 'em—"Private Property—No Trespassing. Beware of the dog!"
Carmen. I guess I don't believe in signs.
Jimmy. You don't have to. You've got woof.
Deming (*Offstage*). Cut! Okay, Otto?
Cameraman (*Offstage*). Okay.
Deming (*Offstage*). Good for me. Oh, Vern!
Carmen. Now looky, cooky. You're not so un-dynamic yourself.
Jimmy. No. That's a girl's racket. Those sign owners wear pants. A guy's got to get in the hard way.
Carmen. M-m. Not if he's got a drag with the sign owner's girl friend.

Jimmy (*Shaking his head*). I'd make a lousy gigolo.
Carmen. Oh, member of the Purity League, huh?
Jimmy. If you want to call it that.
Carmen. But you could use some of that good earth, couldn't you?
Jimmy (*Nodding*). Just give me a shot at it. That's all I ask—one good, fat shot.
Carmen. Stick around. Maybe I will.
Jimmy (*After a long look*). Shall we go ahead with the Frank Merriwell?
Carmen (*Shaking her head*). Mm-mm. I've lost the mood.
Jimmy. Okay. (*Sol Herzog, the president of Phoenix Pictures, Inc., comes on from the left. He is accompanied by James Tillinghast, a handsome keen-eyed man of about fifty.*)
Herzog. Here she is. Well, you're lucky, Mr. Tillinghast, that she's not working. Carmen, darling.
Carmen. Hello, Sol.
Herzog. I want you to meet a very special friend of mine—Mr. James Tillinghast.
Carmen. How do you do?
Tillinghast. I'm delighted to meet you, Miss Sherry.
Herzog. Mr. Tillinghast is the president of the Hapwood Aircraft Company.
Carmen. Well—(*Indicating Jimmy.*) This is Mr. Galahad, Mr. Tillinghast. His strength is as the strength of ten.
Tillinghast. Glad to know you.
Jimmy. Hi'ya. She's kidding you.
Tillinghast. Oh, I don't know. You look pretty husky.
Jimmy. Yeah. Well, my name's Aquilina.
Herzog. Which, believe me, young man, is entirely *irrevelant*.
Carmen. Don't mind Sol, Mr. Tillinghast. He knows it's irrelevant. He's just trying to horn in on that Goldwyn publicity.
Herzog. I'm doing nothing of the kind. With me it's natural. With Goldwyn it's absolutely infected.
Carmen. I'm sorry I mentioned it.
Herzog. Darling, Mr. Tillinghast is going to produce a picture. He's got a wonderful story—really wonderful. And what a title! *March On, America!* Do you like it?
Carmen. Sounds very thrilling.

Herzog. I should say so. And what a part for the girl! What a part! Simply omnipotent! I'm telling you. Look, couldn't we go someplace where it's quiet?
Carmen. What about my dressing room? If Mr. Aquilina will excuse us—
Herzog. Certainly he'll excuse you. Why shouldn't he?
Jimmy. You got me there. (*They start into the dressing room. Vern Jones appears and interrupts.*)
Jones. Excuse me, Mr. Herzog.
Herzog. Yes—what is it?
Jones. Mr. Deming is ready to rehearse with Miss Sherry on the set.
Herzog. Oh, for goodness sakes!
Carmen. Won't you come with me, Mr. Tillinghast? It's not a very long scene.
Tillinghast. I'd love to watch if it won't bother you.
Herzog. Come ahead. Come ahead. It'll be a pleasure.
Tillinghast. Well, thank you. (*They cross toward the set.*)
Herzog. Mr. Tillinghast has his heart set you should play the lead in his picture. I want you to read it. (*Chuck comes in with Art. Babe sees him.*)
Babe. Hey, here's Chuck.
Stunt man. Let's split the pot and call it off. Nobody's drawn yet.
The rest. Okay—sure. Split it seven ways. You count it, Peewee.
Flabby. Hey, wait a minute.
Babe. What's the matter?
Flabby. Four queens is the matter. Look. I had 'em natural.
Stunt man. Too bad, Flabby. Look at that! He really had 'em.
Flabby. There was over seven bucks in that pot!
Babe. What happened, Chuck? How'd you make out?
Chuck. Not bad. Fifty apiece, and a hundred and fifty for me.
Babe. Damn right it's not bad. You hear that, Flabby?
Flabby. Eight dollars and thirty cents!
Chuck. Anybody got any aspirin? That argument gave me a headache. I think I'll sit down a minute.
Babe. That maid of Sherry's has. Probably got some in her dressing room.
Stunt man. Don't forget to tip your wig when you ask her.
Babe. Quiet. (*He exits into the dressing room. Gladys, an overblown blonde in a cigarette girl's outfit appears and walks up behind Flabby.*)
Gladys. I thought you weren't working. (*Flabby turns and recognizes the blonde.*)

Flabby. Hello, Gladys. I'm not. I—just came over to watch the boys. You ain't with Mr. Deming.

Gladys. I'm working on the Dixon set. It says on the call sheet you're working.

Flabby. Aw! That assistant got it balled up.

Gladys. I'll see you at the cashier's window when I'm through. Or do you want to write me an order to pick up your check?

Flabby. Look, Gladys. I know I'm behind in my alimony.

Gladys. Behind! Huh! For what you are, "behind" is a very polite word.

Flabby. Never mind now. The point is next week I got a real job coming up. I'll send you the whole check.

Gladys. I'll see you at that window at 6:30. (*Babe comes from Carmen's dressing room with two aspirin tablets in the palm of one hand and a lily cup full of water in the other. He holds out the aspirins. Chuck doesn't notice him.*)

Babe. Here you are, Chuck. (*Chuck turns and gropes toward Babe with his right hand.*)

Chuck. What's happened to the lights?

Babe. Nothin'.

Chuck. What did they turn 'em off for? (*Babe regards him uneasily. Flabby turns from Gladys. Jimmy and the stunt men move closer. The distant sounds of Deming's company preparing to shoot have been heard faintly during this.*)

Deming (*Offstage*). Quiet! CAMERA!

Babe (*Whispering*). The lights ain't off, Chuck.

Stunt Man [Peewee] (*Whispering*). What's the matter with his eyes?

Flabby (*Whispering*). Shh! (*He moves close to Chuck. So does Jimmy.*)

Chuck. You're not kidding me, Babe?

Babe. No, Chuck.

Chuck (*After a pause*). I can't see a damn thing. (*Another pause.*) Gimme that aspirin. (*Babe guides his hand. Chuck swallows the aspirin. Babe helps him with the water.*) Head still aches. Gotta get that dough. (*He tosses the cup away, then sits thinking a moment.*) Is Flabby there?

Flabby. Right here, Chuck.

Chuck. Gimme your hand. (*Flabby does so. Chuck rises and takes Flabby's arm.*) Let's take a walk. (*They do so.*) Uh-huh. How many steps in that stairway?

Jimmy. I'll check it for you. (*He tiptoes off toward the set.*)

Deming (*Offstage*). Cut! (*The usual buzz follows.*)

Chuck (*Suddenly to Flabby*). Flabby. Grab me here. (*Indicating his lapels. Flabby does so.*) Now take a poke at me. Count under your breath. One—two—okay. Right now!
Flabby. Here we go. One. Two. (*On two he swings his right. Chuck ducks and counters with his own right to Flabby's chin.*)
Chuck. Not bad—huh, Flabby?
Flabby (*Rubbing his chin*) Very good.
Jimmy (*Reappearing*). There's twenty-one steps.
Chuck. Thanks.
Jones (*Coming from the set*). Whenever you're ready, Chuck. We're setting up. Three cameras.
Chuck. Be right with you.
Babe. Chuck!
Chuck (*Whispering*). Shut up!
Jones. We'll wait for you. (*He goes.*)
Chuck. On the fire. (*Everyone remains quiet until Jones is gone.*)
Babe. You're not going to try it, Chuck!
Chuck. Why not? Listen. We'll walk over there right now and count it out. All you got to watch is when the ladder falls on those boxes, about three of you break the fall without spoiling it. I'll handle the rest easy.
Flabby. But, Chuck—
Chuck. Shut up! Come on. Stay close to me, boys. (*They start out for the set. Carmen, Herzog, and Tillinghast are coming off.*)
Carmen. Good luck, Chuck. Knock 'em silly.
Chuck. Thanks, Miss Sherry.
Carmen. Don't do anything I wouldn't do.
Chuck. Okay. I'll remember that.
Carmen. You want to watch this, Mr. Tillinghast. It's the shot Mr. Deming told you about. We can see it perfectly from this parallel.
Tillinghast. Fine. Thank you. (*He helps her up onto the parallel.*)
Carmen. Chuck Burden is the best damn stunt man in the business.
Herzog. And expensive.
Carmen. Look at the retakes he saves you.
Herzog. I should hope so. (*Meanwhile, Chuck and the others are working things out by the ladder. Chuck pantomimes socking Flabby then climbs the ladder, grabs the wall, and tilts the stepladder over the brink of the stair. A grip kneels and loosely nails the forward legs of the ladder. Finally, Chuck comes down and the stunt men disperse down the stairs, Flabby and Babe on either side of Chuck.*)

Tillinghast. I hope you'll be able to read *March On, America!* over the weekend, Miss Sherry.
Carmen. I will—unless we work on Sunday.
Herzog. I'll guarantee it that you don't.
Carmen. Why, Sol, you must be asking three times my salary.
Herzog. What a kidder. Carmen—the way I look at it, *March On, America!* is a patriotic duty.
Carmen. But will it make any money?
Herzog. I tell you, it's sure-fire.
Carmen. Hmm. Mr. Tillinghast, I'd like to have something to say about the cast, if that's possible.
Tillinghast. I don't see why not. We want the very best, and we'll pay for them.
Carmen. That would certainly help.
Jones (*Offstage*). Quiet, everybody, please! Quiet. Turn 'em over.
Sound man (*Offstage*). Turning.
Carmen. There they go. Watch now.
Deming (*Offstage*). Start your action, boys. (*The stunt men are heard starting to shove each other around.*)
Sound man (*Offstage*). Speed.
Sound grip (*Offstage*). Scene 79A—Deming—Sound.
Deming (*Offstage*). CAMERA! (*Chuck appears running up into the set at the head of the stairs. He guides himself by the rail. Flabby runs in, grabs him by the lapels and swings. Chuck ducks and clips Flabby on the chin. Flabby goes out of sight down the stairs. Chuck feels for the ladder and goes up it.*)
Flabby (*Offstage*). Come on, boys. Let's get him! (*The others take up the cry and we hear them start for the stairs. Chuck grabs the wall and shoves off. The ladder swings out, gathers speed, and with its base as the axis, topples over down the stairs. There is a terrific crash.*)
Carmen (*Whispering*). Wow! What did I tell you? (*The sound of the fight continues. Blackout. The curtain falls on Act One.*)

Act Two: Scene One

About 10:00 in the evening, several weeks later.

The scene is the stunt men's hangout in the Villa Murietta Bungalow Court in Hollywood. We are in the living room; the door to the entrance court is just about center. When it is open, the tropical vegetation of the court's "garden" can be seen. On either side of the entrance door are two small windows. In the upstage left wall of the living room is an entrance leading to a bedroom. Directly opposite, in the right wall, is a door leading to a kitchenette and breakfast alcove. Downstage in the left wall are double doors that conceal a folding bed. Opposite these doors, in an inset space in the right wall, is a large sofa. The furnishings and decorations are in the typical Hollywood "Spanish" style. One of the floor lamps displays a shade with fringe hanging from it. It is immediately obvious when the lights are turned on that the occupants of the place are not "easy" on the furnishings. For example, one arm of the sofa is broken and dangles loosely. A picture of Jig Smith in his wheel chair is on the upstage wall.

When the curtain rises, the lights are all out. The only illumination comes from the court through the windows. Someone inserts a key in the entrance door and unlocks it. Two figures come in, close the door and turn on the lights. They are revealed as Jimmy Aquilina and Carmen Sherry. Carmen is wearing slacks, a sweater, a beret, a nutria topcoat, and dark glasses. Jimmy has on greenish trousers, a polo shirt and scarf, a sport jacket, and a light overcoat. He is hatless.

Jimmy. Well—this is it. The Vista del Stunt Men.
Carmen. On a clear day you can see Aquilina.
Jimmy. Take off those cheaters and you can see him right now.
Carmen. You're sure everybody's out?
Jimmy. Sure. I told you. They're all at the Soldiers' Home. Come on, take 'em off. They give me the willies. One pair in the family's enough.
Carmen. How *is* Chuck?
Jimmy. He's all right. He can see perfect. Be able to work in another week.
Carmen (*Taking off her glasses*). You tell him to take it easy. (*Looking around.*) Well, well, well. Memory Lane.
Jimmy. You've been in this joint?

Carmen. It wouldn't surprise me! I must have lived in fifty just like it. Villa! Vista! Chateau! In plain English—"La Dump." If I missed this one it wasn't my fault. How long have you been here?
Jimmy. About three weeks. The boys have been here a year. How about a drink?
Carmen? M-m-m. A little later. That last roller coaster did things to my alcoholic content.
Jimmy (*Taking off his coat*). You shouldn't have stood up to swipe that guy's hat.
Carmen (*On the coy side*). I wanted the feather on it. I wanted to tickle you. We gave it back.
Jimmy. You mean, *I* gave it back. The guy was going to poke me one.
Carmen. And did you see the look he gave me? You know, I think he recognized me.
Jimmy. Well, what if he did?
Carmen. M-m-m-m. Nothing.
Jimmy (*After a moment*). I guess maybe I should have worn the cheaters.
Carmen. Jimmy!
Jimmy. No, I mean it. You just don't want to be seen with me.
Carmen. That's not true. And you know it. It's that damn studio.
Jimmy. What's the studio got to do with it?
Carmen. Sol Herzog is allergic to gossip. If there's one squib about me in the *Reporter*, he calls me right in on the mat and cries down my shirt front. He says my fans won't stand for it. So I've been trying to be careful.
Jimmy. Why didn't you tell me that?
Carmen. I'm telling you now. Look, Jimmy. How about having that drink at my place?
Jimmy (*Shaking his head*). Not me. First time I pay you a visit, I'm gonna drive up in my own kiddie car. And I'll be dressed right, too.
Carmen. Oh, hey! How are you doing with those "No Trespassing" signs? Have you crashed any yet?
Jimmy. You just wait.
Carmen. Maybe I won't wait. Sit down a minute. There's something I want to talk to you about.
Jimmy. Okay. (*He indicates the sofa. She sits down, Jimmy follows suit. The end of the sofa with the broken arm collapses, depositing them in a heap on the floor. They laugh. Jimmy helps Carmen up.*) I told Flabby not to practice bumps on that. Here, wait a minute. (*He crosses, opens the double doors, and lets down the folding bed.*)

Carmen. My God! A collapsible casting couch! M-m-m-h-m-m! Does that remind me!
Jimmy (*Not liking it*). I'll bet.
Carmen. Oh, don't worry. I was the girl Houdini. I was like you—the best or nothing.
Jimmy. I'll bet.
Carmen. No kidding. I did nip-ups off those things that Chuck would have envied. (*Jimmy reaches out and starts to put the bed up.*)
Jimmy. Suppose we sit on the floor.
Carmen (*Stopping him*). Leave it alone. With you, Jimmy, it's perfect. (*They sit down.*)
Jimmy. Well?
Carmen. Oh, yes—what I was going to tell you. I've been seeing quite a lot of Poppa Tillinghast lately.
Jimmy (*Nodding*). You were at the Grove with him last night.
Carmen (*Pleased*). Who told you?
Jimmy. I've got spies.
Carmen. Did they tell you what I was talking to him about?
Jimmy. M-m-m. No.
Carmen. The, shut up and listen. I've been trying to sell him the idea that we ought to discover somebody for the lead in *March On, America!* It's a swell part. You could murder it.
Jimmy. Me?
Carmen. Yes, you. You'd have to make a test of course—but that wouldn't bother you. You'd make it with me.
Jimmy. Now, wait a minute. What kind of a part is it?
Carmen. It's you—to the life! Honest, the minute I read it I couldn't see anybody else. It's a kind of Cagney part. He's a young truck driver who thinks America has got to fight for democracy and enlists in the British army.
Jimmy (*Slowly*). Oh.
Carmen. I brought a script with me. (*She rises and picks up an envelope which she dropped on a table by the door when she came in.*) Here. You read it. I turned down the page we'll use for the test. Look it over tonight and I'll call you tomorrow.
Jimmy. Jeez. I—I—don't know what to say.
Carmen. Listen. I'm doing myself a favor. You're going to be great.
Jimmy. I'll bust a gut trying.

Carmen. Just be yourself and you're a cinch. Now, here's the gag. We'll rehearse the scene at my place. Then when you're okay, I'll have Tillinghast in for tea and I'll introduce you. You're a young actor—from New York. I'll ask you to read the scene as if you'd never seen it before. Then I'll get him to suggest a test.
Jimmy. Jeez. I'm groggy.
Carmen. You read it tonight, and I'll call you about eleven.
Jimmy. Okay. Jeez! (*They sit a moment.*)
Carmen. Penny?
Jimmy. Hm?
Carmen. For your thoughts.
Jimmy. You might not like 'em.
Carmen. Two pennies.
Jimmy. If I tell you this, you've got to understand it's got nothing to do with what you're trying to promote for me.
Carmen. Sure. All right. Go ahead.
Jimmy. Well—it goes back to when I was in New York—shoving my hack around.
Carmen. M-m-m.
Jimmy. I used to see every picture you ever made. I guess I told you that.
Carmen (*Nodding*). On location that day.
Jimmy. Yeah. Well—I was nuts about you, see! It got me down. I'd try to forget it. I'd take some dame out. You know. But it didn't mean anything. Nothing happened. She wasn't you. And now you're sitting there. (*He puts his hand on hers.*) You.
Carmen (*Nodding*). Believe it or not.
Jimmy (*Suddenly*). Carmen.
Carmen. Yes, Jimmy? (*Jimmy sits staring at her. Then suddenly he jumps up.*)
Jimmy. It's no good. It's no damn good. You'd think back, and all you'd remember is—this! (*He gestures, then stands looking at her. There is a sharp knock at the entrance door. They both turn. The knock is repeated. With a sudden instinct, Jimmy steps forward and folds up the bed. Carmen squawks. There is a flurry of legs and skirt as she disappears upside down. Jimmy closes the double doors. The entrance door opens suddenly and Gladys, Flabby's ex-wife, appears in the doorway.*)
Jimmy. Ah—er—hi there.
Gladys. Where's Flabby?

Jimmy. He's out. (*Gladys looks at him sharply, then barges into the bedroom. Jimmy opens the doors and pulls down the bed.*)
Carmen. Hey! What goes on?
Jimmy (*Whispering*). It's a dame. She's looking for Flabby. You better blow.
Carmen. I'll call you tomorrow. (*She kisses him quickly and exits. Jimmy readjusts the bed as Gladys returns from the bedroom.*)
Gladys (*Looking at him closely*). I know you. You were on the set that day with Flabby.
Jimmy. That's right.
Gladys. When's he coming back?
Jimmy. He didn't say.
Gladys. I've got to have twenty bucks.
Jimmy. I'll tell Flabby.
Gladys. I got to have it tonight. They're going to throw me out on the street.
Jimmy (*After a moment*). Here. (*He pulls out his wallet and gives her the money.*) I'll get it from Flabby when he works again.
Gladys. Thanks. Say, are you in love or something?
Jimmy. I can't let you walk the streets, can I?
Gladys. How long have you been in Hollywood?
Jimmy. Couple of months.
Gladys. M-m-m. Well, kid, I hope you stay this way, but I doubt it.
Jimmy. What's the matter with you and Flabby?
Gladys. What's the matter with everybody?
Jimmy. Huh?
Gladys. Never mind. I'll answer that myself. Can I sit down?
Jimmy. Help yourself.
Gladys (*She sits*). Thanks. The matter is fairy tales.
Jimmy. I don't get you.
Gladys. "So they got married and lived happily ever afterward." Remember that one?
Jimmy. Yeah—I remember it.
Gladys. Did you believe it?
Jimmy. M-m-m. I sort of half-believed it.
Gladys. Well, it's a lie. It's a dirty lie people tell their kids, because if they told 'em the truth, they'd stay single. "Love conquers all." That's another lie. That one sells a million seats at the box office.
Jimmy. People got to believe in something.

Gladys. Listen, kid. Love's a luxury. And it don't last. Believe in that one. It ought to be lesson number one in McGuffey's First Reader.
Jimmy. Yeah, but if people didn't believe in that stuff, you'd have race suicide.
Gladys. So what? The rich have it. They're doin' fine.
Jimmy. You're kind of pessimistic.
Gladys. Who, me? Why, mister! I'm in the movies. I've got a rich husband who pays me alimony every leap year. How can you talk that way?
Jimmy. Now, look. There's plenty of weeks when Flabby don't make a dime.
Gladys. Listen, little boy. I don't blame Flabby, see. When a man's through sleeping with a dame, he hates like hell to give her money. That's only human. Only when you gotta eat, you gotta eat.
Jimmy. I know that.
Gladys. And when you're a woman, and you're all alone, you begin to think about things. You begin to hate those lies they told you. You remember how you believed that being stuck on a guy was all that mattered. As long as he was hot for you, things just *had* to come out all right, you thought. When you had a job and he didn't, you got a big boot out of keeping the both of you alive when there wasn't enough for one. Then one day, you take a peek at yourself in the glass, and you see those things under your chin and around the corners of your eyes, and it's like the truth looking out at you. "Independence," you say to yourself. "That's what a woman's got to have—independence!"
Jimmy. That's what everybody's got to have. But how do you get it?
Gladys. That's your question, kid—you answer it. I don't know. But I can tell you one thing. Nine girls out of ten have got to support themselves by grabbing a man who's got a stake. Of course, there's a few lucky ones who've got brains or some kind of a trick they can cash in on. They play piano, or they're double-jointed or something. Then there's the ones with looks and a good figure, and they sell that—one way or another. Then there's the big mob—the two-for-a-nickel average—like me. Believe me, baby, if they haven't got a little dough to start with, they really take it on the chin.
Jimmy. Money, money, money. Yep. And if the girl's got it and the guy ain't, that's no bowl of cherries either.
Gladys. So that's what's eatin' you?
Jimmy. That's it all right.

Gladys. I thought I caught a whiff of Quelques Floosie when I came in here.
Jimmy. Hey, sister, you ought to be more careful of your language.
Gladys. Oh, pardon me. Well, dreamer, I'll shove off. Thanks again for the room rent. I certainly was flat. Say, I haven't had a call from Central Casting since that day you saw me on the set. It's been like that ever since the war started. That's a fine mess! I can't understand those dopes. Why don't they just turn around and go on home? What's it getting them? They must be nuts! Well, so long, kid. Good luck to you. There's one thing you can count on, anyway. Tomorrow is another day—God forbid! (*She goes. Jimmy picks up the script left by Carmen and turns to the sofa. It's condition stops him for a moment, then he goes into the kitchenette, returns with an empty box, places it under the broken down end of the sofa, and sits down to read the script. Babe's face appears at one of the windows. Next moment, he steps inside. Jimmy shoves the script under a pillow.*)
Jimmy. Hello, Babe—how's Jig?
Babe. He's on the crest. We brought him with us. He's got a yen to gamble. Wants to play Hearts. Come on, we'll set up the table.
Jimmy. Sure. (*He follows Babe into the kitchenette. Chuck's back appears in the entrance doorway. He has hold of Jig's chair. The chair, with Jig in it, comes next. Flabby brings up the rear. He boots the chair over the threshold.*)
Jig. Whoop's a daisy! Easy now, Flabby—easy. Okay. Set her down.
Flabby (*Putting the chair down*). How's that?
Jig. Lousy. You got to get her tail down sooner. You're a hell of a navigator.
Chuck. He's out of practice.
Jig. He never *was* any good. I wouldn't let him fly a kite. (*Babe and Jimmy come in with a small table and two chairs.*) Hi there, Jimmy. How's the boy? (*Flabby goes into the bedroom.*)
Jimmy. I'm pretty good, Jig. How's yourself?
Jig. Never better. Been talking my head off. The boys brought me a bottle of Scotch. I'm just a "leetle" high.
Jimmy. Better watch yourself. (*He holds up the deck of cards which he was about to toss on the table.*) They'll take you to the cleaners.
Jig. Like hell they will. They're higher'n I am. Anyway, Chuck and I have got a system. (*Flabby comes in with two chairs from the bedroom.*)
Flabby. Yeah—it's colossal. (*He pronounces it "col-lou-sal."*) Combination play. Jig's brains and Chuck's dealing. Which cancels.
Babe (*To Jig*). Want a pillow?

Jig. Thanks. (*Babe picks one up from the sofa, exposing Carmen's script.*)
Babe. Hey, what's this?
Jimmy. It's a script I'm reading. (*He takes it.*) I'll round up the drinks. (*He goes, taking the script with him. The others exchange looks.*)
Babe (*Stage whisper*). It's the Woof Girl's. Her name's all over it.
Flabby. So that's who he was out with.
Chuck. Sure. She's got hot zippers for him.
Jig. You mean that Sherry number?
Babe. That's who.
Jig. He's doin' all right.
Flabby. I wonder what she gave him that script for.
Chuck. She's trying it out on the dog. De Mille gives 'em to his cook.
Babe. It had a hoopla title. Something about America. I couldn't quite make it out.
Chuck. Some more of that patriotic junk, huh?
Babe. I guess, maybe. (*Jimmy appears in the doorway with a tray on which are glasses, a whisky bottle, ice, and a siphon of soda. He stands, listening.*)
Jig. Before long, they'll all be lining up to shove us in. The papers—radio—pictures. The call to arms will have a million tongues. The voice of peace is a whisper.
Chuck (*Nodding*). Which is tough to amplify.
Jig. And tougher to dramatize. The thunder and the lightning steal the show. The peaceful sunlight draws nothing but flies. We've got to think of something.
Jimmy (*Coming forward with the tray*). What are we playing for? I'm not so flush.
Flabby (*Winking at the others*). Why, what have you been doing since this morning? You were flashing a double sawbuck at breakfast.
Jimmy. Yeah? Well, I gave it to your ex-Missus. They were gonna throw her out on the street. She was in here just before you came.
Flabby. Well, for God's sake. Thanks, kid. Here. (*He takes out some money.*) Here's ten till next week. I had a call yesterday but I turned it down. Fifty bucks to jump four stories into a fire net. Phooey! Do you think she was on the level?
Jimmy. She sure sounded on the level.
Flabby. Jeez. Poor Gladys. Sometimes I go to sleep and I dream that Gladys has found herself a nice fat chain-store owner with a million bucks—but I always wake up.

Babe. Well, wake up now, slug, and answer Jimmy. (*To Jimmy.*) It's a penny a heart—thirteen for the Black Lady—and twenty-six apiece to the gang if you get 'em all. (*Chuck is pouring the drinks.*) I want plain water. (*He takes his glass and goes to the kitchenette as Jimmy answers.*)

Jimmy. I guess I can stand that. (*They arrange themselves at the table. Chuck sits next to Jig's chair. Chuck finishes pouring drinks. Babe comes back and starts shuffling the cards. Flabby goes to get himself a pillow from the sofa.*)

Babe (*Spreading the deck*). Low deals. Ace is high. (*Flabby observes the box under the couch and kicks it out. The sofa collapses.*)

Flabby (*The "little bear"*). Who's been layin' on *my* sofa?

Jimmy. I *sat* on it. I told you those bumps would ruin it.

Flabby. Now, Jimmy. Woof, woof!

Jimmy. Aw, shut up.

Babe. Lay off, Flabby. *Low deals!*

Flabby (*Returning to the table*). I didn't say a thing. (*Softly.*) Woofa, woofa, woofa! (*They draw.*)

Babe. Jig's deal. (*Chuck collects the cards and starts to deal.*)

Jig. Did you read that speech the guy made in the Senate this morning?

Flabby. No—what was that?

Jig. Very cute. The gentleman from Honky-Tonkus says he's for peace—but he wants to lend the boys fifty million smackers.

Babe. That's nice. Well, they won't get away with it. Look at the last Gallup poll. Over ninety percent against our going in.

Jig. I know, Babe, but things can switch like *that*. In 1916, Wilson got elected because he kept us out of war. Six months later, he was leading us into it.

Jimmy. But don't you think people are smarter today?

Jig. Sure. And so are the pop-gun salesmen. Don't kid yourselves, boys. Uncle Sam's got to protect his investment. I told you what would happen when we made that first loan. From now on they'll lay it on thick. A big build-up for the good old bill collector. Get that dough back! Send for the marines!

Babe. What a racket! (*Babe plays. Flabby looks at the card.*)

Flabby. King of diamonds, huh?

Babe. Ought to be safe once around.

Flabby. Sorry, pal—I'm fresh out of diamonds. Have a heart. Little ace.

Babe. Son of a—son of a—*son* of a—!

Jimmy (*As he plays, to Flabby*). I hope you're holding another high one, sucker.
Flabby. Listen, Woofy, you play your hand and I'll play mine.
Jig. Nuts! We've got the ace of diamonds singleton. (*Chuck takes the trick.*)
Babe. Thank you.
Jimmy. Better watch 'em, boys. They might be trying to run it.
Jig. Fat chance. Let's see now. Flabby *must* have a club, Chuck.
Chuck. Sure. We're safe as a church. (*He plays.*)
Jimmy. Watch 'em. Watch 'em. I don't like those ace leads.
Babe. We'll soon find out. (*The play goes around. Chuck takes the trick.*)
Jig. Hmm. No hearts. We got away with it. Try it again. (*Chuck plays.*)
Jimmy. Queen of clubs. Watch 'em, boys. Watch 'em.
Babe. I'm watching. King! (*He plays. The play goes around. Babe takes the trick.*) All clubs again. Well, let's see about this. I lead a little heart.
Flabby. I got one that's littler.
Jimmy. Okay. I'll be the fall guy. (*He plays.*) Queen.
Jig (*Very British*). Awf'ly sorry. (*Chuck takes the trick with the King.*)
Jimmy. What did I tell you! They're after 'em!
Jig. No, Jimmy. We got 'em. Lay 'em on the table, Chuck. (*Chuck lays down his hand.*)
Jimmy. Jack—ten—and look at those spades. (*To Flabby.*) Well, smarty, are you happy?
Jig. Write it down, Chuck. Twenty-six apiece.
Flabby. Hey, wait a minute!
Babe. It's too late, dope. You've been blitzkrieged.
Flabby. I was holding the Black Lady.
Jimmy (*Bitterly*). But they had the ace, stupe!
Flabby. Well, Jeez!
Babe. What a brain! What a brain! See if it's connected to anything, Jimmy.
Jimmy. Yeah, must be a short some place. (*He pulls back the collar of Flabby's polo shirt. Flabby turns to him. Babe quickly empties the ice and most of his highball down Flabby's neck.*)
Flabby. Ow! Goddamn it! (*He leaps to his feet, wriggling and writhing. Finally, he starts to pull his shirt over his head. The moment his eyes are covered, Babe and Jimmy whip off their belts and start flaying the seat of his pants.*) Hey, cut it out. I'll murder you!
Jig (*Singing*). Strike, while the iron is hot—
Chuck (*Joining in*). The merry steel resounding!

Flabby. Cut it out, I tell you! (*There is a knock on the door. No one hears it. The door opens. A policeman strides in.*)
Cop. Hey, what goes on? (*The attack on Flabby subsides.*)
Babe. Just a friendly game, officer.
Jimmy. We're playing "Consequences."
Cop. Oh, you are, huh? Well, who belongs to that Chevy that's parked next to the fire hydrant?
Chuck. Oh, I guess that's mine, officer. I'm sorry. I had to park close to the entrance on account of his wheel chair. (*He indicates Jig.*)
Cop. Let's see your driver's license.
Chuck. Sure. Right here. (*He fishes it out.*) Look, officer, we're taking our friend back to the Soldiers' Home in fifteen minutes.
Cop (*Taking the license and starting to fill out a ticket*). Yeah? Well, you're moving away from that hydrant right now. Suppose a fire started.
Flabby (*Helpfully*). Oh, we'd put it out.
Cop. Well, now isn't that nice.
Chuck. Look, officer—before you sign that—Jeez—don't spoil my record. This would be my first offense.
Cop. Oh?
Chuck. Yes, officer. I'm a very careful driver.
Cop. Oh, I see.
Chuck. Never even went through a boulevard stop.
Cop (*Looking at the card*). Horatius Burden—huh.
Chuck. Yes, sir.
Cop. Haven't I seen you some place?
Chuck. I can't imagine where. Maybe you're thinking of Henry Burden, downtown in the Mayor's office—know who I mean?
Cop. Sure, I know. And I know you—Mr. Chuck Burden.
Chuck. Er—who?
Cop. Why, certainly. The first time I saw you was in the Cole Avenue Police Station. You were drunk and disorderly, and you'd just driven your jalopy in front of a west-bound trolley car that was doing thirty miles an hour.
Chuck. Why, that's impossible!
Cop. Yeah, you found that out. Why, certainly. I remember you perfectly. Say, that was the craziest trick I ever heard of. (*To the others.*) You know what that screwball was trying to do? He had a bet on with the guy who was with him that he could run over the cowcatcher of that trolley without getting nicked. And he damn near made it. (*His eyes on Babe.*)

Hey, wait a minute! If I ain't very much mistaken, you're the little runt who was with him.

Babe. Who me?

Cop. Yes, you. Why, sure! (*He turns to Chuck.*) Now, look, you. You be there next Tuesday at ten o'clock—and bring your pocket book. And if your Chevy isn't away from that hydrant in ten minutes, I'll slap another tag on it. Good night. (*He goes. The group is motionless for several seconds.*)

Babe. Little runt, huh?

Chuck. I'll get that blabbermouth—if it's the last thing I ever do. (*He takes his car keys from his pocket.*) I'll move the Chevy. (*He goes out.*)

Jimmy. He won't start anything, will he?

Babe. Don't worry. Chuck's smart. But he's an elephant. He don't forget things. It's my deal. (*They start back to the table. The telephone rings. Jimmy picks up the receiver.*)

Jimmy. Hello. (*Embarrassed.*) Oh, hello. No, I'm not. No. They just came in. Mm-hm. Sure. You bet I will. Uh-huh. That's right. Eleven o'clock. (*Chuck comes in.*) Mm-hm. Mm-hm.

Flabby. Mm-*hm*!

Jimmy (*To Flabby*). Shut up! (*Into the phone.*) What? No. I said, "mm-hm." Mm-hm. Okay. Bye. (*He hangs up.*) Hey, listen!

Flabby. I was listening. But all I could hear was you. You should have told her to talk louder.

Jimmy. That's not funny.

Chuck. Hey, let's get goin'. What happened to your drink, Babe?

Flabby. It's down my neck.

Chuck (*Grinning*). Okay. Here y'are, Babe. (*He starts to pour.*) Soda?

Babe. Plain water. I'll get it.

Chuck. Go ahead and deal. (*He goes to the kitchenette.*)

Babe. Thanks.

Flabby. I didn't mean to rib you, Jimmy. But you want to watch yourself with that Woof dame.

Jimmy. Forget it, will you.

Flabby. No kidding. I've seen a lot of ten-cent Romeos get in over their heads out there, and it's the bunk. You can't keep up with that four-figure competition. You just can't do it. Why, the first thing you know, you'll be in hock for life!

Jimmy. I won't either.

Babe. Flabby's right, Jimmy, and there's another angle—Carmen's a good kid, see. We all knew her when. But she ain't for you, Jimmy boy. The boys at Phoenix Pictures just won't stand for it.
Jimmy. What do you mean they won't stand for it?
Babe. Look, fella! As far as they're concerned, anything under a thousand bucks a week is out. Know what I mean? Out! So lay off quick, little boy, before she busts your trustin' heart.
Jimmy. Maybe some day I'll be making a thousand a week.
Flabby. Oh—oh. He's got an oil well.
Jimmy. Never mind what I got. (*Chuck comes in with Babe's drink and Carmen's script.*)
Babe. Don't kid yourself, Jimmy. It's no good!
Chuck. Say, listen, boys—this thing is dynamite.
Jimmy (*Jumping up*). Hey! Gimme that.
Chuck. Wait a minute, Jimmy. Maybe you can do something about this.
Jimmy. Never mind—just hand it over.
Chuck. Now, take it easy, son. She wants you to tell her what you think of this, don't she?
Jimmy. Well, what of it?
Chuck. I'm going to tell you what of it. If you say to her, "Lookit, kid—I think this is lousy. I think it's so lousy that if you do it, you'll be absolutely washed up." Why, maybe she'll give it the go-by.
Jimmy. But is it so lousy?
Chuck. From the little hunk I saw, it's plenty lousy. Why, it's the goddamnedest pro-war propaganda I ever read in my life.
Jig. Let's see, Chuck.
Jimmy. You give that here! (*Chuck pauses.*)
Jig. Go ahead, Chuck. Let him read it. If it's like you say it is, Jimmy'll do what's right.
Chuck. Okay, Jimmy. (*He hands him the script.*) That's a job for you. You know, I was just thinking—if Carmen Sherry should decide not to play that part, I'll bet they never make the goddamn picture. You give her the works. (*Jimmy takes the script, puts it in his chair, and sits in it.*) Boy, I'm hungry! Anybody like some cold chicken while Babe is stacking those cards?
Flabby. Yeah. I could toy with a wishbone.
Chuck. Okay. Comin' up. (*He goes out. Babe starts to shuffle the cards.*)
Babe. That's a hell of an idea Chuck had. Do you think you can sell her, Jimmy?

Flabby. He's a cinch.
Jimmy. How do you figure that? Why should she give a damn what I think?
Flabby (*Very cute*). Oh, just 'cause.
Jimmy. Well, I wouldn't count on it.
Babe. I'll tell you what you do. You just say you read it to us—she knows we're all fans of hers—and that confidentially we think it stinks.
Jimmy. Listen—she's got a mind of her own.
Flabby. Don't be so goddamn modest. You just give her the business. (*Chuck appears with a platter of chicken.*)
Chuck. Look here, men! That's what I mean chicken!
Babe. Holy Christmas! Will somebody please say grace.
Jig. Damned if I won't. Set her down, Chuck. (*Chuck does so and seats himself next to Jig.*)
Chuck. Go ahead, deacon—give! (*They all kiddingly bow their heads.*)
Jig. God almighty—for this, which we are about to receive, make us deeply thankful—and I ain't kiddin'. God almighty, this is America—and America's at peace. We got chicken, God, and we've got butter and eggs and milk. We remember the last war, God almighty, and we remember those meatless Mondays—God almighty, yes—meatless Mondays invented by that great American who also gave us foodless Friday. God almighty, there's a big meeting for peace the fifteenth of this month. But some of your children are losing heart. They don't know what to say. God almighty, give us a sign and a slogan! Give us a red-hot gag to rally 'round for peace. And one more little thing, God almighty. God almighty, I almost forgot this. There's a kid, sitting right here at this table, named Jimmy Aquilina. He's got a little job to do, God almighty, that'll help give the finger to those blood-money bastards who would send their own sons to be slaughtered for ten cents extra profit on a dollar. God almighty, give Jimmy the low-down on what to say and how to say it. We want peace, God almighty—and, in spite of the way your name is being kicked around, we think you want it too. God almighty, give America peace! For Christ's sake. Amen. (*They raise their heads. But now everyone is intensely serious.*)
Flabby. God almighty. Pass the chicken. (*They reach for the platter. Blackout.*)

ACT TWO: SCENE TWO

The next morning. The stunt men's living room has been cleaned up and is now as presentable as its basic shortcomings will permit. The sofa has been repaired and the personal belongings of its occupants have been stowed out of sight. The California sun streams in through the windows. Jimmy—dressed as he was the evening before, except that his sports jacket is over the back of a chair—is running a small vacuum cleaner up and down the carpet, pausing every once in a while to look down at Carmen's script which is open on the sofa, and to throw a glance toward one of the windows. At last, he sees someone coming. He detaches the vacuum, heaves it into the kitchenette, and gets into his jacket as the front entrance knocker begins to rat-tat-tat. Jimmy opens the door and admits Carmen. She is dressed in a smart sports outfit.

Carmen. Now, what the hell is the matter?
Jimmy. Sit down a minute. (*They move toward the sofa. Carmen gives it a wary glance.*) It's okay. I fixed it. (*Carmen sits down. Jimmy pulls up a small chair and sits facing her.*) The matter is I'm worried.
Carmen. You sounded worried when I telephoned. That's why I came right over. What is it—stage fright?
Jimmy. N–no. I'm worried about the whole setup. (*He gestures toward the script.*) This script is kind of phony, isn't it? I mean, do you really think you ought to do it?
Carmen. Why, what's the matter with it?
Jimmy. It don't sound to me like the way people talk. I read some of it to Chuck and the boys. They don't like it either. They think it would ruin you.
Carmen. Well, they're crazy. Why, it's a swell part. It may be a little hammy in spots, but that doesn't mean anything. I'll make Tillinghast get a new writer to fix it up. John Barrett would do a swell rewrite job. I think a lot of it's swell. That scene I marked for the test is certainly okay. Look. You come out to my place right now and we'll go to work on it. The main thing is to sell you to Tillinghast. Once that's set, we can switch the script around any way we want it. Come on.
Jimmy. You mean you would really change it?
Carmen. Baby face! What do you suppose I've been "gooing" around Tillinghast for?
Jimmy. I'd hate to tell you.

Carmen. Now, is that nice?
Jimmy. You seem to like it.
Carmen. Jimmy!
Jimmy. All right. I'm sorry. Let's go. (*They cross to the entrance door. Jimmy opens it. Carmen starts out, then steps quickly back into the room and shuts the door.*)
Carmen. He's out there!
Jimmy. Who?
Carmen. Tillinghast. He's talking to people in the first bungalow.
Jimmy. You didn't tell him you were coming here?
Carmen. Of course not. He must have seen me leave and followed me.
Jimmy. He's headed this way.
Carmen (*Thinking fast*). Wait. I'll fix it. You just play straight. (*She opens the door and steps outside.*) Tilly! How wonderful! (*She dashes off to the left. Her voice is heard calling:* "Tilly! You're just the person I want to see. Come here, darling." *She reappears in the doorway with Tillinghast who is not entirely sure what exactly is going on.*) Mr. Tillinghast, this is Mr. Douglas Davis of the New York Theatre League. His sister is an old friend of mine. She wrote me to look him up. He's here on his vacation.
Tillinghast (*Looking at him keenly*). How do you do, Mr. Davis?
Jimmy. How are you? Come in.
Tillinghast. Thank you. (*They enter.*)
Jimmy. Sit down, won't you?
Tillinghast. Thank you. (*He sits on the sofa. There is an uncomfortable pause. The end of the sofa starts to give way. Jimmy steps guiltily forward and straightens it.*)
Jimmy. I—er—sorry. (*Tillinghast reassures himself that the sofa is secure. In doing this, he sees the script.*)
Tillinghast. Why this looks like *March On, America!*
Carmen (*Brightly*). It is. I never go any place without it. I was reading some of it to Mr. Davis.
Tillinghast. Well, how did you like it?
Jimmy. Why—
Carmen. He thinks it's wonderful. How could he help it? He's exactly like the boy in the story himself—don't you think so?
Tillinghast. Why, yes—now that you mention it—he does look quite a bit like a truck driver.
Carmen (*Slightly hysterical*). Doesn't he, though? Of course, that's only natural. That's the kind of part he always plays.

Tillinghast. I see. When did you get in, Mr. Davis?
Jimmy. Oh—I—
Carmen. Yesterday. I called him this morning.
Tillinghast. Funny. You know, there's something about you that's very familiar.
Jimmy. Is that so? Well, I've got one of those faces. I used to do imitations. Ever since then, I look like everybody.
Carmen. You certainly do. It's amazing. You know, you even remind *me* of somebody.
Jimmy. Oh, sure. I never miss. Everybody's long-lost brother. That's me. (*Flabby appears at the window on the right side of the entrance doorway. He peers in, trying to see who the visitors are. Neither Tillinghast nor Carmen, who is sitting next to him on the sofa, is aware of the danger. Jimmy sees him and thinks quickly.*)
Carmen. It's someone in pictures, too. It's not John Garfield—though there is something about your eyes—(*Jimmy has jumped up and flung open the door. Flabby has his hand in his pocket, just about to reach for his key.*)
Jimmy (*Quickly*). Now, look here. I told you yesterday I don't want to subscribe to any magazines.
Flabby. Huh?
Jimmy. I'm just not interested. Now, go away and *stay* away! (*He slams the door in Flabby's astonished face. A few seconds later, Flabby can be seen peering in again, backed up by Chuck and Babe. They finally pull him away from the window.*) I'm sorry, but that guy is beginning to annoy me.
Tillinghast. I don't blame you. This town is certainly full of the strangest characters. Tell me, Mr. Davis, how much of *March On, America!* did Miss Sherry read to you?
Jimmy. Oh, just one scene.
Tillinghast. And you liked it?
Jimmy. Sounded very interesting.
Tillinghast. I don't suppose you'd be willing to read a little of it with her now?
Jimmy. Well—
Carmen. That's a wonderful idea, Tilly, but I've really got to be going. Why don't you both come to my place on Friday for tea and we could read it then? I imagine what Mr. Tillinghast has in mind, Mr. Davis, is that you might be interested in playing the part.
Tillinghast. Well—er—yes.

Jimmy. That's very nice of you.
Tillinghast. You're not under contract to those people in New York, are you?
Jimmy. No. No, I'm not.
Tillinghast. Then, suppose we do as Miss Sherry suggests.
Jimmy. It's all right with me.
Tillinghast (*Rising*). Good. I'll see you then, Mr. Davis. Goodbye. It's been a pleasure.
Jimmy. Thanks. The same to you.
Carmen. Bye-bye, Mr. Davis. When you write to Joan, send her my love.
Jimmy. Er—what?
Carmen. Your sister.
Jimmy. Oh, sure. I'll do that.
Carmen. Friday at five, then. I'll send my car for you.
Jimmy. Thank you.
Carmen. Goodbye, Mr. Davis.
Jimmy. So long, Miss Sherry. (*Carmen and Tillinghast go. Jimmy stands a moment, peering out the door, then walks over and picks up the script, leaving the door ajar. There is a crash offstage. Jimmy turns and starts toward it. The bedroom door opens and Flabby appears.*)
Flabby. Chuck shoved me in the window so they wouldn't see us. (*Babe and Chuck come in from the bedroom. Flabby continues, to Jimmy.*) Hey, what was the idea, giving me the bum's rush?
Jimmy. You big lug. That was Mr. Tillinghast—the guy that's putting up the dough for Carmen's picture.
Flabby. So what?
Jimmy. So he came in while I was giving her the big sales talk.
Flabby. I still don't see—
Babe. Never mind, dough head. What happened, Jimmy? Did you sell her?
Jimmy. This feller Tillinghast interrupted me. I had to pretend I was a friend from New York.
Flabby. Oh, now I get it. The guy thought you was cutting in on him.
Jimmy (*Savagely*). No, you don't get it!
Flabby. Well, Jeez!
Babe. Just relax. How far had you got with her?
Jimmy. I just started. I've got a date on Friday.
Chuck. You better be good, kid. Did you see this? (*He shoves a morning paper in front of Jimmy.*)

Jimmy (*Reading*). Defend Democracy Demonstration set for March 15 at Coliseum. Why, that's the date of Jig's peace meeting.
Chuck. That's right. And don't fool yourself it's a coincidence either. They're trying to wreck the meeting. We just came from seeing Jig, and half of the peace bunch were talking about changing their date. Jig told 'em it's too late to change. Their publicity's been out for weeks. There's a committee meeting of all the peace organizations tonight. I'm telling you, boys, the war drive is really on. That picture has got to be stopped.
Jimmy. Well, I can tell you one thing. It's not going to be easy. About the best you can hope for is that it could be changed some.
Chuck. That's no good.
Jimmy. It's better than nothing, ain't it?
Chuck. You've got to really work on her.
Jimmy. I did work on her. But she thinks it's swell. I tell you, all she'll do is get some guy to rewrite it—a fella named John Barrett, I think she said.
Babe. Hey, I know Johnny. He's all right, too. Hates war to beat hell. I'll talk to him.
Jimmy. Sure, that's it.
Chuck. Boys, you're kidding yourselves. You know who Tillinghast is? He's the president of the Hapwood Aircraft Corporation. Oh, no. The money behind this picture knows exactly what's what. Those babies are after big war profits, and they're going to get 'em or else. This picture is just a little item in their advertising budget, and they won't change a word of it. But if Carmen Sherry walks out on it, there's a damn good chance they can't make it. (*Carmen opens the entrance door on the last speech. As Chuck finishes, she closes the door behind her.*)
Carmen. What was that?
Jimmy. Where's Tillinghast?
Carmen. He's gone to his office. Did you tell 'em, Jimmy?
Jimmy. Yeah. I told 'em you thought the story could be fixed.
Carmen. I don't mean that. That's nothing. I mean, did you tell 'em the gag? What a hit you made as a member of the New York Theatre League?
Jimmy. I'll tell 'em tonight. Let's you and me go and talk things over.
Carmen. Okay. But, boy, was he marvelous!
Babe. What is all this?
Flabby. Yeah. Let us in on it.
Jimmy. I'll tell you later. Come on, Carmen.
Chuck. What's the big rush?
Jimmy. We've got to go.

Carmen. It'll only take a minute. Go on. They'll love it.
Jimmy. No.
Carmen. All right, sour puss. (*They start for the door.*) But, believe me, if I had a chance to be the new Clark Gable, I'd be broadcasting the news.
Chuck. Here, wait a minute! What are you talking about?
Carmen. Listen. It's practically set that Jimmy is going to make a test for the leading part in my new picture.
Chuck. Not for *March On, America!*?
Carmen. That's right. Isn't it marvelous? Why, what is it? What's the matter?
Flabby. Well, God almighty!
Carmen. I suppose you don't think he can do it. Well, let me tell you something. Jimmy's a hell of an actor. I've heard him read. He's going to knock 'em dead.
Babe. Jeez! How do you like that?
Carmen. I don't get this. What are you looking at each other that way for? I should think you'd be doing nip-ups.
Chuck. Would you sit down a minute?
Carmen (*After a moment, she sits*). Now, what *is* this?
Chuck. How old are you?
Carmen. Twenty-two.
Chuck. 1918. Just when the last one ended.
Carmen. The last what?
Chuck. The last war.
Carmen. Oh, that. What of it?
Chuck. Well, you see, we were in that one—Babe and Flabby and me—and our friend, Jig Smith. You never met Jig?
Carmen. I've heard about him.
Chuck (*Indicating the wall*). That's his picture. That's *after*. *Before*—well, before he looked like a lot of other guys. Like Jimmy there, for instance. Yeah, he was younger than Jimmy a little bit, but he was a hell of a lot like him. Same eyes. Same bounce when he walked. Fade out. Fade in. Twenty-two years. Am I boring you?
Carmen. Go ahead.
Chuck. Twenty-two years. And over there they're hollering for help again. Over here? "Let 'em holler," says we, and that's great. Only, look out for that last reel switch. Like in '17. Boy, that's one we'll never forget! All of a sudden: BOOM! Poor little Belgium! Spies! Jail 'em! Preparedness! Save democracy! Let's go! And we went. How did they swing it? Baby, in

America it pays to advertise—and what a stake they had. What a chance for Yankee Doodle to be the "Big Shot Businessman" of the world. So they went to work. Cartoons—editorials! They even made a picture—*The Battle Cry of Peace.* Beautiful! It paved the road to war. Do you see what I mean?

Carmen. I see. And I think you're crazy. Listen. There's not much propaganda in *March On.*

Chuck. There's enough in one speech I read—

Carmen. We'll change it.

Chuck. They won't let you.

Carmen. Then I won't do it.

Chuck. Will you shake on that?

Carmen (*Suddenly*). Why—no! I'll be damned if I will. What the hell difference is one picture going to make?

Chuck. With *you* in it? Ho-ho!

Carmen. Well, I still think you're nuts. And what's more, I don't believe there's a chance of us going to war. You're acting like a lot of old women with the jitters. You're just prejudiced, and if you ask me, you're being goddamn selfish, Do you realize what this can do for Jimmy?

Chuck. I realize.

Carmen. Well, then, how can you be that way? Chuck, he's got a chance to be a star. I'm telling you.

Flabby. Looks to me like he's got a chance to be a first-class louse. What about it, Jimmy?

Jimmy (*Passionately*). I'll tell you what about it. You guys don't know Carmen. You don't know her at all. She's not going to make any pro-war propaganda. She told you that—and she'll tell Tillinghast.

Chuck. Let her shake on it, then.

Jimmy. That's not fair. You can't ask her to put herself on the spot like that. But she's telling you. The picture's going to be all right.

Babe. All right for who?

Jimmy. For what you want. You wait and see.

Chuck (*Slowly*). That's crap, Jimmy. You don't believe a word you're saying.

Jimmy. All right, so it's crap. It ain't—but all right, if you think so. Well—I'm going to do it, if they ask me. I've got to do it. It's the chance of a lifetime. Jeez! I just can't give it the go-by. You wouldn't ask me to.

Chuck. We would, Jimmy.

Flabby (*Nodding*). Yeah.

Babe. We are asking it.
Jimmy (*After a long pause*). Then—I guess that's that. (*Another pause.*) Will I be seeing you?
Chuck. That's up to you, Jimmy.
Carmen. Let's get out of here. (*Jimmy hesitates.*)
Chuck. Go ahead, Jimmy. And when you're a star, and the war comes and you're drafted—or maybe you'll enlist—we'll be rooting for you to come back—all of you, in one hunk. We'll be waiting for you, kid—and we hope she will.
Carmen. Jimmy! Come on! (*Jimmy and Carmen go. Chuck, Babe, and Flabby stand looking at each other. The voices of newsboys can be heard growing gradually louder: "Extra! Read all about it. American liner sunk! Get an extra!"*)
Chuck. Three old women. With the jitters. (*Chuck moves to the window. The curtain falls on Act Two.*)

Act Three: Scene One

The living room of Carmen Sherry's house in Beverly Hills. The house is an excellent example of the best type of California Spanish architecture. It has been decorated by an expert. Large doors in the upstage wall give out onto a patio. The front entrance is off to the right. There is a door at the left leading to a library. When the curtain rises, Carmen, Jimmy, and Mr. Tillinghast are posing for a half-dozen news photographers and reporters. Carmen is holding a legal-looking document. Jimmy and Tillinghast both have fountain pens.

1st Photographer. Okay, folks, this is the last one. Get a little closer together, will you? That's it. Now you be signing the contract, Mr. Davis. You just hold your pen ready, Mr. Tillinghast—and smile at Miss Sherry. That's it. All right, boys. Here we go. Hold it now. Hold it. Still! (*He takes the picture. The rest of the flash bulbs explode.*) Thank you.
The others. Thanks. Okay, boys, let's go. Thank you, Miss Sherry, etc., etc.
Reporter. I'll drop around Monday for that interview, Mr. Davis. Hotel Roosevelt, isn't it?
Jimmy. That's right.
Reporter. Four o'clock okay?
Jimmy. That's fine.
Reporter. See you then. 'Bye, Miss Sherry. Thanks for the drinks.
Carmen. You bet, Harry. Goodbye, boys.
The others. 'Bye, Carmen. 'Bye, Miss Sherry. (*They go. Carmen throws herself into a chair.*)
Carmen. Wow. I'm exhausted.
Tillinghast. I don't blame you. It was quite a party. Well—I'll be running along. Can I drop you off, Mr. Davis?
Jimmy. Thanks. I'd like to talk to Carmen about the first day's work if she can take it. We've only got two weeks more. I want to be as good as possible.
Tillinghast. That's very commendable. I'll pick you up at 7:30, Carmen. (*Jimmy reacts to this.*)
Carmen. Okay, Tilly.
Tillinghast. We're dressing. (*To Jimmy.*) You'll go easy on that interview, Monday?
Jimmy. How do you mean?

Tillinghast. I mean, don't rub it in about my falling for that Theatre League story.
Jimmy. Oh, that. All right.
Tillinghast. Thank you. See you at 7:30, Carmen.
Carmen. Yes, sir. (*Tillinghast goes. Jimmy looks after him for a few seconds, then turns to Carmen. She puts up both hands and beckons to him by wiggling her fingers.*)
Carmen. Come here. (*Jimmy crosses slowly and stands, looking down at her.*) Aren't you going to kiss me? (*He does so, but something is troubling him.*) Hey, what's the matter?
Jimmy. You know damn well what.
Carmen. It's the last time. I've had the date for over a week.
Jimmy. Are you going to tell him about us?
Carmen. If you want me to.
Jimmy. I want to tell everybody.
Carmen. All right. I'll tell him. Why not? The contract's signed. The hell with him.
Jimmy. And you're not going to see him again?
Carmen. I told you. It's the last time.
Jimmy. He burns me up. He acts as if he had a mortgage on you.
Carmen. Let's forget about him.
Jimmy (*After a second*). Will you call me when you get in?
Carmen. The minute I'm home.
Jimmy. Okay. (*He bends over and really kisses her.*)
Carmen. Now you're talking.
Jimmy. Don't you forget, now. I'm going to murder the first guy that looks at you cross-eyed.
Carmen. You're pretty cute.
Jimmy. I'm so nuts about you—(*He kisses her again.*) Did he ever kiss you?
Carmen. Who?
Jimmy. Tillinghast.
Carmen. I thought we were going to forget about him.
Jimmy. You didn't answer me.
Carmen. Jimmy! What do you want to stick knives in yourself for? I've been kissed by half the hams in Hollywood. I want to forget 'em. All of 'em. The first and the last.
Jimmy. Was he the last?

Carmen. What's the point of this? If I say no, you won't believe me. If I say yes, it'll just hurt you. I told you I'm not going to see him again. Isn't that enough?

Jimmy. What did you do it for? What for?

Carmen. Jimmy! This is so stupid!

Jimmy. But that was smart. Sure. Playing up to money is always smart.

Carmen. All right. You're going to make the picture, aren't you? Well, what are you kicking about?

Jimmy. Okay. That stops me.

Carmen. Jimmy. It's over. It's through. I love you. Don't you believe me?

Jimmy. Knives, you said. And are you right! A belly full of knives! I don't know what to believe.

Carmen. Yes, you do. You must know. Jimmy, I didn't want to hurt you. Maybe that was wrong—maybe I should have told you the minute I knew it was you. But I thought, no. What's done is done. I've never asked about you, Jimmy. I don't want to ask—ever. All I want is now. I want you to love me. It's all I give a damn about.

Jimmy (*Suddenly*). Come here. (*He takes her in his arms. A reporter with a news camera comes in from the patio, sees them, and goes right out again. A moment later, the front doorbell rings. Jimmy and Carmen separate.*)

Carmen (*Calling off*). I'll answer it. (*She goes to the door. The reporter steps in.*) Oh, hello, Jack. Did you forget something?

Reporter. Nope. I got an idea.

Carmen. Take it easy, Jack—they'll fire you.

Reporter. No kidding. I got a gag for a swell shot—if you and Mr. Davis will cooperate.

Carmen. Have I ever said no?

Reporter. Gee, that's swell. I'll tell 'em to come in. (*He starts toward the patio.*)

Carmen. Hey, wait! Who is it? No animals now—no livestock.

Reporter. Naw. (*Calling off.*) Come ahead, boys. No. It's his buddies. The boys he used to work with. I sold 'em the idea they should pose for a little family group.

Jimmy. Say. Wait a minute!

Reporter. Come in, men. (*Chuck, Babe, Flabby, and Jig appear in the patio. Flabby is shoving Jig's chair.*)

Chuck. Hello, Jimmy.

Jimmy. Hello, Chuck. (*There is a moment's embarrassed pause. Finally, Chuck turns to Carmen.*)

Chuck. Afternoon, Miss Sherry. Er—this is Jig Smith.
Carmen. Er—how are you, Mr. Smith?
Jig. I'm fine, Miss Sherry. And glad to meet you.
Carmen (*Staring at him*). Thank you.
Reporter. Oh, excuse me, Carmen. I thought you knew all the boys. Er—Mr. Smith's accident happened a long time ago, they tell me. Doing a stunt, wasn't it?
Jig. That's right. A feller named Krupp threw a firecracker at me and I forgot to duck.
Reporter. Oh. Oh, yeah. Well, let's go. Right over here, Carmen—next to Mr. Smith. Mr. Davis—you stand on the other side. You boys fill in close. That's it. (*He arranges the group.*) All right now—a big smile, everybody. Hold it. Hold it. Still! (*He takes the picture and starts to change bulbs.*) Now, let's see. How about a human pyramid? Babe on Flabby's shoulders. Chuck and Mr. Davis, you get on either side of Flabby. Carmen, you stand next to Jig and be showing the contract to the bunch. Got the idea? Here. (*He picks up the contract and shoves it into Carmen's hand.*) Okay now. Let's go. (*They arrange themselves. Flabby gets behind Babe, spreads the latter's legs, puts his hand between them, and boosts Babe into the air.*)
Jimmy (*Next to Jig*). How's the meeting coming along, Jig?
Jig. Not so good, Jimmy. The Defend Democracy party is stealing the show. Two of our societies are going to that one instead of the Peace and Progress meeting. The rest are all sticking but, confidentially, the ticket sale is not so hot.
Reporter. All set. Hold that now. Give with the teeth. Hold it. Hold it. Still! (*He takes the picture.*) Thank you. (*Flabby lets Babe down. The reporter bustles forward.*) Okay now. Just Mr. Davis and the boys. I want a couple of trick shots doing stunts. There's a spot out in the patio that's perfect. Come on. (*They all go, leaving Carmen and Jig alone. There is a moment's embarrassed silence.*)
Carmen (*Suddenly*). You're a lot like him.
Jig. Like who?
Carmen. Like Jimmy. Chuck said you were, and he's right.
Jig. I'm enough like him so I can understand him, I hope. Looking at you makes that pretty easy.
Carmen. You don't like me. Why not? I want to help him.
Jig. I'm sure you do. Why do you think I don't like you?
Carmen. You think I'm a pig.
Jig. I just think you're a little balled up.

Carmen. I want him to go places—to the top. Don't you want that for him?

Jig (*Nodding*). But first we want him to live—him and a million other Jimmies.

Carmen. We're not going in the war. I don't believe it.

Jig. Once upon a time, I didn't believe it. But they crossed me up. They double-crossed me right into this chair. This time, I'm not taking any chances.

Carmen. How can you stop it?

Jig. With an army.

Carmen. What?

Jig. An army of peace. Over a million men who aren't going to fight in a foreign war. Signed on the dotted line. Signed and sealed and delivered to Uncle Sam. And ours isn't the only meeting. There's twenty of 'em—all over the country—where they're taking the pledge not to fight. Why don't you drop in on this one and take a look?

Carmen. Maybe I will.

Jig. And why don't you forget to make that picture?

Carmen. No. Jimmy'd never get another chance.

Jig. Why not? He made a swell test.

Carmen. Yes, but right now he's hot. If he doesn't make this one, they'll forget all about him.

Jig (*After a pause*). You're such a pretty pig. Eighty million people will see that picture. Eighty million guinea pigs you'll inoculate with the war bug. (*Carmen stands looking at him. The front doorbell rings again. Carmen moves toward the door.*)

Carmen (*Calling off*). I'll get it. (*Carmen opens the door. The Reverend David Ely is standing there. He is spectacled, slightly rotund, and a ball of energy.*)

Ely. Excuse me. I'm Dr. Ely of the First Methodist Church. I'm looking for Mr. Smith.

Jig. Hi'ya, parson. This is Miss Carmen Sherry.

Ely. Now you don't have to tell me that. I'm a fan of hers. How are you, Miss Sherry? I hope you'll pardon my intrusion.

Carmen. Why, of course. I'm very happy to know you.

Ely. I'm afraid that's a slight exaggeration—but I'll forgive you.

Jig. What's up, parson? (*To Carmen.*) Dr. Ely is the chairman of our meeting.

Ely. Yes, ma'am. That is if there is a meeting.

Jig. Why, what happened?
Ely. Your damn Disabled Veterans are threatening to walk out.
Jig. Why, I'll bat their ears down.
Ely. There's a meeting downtown at 5:00—in twenty minutes. We've been trying to get you all afternoon.
Jig. Well, let's go. Take me out to the boys, will you, parson? They're in the patio.
Ely. Right. (*He starts wheeling Jig out.*) I've got a damn good idea who's been talking to those pals of yours.
Jig. I'll straighten them out.
Ely. You'll pardon us, Miss Sherry?
Carmen. Certainly.
Ely (*To Jig*). That Defend Democracy delegation is really raising hell with us.
Jig (*To Carmen*). Hmm. You bring Jimmy to that meeting!
Ely (*To Jig, as he wheels him out*). Dearie me! We little doves of peace have hardly got a spot to kiss in. (*They disappear into the patio. Carmen walks to a downstage table and lights a cigarette. The reporter comes in from the patio.*)
Reporter. They're on their way. What a bunch of cuckoos. I got some great stuff though. Thanks for helping me out.
Carmen. Okay, Jack.
Reporter. The boss'll give this a great play. Half a page at least. I knew it was hot the minute Chuck called me.
Carmen. Oh, it was Chuck's idea.
Reporter. Sure. Smart guy, that one.
Carmen. He's not exactly dumb.
Reporter (*Picks up a half-empty highball glass and finishes it off*). Well, good luck with the picture, Carmen. I'll duck along. (*He goes. Carmen sits thinking. Jimmy comes in from the patio. He is carrying his coat.*)
Jimmy. Thank God, that's over! Jig say anything to you?
Carmen. He gave me a little workout. He called me a pig. He wants us to come to the meeting.
Jimmy. Oh. Well, that's out.
Carmen. Why?
Jimmy. Didn't Tillinghast tell you? We're supposed to go to the other shindig.
Carmen. No. He didn't say a word. Maybe we can get out of it.

Jimmy. Not the way he put it to me. It was just plain, "Be there!" (*Carmen studies him a moment. There is an uncomfortable silence. Carmen notices that the reporter has left the empty highball glass on the table top. She rises and crosses to the table where she picks up the glass and wipes the table top with a napkin from the tray on which the highball was originally standing. Jimmy pulls a chair forward so that it is just about where Jig's chair was when he talked to Carmen. Jimmy throws his coat over his shoulders and sits down, watching Carmen as she works. Carmen puts the glass on the tray and picks up the latter.*) You're an awful pretty pig. (*Still holding the tray, Carmen turns. The loosely hanging sleeves of the coat and his position give Jimmy a startling resemblance to Jig. Carmen drops the tray. Jimmy jumps up. His coat falls to the floor.*) What's the matter?
Carmen. You looked just like him. As if they'd done it to you—(*He comes quickly toward her, his arms out. She goes to him, grasping his arms, then clasping her own around him.*) Put them around me. Hold me, Jimmy! Hold me! (*He holds her tight, comforting her. Blackout.*)

Act Three: Scene Two

Backstage, a half hour before the peace meeting starts. The set is simply a curtain that hangs in 1, with an opening in the center. The stage of the auditorium is beyond the curtain. When the lights go up, two stagehands are carrying a speaker's rostrum through the curtain onto the stage. They are followed by two sound men with a public address microphone and a portable loudspeaker. As the last two start toward the opening in the curtain, Dr. Ely comes through it from the stage.

Sound man. Where do you want the loudspeaker, Dr. Ely?
Ely. That's for the radio hookup?
Sound man. Yes, sir.
Ely. Oh—anywhere. On the right side of the stage will be all right.
Sound man. Okay. Come ahead, Eddie. (*They go off through the curtain. A disabled world war veteran on crutches, a woman representing a peace society, and a trade union delegate come on. They are all wearing badges.*)
Ely (*To the veteran*). Hello there, Henry. Glad to see you—and you're early.
Henry. Well, the way I figured it, I thought I'd get here before that committee of ours changed its mind again.
Ely. I don't blame you. Those ruffians. Why don't you go right in on the stage and find yourself a comfortable chair? Oh, good evening, Mrs. Barney. Do you know Henry McGowan of the Disabled Veterans? Mrs. Barney is the secretary of the Women's Peace League.
Henry. How are you, Mrs. Barney?
Mrs. Barney. Good evening. We're certainly glad you veterans didn't run out on us.
Henry. Yes. That was quite a party, until Jig Smith got there. Say, when he finished with them, they were damn well ashamed of themselves. Shall we go in?
Mrs. Barney. Thank you. (*Henry holds open the curtain and they go in. The trade union delegate comes up to Ely.*)
Daggett. Good evening, Dr. Ely. I'm Bill Daggett of the Studio Painters.
Ely. Glad to know you.
Daggett. How does it look?
Ely. Not bad. Not bad. The unions are about sixty percent with us. The rest of the delegates sounded very good at five o'clock.
Daggett. That's fine. (*A Telegraph boy appears.*)
Boy. Dr Ely?

Ely. That's right.
Boy. Flock of telegrams. Sign right here.
Ely. Thank you. (*He signs.*) Yes, those Defend Democracy devils didn't hit us as hard as I expected. (*The boy goes.*)
Daggett. They're going to have a big turnout just the same. I live right near the stadium—it certainly looked like a lot of people when I went by.
Ely (*Opening telegrams*). Yes, no doubt. (*Reading.*) Good luck. Best wishes. (*To Daggett.*) I suppose they'll really put on a great ballyhoo.
Daggett (*Lighting a cigarette*). I wish we could do something about it.
Ely. And don't I! Yes, sir—we could certainly use a few miracles tonight. Here, what's this? (*He studies one of the telegrams.*) "Deeply regret"—hmmm—Local 36 is dropping out.
Daggett. That's that phony leadership. I heard about their meeting. They called it on four hours' notice and railroaded the resolution through. The rank and file will be here just the same.
Ely. I hope so.
Daggett. Yes, I talked to quite a lot of 'em. Oh—oh. Here's Jig Smith. (*A male nurse wheels Jig on.*) Hello there, Jig.
Jig. Hello, Bill. Glad to see you. Evening Parson. Chuck and the boys show up yet?
Ely. I haven't seen them.
Jig (*Nervous*). They ought to be here.
Ely. Why, it's early. We've got half an hour yet.
Jig. I know. This is something special. (*To the male nurse.*) Look, Tom. I'm all right. Will you take a peek out front?
Tom. Okay, Jig. (*He goes through the curtain. The cop of Act Two steps through the opening. He spots Daggett's cigarette.*)
Cop. Hey, *you*! No smoking.
Daggett. My name's Daggett.
Cop. Well, put that out.
Daggett. —Mr. Daggett.
Cop. Just put it out.
Ely. Can't you be civil, officer?
Daggett. It's all right, Dr. Ely. (*He steps on the cigarette, then turns to the cop.*) Only don't talk to people like a brown-shirt. This is still America.
Cop (*Nasty-nice*). Okay, Mr. Daggett. (*He goes through the curtain again.*)
Daggett. Damn Nazi.
Jig. I know that bird. He's poison.

Daggett. They're just warming up his wartime technique. See you later. (*He goes through the curtains. Chuck, Babe, and Flabby come in quickly.*)
Jig. Hey. Where the hell have you been?
Ely. Well—good evening, boys. Jig's been worried about you.
Chuck. We got held up. How are you, Dr. Ely?
Babe and Flabby. Good evening, doctor.
Ely. I'm rearing to go. What's this big special event you and Jig are cooking up?
Chuck. Oh, it's nothing. Just some ideas for Jig's speech. Are you still goin' to broadcast some of that stadium powwow?
Ely. That's right. 9:30 sharp—just before Jig speaks.
Chuck. You're not afraid some of our weak sisters will fall for that flag kissing, are you?
Ely. On the contrary, I think it will make them fighting mad. (*Carmen walks through the curtains as Ely finished speaking.*)
Carmen. Well, if it doesn't, you'd better give up. I just came from there.
Jig (*Astonished*). Well!
Carmen. What a sanctimonious collection of slaughter salesmen!
Jig. Where's Jimmy?
Carmen. With Tillinghast. I walked out on both of them. Well—gentlemen—what about it? Have you room out there for one more fanny?
Ely. For your fanny, Miss Sherry, we'll make room.
Carmen. Thank you, doctor. Oh, and by the way, boys, how about a job in the stunt girls' department?
Babe. How do you mean—job?
Carmen. I mean, I'm through. I quit. I'm not going to make their damn picture!
Jig. Jeez, baby! But what about Jimmy?
Carmen. He's still trying to patch it up with Tillinghast. I wouldn't stop to argue. I just left.
Jig. Take her in, doctor, and give her the softest seat on the platform.
Ely. An honor. (*He offers her his arm. They go through the opening in the curtain.*)
Babe. What a break!
Flabby. Yeah. If only Jimmy doesn't talk her out of it.
Jig. Don't worry. She's hot. Now tell me—(*A stagehand enters with a peace slogan cutout and a stage brace and starts to go through the curtain to the auditorium stage. Then he remembers something, leans the two props*

against the curtain, and goes back where he came from. The boys watch this intently. As soon as they are alone, Jig speaks.) Well—what about it?
Chuck. We're all set.
Jig. You heard what the parson said—9:30.
Flabby. That's perfect. She'll be all ready to take off at 9:20. (*The stage brace slips and falls to the floor. Chuck walks over and picks it up. He has some trouble balancing it against the curtain.*)
Jig. How about the sign?
Babe. It's terrific. We tried it over the desert this afternoon. That's why we were late. And the radio sounds swell. (*The cop comes through the curtains. His back is to Chuck. Something about the other three strikes him as very familiar. He listens intently.*)
Jig. How the hell did you get that ham actor to lend you his ship?
Flabby. We didn't have to. He's out of town. We just borrowed it.
Jig. Jesus. Wasn't there anybody around?
Babe. Sure. We gave 'em some fast double-talk and they wrote us an order. Nothing to it.
Jig. You better leg along before somebody gets hep.
Flabby. Okay.
Cop. Hey. Just a minute. Hi'ya, boys. (*Chuck picks up the stage brace and edges his way along the curtain until he comes to the opening. A second later, he slips through to the stage.*)
Flabby. H-hello, there.
Cop. Now, what is all this?
Flabby. All what?
Cop. Listen. I heard every word you said. Whose airplane have you stolen?
Babe. Now, listen, officer—don't get the wrong idea about this. The whole thing's a joke.
Cop. Well—I'd love to hear some good laughs. Suppose we take a little walk.
Flabby. Now, wait a minute—
Cop (*Tough*). Come on! (*He grabs them—one on either side. Suddenly they back him into the curtain. There is a terrific thud as Chuck socks the cop on the back of the head with the stage brace through the curtain. The cop slumps to the floor. Chuck reappears through the split in the curtain. The other two are already on their way.*)
Chuck (*Whispering, to the fallen cop*). So long, blabbermouth. We're quits. Bye, Jig.

Jig. Scram, you bastard! (*Chuck disappears on the run. Dr. Ely and several others come pouring through the curtain.*)
Ely. Good Lord, Jig. What happened?
Jig. I don't know. Maybe he ate something!
Ely (Looking around). Where's Daggett? (*The delegates bend over the prostrate officer, and Ely goes onstage to look for Daggett. Blackout.*)

Act Three: Scene Three

The peace meeting. The curtain of the previous scene is now the backdrop. Flags and peace signs decorate the stage. In front of them and the curtain is a row of chairs reaching across the stage behind the speakers' rostrum, which is downstage center. In these chairs sit the speakers and special guests. Daggett is speaking, using a public address system. He delivers his speech to the "real" audience in the theatre.

Daggett. So history repeats itself. In 1914, the American Secretary of State declared that—quote—"Loans by American bankers to any foreign nation which is at war are inconsistent with the true spirit of neutrality"—unquote. Two months later, that policy went into the ashcan. The government okayed short-term loans to the Allies. A year later, we gave America's blessing to long-term credits. Meanwhile, the war dragged on, and it became gradually clear that, unless we jumped the ante once more, world trade would hit the toboggan, and the whole financial setup in Europe would go boom. So, what happened? Overseas went truckloads of American dollars—and when the time came, our doughboys followed the dough. That's the gag we've got to remember. They *had* to follow. When you bet on a horse, you've got a stake in the race. When you lend money to a country's that's at war, you're backing that country to win. So, watch it. Don't sit around and let the big time gamblers take the play away from you. Because if you do, you'll wind up behind the eightball. You'll finish by betting your life! (*Daggett returns to his seat on the stage as the delegates applaud. Dr. Ely takes the stand.*)

Ely. Thank you, Mr. Daggett. I have a short announcement to make. As most of you know, the Peace Pledge which we are presenting at this meeting tonight is being simultaneously presented in twenty cities throughout the nation. What I wish to announce is that one of our meetings—the one in Denver—will reach the moment of signing the antiwar pledge in five minutes. We have arranged a radio hookup whereby the ceremony of obtaining signatures can be heard in this auditorium. I have been asked by your committee to tune in on the Denver meeting immediately. (*To the sound man.*) Are you ready with the hookup?

Sound man. All ready, Dr. Ely. (*A man rises in the front row of the audience.*)

Man. Mr. Chairman. I want to protest against this procedure. We can't sign a document like that. It'd be treason. (*There is a storm of protest from the audience.*)
Ely. Order, please. I assure you that it is not. America is at peace. A refusal to serve in a war which has not been declared is within the constitutional rights of any citizen. (*Cries of "You're damn right!" "Treason, my eye!" etc., are heard.*) Order. Order.
Man. All right. Then I'd like to suggest that you tune in on the Defend Democracy Meeting that's going on here in Los Angeles. As a matter of fact, there's a lot of us here tonight that feel this whole audience should be at that meeting. (*Cries of "Boo! Boo!" and some applause.*)
Ely. We have arranged to do exactly that. In fact, that is the next event on our program. In the meantime, if there is no objection—
Man. I do object. If you ask me, this whole signing up business might be a racket. (*Cries of "What?" "How do you mean racket?" etc.*) I mean, how do we know it's on the level? What's to prevent it from being staged? (*Cries of "Shut up! Aw, throw him out!" and a violent reaction from the audience. A policeman moves down the aisle to the man.*) I won't shut up. I'm not the only one who feels this way! (*An even more violent reaction. Dr. Ely raps for order. The sound man comes forward and whispers to him.*)
Ely. Order! Order! Ladies and gentlemen, I must ask for order. (*The meeting quiets down.*) I'm afraid the gentleman has won his point. The radio people have just warned me that the time we had scheduled to listen to Denver is nearly up and that we should proceed to tune in immediately on the Defend Democracy Meeting. (*There is another grumbling response to this announcement. A member of the audience comes down the aisle to the objector. The police take several seconds to quiet things down. Ely nods to the sound man. They go to work.*) Order, please! Order! I must ask for absolute quiet. We are just about ready to listen in. (*The meeting quiets down. Suddenly, the voice of a radio announcer breaks the stillness.*)
Radio announcer (*In the middle of a broadcast*).—and the giant searchlights playing over the field. Those two captive balloons I told you about are still very much in evidence, and that big sign that's stretched between 'em is still the highlight of the display. Yes, sir. It's right up there where everyone can read it. "Defend Democracy," it says, and that's been the slogan of every speaker on this amazing program. "In time of peace, prepare for war." That's been the battle cry of freedom here tonight. We've heard it again and again. And, by the way, those airplanes that hummed over the stadium a few minutes ago, dropping those little "Defend

Democracy" parachutes, were all fueled by Streamline High-Octane Gasoline—the gasoline that changes riding into gliding—the gas that gives you the silky smoothness of a sealskin coat. Hop aboard, everyone. Step on it—with Streamline! Well, well, well. Here they come back again—those Streamline Seagulls. Yes, sir. The news cameramen are lining up to catch 'em as they come into the range of the searchlights. Oh, oh! But this time there's only one of them. It comes sailing right down toward the field. No. Wait a minute. This is a different plane. (*The lights dim down until one spotlight focused on Jig's face is the only illumination on the stage.*) It's carrying a sign behind it. The sign says: KEEP—OUT—OF—WAR. (*Jig leans forward in his chair.*) Just a moment now. This wasn't on the program. (*The spotlight dims completely out. A moving picture screen is lowered. The events which the announcer is describing appear on the screen.*) Why, there's a man hanging below the fuselage. They're coming toward the balloons—the man is going to tangle up in that sign. No. He's cutting one end of it loose. He has cut it loose. He's caught in the sign. No—he's all right. He's pulling himself up to the plane—hand over hand. He's in the plane again. This is amazing. Nothing like this has happened since the Graf Spee was blown up. They're broadcasting—we'll try to pick it up for you. (*The muffled sound of Chuck's voice is just discernible.*)

Chuck's voice. Keep out of it! You can't defend democracy by fighting in someone else's war. We've got to stay out. America wants peace—(*The voice fades away.*)

Radio announcer. They're circling 'round the field. There's quite a commotion down below. Here they come again. They're diving at the news cameras. Here they come. (*The sound of the plane roars closer, then fades away.*) Boy! That was right over us. Here, wait. They're going to send up a plane. They're going to try and force them down. Here they come again! (*The motor roars.*) They're throwing leaflets into the crowd. There goes that plane from the field—there's three of 'em. No—five. And they mean business. Here comes the peace plane. Right across in front of those news cameras. Those other planes have disappeared. No. They're up high. They're coming down. The peace plane is on its way. They're after it—they've turned it back. It's coming this way again. They're trying to get in front and give it their propeller wash. Hey! That was close. They almost collided. They're right over the field now. They're forcing them down. Here they come. (*Suddenly—an involuntary cry.*) Look out, there! (*On the screen, the plane hits a flagpole and crashes to the ground. There is a terrific explosion. The plane bursts into flames.*) They hit a flagpole! The gas tank exploded. The plane's on fire. Someone's driving over to them. They're using an extinguisher. But it's no use. She's going up like a box of matches. (*The scene on the screen fades out. The screen is pulled up out of sight.*) The whole stadium is in a panic. People are rushing on to the field. (*A siren sounds.*) Here comes an ambulance. But it's too late. Those poor devils haven't got a chance in the world. Not a chance. (*The lights come up as the announcer's voice stops. A moment of breathless silence—then a rumble from the audience. Dr. Ely steps forward and raises his arms.*)

Ely (*Deeply moved*). Order. Order, please. (*The rumble quiets down.*) I—what you have just heard—I—I knew these men. They were soldiers. They were comrades in arms of Jig Smith—here on this platform. They hated war. They understood what was happening tonight—and they hated that. They knew what it meant. By profession they were daredevils. Every day they risked their lives to thrill and entertain us. Tonight, they gambled their lives for peace. What they tried to do was madness. But they were desperate—cornered—and they died. May God rest their souls.

Jig (*A cry*). How can they rest? How can they? (*He lifts his stump of an arm and his eyes.*) God almighty, my buddies are dead. They were fighters, God almighty—unknown soldiers of peace. They belonged to the great army of plain men who are asking not to die. Is that too much to ask? Answer me, God almighty. Answer me. (*A long silence, then Jig begins to whisper.*) Help yourselves! Help yourselves! God helps them that help themselves. Okay, God almighty. We pledge ourselves to live. That's our answer. Who takes that pledge? Who is the first? (*Jimmy Aquilina steps forward on the platform.*)

Jimmy. Right here. I'm signing it.

Jig. Jimmy. God almighty, it's Jimmy.

Jimmy (*Reading*). We, the undersigned, loyal Americans of military age, proud and ready to fight in defense of our country against invasion, but vigilant to safeguard the precious gift of peace which is our heritage, hereby pledge ourselves to preserve that peace and to refuse to bear arms in any war waged by foreign powers upon an alien soil. (*He signs. Several others crowd forward to follow his lead. He turns to Carmen. In the crowd, someone starts to beat time with his feet and to sing: "The Yanks aren't coming! The Yanks aren't coming! THE YANKS AREN'T COMING!" The chant becomes a roar. It fills the auditorium. Its message cries out to the world. The curtain falls.*)

Head over Heels

Screenplay by Frank Tuttle
From a story by Walter Brooke

FADE IN

1 EXTERIOR CLOSE SHOT—MOVING BACKGROUND—DAY
The front seat of a speeding Dodge convertible. The man at the wheel, Shad Burtis, is closer to the CAMERA *than his companion, Doc Beauregard. Shad's Stetson shadows a square head with two narrow slits for eyes and a larger slit for a mouth. Doc Beauregard wears a wide-brimmed Homburg. His face is soft and handsome. He looks at his wrist watch. Both men speak with a drawl.*
    Beauregard. Step on it, Shad.
Shad nods and shoves his foot to the floor. Beauregard studies the speedometer and relaxes. Shad sneaks a look at him.
    Shad. Yankee, ain't she, Doc?
    Beauregard. Boston.
    Shad. Millionaire, ain't she?
    Beauregard. I *said*, "Step on it."
Shad's larger slit widens to a grin. Doc Beauregard sees something straight ahead.

2 EXTERIOR TALBOT ESTATE
The angle takes in the speeding Dodge. As the CAMERA PANS TO THE LEFT *and the convertible goes away from us, we see that it is pulling an open army trailer in which two young men are riding.* THE CAMERA MOVEMENT *also reveals the driveway entrance to the Talbot estate. The Dodge and the trailer head for the beautiful Georgian mansion in the background.*

3 MEDIUM LONG SHOT—TALBOT MANSION
The Dodge pulls up in front of the entrance. Beauregard gets out, picks up a small black bag, walks up to the door and bangs the knocker. Shad joins the two young men as they jump down from the trailer. A Negro servant opens the door and Beauregard goes in.

4 LONG SHOT—INTERIOR TALBOT MANSION
The Talbot interior is right out of Gone With the Wind. *The servant and Beauregard have just left the entrance door which is in the extreme*

background of the hallway. An aura of tension hangs over them as they mount the stairway. Beauregard removes the Homburg halfway up the stairs.
Dissolve to

5   Full shot—interior Mrs. Talbot's bedroom
Agatha Talbot is seated on a chaise longue in the foreground. In her early fifties, Mrs. Talbot exudes Back Bay Boston. She is stirring powder in a small glass of water as she stares just below the CAMERA *with marked concern. The bedroom door is behind her. Someone knocks.*

    Servant's voice. Doctor Beauregard, Mis' Talbot.
    Mrs. Talbot. Send him in, Elijah.

Beauregard comes in and walks to the foreground, just behind Agatha Talbot, as the Negro closes the door. The doctor's eyes look under CAMERA *in the same direction as Mrs. Talbot's. She senses that he is there, shudders ever so slightly, and speaks in a whisper.*

    Mrs. Talbot. What do you think, Doctor?
    Beauregard (*After a pause—also whispering*). I'm afraid it will have to come off.
    Mrs. Talbot (*Shivering again*). The whole limb?
    Beauregard. I'll do what I can, ma'am.

6   Reverse angle—shooting out the window
(Note: this is shot from a parallel platform with a built wall and window "tarped" over.) In the clearing below stands a lone tree. The lowest branch—about eight inches in diameter—has been shattered a few feet from the tree trunk, and there is a great gash in the tree itself. The broken branch dangles to the ground. Mrs. Talbot's voice goes right over the scene, rattling along at full speed. (Note: we may need a close-up of tree DISSOLVING *to Scene 6.)*

    Mrs. Talbot's voice. I'd appreciate it if you would. It cost a fortune transplanting it, and it's such a darling tree. A poverty birch they call it, I believe. Isn't that quaint?

The camera dollies back, *until it includes Mrs. Talbot and Beauregard in the foreground. The dialogue continues during the* camera movement.

    Mrs. Talbot. I was in the closet when the lightning struck it last night. I can't endure thunderstorms. I'm still jumpy. Really, I am.

Mrs. Talbot gives the power in the glass a final stir and downs a jittery gulp.

Mrs. Talbot. Do try and fix the branch, won't you? I'm going to miss it at breakfast. It looked *so* charming.
Beauregard (*The statesman*). Fixin' it might be quite expensive, ma'am. There's that hole too. That's a powerful big cavity.
Mrs. Talbot (*Suddenly sharp*). How much?
Beauregard (*Stretching out the first word*). Well. That could run into thirty or forty dollars.
Mrs. Talbot. Chop it off! And fill that cavity—with amalgam—cement—er—anything! (*Reacting to the doctor's crafty look with sarcasm.*) No! Not gold.

Mrs. Talbot makes a gesture of dismissal. Beauregard bows and leaves past CAMERA. Mrs. Talbot throws a nasty look after him and goes to the window. On the lawn below, Shad and the two assistant tree surgeons are pulling the trailer into the scene.

7   REVERSE ANGLE—SHOOTING INTO WINDOW
    Mrs. Talbot comes close to the window and looks down.
8   MEDIUM SHOT—THE LAWN
    The three men are unloading the trailer on which is painted HENRY BEAUREGARD, TREE SURGEON. *Shad and a freckled-faced oaf named Catfish Johnson, who is Beauregard's first assistant, take a ladder and some utensils from the trailer and walk out of the scene carrying them. The remaining assistant is tall and lean. He tosses several instruments on the lawn. Then he picks up a large book from the trailer. He turns toward us, revealing an appealing, sensitive face, and begins to thumb the pages. His poet's eye alternates between the book and the tree's gaping wound which is close to us in the foreground.*
9   CLOSE SHOT—MRS. TALBOT
    She is peering through the window at the second assistant.
10 CLOSE-UP—THE SECOND ASSISTANT
    The voices of Shad and Catfish (off-scene) are augmented by Beauregard's voice giving orders. The assistant finds the page he is looking for. On the cover of the book is printed FLORA AMERICANA. *The sensitive young assistant looks at the tree (off-scene) with honest sympathy.*
    The assistant (*Almost a sigh*). Poverty birch. Tsk! Tsk! (*Meaning, "What a pity!"*)
11 CLOSE-UP—MRS. TALBOT
    She reacts to the attractive young man.
12 MEDIUM CLOSE SHOT—THE ASSISTANT

He looks at the tree, then down at the book.
   Beauregard's voice (*Off scene*). Jonathan!
The assistant goes on studying the book.
   Beauregard's voice. JONATHAN!!!
The young man looks up.
   Beauregard's voice. Fetch me my saw!
Jonathan automatically closes the book, shoves it under his arm, and takes a two-man woodsman's saw out of the trailer. Suddenly, he realizes what it is. He is shocked. He goes off toward the tree, holding the saw as though it were a snake.

13   GENERAL VIEW
Jonathan walks around the birch. Shad and Catfish have propped up the ladder against the tree. Beauregard is descending the ladder. He adjusts his black bag in the crotch made by the shattered branch and the tree trunk. He takes a pair of gloves out of the bag and pulls them on as Jonathan comes up to him. During the dialogue that follows, a gardener and a kennel man, with two hounds on a leash, wander into the background. Jonathan walks breathlessly up to the bottom of the ladder.
   Jonathan. Dr. Beauregard! You're not going to—amputate?
   Beauregard. That's what I'm doin', son. Hand her up here.
He stretches out his hand for the saw. Jonathan shakes his head. THE CAMERA STARTS TRUCKING CLOSER *until the shot takes in only Beauregard and Johnny.*
   Jonathan (*Passionately*). But, doctor—that branch isn't dead. You can save it.
   Beauregard (*Sternly*). Jonathan Boone. You hand me that saw!
   Jonathan (*Just one more chance*). Doctor!
   Beauregard (*Turning to Shad off scene*). You were right, Shad. Your neighbor here is uppity!

14   CLOSE SHOT—SHAD AND CATFISH JOHNSON
Shad is smirking.
   Shad. I told you the trouble I had with him three years ago. And he ain't changed a mite—
Shad points an accusing finger toward Jonathan.
   Shad. Look what he's got there—a book! Uppity? He's downright dangerous! Come on, Catfish.
Shad and the chinless Catfish start toward Jonathan.

15   LONG SHOT

Shad and Catfish move in on Jonathan.

Shad. Hand over that saw!

Jonathan moves back. The two men close in. Jonathan puts the saw behind him. Shad lowers his head and charges forward like a goat. Jonathan steps aside. Shad butts the tree and crumples to his knees. The impact dislodges the doctor's bag. It conks Shad on the back of his noggin and flattens him. Still backing away, Jonathan trips over the ladder, bringing it and Beauregard down on top of him. Jonathan struggles to his feet. In the process of untangling himself, he yanks at the saw. One handle catches the base of the ladder which has slid halfway down the tree trunk. The yank brings the top of the ladder down on Shad's head. A perfect rabbit punch! Catfish steps forward and stares down at the fallen man. He is out—like a smitten ox.

Catfish (*Solemnly*). He's deader than a doorknob!

Catfish fixes a moronic and murderous eye on Jonathan, draws an ugly-looking case knife from his belt, and shambles forward. Jonathan retreats. Catfish goes into high gear. Jonathan frantically flings the saw at his assailant's feet and runs for his life out of the shot. Catfish trips and goes down as though he had been hit by a Notre Dame tackler. Beauregard is on his feet. He waves to the kennel man and the gardeners.

Beauregard (*Shouting*). He'll head for Boonesville. Go get him!

Now everyone is yelling. Bedlam breaks loose. Catfish staggers to his feet and the improvised posse, including the dogs and the gardeners, takes off after Jonathan. Mrs. Talbot's imported chauffeur and her French chef, brandishing a ladle, run into the scene. As he goes by, the chauffeur steps on Shad's neck.

16 CLOSE SHOT—SHAD

He groans and lifts his head. The chef's foot steps on it, driving Shad's puss into the earth. This time the sound is a muffled moan.

17 CLOSE SHOT—MRS. TALBOT

She reaches for the window shade to pull it up for a better view, but the yank she gives it brings the roller out of its socket. The shade drapes itself around her shoulders.

18 LONG SHOT—TALBOT ESTATE

The Georgian mansion is in the extreme left of center background—the entrance driveway is twenty yards from CAMERA. *The road comes forward at a slight angle that takes it past us to the right of* CAMERA. *Jonathan is sprinting through the entrance. And he can sprint! Thirty*

yards or so behind him come his pursuers. By now there are about fifteen of them and six yelping dogs, all on leashes. Jonathan whizzes by CAMERA quick as Flash Gordon. The posse trails after him.
DISSOLVE TO

19 LONG SHOT—MOUNTAIN ROAD
Again the road comes toward us at a left-to-right angle, but this time over a hillock. The Blue Ridge Mountains are in the background. In the foreground, a Lincoln Continental convertible is slowing down so that the girl who is driving it can look at a broken-down signpost.

20 CLOSE SHOT—GIRL IN CAR AND SIGNPOST
The girl's face is turned away from CAMERA as she drives into the shot and studies the signpost, which is so weather-beaten that it is unreadable. The girl shrugs, turns and looks behind her. We get a good view of her. She wears a simple, smartly tailored outfit. Her pert face displays a disarming directness, but two little devils are turning somersaults in her eyes. She sees someone. The devils stop somersaulting.

21 LONG SHOT—ROADWAY
The convertible is in the right foreground. Jonathan has run into view at the top of the hillock. He legs it downhill toward us, hell-bent for home and mother. When he is several yards from the car, the girl puts it into gear and coasts forward. As she gets the Lincoln into high, Jonathan throws a quick look over his shoulder and sprints past her out of the shot. The car picks up speed and follows him.

22 CAMERA CAR SHOT
Jonathan sprints into the scene and keeps on going. The Lincoln pulls alongside. The girl calls out.

The girl. Hey there! Where's Boonesville?

Jonathan (*Scarcely looking at her*). Follow me!

He hotfoots it out of the scene. The devils start somersaulting again as the girl steps on it and catches up with Jonathan. She screams at the back of his head.

The girl. I'll give you a lift.

Jonathan slows down. The car slows down. Jonathan vaults into the seat beside the girl.

23 CLOSER SHOT, ALMOST STRAIGHT BACK
Jonathan finishes the leap into the seat. He is a bit winded. He looks beyond the girl at the road behind, then turns back and stares straight ahead. The girl's eyes give him a thorough going over. What they see

pleases her. She slows down. Jonathan turns to her. She smiles at him. He smiles impersonally at her. Then he looks ahead again. The car is really coasting. Jonathan gives the girl an accusing look and, without saying a word, gets up and vaults out of the car.

24 LONGER CAMERA CAR SHOT—THREE-QUARTER SIDE ANGLE

Jonathan lands on the road and sprints forward out of the shot. The girl reacts, steps on it again, and catches up.

The girl. What'd I do?

Jonathan. Too slow, ma'am.

The girl reacts, burns, and issues a challenge.

The girl. You get back in!

Jonathan considers as he runs, then accepts the challenge and lands once more beside the girl. She gives him a vicious look. The convertible leaps forward out of the shot.

25 LONG SHOT—MOUNTAIN ROAD

The car skids around an uphill curve at sixty miles per hour.

26 CLOSE CAMERA CAR SHOT

The background is whizzing by. Jonathan looks back, then smiles gratefully at the girl.

Jonathan. Thank you, ma'am.

The girl burns again and gives the accelerator the works.

27 DOLLY SHOT (WITH DOUBLES)

THE CAMERA IS TILTED DOWN *and focused on the road where a broken board with a spike sticking out of it is lying.* THE CAMERA TILTS UP AND PULLS BACK. *The Lincoln is doing eighty as it comes toward us and goes over the board.* THE CAMERA SWINGS *as the car passes and speeds away from us up a steep hill. The tire blows out with a nasty bang. The Lincoln skids and crashes into a fence.*

28 CLOSE SHOT—THE CAR

The air is full of dust and splinters as the front left tire slides down the fence onto the road. Jonathan's face shows real concern as he leans toward the girl.

Jonathan. You all right, ma'am?

The girl. Never better. You?

Jonathan. I'm a little out of breath.

The girl. You and that tire both. Let's have a look.

The girl starts to open her door but realizes that it is too close to the fence. Jonathan opens the door on his side and helps her out. They exit from the scene.

29 MEDIUM CLOSE SHOT—REAR OF CAR

The girl and Jonathan come into the scene. The girl looks over the situation and kicks the flat tire. She makes a face and turns to Jonathan.

    The girl (*Rolling up her sleeves*). My spare, James.

Jonathan doesn't know from sophisticated small talk. He takes her seriously.

    Jonathan. Jonathan, Miss—er—
    The girl. Lyon. Dandy Lyon.

30 CLOSE TWO-SHOT

    Jonathan (*With a sudden new interest*). That's a flower. Taraxacum Officinale.
    The girl (*After a wolf whistle*). Get *me*! Hey, are you a botanist?
    Jonathan (*Proudly*). The University—class of '47. Under the G.I. Bill. I made it in two years. Magna cum laude.
    The girl. And the track team, I'll bet. Magna cum sprint-a.

31 LONGER SHOT

Jonathan smiles. Very faintly the sound of the baying hounds comes over the scene. Jonathan hears it. The smile fades. With an almost imperceptible start, he goes to work on the spare at a frantic tempo. Dandy starts to get out her tools, then stops, fascinated by his almost hysterical intensity. She studies his actions for a moment before she speaks.

    Dandy. Hey! What's eating you?

Jonathan doesn't even hear her. If anything, he redoubles his frantic efforts. Dandy bends over and studies his face.

    Dandy (*Continued*). Look, Johnny-jump-up. What's so special in Boonesville?

Jonathan straightens up. He realizes that his frenzy needs an explanation. He is a bad liar, but he's got to try.

    Jonathan. It isn't that. It's—

Once again the dogs bay—but this time, Dandy hears them too. She sees the hunted look in Jonathan's eyes. She walks over to the fence and mounts the lowest rail to look down into the valley where the baying is coming from. Jonathan tenses as he watches her.

32 LONG SHOT—THE VALLEY

The back of Dandy's head comes into the foreground. Down below, the hounds have lost the scent where Jonathan jumped aboard the convertible. They are circling about, sniffing the ground. Jonathan's pursuers are watching them.

33 CLOSE-UP—DANDY
    She turns back to Jonathan, and the eye devils are sitting in judgment.
34 CLOSE-UP—JONATHAN
    He watches her. The corners of his mouth are tight. He stops breathing.
35 CLOSE-UP—DANDY
    She indicates the posse with a toss of the head.
    Dandy. That's for *you*.
36 GENERAL VIEW—JONATHAN—DANDY—THE CAR
    In the foreground, Jonathan releases his breath and nods.
    Jonathan. Yes. You see they're after me because—
    Dandy. Tell me later.
    She steps over to the tire and goes to work. Jonathan breaths freely and joins her. They work fast.
37 LONG SHOT—VALLEY ROAD
    Beauregard and Catfish walk into the foreground. The rest of the pursuers are some distance away in the background still watch the dogs. The two men stop as they see the tire marks where the Lincoln made its first skid. They look at each other.
    Catfish. That car was travelin'—
    Beauregard. Maybe that Johnny hooked a ride—
    Catfish. I'll betcha.
    They look up at the road above them.
38 LONG SHOT—CREST OF HILL
    The Lincoln and the fence. The tiny figures of Dandy and Jonathan can be seen as they finish changing tires and start for the front seat.
39 LONG SHOT—VALLEY ROAD
    The two men turn and call out to the posse.
    Catfish. Come a-runnin'. We found him!
    The posse runs up from the background. The pursuers look up toward the car.
40 LONG SHOT—CREST OF HILL
    Dandy backs the Lincoln up to clear the fence and takes off for Boonesville. The car leaps forward out of the shot.
41 CLOSE SHOT—THE POSSE
    Catfish looks down and fingers the point of his knife.
    Catfish. Aw, shucks! We was goin' to have *fun*!
    He hacks off the head of a roadside sunflower. The rest of the posse echo his disappointment.
42 LONG SHOT—MOUNTAIN ROAD

A scenic composition, featuring the Blue Ridge Mountains and a signpost in the background. The Lincoln whirls through the shot at about fifty.
DISSOLVE TO

43 CLOSE SHOT—SIGNPOST

This sign is in better shape than the one Dandy was trying to decipher when we met her. It reads: BOONESVILLE—5 Miles.
DISSOLVE TO

44 CLOSE SHOT—JONATHAN AND DANDY

Jonathan is somewhat relaxed. He is just finishing his version of what happened at the Talbot estate.

    Jonathan. And then—and then, I ran.
    Dandy. What for?
    Jonathan (*With simple logic*). They were chasing me. And besides, Shad was lying there—deader than a doornail.
    Dandy. Good.
    Jonathan (*Startled*). Good?
    Dandy. That's right. He started it, didn't he?
    Jonathan. Yes—but it was my fault, in a way. I mean, maybe I should have given Shad that saw.
    Dandy (*But really sarcastic*). Naturally. And apologized too.
    Jonathan. I didn't mean that exactly.
    Dandy. Oh, yes you did—exactly. Once you start letting mean characters kick you around, you've got yourself a lifetime job as a football.

45 CLOSE-UP—JONATHAN

He is thoughtful.

    Jonathan (*Seriously*). But all people are mean—mostly.

46 CLOSE-UP—DANDY

She reacts sharply.

    Dandy. Hey! That's not very polite. I'm people. Do I look as if I wanted to bite you?

47 TWO-SHOT

Jonathan weighs this carefully. Finally, he reacts as if the idea were neither improbable nor unappetizing. Dandy's eye devils do a triple handspring.

    Dandy. Hmmm. Could be.

By now, Jonathan is quite aware that Dandy is a woman.

48 CAMERA CAR SHOT—FROM BEHIND LINCOLN

The CAMERA CAR *is just a bit to the right of the convertible. A broken-down jalopy comes toward the Lincoln and passes it. The lone figure at the wheel is a bearded mountaineer. Jonathan turns around and looks at him.*

49 CLOSE SHOT—DANDY AND JONATHAN

Jonathan turns back from watching the jalopy. Dandy notices the concern on his face.

Dandy. Friend of yours?

Jonathan (*Nodding*). That was Shad's brother, Zeke.

Dandy's left eyebrow goes up.

Dandy. I see what you mean. Now Simon Legree and company get a free ride. Okay, hold your hat!

The car spurts forward. Jonathan instinctively puts his hand up for the hat that isn't there. Then he glances down at the speedometer and edges gratefully closer to Dandy.

50 LONG SHOT

The Lincoln whizzes around a curve.

51 CLOSE SHOT—DANDY AND JONATHAN

Jonathan, under Dandy's direction, is fishing a folded tabloid clipping out of Dandy's shoulder-strap bag.

Jonathan. This it?

Dandy. Take a look.

Jonathan unfolds the clipping.

52 INSERT—THE CLIPPING

It features a two-column headline that reads:

BLUE RIDGE BUNNIES BOW

TO BOUNDING BETSY BOONE

The cut below the headline shows Mrs. Boone leaning against a fence. She is holding two kicking rabbits in either hand. Underneath the picture we read:

Mrs. Betsy Boone

At Fifty She Catches Rabbits on the Run

53 CLOSE SHOT—JONATHAN AND DANDY

Jonathan's face shows considerable astonishment. Dandy tosses a glance his way.

Dandy. You know her?

Jonathan. Yes.

Dandy. She as cute as she looks?

Jonathan (*Smiling*). Mrs. Boone is what was so special in Boonesville. She's my mother.

Now it is Dandy's turn to show astonishment. She recovers somewhat and speaks.

Dandy. Either that's a coincidence, Mr. Boone, or it'll do till one comes along.

Jonathan. How do you mean?

Dandy. Ever hear of the Palisades?

Jonathan. On the Hudson in New York?

Dandy. Jersey.

Jonathan. Oh, I'm sorry.

Dandy. Please! They're still allies.

Jonathan is somewhat bewildered. Dandy is serious again.

Dandy. Here's the gag. I hurt my ankle. So I came down here to the Mayfair Clinic.

Jonathan (*The proud native son*). Best in the country!

Dandy. While I was there, I saw that clipping and decided to ask your mother to come back with me to Palisades Park.

Jonathan. What for?

Dandy. I called my boss long distance. He's nuts for the idea. He wants her for his "House of Wonders."

Jonathan. House of what?

Dandy. Wonders. It's a concession there—in Larry Ellis's Amusement Park. Think your mother would go for it?

Jonathan. She might—if *you* ask her.

Dandy smiles back. Suddenly Shad-conscious, Jonathan stops smiling and throws a look behind them. A new idea turns him back to Dandy.

Jonathan. I don't suppose *I* could get a job there?

Dandy. Now *that* has possibilities.

Jonathan is too worried about the posse to give Dandy's lateral pass more than a casual tumble. He frowns and speaks a thought aloud.

Jonathan. I'd take my botanical stuff—my aloe extract—and Julius.

Dandy. Who?

Jonathan doesn't answer. Dandy looks at him quizzically.

Dandy. Who's Julius?

Jonathan shows real embarrassment.

Jonathan. Er—nobody—really.

Dandy registers her curiosity. To cover up, Jonathan looks behind him again, then stares straight ahead. Dandy shrugs and steps on it.

54 MEDIUM SHOT—THE POSSE
The bearded Zeke's jalopy drives into the scene past CAMERA *and stops. The posse crowds around the car.*

55 LONG SHOT—MOUNTAIN ROAD
The Lincoln flashes by on its way to Boonesville.

56 CLOSE ANGLE FEATURING ZEKE, BEAUREGARD AND CATFISH
Zeke quiets the others and pats the shotgun on the seat beside him. His face is drawn. When he speaks, he isn't kidding.

Zeke. That's fo' neighbor Boone!

Beauregard. Catfish, we're goin' to have *plenty* of fun.

A savage roar goes up. Catfish and Beauregard climb into Zeke's car.

57 LONGER SHOT
The mob, still yelling and muttering, pile into the jalopy. It turns around and heads for Boonesville.

58 LONG SHOT—ROAD NEAR BOONE CABIN
Dandy and Jonathan drive up and stop. Jonathan jumps out and indicates the Boone "estate." Off scene, he calls out.

Jonathan. Ma!

59 MEDIUM CLOSE SHOT—RABBIT CORRAL
Ma Boone has just cornered a rabbit. She turns as she hears Jonathan call, still holding the cottontail by the neck. She smiles at her son, drops the rabbit into a crate which holds several bunnies, and starts forward.

60 LONG SHOT—BOONE PROPERTY
The Lincoln is in the foreground. Jonathan helps Dandy out of the car. Beyond them, the Boones' acre contains a cabin and an outhouse. The rabbit corral is to the right of the cabin. Ma Boone vaults over the corral fence and walks briskly toward the foreground. It is easy to see from whom Jonathan got his winged legs.

61 CLOSE SHOT—REVERSE ANGLE
Dandy reacts to Ma's unorthodox approach. Jonathan glances down the road in the direction of the posse. The CAMERA PULLS BACK *as Mrs. Boone comes into the scene. Jonathan greets his mother with a nervous smile. She studies his face.*

Ma. What happened, son?

Jonathan. This is Dandy Lyon, Ma.

Dandy and Ma (*Together*). Hello, Mrs. Boone. Miss Lyon.

Jonathan (*Breathlessly*). I—I have to get out of town. Miss Lyon will explain. I've got to pack my things.

62 CLOSE THREE-SHOT—FAVORING MA BOONE

Ma. All right, Jonathan—

63 REVERSE THREE-SHOT—FAVORING JONATHAN AND DANDY

Jonathan walks quickly out of the scene. Ma swings around to look after him. THE CAMERA MOVES CLOSER.

Ma (*Almost to herself*). He hain't done nothin' bad. Not Jonathan.

Dandy. That's right.

Ma Boone gives Dandy a quick look. Her instinctive mistrust of a stranger begins to thaw out.

64 MEDIUM CLOSE SHOT—CABIN DOORWAY

Jonathan hurries into the scene. On one side of the shot, part of a hammock is visible. The rest of the hammock is out of the scene. The third that is visible reveals the crossed legs of a recumbent sleeper. One foot is bare. Several yards of strong twine, attached to the man's big toe, go up at an angle out of the shot. The foot is seesawing up and down. Jonathan glances at the hammock, as he starts inside, but decides not to disturb the occupant. As Jonathan disappears, the CAMERA PANS QUICKLY OVER AND PULLS BACK. *The entire hammock is revealed. The sleeper, his hands behind his head, has rigged up a rectangular strip of cloth like an East Indian punka. The action of the bare foot and the twine causes the cloth to fan the man in the hammock. He is his own punka-walla. Several other conveniences are around the hammock. Tipped into the shot is the end of a clothesline from which a shirt is hanging.*

65 INTERIOR BOONE CABIN BEDROOM

Jonathan runs in from the main room and begins dumping his things into an old army duffel bag. A small, weed-like plant with a tiny blossom or two, stands on the window sill. Jonathan, the botanist, picks up the potted plant, studies it a brief moment, and puts it on the floor near the duffel bag.

66 MEDIUM CLOSE SHOT—BOONE FRONT YARD

We are shooting away from the cabin. Dandy and Ma Boone are walking quickly toward the house which is BEHIND CAMERA. *They pause when they are close to* CAMERA.

Ma. That Shad's always hated Jonathan. What did you say they'd pay me?

Dandy. Mr. Ellis authorized me to offer you twenty per—for three months.
Ma. Hmm. That's sixty dollars.
Dandy is about to speak when a man's voice calls out from off scene.
Voice. Hold on, Ma. It's wu'th a hundred.

67 CLOSE SHOT—THE HAMMOCK
The man in the hammock sits up. He has a shrewd, perpetually indignant face, and blue eyes that alternate childish innocence with sudden craft. He continues talking, as he unwinds the twine from his toe.
Man (*Shrewdly*). Whut's it for?

68 DOLLY SHOT—MA AND DANDY
As the scene goes on, the CAMERA PULLS BACK *until Pa Boone, the man in the hammock, is included in the foreground.*
Ma (*Talking fast*). Jonathan's in trouble, Pa. We're all leavin'—in a hurry. Git yore things and tell cousin Jed to look after the hogs while we're gone.
Pa (*With insistent irrelevance*). It's wu'th a hundred and whut is it?
Dandy. But I meant twenty *a week*. Two hundred and forty dollars.
Pa. Well, why didn't you say so?
Pa's whole tempo changes to double quick. He reaches out and releases a string, wound about a nail. A tree-bark megaphone comes down into the shot. Pa seizes it and puts it to his mouth.
Pa (*Lucky-Striking*). Fuddle-dee, fuddle-dee, fuddle-dee, *fud*! American! Tune in, Jed Boone! Tune in!

69 LONG SHOT—NEIGHBORING FIELD
A lanky tenant farmer is in the middle foreground, feeding some pigs. He hears the call, cups his hands to his mouth, and calls back.
Jed. Fuddle-dee, fuddle-dee, fuddle-dee, *fud*! American! I'm a-listenin'.

70 MEDIUM SHOT TOWARD CABIN—PA, MA, AND DANDY
Pa yells back through his megaphone. His free hand catches the clothesline.
Pa. We're headin' no'th, Jed. Keep an eye on the property!

71 MEDIUM CLOSE SHOT—JED AND THE PIGS
His hands still cupped, Jed hollers back.
Jed. Sho' nuff, will, Pa. Business or pleasure trip?

72 MEDIUM SHOT

Pa is loosening his shirt from the line as he yells.
   Pa. Business, Jed.
   Ma (*Yelling*). Show business!
Ma hurries into the house. Pa goes to work bundling up his things and putting on his shoes. Dandy watches him, amused.
   Dandy. Can I help?
   Pa. Practically set. Go on in and help Ma.
Dandy salutes and starts into the house. As she reaches for the latch, Pa calls out to her.
   Pa. Whut's yore name?
   Dandy. Dandy.
   Pa (*Still packing*). Yo're purty.
   Dandy (*Smiling*). You're a flirt.
Dandy makes with a corny out-of-the-corner-of-her-mouth tch-tch, and starts into the cabin. She bumps into Jonathan on his way out, his duffel bag over his shoulder, the plant under his arm. Dandy hurries on in. Jonathan calls out to his father as he runs out of the shot toward the Lincoln.
   Jonathan. Hurry it up, Pa!
Pa nods, picks up his bundle and a jug, and starts after his son.

73 LONG SHOT—MOUNTAIN ROAD
Zeke's jalopy, loaded to the gunwales with posse and hounds, skids and "rattle-ty" bangs through the shot.

74 MEDIUM SHOT—DANDY'S CAR
Jonathan and Pa have practically finished stowing their stuff in the Lincoln. Jed Boone is helping them. Dandy and Ma Boone hurry into the scene, Dandy carrying Ma's bundles, Ma with the rabbit crate on her shoulder. They dump the stuff, and the men help them pack it into the convertible. Dandy moves around to tune up the motor. As she starts into the front seat, she bangs her ankle. She emits a little "Aiee!" and sinks into the seat. Jonathan runs to her.

75 CLOSER SHOT
Jonathan's face is troubled.
   Jonathan. Bad, hmmm?
   Dandy. Not good. It's the ankle I twisted.
   Jonathan. Anything I can do?
   Dandy (*Nodding, with a forced smile*). Rub it.

She pulls up her skirt and sticks out a streamlined, strictly-from-Varga gam. Jonathan is flustered, but not that flustered. He rubs the leg, but gingerly.

    Dandy (*Continued*). M-m-m-m! That helps.

76 CLOSE SHOT—PA AND MA
Pa is giving the leg a healthy gander. Ma clunks him with a bundle. Pa snaps out of it and goes back to work.

77 CLOSE SHOT—DANDY AND JONATHAN
Just their heads. Dandy is smiling like a stroked cat, as Jonathan's fingers work on the ankle out of the shot. Suddenly, the smile vanishes. Dandy has seen something behind the car. She punches Jonathan's shoulder. He straightens up and looks behind him.

78 LONG SHOT—MOUNTAIN ROAD
Zeke's jalopy comes over the rise of a hill, something over a quarter of a mile away, and starts downhill toward the Boone cabin.

79 MEDIUM SHOT—REAR END—THE LINCOLN
The whole group reacts to the approaching nemesis. Dandy swings back into the seat and presses the starter with her good foot. It whirs but doesn't start anything. Everybody looks back again.

80 LONG SHOT—MOUNTAIN ROAD, AS BEFORE
The jalopy is rattling closer and closer. The posse is yelling bloody murder.

81 MEDIUM SHOT—GROUP AT LINCOLN
Jonathan whispers something to Pa and Jed. Pa nods and streaks it out of the scene. Jonathan and Jed tear off in the opposite direction. Dandy keeps working at the starter. Jonathan watches her as nothing happens. The sound of the yelling posse comes over the scene.

82 LONG SHOT FLASH
The approaching posse.

83 MEDIUM LONG SHOT—REAR OF LINCOLN
Jed and Jonathan come running into the foreground, each carrying two pails of hogwash which they start dumping onto the road so that it covers the entire width. There are open fences on both sides of road. Pa Boone runs into the shot with his megaphone. He puts it to his mouth.

    Pa (Hog calling). Come-a, come-a, come-a, come-a, come-a. COME-A-PIGGY-PIGGY-PIGGY!

84 MEDIUM SHOT—JED'S PIGS
Just as we last saw them. They lift their heads and take off.

85 LONG SHOT—COUNTRY ROAD

Pa is in the foreground, back to CAMERA. *Jonathan and Jed are watching him call. The approaching jalopy is in the background. Jed's pigs run into the scene and start rooting in the hogwash. Then comes the deluge. Every neighbor's pig in the district runs into the scene and goes for the feast. The road is completely blocked. The jalopy skids to a stop just beyond the pigs. The three men turn and run for the Lincoln.*

86 MEDIUM SHOT—THE LINCOLN

The starter starts. The engine turns over. Jonathan and Pa jump in. The Lincoln takes off. The occupants wave to Jed. He waves one of his pails at them.

87 MEDIUM SHOT—THE JALOPY

Zeke steps forward and fires his shotgun over the scrambling hogs.

88 CLOSE SHOT—JED

The birdshot hit his pail. Its contents spurt out. Jed dives for cover. The CAMERA *whips over and shows the vanishing Lincoln.*

FADE OUT

FADE IN

89 LONG SHOT—PALISADES PARK—DAY—CONCEALED CAMERA

The shot is from a high angle. The CAMERA PANS OFF *a sign reading,* LARRY ELLIS'S PALISADES PARK *and* TILTS DOWN *to show the park on a busy afternoon. The crowds are milling around the concessions. In the distance, the Lincoln comes through the entrance gate with Dandy and Jonathan in the front seat and Ma and Pa Boone in back (all doubles). The convertible winds around the back of the Administration Building.*

90 FULL SHOT—FRONT OF ADMINISTRATION BUILDING

The shot shows the building in the background, as the Lincoln comes to a stop in front of the main office, which carries a sign: LARRY ELLIS—EXECUTIVE DIRECTOR. *Dandy sounds her horn—three short ones and one long one—and jumps out of the car. She turns to the Boones, her eyes shining. Jonathan is carrying the plant we saw in his bedroom.*

Dandy. You're going to love this guy.

The Boones look at the door leading to the offices. It opens.

91 FULL FIGURE SHOT

The opening door and the sign. Larry Ellis comes out. In the vague thirties, Larry is dashing, debonair, and, from Jonathan's point of view, definitely Dandy's dish. He waves a greeting.

Larry. Hi, character!

92 REVERSE ANGLE—FROM LARRY'S POINT OF VIEW

Dandy waves back. The Boones watch her.

Dandy. 'Lo, character!

She runs out of the scene. Jonathan's heart sinks as he watched her go. Ma and Pa Boone look at him, then back at the office.

93 CLOSER SHOT—PORCH

Dandy runs in and throws her arms around Larry's neck.

Dandy. Miss me, Larry?

Larry (*Grinning*). I didn't catch the name.

Dandy. Nature Girl. Look!

She detaches a blossom from her corsage and fastens it in Larry's lapel.

94 CLOSE GROUP SHOT

The Boones. Jonathan hitches up the potted plant and looks down at it. Ma Boone watches his reaction. Pa's eyes wander skyward.

Pa (*Almost to himself*). I'm a flirt, huh?

95 MEDIUM SHOT—OVER THE BOONES TOWARD THE OFFICE

Dandy gives Larry's shoulder a pat and takes his arm.

Dandy. Come on, boss. Meet the Bounding Boones.

Dandy and Larry come down the steps into the foreground. The Boones get out of the car. Larry extends his hand with genuine cordiality to Ma.

Larry. Mrs. Boone, I'm delighted you're going to be with us. (*His eye goes to the crate.*) And you brought your famous rodents.

Ma (*Quickly, disregarding his remark*). My husband, Dawson Boone, and my son, Jonathan.

Larry (*Shaking hands with the two men*). Glad you could come.

Pa. Nice little place you got here.

Jonathan. Your trees are beautiful.

Larry. Thank you. (*Calling over his shoulder.*) Jimmy! Bud! (*To the Boones.*) My boys'll help you with your things. I'll take you to the Waldorf—Mrs. Waldorf's Chowder House. I think you'll be comfortable.

Ma (*Making conversation*). Fish chowder's right tasty.

Larry turns to Jonathan as two park attendants appear and start down the steps.

Larry. Like our trees, hmm?

Dandy (*Cutting in quickly*). That's Johnny's racket. He's a fugitive from a nursery.

Larry. I don't blame him. At his age, I was in kindergarten.

Dandy. A *tree* nursery, smarty pants. He's a botanist. We've got to find him a job here.

The attendants are abreast of the group. Larry tosses one of them an order.
Larry. The luggage goes to Mrs. Waldorf's, Jimmy.
Jimmy replies "Yes, sir," and the two men go to work. Ma and Pa move with them to the rear end of the car. THE CAMERA MOVES CLOSER TO HOLD THE THREE. *Larry addresses himself to Dandy.*
Larry (*Continued*). What about Joe Donatello's, till I can find Johnny something better? (*To Jonathan.*) Donatello's our florist. With delusions of grand opera—but a sweet layout.
Jonathan. Sounds wonderful, sir.
Larry (*Correcting the "sir"*). The name is Larry. (*To Dandy.*) Tell Joe I said to put Johnny to work, will you, angel?
He turns to Ma and Pa (off scene) as he tosses a bundle to Bud.
Larry (*Continued*). Let's shove, hmm? Unless you've stowed another offspring in my rumble seat.

96 CLOSE SHOT—MA, PA, JIMMY, AND BUD
Ma and Pa are at a loss for an answer.

97 CLOSE SHOT—DANDY, JONATHAN, AND LARRY
Dandy cuts in and taps Jonathan on the shoulder.
Dandy. Hear that, Johnny? Whatever happened to Julius?
Larry (*Tossing another bundle to Jimmy off scene*). Who's he?
Dandy. That's what I want to know.
Jonathan. I—I'll tell you some other time.
Larry (*Laughing it off*). Fair enough. If he's not in my trunk rack. (*To Ma and Pa, off scene.*) Follow me, Mister and Missus. (*To Jonathan.*) See you, Johnny.
Larry goes. The Boones and the two park attendants go through the scene after him. As Pa passes Dandy, he makes with the corner-of-the-mouth "Tch! Tch!" that she gave him. Dandy throws a kiss after the cavalcade, then turns to Jonathan. He looks down at the plant, then back at Dandy.
Jonathan. Mr. Donatello's?
Dandy takes a second flower from her corsage and puts it in Jonathan's lapel.
Dandy (*Phony melodrama*). All in good time, my friend. But first, the missing mystery man.
She steps back and regards the effect made by the boutonniere.
Dandy (*Continued*). M-m-m. Very attractive!

Jonathan *blushes. Dandy comes close again and resumes the stage-whisper approach.*

Dandy (*Continued*). *Where* is the body? And *who* is Julius?

Jonathan. If I tell you, you'll laugh.

Dandy (*Gesturing toward the car*). Inside, bub.

They get into the rear of the Lincoln.

98 CLOSE SHOT—BACK SEAT OF THE LINCOLN

Dandy and Jonathan sit next to each other. Jonathan is somewhat mystified.

Dandy. Now then. I practically never laugh when I'm sitting down.

Jonathan (*Not quite sure how to take her*). Promise?

Dandy. Word of honor.

Jonathan (*Slowly at first*). Well. About three years ago—just after I got home from overseas, I was kind of low in the mind.

Dandy (*Reminiscing*). I remember that one. No bright new world. The black market stay-homes shoving you around. So that's where you got the idea that people are mean.

Jonathan. I guess maybe. Say, were you a WAC or something?

Dandy. Something.

Jonathan. Anyway. I'd just found out someone had my old job. I must have been pretty desperate because I asked Shad if I could work for him. His place is next to ours. Opposite Cousin Jed. You remember Jed?

Dandy. I remember his pigs.

DISSOLVE TO

99 EXTERIOR SHAD'S FENCE, BOONESVILLE

The action told in the next speech is photographed as the voices come over.

Jonathan's voice (*After an appreciative grin*). Shad was weeding out his field. He'd never liked me, particularly after I went to night school. He thought book-learning was uppity. When I asked him for a job, he just laughed and shoved me over the fence.

Dandy's voice. And you jumped back and socked him.

Jonathan's voice. It was his property. I just walked away. Shad dug up a big weed and threw it at me.

DISSOLVE TO

100 CLOSE TWO-SHOT

Dandy is incurably hopeful.

Dandy. And you threw it back.
Jonathan. N–n–no.
Dandy. Why not? It was his property.

Jonathan has to laugh. He sobers and goes on.

Jonathan. I picked it up. It was a skunk parsnip. *Julicarpus Foetidus.*
Dandy. Julius.
Jonathan (*Nodding*). Pa called it that when I brought it home and patched it up. It got to be the family mascot—sort of. Sounds pretty silly, I guess—

They both look down at the plant.

Jonathan (*Continued*). But it had been pulled up by the roots and thrown away—
Dandy. Like you.
Jonathan. Like a lot of us then. And, anyway, I'd been working on an idea to save dying trees—an aloe extract—I tried it out on Julius.
Dandy (*Impressed*). And?
Jonathan. I'm still working on the idea. Does Mr. Donatello have a refrigerator?
Dandy. I imagine. Let's ask him.

Jonathan gets up and leaps over to open the door. Dandy's boutonniere falls out of his lapel. He picks it up and sits down to replace it. Dandy leans close and reaches across him to help.

101 CLOSE SHOT—THE TWO HEADS

Dandy's movement has brought them cheek to cheek. As she puts the flower back in Jonathan's lapel, her eyes begin to study the sensitive face. Her fingers fumble with the flower. Jonathan becomes conscious that she is looking at him. He turns to her. Their eyes hold. Dandy's eyes are saying, "Well?" and Jonathan is sorely tempted. Then he gets a hold of himself. He is thinking, as he did with Shad, "This is someone else's property." He moves back. He retreats.

102 MEDIUM SHOT

To cover his embarrassment, Jonathan pulls a small preserve jar from his coat pocket. It is full of something that looks like cold tea. He holds it out to Dandy.

Jonathan. This is the stuff. It's an extract from the century plant.

Dandy is female to the core. From her point of view, any man who could come that close to kissing her and not even try is beyond the pale. She is burned to a crisp. She steps quickly out of the car.

103 SHOOTING ACROSS THE CAR

Jonathan follows Dandy. He feels like a fool, but he has to do something. He goes after Dandy like Tom Sawyer following Becky Thatcher with the doorknob. He holds out the aloe extract.

Jonathan. It has to be cold as ice before you can use it.

Dandy (*Nasty nice*). That's no problem. With the company it keeps.

This throws Jonathan for a complete loss. Before he can answer, a six-foot easel poster comes into the shot. The legs of two men behind it show underneath. The poster bears the legend, MARKO THE GREAT, *and displays a lurid picture of a hypnotist, with devils on his shoulders, staring straight front with piercing black eyes. The rest of the printing says:* HYPNOTIST AND MAGICIAN. *A voice comes from behind the poster as Jonathan stares at it.*

The voice. Got it, Tony? It goes in front of the House of Wonders. And don't fence me in.

Second voice. Okay, Mr. Marko.

One pair of legs walks off with the easel, revealing the original of the poster. The hypnotist is smoking a meerschaum pipe. His ring finger sports an enormous diamond. His sardonic eyes light up as he sees Dandy. He comes forward.

Marko. Well, well, well, *wel*-come! What luck with your Boone-doggling?

Dandy. That's the question. This is Jonathan Boone.

Marko (*Eyeing the profile*). M–m–m. Good luck. (*To Jonathan.*) And good luck to you, Lochinvar.

Jonathan bows and pockets the jar. Dandy cuts in quickly.

Dandy. I'm taking this genius to Joe Donatello's.

Marko. Perfect. (*To Jonathan.*) I work at the House of Wonders next door to Joe's.

104 DOLLY SHOT—THE THREE AS THEY STROLL ALONE

Jonathan stares at the diamond ring as Marko pulls on his meerschaum.

Jonathan. That's where my mother's going to be.

Marko. My condolences. Does she suffer from headaches, pains in the back, heartburn, that tired feeling?

Jonathan (*Indignantly*). Ma's never been sick in her life.
Marko. What a pity.
Jonathan is startled. Dandy explains.
Dandy. Marko's got a nice little racket on the side. Neurotic females. He sells them doses of hypnosis at a hundred bucks a "hyp." But not me. My complex, right or wrong. That's my motto.
Marko (*To Jonathan*). A defense mechanism. She's afraid to let me cure her headaches. She gets them whenever she has a tantrum—which is practically daily. Well—here we are.

105 MEDIUM LONG SHOT—SIDE ANGLE

The trio comes to a halt in front of the House of Wonders. The posters ballyhooing the Bearded Lady, the Strong Man, etc., are all less prominent than Marko's—the one we saw earlier.
Marko (*Eyeing his poster*). Hmmm. Hmmm. Vulgar, but effective. (*He gestures to Jonathan to go ahead.*) There's a shortcut to my dressing room through Joe's place.
The CAMERA SWINGS OVER *as they walk into the florist's shop next door. The window displays the name of the owner,* GIUSEPPE DONATELLO.

106 MEDIUM SHOT—INTERIOR FLORIST SHOP

The interior is typical. Near the entrance door is a table for writing cards with a mirror above it. In the right wall is a closed door which (we find later) leads into a corridor that goes down some steps into the CHAMBER OF HORRORS *in the Waxworks Museum. Further along this wall is a shelved closet that contains cans, tools, and other odds and ends. In the wall facing the entrance is the door Marko spoke of that leads into the House of Wonders. Only the entrance, some floral displays, and the table in front of the mirror are included in the present shot. As the trio enters, Joe Donatello is mi-mi-ing, "My Leonora, fare thee well!" as he arranges some flowers on the table. The Italian has put them in front of the mirror so that he can watch himself as he sings.* THE CAMERA DOLLIES IN CLOSE, *eliminating Donatello. Marko joins in the last, "Fare thee well," and blows a smoke ring over Dandy's ring finger.*

107 CLOSE SHOT—DONATELLO

He turns and regards the by-play (off scene) with a baleful eye. As he coughs and walks to the three, the CAMERA SWINGS WITH HIM.
Donatello. Put out that stink-a-pot, Mister Marko. You are strangling my beautiful begonias.

Marko looks around for an ashtray, sees none, and shoves the offending meerschaum in his trousers pocket as he speaks.

Marko. What he really resents is my strangling his beautiful "baritonia." Never mind. I go on in twenty-five minutes. My "Dandiora," fare thee well. Happy days, Jonathan.

He walks past CAMERA *toward the rear door. Dandy plucks Donatello by the sleeve and takes him out of the shot as Jonathan steps forward and the* CAMERA MOVES CLOSER.

Jonathan (*Gesturing after Marko*). 'Bye, sir. Happy—er—hypnotism.

108 CLOSE SHOT—REAR DOOR

Marko enters, puts his hand on the doorknob, and turns. He fixes a piercing eye on Jonathan.

Marko. *You* would make a perfect subject.

He exits quickly into the House of Wonders.

109 CLOSE-UP—JONATHAN

He swallows uncomfortably. Dandy's voice comes over the scene.

Dandy's voice. Johnny!

Jonathan moves over and joins Dandy and Donatello, the CAMERA FOLLOWS *him.*

Dandy. You're all set, Mr. Einstein. Joe's delighted.

Donatello. I gotta be delighted. Larry Ellis—he's the boss.

His eye falls on Julius in the crook of Jonathan's arm. His expression changes.

Donatello (*Continued*). What's-a that?

Jonathan is embarrassed. Before he can answer, Dandy jumps in.

Dandy. That's Johnny's skunk parsnip, Julius. He gets the bridal suite in your refrigerator.

Donatello's eyebrow goes up, but before he can reply, Dandy looks beyond him at the wall clock. As Donatello follows her gaze, Jonathan sneaks Julius behind him to the table on which is a watering can.

Dandy (*Continued*). Is that clock right?

Donatello. Abso-positively.

Dandy. Murder! *I* go to work in *fifteen* minutes. 'Bye Einstein. You'll see me later.

She dashes out the entrance door, leaving Jonathan somewhat bewildered by her cryptic reversal of the conventional, "See you later." Donatello loses no time in resuming his role of a frustrated Ezio Pinza.

He carols to Jonathan in recitative, following, note for note, the famous prologue from Pagliacci.

Donatello. Tomorrow mor–r–ning, you start-a to sweep out the store. At seven o'clock—at seven o'clock. (*He shoves Jonathan aside and points at Julius.*) And put-a that stink-weed-a in the garbage can-a.

I need-a some cash-a. I'll be back in a flash-a.

Good-a-bye, John, good-a-bye-a.

Please mind-a the shop-a while I'm away.

Vesti la guiba! On with the play!

He gives the aria a laugh-clown-laugh finish (corn plus!) and sobs his way out the front door. Jonathan reacts and turns to Julius.

110 VERY CLOSE SHOT—JULIUS'S LEAVES

The spout of the watering can is tipped into the shot. THE CAMERA MOVES EVEN CLOSER. *Like one of Donatello's tears, a drop of water rolls down a leaf and plops onto the glass-topped table.*

Jonathan's voice. You, too. *What* a performance!

Jonathan's hand, holding a handkerchief, comes into the shot and wipes the "tear" away.

111 CLOSE SHOT

Jonathan picks up Julius and begins to look for a place to hide the potted parsnip. He moves toward the display window. THE CAMERA PANS WITH HIM *as he makes room for the plant near a particularly lovely vase of tuberoses. Outside, although it is still daylight, the first streetlights come on.*

112 MOVING CAMERA SHOT—THE SIDE DOOR TO THE WAXWORKS

The door opens. A little man, with vacant, staring eyes, comes into the florist's shop. The man is carrying a knife. The thin blade has been broken off halfway to the handle, leaving an ugly, jagged edge. THE CAMERA GOES WITH HIM *as he slithers up to Jonathan and taps him on the shoulder. Jonathan turns and gasps. The man thrusts the knife under Jonathan's nose.*

The man. I'm Gerald Briggs. I broke this cutting Du Barry's throat.

Briggs smiles pleasantly. Jonathan gulps.

Jonathan (*With forced interest*). You don't say so?

Briggs nods. He glances furtively around the shop with his vacant eyes.

Briggs. Mr. Donatello has a beautiful knife. I'd like to borrow it.

113 CLOSE OVER-SHOULDER SHOT—JONATHAN

He swallows again. He can taste his tonsils. The suggestion he makes carries no enthusiasm.

Jonathan. I just started to work here. Er—help yourself.

Briggs nods and walks out of the scene. Jonathan stares after him.

114 CLOSE SHOT—AT CLOSET

Briggs enters and selects a pruning knife from the assortment of tools and junk. He tests the blade's point with practiced fingers. He smiles and gives Jonathan an approving nod.

Briggs. Perfect!

He walks out of the shot.

115 CLOSE SHOT—JONATHAN

His eyes follow Briggs as the latter crosses (off scene) to the door through which he entered.

116 CLOSE SHOT—SIDE DOOR LEADING TO WAXWORKS

Briggs enters the scene and turns back to Jonathan.

Briggs (*With ghoulish enthusiasm*). Would you like to see what I did to Du Barry?

117 CLOSE-UP—JONATHAN

He shivers slightly and shakes his head emphatically. The shaking slows down.

118 CLOSE-UP—BRIGGS

He is beckoning to Jonathan with the knife.

119 CLOSE SHOT—JONATHAN

The head shaking gradually becomes a nod. Jonathan finds himself walking over to the little man like a hooked salmon. THE CAMERA FOLLOWS HIM. *When he gets to the side door, Briggs steps aside.*

Briggs (*Pointing*). Down there.

He gestures toward the passageway beyond. Jonathan goes in. Briggs follows him. Both men disappear. The door closes.

120 TRUCKING SHOT—PASSAGEWAY AND CHAMBER OF HORRORS

Jonathan, with Briggs behind him, moves toward CAMERA *along the dark passageway.* THE CAMERA DOLLIES AHEAD OF THEM BUT FASTER THAN THEIR SLOW WALK. *As the shot reveals their full figures, they start down some steps.* THE CAMERA PULLS BACK AND TO ONE SIDE AND STOPS. *Tipped into one corner of the shot is a seated figure—a gagged man with a dagger in his heart. Jonathan is paralyzed with terror. He turns to run back, but Briggs prods him on with his knife. The men continue walking.* THE CAMERA SWINGS OVER, *revealing the Chamber of Horrors. In the background are famous criminals, an Indian torture group—the usual display of horror waxworks. The grouping nearest the* CAMERA, *where Briggs and Jonathan stop, features Mme. Du Barry. The wax figure is reclining on a chaise longue, staring at the order for her execution which a French deputy of the period, with a tri-colored cockade on his liberty cap, is holding out for her to read. A wide band of modeling wax encircles Du Barry's throat. It is obvious that Briggs has been doing a repair job.*

121 CLOSE-UP—MADAME DU BARRY

Briggs's voice comes over the scene.

>**Briggs's voice.** She fell off the couch and broke her neck. I'm fixing it.

122 LONG SHOT—CHAMBER OF HORRORS

Briggs, Jonathan, and the Du Barry group are in the foreground. Many other groups are in the background. The whole exhibit has been rigged up as a cave with stalactites hanging, and a few stalagmites poking up from the floor. A big sign is on display, reading: CHAMBER OF HORRORS—CLOSED FOR REPAIRS. *Briggs goes right on talking.*

>**Briggs.** I created Du Barry. (*A broad, godlike gesture.*) I made all these people.
>
>**Jonathan** (*Looking over the works*). You do very nice work.

123 MEDIUM CLOSE SHOT—OVER DU BARRY TOWARD BRIGGS AND JONATHAN

Briggs is flattered. He bends down and picks up an electric plug with a wire attached, talking as he completes the operation of plugging in.

>**Briggs.** Watch what happens when the mechanism's connected. My own invention.

124 CLOSE-UP—DU BARRY

The hand holding the execution order and the scroll itself are in the foreground. A slight humming sound comes over the shot. Du Barry's eyes open and close slowly. The "invention" gives the startling effect that the waxwork is reacting to the death sentence.

>**Briggs's voice** (*Happily*). Gruesome, isn't it? I had them wire both eyes separately just to amuse myself. It gives an entirely different effect.

125 CLOSE SHOT—BRIGGS AND JONATHAN—OVER DU BARRY'S BACK

Briggs gives the switch he is holding a thumb movement.

>**Briggs.** You see!

We do not see the alternating eye effect, but Jonathan does. He is sincerely impressed by the whole show.

Jonathan. It's wonderful, Mr. Briggs, you're an artist.
Briggs accepts the compliment with the attitude of a genius who knows he is great. Then he frowns.

Briggs (*Bitterly*). They don't appreciate me. They pay me nothing. I have to work as a hypnotist's stooge to earn a living. You know Marko?

Jonathan. I met him. (*Hopefully.*) Don't you have to go to work next door—pretty soon?

Briggs (*Nodding*). It's humiliating. Marko has no heart. No consideration. Ten shows a day!

Jonathan. Then I—er—won't keep you. Thank you, Mr. Briggs.

But Briggs doesn't even hear him. He leans forward and gives the wax around Du Barry's neck a deft touch with Donatello's knife. Jonathan tiptoes away toward the passageway. Briggs looks at his wrist watch and goes on working.

126 MEDIUM SHOT—INSIDE DONATELLO'S—NIGHT

The angle takes in the entrance door and part of the window display. Outside, it is completely dark, except for the streets lights and a few illuminated concessions, like the Ferris wheel in the distance (miniature light effects). A few passersby give the window a casual glance. Donatello comes in from the street, counting some money. He sees Julius in the window, pockets the dough, and picks up the skunk parsnip. THE CAMERA SWINGS OVER *with him. Jonathan comes hurriedly into the scene. Donatello faces him with the plant. He speaks before Jonathan can say anything.*

Donatello. Downstairs your little parsnoop is going to freeze its buds off.

Jonathan. Oh, we don't have to keep Julius in the refrigerator.

He takes the preserve jar of aloe extract out of his pocket.

Jonathan (*Continued*). It's this—for my experiment. If you'll leave it in a sub-zero temperature for twelve hours, we'll find out if it really works.

Donatello hands Julius to Jonathan and takes the aloe jar.

Donatello (*Studying the jar*). What's this-a monkey business?

Jonathan. Well, you see—

The explanation is cut short by the park band which cuts loose with a fanfare—fortissimo! A few hundred yards away, flood lights hit the sky. Drums roll. The fanfare segues into "Yankee Doodle." Jonathan turns to Donatello with question marks in his eyes.

Donatello. You hear that? That's our Yankee Doodlum DANDY!
Jonathan stares at the Italian bewildered. Donatello smiles.
   Donatello (*Continued*). Go look-a. I put your bug juice in the cooler.
Jonathan nods. THE CAMERA PANS OVER *as he goes out the door.*

127 TRUCKING SHOT—EXTERIOR DONATELLO'S—NIGHT

Jonathan comes out of the door, carrying Julius, and moves along with a crowd (about forty people in this shot) which, for the most part, is hurrying past him toward the band and the floodlights (off scene). THE CAMERA DOLLIES ALONG IN FRONT OF HIM. *The music comes to a brassy finale. Silence. Then a slow drum roll. Jonathan jumps up on the counter of a concession. He looks off. The crowd mills around below him.*

128 HIGH-ANGLE LONG SHOT—REVERSE ANGLE

The back of Jonathan's head and shoulders repeat the action of his coming into position on top of the counter. Beyond him, near the Hudson River, is an outdoor theatre. The seats seem to be filled. (Actually a very few people lighting matches will take care of this section.) CLOSER TO CAMERA, *an area about twenty feet square has been roped off with heavy white ropes. Park attendants and policemen keep the crowd from entering the space. The crowd that shows is jammed against these ropes. A smaller crowd is moving from the foreground toward the roped-off area. (The silhouette of Jonathan's head and back eliminates the necessity of another space being filled with people. Something under a hundred extras should do the whole trick, if the shot is carefully planned in advance.) Above the roped-off square is a slack wire, supported by two columns of steel framework capped by fringed platforms with white railings around three sides. A white rope ladder dangles from the nearer platform. A tiny figure (a double) in white tights, a sequined bodice, and a ballet tutu, feathered like an overblown dandelion, begins to climb the ladder in the beams thrown by the floodlights. As the girl ascends, an announcer's voice blares out over the park loudspeaker.*

   Announcer's voice. La–dies and gentlemen! Your attention, please! You are about to witness one of the most dazzling feats of skill and daring ever seen. Watch her! Watch that exquisite mite of thistledown. There she goes. Up and up till she reaches that platform—*thirty feet about the ground, and no net beneath her!*

129 CLOSE SHOT—JONATHAN—REVERSE ANGLE

We are shooting up at Jonathan. A few heads are in the foreground. The concession roof and the park lights are behind him. The announcer's voice continues over the scene.

> **Announcer's voice.** She's going to make it! The foremost slack wire artist in the world—DANDY LYON.

The off-scene crowd bursts into applause.

130 FULL FIGURE SHOT—DANDY

She arrives on the platform. An attendant steadies her and hands her a closed parasol. As the applause rises in a crescendo, Dandy kisses her hand to the crowd.

131 CLOSE-UP—JONATHAN

He watches the vision with rapt attention. (Note: take enough footage for several reactions.)

> **Announcer's voice.** I thank you. On behalf of Dandy Lyon, I thank you. Miss Lyon was brought to you from the Greatest Show on Earth by that prince of showmen—Larry Ellis.

132 CLOSE SHOT—DANDY

She tests the wire, resins her shoes, etc., as the crowd simmers down and the announcer continues.

> **Announcer's voice.** And, ladies and gentlemen, this amazing artiste will dance upon that slender wire with absolutely no extra charge to you.

133 CLOSE SHOT—LARRY—AT BASE OF STEEL FRAMEWORK

One hand on the rope ladder, the other holding a box with rose stems sticking out from one end, Larry Ellis is looking up.

> **Announcer's voice.** Mr. Ellis presents this artiste of artistes as one of the many free features to which your fifty-cent admission ticket entitles you.

134 LONG SHOT—OVER JONATHAN'S SHOULDER

As before, Jonathan is watching Dandy's preparations as the crowd still mills around.

> **Announcer's voice.** And now I must ask you, one and all, to remain as quiet as you can while Miss Lyon is on the wire. One distracting sound might break her concentration and endanger her life. Are you ready, Dandy Lyon?

135 CLOSE SHOT—PLATFORM

The angle is from above, so that Dandy is close in the foreground, and the crowd below is in the shot. Dandy waves the closed parasol. The announcer's voice comes over.

Announcer's voice. She is ready! Remember please. Absolute silence—

Dandy turns her back and opens the parasol close to CAMERA. *The action blots out the scene. (During the next three seconds, as the parasol spins, the actress hands the spinning sunshade to the professional tightrope walker who is doubling for her, and the actress ducks down the ladder.)*

Announcer's voice. All right, Dandy Lyon. GO!

The parasol moves away from CAMERA, *revealing the full figure. It goes out on the wire. The wire goes away from* CAMERA *at a slight angle. (In this shot there is a net a few feet beneath the wire, but the net doesn't show in the camera angle—as in all so-called high-and-dizzy-safety-last shots.) As the figure goes away from us, it whips the parasol back and forth. White blossoms start falling from a net jiggled by two stagehands above. Once again, the drums roll.*

136 CLOSE-UP—JONATHAN

He takes a deep breath.

137 LONG SHOT—OVER JONATHAN'S BACK

The figure dances on the wire in the floodlights as the blossoms float down. (Note: the net is there but painted black—or we use a split screen shot. The figure bounces up and down in one spot so that the floodlights don't have to move.)

138 CLOSE SHOT—SPECTATORS

They are looking up, their faces tense.

139 FULL FIGURE—DANDY (STUDIO SHOT)

*(This is the real actress. The black sky is behind her. Actually, Dandy is standing on a springboard covered with black velvet. Along the toward-*CAMERA *edge of the springboard, a white rope runs under a black nail. The* CAMERA LENS *is on the exact level of the rope. Therefore, when Dandy walks and the springboard goes up and down with her weight, she seems to be on the rope, because the nail makes it follow the movement of the springboard.) Dandy, her parasol whipping back and forth for balance, executes several difficult movements on the wire. The white blossoms flutter through the floodlighted area. (Note: all these studio shots will be taken later, after the sequence is cut, so that we can match the lighting, etc.)*

140 CLOSE-UP (FLASH)

Jonathan is watching.

141 CLOSE-UP (FLASH)

Larry looking up.

142 CLOSE SHOT

Another crowd of spectators watching.

143 LONG SHOT—OVER JONATHAN'S BACK

Jonathan jumps down and starts toward the nearer platform—the one where Larry is standing.

144 MEDIUM SHOT—LOW ANGLE—JONATHAN

He repeats the action of shot 143. Only a few heads are in the foreground.

145 FULL FIGURE—DANDY (STUDIO SHOT)

The real Dandy starts to do a split. The announcer's voice comes over.

Announcer's voice. Miss Lyon is attempting a feat never executed by any other artiste in the world. A split and a pull-up to her feet on the wire. I must ask you not to applaud until Dandy Lyon has recovered her balance on the slack wire. Quiet *please!*

146 SHOOTING DOWN FROM ABOVE—DOUBLE

*The real wire walker does the trick with the out-of-*CAMERA-ANGLE *net below her, and the crowd at the edge of the roped-off space in the shot.*

147 CLOSE SHOT—LARRY—AT BASE OF FRAMEWORK

Larry is still looking up. Jonathan comes into the shot behind him.

148 FULL FIGURE—DANDY (STUDIO SHOT)

Dandy finished the pull-up from the split and starts for the platform.

149 HIGH SHOT—DOWN—DOUBLE

The double dances toward the platform and lands on it. The crowd starts to applaud—a thunderous burst of approval.

150 CLOSE-UP—DANDY (STUDIO)

A waist figure. Dandy lands on the platform, grabbing the rail and bowing as the applause becomes deafening. She starts down the ladder.

151 MEDIUM LONG SHOT—FROM LOW ANGLE

The double starts down the ladder.

152 CLOSE SHOT SHOOTING DOWN—LARRY AND JONATHAN

As the applause continues, it is augmented by horns and ratchets. Larry notices Jonathan looking up. He pulls Jonathan closer. Larry has to yell to be heard.

Larry. Ever see anyone like her?

Jonathan shakes his head.

Larry (*Continued*). And you never will. The world's greatest.

Jonathan manages to nod. Larry tightens his grip on Jonathan's arm.

Larry (*Continued*). Come on over to the dressing room, when you've said hello to your folks. They're knocking the yokels dead at the House of Wonders.

Jonathan nods again and looks up.

153 MEDIUM LONG SHOT

THE CAMERA IS TILTED UP *at the real Dandy, who is coming down the ladder.* IT TILTS GRADUALLY DOWN *as it follows her descent. When the shot includes Larry and Jonathan, the latter loses his nerve and backs away, out of the shot. Larry helps Dandy down. The crowd breaks through the ropes and surrounds Dandy and Larry.*

154 MEDIUM SHOT—CANDY BUTCHER'S CONCESSION

Jonathan backs into the scene. A flying wedge of autograph fiends dashes toward Dandy, waving their books. A big man's shoulder hits Jonathan as the man is shoved back. Jonathan ricochets against the candy butcher's counter. As he tightens his grip on Julius, he comes face to face with the candy pull machine and an amazing collection of confection—from salt water taffy to the pièce de resistance—*Dandy Lyon Lollipops (fluffy skirt and all). Jonathan looks back toward Dandy.*

155 MEDIUM SHOT—DANDY AND LARRY

They escape from the autograph fiends and go off toward Dandy's dressing room.

156 CLOSE SHOT—JONATHAN AND CANDY BUTCHER

Jonathan beckons the white-coated concessionaire closer. The man has a smart-cracker's face. He leans toward Jonathan.

    Jonathan (*Breathlessly*). Could you make me something special?
    Candy butcher. Just name it, son.
    Jonathan. Er—perhaps I'd better draw a picture for you.

Jonathan puts Julius on the counter, reaches out for a paper bag, and begins to draw. While he is doing this, the candy butcher goes on talking.

    Candy butcher. Go right ahead, all day sucker—go right ahead.

157 MEDIUM CLOSE SHOT—INTERIOR DANDY'S DRESSING ROOM

Dandy has taken off her costume and is putting on her street make-up. She wears a dressing gown. Larry's long-stemmed American beauties are in the foreground, with Larry's card sticking out of the envelope. Larry is facing Dandy, leaning close.

    Larry. Here I go again, darling—
    Dandy (*Gently*). Larry. I promised I'd tell you Wednesday. And I will.

Larry. This feels like Wednesday.
Dandy puts down the lipstick. Her eyes are thoughtful. Larry leans close.
    Larry. Darling. Don't make me wait any longer.
He kisses Dandy as the CAMERA MOVES TO A TIGHT TWO-SHOT. *He kisses Dandy's hair, her eyes, her lips. Dandy kisses back. The loose end of Larry's necktie dangles into an open box of face powder. As they separate, Dandy sees the powder on the tie. She picks up a wad of crumpled Kleenex and rubs the tie with it. The rubbing leaves a smear of lipstick. They both look at it. The tie is a mess. Larry grins. Then he opens one of the dressing table drawers. Dandy takes out a plain blue tie.*
    Dandy. This one?

158 CLOSE TWO-SHOT—FAVORING LARRY

Larry whips off the ruined tie and starts putting on the blue one.
    Larry. What I said still goes. That license is burning a hole in my pocket. Don't make me wait, Dandy.
He turns to her, his fingers knotting the tie. Dandy helps him.
    Dandy (*Gently*). So it's Wednesday. So it's yes.
Larry holds her close.
    Larry. I'm so crazy about you—so crazy. I just can't believe this. Cross your heart.
    Dandy (*Her eyes shine*). You cross it.
Larry traces a cross on Dandy's heart and holds her close.
    Larry. I'll call Judge Conovan tonight. He's a bit miffed at us for calling it off the last time.

159 CLOSE TWO-SHOT—FAVORING DANDY

Dandy draws a little bit away from Larry.
    Dandy. I haven't changed my mind about being married up there on the platform—as if it were a publicity stunt. That's still out.
    Larry (*Frowning*). Please, darling, don't start that all over again.
    Dandy. I know that press-agent look.
    Larry. What press-agent look?
    Dandy. Oh, I suppose Scoop Kenton did the dirty work, but *you* put the idea in his head.

160 CLOSE SHOT—FAVORING LARRY

Larry is angry, but he knows he is in a tough spot. He throws his best punch.

Larry. All right. All right. What if I did? Is it so horrible that I want to give you things—publicity as well as roses—

161 CLOSE SHOT—FAVORING DANDY

She is beginning to weaken, but she won't give Larry the satisfaction of knowing it. He goes right on.

Larry. You're an artist. You live on publicity—and anyway, that's not the point.

Dandy (*Coldly*). What is the point?

Larry. Just this—I want everyone to know I'm marrying the most wonderful girl in the world.

Dandy seems for a moment to have been persuaded. Then her mouth tightens and she gets up.

162 MEDIUM SHOT

Dandy rises and begins to walk angrily back and forth. Larry watches her.

Dandy. Who—incidentally—can be seen every night at Larry Ellis's Palisades Park—and for only FIFTY CENTS—plus tax.

Larry. Dandy!

Dandy. And who is now mine—all mine—signed on the dotted line. Unquote. No, thank you. I won't be your favorite freak. And I'm getting a headache! And I've got another performance—so, please stop it—or this time, I'll *break* my leg!

Larry rises angrily, grabs Dandy by the shoulder, and whirls her around so that she is facing him.

Larry. The way you twist things.

163 CLOSE SHOT—LARRY AND DANDY

Larry goes on, but tenderly.

Larry. You know what I want—all I want.

Dandy. Tell me.

Larry. This.

He kisses her. Someone knocks. They keep right on kissing.

164 MEDIUM SHOT—INTERIOR HALLWAY OUTSIDE DRESSING ROOM

Jonathan is standing facing the door, his back to CAMERA. *One hand has just knocked. In the crook of that arm is Julius. In the other hand, conspicuously displayed behind his back, is the chrysanthemum that the candy butcher dreamed up from Jonathan's drawing.* THE CAMERA DOLLIES IN CLOSE. *The flower is made from spun taffy. It is attached to a long wire stem, wrapped with green tissue paper, and it sports a cluster of artificial leaves. Jonathan knocks again. After a moment,*

Larry opens the door. Dandy is close behind him. Larry is fiddling with his tie. There is a smear of lipstick on his collar.

Larry. Johnny! Come on in.

Jonathan hesitates a moment, then enters the room.

165 PAN SHOT—INTERIOR DANDY'S DRESSING ROOM

The angle starts as a reverse of the last scene. As Larry ushers Jonathan into the room toward the dressing table, the dialogue continues.

Larry. What's with your Ma and Pa?

Jonathan doesn't answer. Dandy comes to his rescue.

Dandy. Sit down, Johnny. Larry has something to tell you.

Jonathan shakes his head and remains standing. Larry takes the ball.

Larry. Gosh. That's right.

He puts his arm around Dandy.

Larry (*Continued*). You probably guessed it anyway. But we just gave it a date. Next Wednesday—wedding bells!

166 CLOSE-UP—JONATHAN

His face shows almost nothing—except the eyes. Larry's voice comes over the shot.

Larry's voice. We're celebrating in my office in fifteen minutes. Just us and our closest friends.

167 MEDIUM SHOT—THE THREE

Dandy picks up where Larry left off.

Dandy. You're the first one we've told, Johnny. You've *got* to come to the party.

Jonathan is still silent. He walks over and puts the chrysanthemum on the dressing table. Larry's discarded tie is right next to it. The roses are at the end of the table.

168 CLOSE-UP—LARRY'S TIE

The shot is close enough so that it is perfectly obvious that the tie is smeared with lipstick and powder. THE CAMERA SWINGS OVER *and shows the open drawer containing the other ties.*

169 CLOSE-UP—JONATHAN

He stares at what he sees, then turns and faces Dandy.

Jonathan. I—I wish you every happiness.

He starts out of the shot.

170 MEDIUM SHOT—THE THREE

Jonathan walks out of the room, clutching Julius. Dandy and Larry look down at the silly-looking candy flower on the table between them.
DISSOLVE TO

171 GENERAL VIEW—INTERIOR HOUSE OF WONDERS—NIGHT

Ma and Pa Boone's booth is in the foreground. Next to it, Lilian, the hooch dancer, is giving out with a grind and a bump. On the other side is Barbarola, the Bearded Lady. A "talker" (a barker in the old days) is spieling as he indicates the Boones with his cane. Ma and Pa are busily signing reproductions of Ma's picture that Dandy showed Jonathan in the Lincoln. (The shot is from behind the "talker." Behind him [off scene] is the entrance. The shot is confined enough so that twenty or thirty extras will cover the action.)

> **The talker.** And now, folks, Betsy Boone, the only woman in the world who can catch a rabbit on the run! The real eighth wonder of the world. She can run like a deer and jump fences like a steeplechase thoroughbred. Okay, Betsy Boone, let's go!

While the talker is spieling, Pa takes a rabbit out of the crate and puts it on the edge of the platform with some lettuce. Meanwhile, Ma has risen and walked back a few steps behind a prop rail fence that goes diagonally across the platform.

172 CLOSE-UP—MA

She hitches her shoulders and takes off.

173 GENERAL VIEW

Ma (a double) does the same fence vault Dandy saw at Boonesville, except that this time, just as her legs are parallel with the top fence rail, Ma clicks her heels together in midair and lands on her feet. The top rail falls off. Ma goes for the lettuce-eating bunny. It escapes into the crowd. Ma dives after it. There is a flurry amongst the spectators' legs as Ma disappears. A couple of women squeal and scream. Ma's head reappears. She holds the rabbit aloft by the scruff of its neck. Those members of the crowd who have not been personally assaulted applaud loudly.

> **The talker.** That's right, folks! A big hand for Bounding Betsy Boone! And step up! Step up, while Mrs. Boone autographs her photographs for ten cents—one dime—one-tenth of a dollar!

As Ma sits down and starts autographing, Jonathan comes into the shot behind the talker. He is thinking about what happened in Dandy's dressing room, and his attitude shows it.

> **The talker** (*Continued*). Who else wants a picture? Come on, folks! Step right up! Some day the autograph of this amazing WONDER WOMAN—just brought here for your entertainment and edification by that great showman, Larry Ellis—will be worth a fortune.

174 CLOSE-UP—MA AND PA

Ma is signing. Pa is shuffling the pictures as though they were an oversized deck of cards. Ma looks up and sees Jonathan.

175 CLOSE-UP—JONATHAN

He smiles a greeting but his heart isn't in it.

176 MEDIUM SHOT—MA AND PA

Ma beckons to Jonathan. He comes into the scene.

Ma (*As she signs a picture*). What's the matter, son?

Jonathan. Nothing, Ma—

Ma regards Jonathan quizzically. Embarrassed, he walks back to the fence and picks up the fallen rail. At this moment, the talker's voice comes over the scene.

The talker. Just a minute, folks. Another Wonder of Wonders! His performance is now going on. Right over there, folks. The man with the gimlet eye—Marko the Great!

Pa and Ma, Jonathan, and the group around them, look off.

177 FULL SHOT—MARKO'S STAGE

Marko's platform is bigger than the rest. Several folding chairs have been set up in front of it. Some of the spectators are in the chairs. A few are standing and some more wander into the scene. A big column in the left foreground cuts off a segment of the side seats. (Fifty extras should cover the longest shot.) Marko has hypnotized Briggs. Marko snaps his fingers. Briggs comes out of it. He looks around bewildered. The customers laugh and applaud.

178 CLOSE SHOT—MA AND PA

The few remaining spectators walk away toward Marko's platform. The Boones watch the hypnotist. Applause and music over the scene.

179 CLOSE-UP—JONATHAN

Still fiddling with the fence rail, Jonathan looks toward Marko.

180 MEDIUM SHOT—MARKO'S PLATFORM

Marko takes a bow and leads Briggs behind a screen. The hypnotist's hand appears above the hiding place and fires a revolver. The screen sways and topples over. A miniature guillotine is revealed. A masked Marko, his hand on the instrument of death, is looking down at Briggs's head, which is rolling back and forth in the basket below the blade of the guillotine. The headless body is kneeling. The crowd gasps. At this moment, another gunshot comes from behind them. They turn and look back.

181 CLOSE SHOT—THE BOONES (A FLASH)

The Boones react to the shot. They, too, turn toward the area behind the crowd.

182 PAN SHOT—MARKO'S AUDIENCE

We are close on a reverse angle of the column we saw in the LONG SHOT. *A second Marko and a second Briggs appear from behind the column. Marko's revolver is still smoking. The two men hurry down the aisle as the* CAMERA PANS WITH THEM. *When they arrive on the platform, we realize that the onstage Marko and the beheaded Briggs are wax dummies. Marko shakes his wax image to show the audience what it is. The crowd applauds as Marko bows and starts down the platform steps.*

183 MEDIUM SHOT—THE BOONES

Still by the fence in the extreme background, Jonathan turns from watching Marko and gives the fence rail his attention again. Lilian, the hooch dancer, joins Ma and Pa. Pa looks at the collection of unsigned pictures and the deserted foreground.

> **Pa**. Huh! What's Dracula got that we hain't?
>
> **Lilian**. Your customers.

Pa gives Lilian a nasty look. A woman with a child ambles by. Pa beckons them to come closer with one hand. With the other, he gives his version of Marko's hypnotic gestures. He screws up his face. He out-Draculas Dracula. The woman screams, clasps her child to her bosom, and flees in terror. Pa snaps his fingers in disgust. Jonathan has finished with the fence. He comes down to the foreground.

184 CLOSER SHOT

Ma reaches out and touches Jonathan's arm.

> **Ma**. What is it, son?

Jonathan doesn't answer. Marko walks into the scene. Pa eyes him suspiciously.

> **Marko** (*To Jonathan*). Dandy telephoned me just before I went on.

Jonathan nods. Marko turns.

> **Marko** (*Continued, to Lilian*). We're invited to Larry's office to toast the lucky couple—(*To Jonathan.*) Coming, Lochinvar?

Jonathan can't take it. He shakes his head and walks off in the direction of Donatello's back door. Marko shrugs and turns to Lilian.

> **Marko** (*Continued*). I simply love short engagements. No presents till the wedding. Come, lovely Lilian.

He offers his arm to Lilian. They exit. Ma and Pa exchange glances and look after the departed Jonathan.

185 MEDIUM SHOT—DOOR TO DONATELLO'S

Four or five House of Wonders customers with balloons, kids, et al., walk by as Jonathan enters the scene. The upper half of the florist's door is glass, so that we can see some of the florist's shop inside. On the lower half of the door is a sign, EMERGENCY EXIT ONLY. *Jonathan tries the door. It opens. He goes inside.*

186 LONG SHOT—FLORIST'S SHOP—REVERSE ANGLE

Donatello is in the foreground near the entrance door, which is BEHIND CAMERA. *The Italian is raising a bottle of Chianti to his reflection in the mirror near the door. He is singing his own somewhat screwed-up version of "Brown October Ale" from* Robin Hood *by Reginald de Koven and Harry B. Smith. In the extreme background, Jonathan comes through the door connecting with the House of Wonders. He is still carrying Julius. Donatello doesn't notice him. His voice drowns out the sound of the door opening and closing.*

187 MEDIUM CLOSE SHOT—INTERIOR FLORIST'S SHOP

Jonathan sinks into a chair and sets Julius down on a table on which there are some plants and a bottle. Donatello's voice comes over the scene.

    Donatello's voice. No stars above me.
                     She does not love me.
                     Can't-a face tomorrow.
                     Must-a drown my sorrow
                     In brown October ale!

The high notes become a gurgle as Donatello downs the Chianti. During the song, Jonathan reaches out to change Julius's position. His fingers touch the bottle on the table.

188 CLOSE-UP—THE BOTTLE AND JONATHAN'S FINGERS

The bottle contains a sticky liquid much darker than the aloe extract. It bears a label, "Mattison's SNAIL KILLER.*"*

189 CLOSE SHOT—JONATHAN

Jonathan studies the label as Donatello's voice reprises the last line with a Shubert finale.

    Donatello's voice. In brown October ale!

Jonathan shudders, pushes the bottle aside as though to resist the temptation to drink it, and sinks his chin in his hands. Off scene, the front door closes. Jonathan doesn't hear it. His eyes wander over to Julius.

190 CLOSE-UP—JULIUS

The parsnip has apparently been affected by the heat and the general crushing Jonathan has unconsciously given it during the lugging around. Its buds look sickly, its long leaves are drooping. Petals from the largest bud fall to the table.

191 MEDIUM CLOSE SHOT—JONATHAN

He reaches out and pulls the potted plant close to him. A few more petals, and some of the smaller leaves, fall off. Automatically, Jonathan reaches for the pocket that held the aloe jar. Suddenly, he realizes that Donatello put it in the refrigerator. He gets up quickly and turns to the front door. The CAMERA LEAVES JONATHAN, SWINGS OVER, *and shows that the shop is deserted. Jonathan comes running into the scene, shouting as he hurries to the door.*

Jonathan. Mr. Donatello! The extract!

192 MEDIUM SHOT—FRONT DOOR

Jonathan runs in and throws open the front door. The street is deserted except for one or two passersby. Donatello is nowhere to be seen. Jonathan hesitates, then closes the door. He walks quickly out of the shot toward the rear of the store.

193 MEDIUM SHOT—TABLE NEAR REAR DOOR

Jonathan enters and picks up the potted plant. He studies the bare expanse of leafless stem and mutters half to himself, as he pats the empty pocket again.

Jonathan. Stuff wouldn't work anyway. Not cold enough yet.

Jonathan moves over to the closet with Julius. He searches the shelves and finds a can of fertilizer. He pokes some into the dirt around Julius and pours a glass of water over the dirt.

194 CLOSE SHOT—MAIN DOOR—HOUSE OF WONDERS

On the street outside, we get a glimpse, between two of the easel posters, of the ticket seller and a few people. Dandy comes through the door, looks around, sees what she's looking for, and exits.

195 MEDIUM CLOSE SHOT—BOONES' BOOTH

Ma and Pa are involved in autograph signing as Dandy comes up to them. There are about fifteen people in the shot.

Dandy. Hello.

Ma and Pa look up.

Pa (*Still harboring his "flirt" grudge*). Marryin' the money, huh?

196 CLOSE-UP—DANDY

Pa's jibe infuriates her.

Dandy. I'm marrying the man I love.

She turns away.

197 CLOSE SHOT—INTERIOR FLORIST'S SHOP—EMERGENCY EXIT DOOR
Dandy comes up to the door and looks through the glass upper half. Behind her, a few people are moving about. The rest of the House of Wonders fades away into blackness and the misty realm of the out of focus.

198 MEDIUM SHOT—DONATELLO'S—INTERIOR
This is from Dandy's point of view. Jonathan is finishing with his emergency treatment of Julius. He puts the potted plant on one of the shelves, turns an electric fan on so that it cools the interior, and reaches out for the light switch.

199 OVER-SHOULDER SHOT—DANDY
Dandy's head and shoulders are in the foreground. Beyond her, inside the shop, Jonathan finishes turning off the switch. All the lights, except an overhead night light near the entrance, go out. Jonathan walks away from CAMERA *toward the entrance. He stops in front of the mirror.*

200 CLOSE-UP—DANDY
Her face pressed against the glass, she watches Jonathan.

201 CLOSE SHOT—JONATHAN
He reaches up for the dangling beaded cord that controls the one remaining light. Then he stops and looks at himself in the mirror. It is Dandy's boutonniere that has caught his eye. He fingers it, inhales its fragrances, detaches it, and drops it into the wastepaper basket. Then he reaches up again for the light string.

202 OVER-SHOULDER SHOT—FROM OUTSIDE SHOP
Dandy is in the foreground. Jonathan pulls the light cord. The shop goes black. The only illumination is from the street. Jonathan goes out, closing the door.

203 CLOSE-UP—DANDY
She reacts to what she has seen.
FADE OUT
FADE IN

204 CLOSE SHOT—INTERIOR LARRY'S OFFICE—DAY
The office has the modern appointments that the exterior suggested. Larry is at his desk telephoning. He holds an open jewel case in one hand. We cannot see what is in it.

    Larry (*Excited, grinning*). Freddy Blenheim, you're a genius. You did it. And overnight! No kidding, she's going to love it. I know, I know—but I'm not going to wait till Wednesday. M-m-m—m-m-m.

She gets it this afternoon—(*A rap on the door.*) the minute she steps off that wire.

Larry turns toward the door (off scene).

205 PAN SHOT—OFFICE DOOR

It opens and Dandy comes in.

Dandy. Hi, character!

She sees Larry is talking and closes the door. Larry's voice comes over the scene.

Larry's voice (*Complete change of tone to business is business*). That's right, Frederick. I'll discuss it with you later. 'Bye.

The receiver clicks as Larry hangs up.

Larry's voice. 'Lo, character.

The CAMERA IS PANNING WITH DANDY *as she crosses to Larry. When Dandy arrives, he is closing the top drawer of the desk.*

Dandy. What are you hiding, character?

Larry. Don't be so snoopy, character—we're not married yet.

Dandy. So, it's my last chance. After Wednesday, you'll beat me if I snoop.

Larry (*Reaching for the drawer*). Okay. One kiss—one snoop.

Dandy sits on his lap. Someone bangs on the door.

Kenton's voice. Open up, boss. I'm hotter'n a pistol.

Larry (*Talking as he kisses Dandy*). Get lost, Scoop, I'm busy.

206 PAN SHOT—THE DOOR

It opens again and Scoop Kenton, the park press agent, bursts in.

Dandy's voice (*Also kissing*). Scoop Kenton—you're fired!

Scoop crosses to the desk. THE CAMERA PANS WITH HIM.

Scoop. Get her. (*To Larry.*) Matter of fact, I want a bonus. The newsreel cameras are going to shoot the whole service. Right up on that platform—

Dandy rises from Larry's lap and gives him an icy stare. When she turns to Scoop, her eyes are blazing.

Dandy. You tell your sharpshooters to stay in New York.

Scoop (*Flabbergasted*). Wh—what? You mean no pictures *at all*?

Dandy. That's right. No pictures—no keyhole peekers—NO PUBLICITY.

Larry. Now, wait a minute—

Dandy (*Not even looking at Larry*). In fact, no wedding!

She dashes for the door. The CAMERA PANS WITH HER. *She goes out. The door slams.*

207 CLOSE SHOT—LARRY AND SCOOP
Larry whips open the drawer and grabs the jewel case.
> **Scoop.** Will you tell me—?
> **Larry.** Tell you nothing. I'll break your neck!

He exits quickly from the scene.
> **Scoop.** Well, shut my mouth!

Scoop emphatically closes his mouth. Simultaneously, the door slams (off scene). Scoop reacts to the sound effect.

208 LONG SHOT—EXTERIOR ADMINISTRATION BUILDING
Larry comes out with the jewel case and looks frantically for Dandy. He sees someone and calls out.
> **Larry.** Barton!

Barton, the park detective, enters the scene.
> **Larry** (*Continued*) Seen Miss Lyon come out here?
> **Barton.** No, Mr. Ellis. Oh! Congratulations.
> **Larry.** Yeah.

He walks off in the opposite direction from Barton's entrance.

209 DOLLY SHOT—INTERIOR FLORIST'S SHOP
The CAMERA *is close on Julius. Jonathan's fingers hold a razor blade with which he is peeling back the bark from the leafless section of the parsnip's stem. Donatello's hands hold the aloe jar in a dish of cracked ice. His baritone comes over the scene. He is humming Mendelssohn's "Spring Song." As the* CAMERA PULLS BACK, *Jonathan finishes the peeling, dips some cotton in the aloe jar, and makes an ice pack around the stem. Jonathan talks as he works.*
> **Jonathan.** Gosh! I'm so excited I haven't even thanked you.
> **Donatello.** For what?
> **Jonathan.** For helping me save a life.
> **Donatello.** You mean to tell me this-a weed could still grow something?
> **Jonathan.** We'll know in a few hours.

He walks over to the icebox that holds cut flowers and puts Julius inside. Donatello follows him, his eyes suddenly shrewd.
> **Donatello.** You take out a patent for this invention?
> **Jonathan.** Not yet. It isn't ready. Besides, that takes money—lawyers—you know.
> **Donatello.** Listen, Giovanni, my little mushroom. This business we make-a together could-a maybe make-a lotta Mazola for us.

Jonathan (*Nodding enthusiastically*). And what it's going to do for flora!

Donatello. Who's-a she?

Jonathan (*Smiling*). Flora's Latin for plants. This aloe might even cure animals and people—if you think they're important.

Donatello (*Regarding the jar in his hand*). Plenty important! When they're us. Look-a, my little cucumber, I put aloha downstairs. You keep flora upstairs.

He starts for the cellar door, then pauses.

Donatello (*Continued*). You need-a money now. Just to get started. Maybe two—three hundred smackers fix everything. When I come up, we talk-a business.

As he vanishes, Jonathan looks toward the front door. He reacts with astonishment at what he sees.

210 FULL FIGURE SHOT—DANDY

She comes through the front door in a hurry. The CAMERA PANS WITH HER *as she rushes breathlessly up to Jonathan and smiles sweetly.*

Dandy. How about a snack?

Jonathan's face is as blank as the first check in a bride's bankbook.

Jonathan. But—

Dandy (*Smiling happily*). I broke the engagement.

Jonathan. But—

Dandy. Stop butting. I'm famished. (*Another smile.*) How about a weenie?

Jonathan. But of course. I—love weenies. I'm famished myself.

Dandy (*Kidding*). Then come on. Wet a giggle on!

They hurry out of the scene.

DISSOLVE TO

211 NEWSREEL SHOT—EXTERIOR TRACK MEET

Three quarter milers are fighting for the inside spot around a curve. Just as we are wondering what the hell this has to do with the picture—

DISSOLVE TO

212 INTERIOR RESTAURANT AND BAR—STUDIO SET

We are shooting toward a corner of the bar. The television set, which is at one end of the bar at a catty-corner angle, shows the track meet. The quarter milers are legging it at top speed. There are just a few people on the bar stools.

213 MEDIUM SHOT—ENTRANCE DOORS

The closed double doors swing open. Jonathan and Dandy come in. They start forward, leaving the doors open, as the announcer's voice from the television set comes over the scene.

    Announcer's voice. They've rounded the curve. Bradshaw, the Yale flash, is leading. Hammersmith of the University of Virginia is right behind him. Yowie! Those boys are really going places.

Jonathan's face takes on a collegiate cheering-section look. He moves forward and stops just beyond a window, through which we see a restricted view of the street outside. Dandy follows him. The CAMERA PANS *with them. The television set is not in the shot. Dandy looks toward the window. Outside, Larry Ellis appears and pauses in profile, looking down the street for Dandy.*

    Announcer's voice (*Continued*). It's the home stretch! Hammersmith is pulling up from behind. Shades of Mel Patton, what a finish! It's—it's—Hammersmith! Yes, sir! The University of Virginia boy broke the tape just two feet ahead of Bradshaw.

Jonathan barely suppresses a cheer. He turns to Dandy. She moves toward him and contrives to stumble, emitting the same little yip she did in Boonesville.

    Jonathan (*The smile vanishing*). Your ankle?
    Dandy (*Nodding with faked pain*). I'd better sit down.

On Jonathan's arm, she hobbles toward the nearest table, near the bar. Larry walks away from the window. The CAMERA FOLLOWS *Dandy and Jonathan as she sinks into a chair.*

    Dandy (*Continued*). Rub it!

Jonathan's back is to the entrance when he kneels. As soon as Jonathan goes to work, Dandy sneaks a hopeful look at the window, and then at the entrance (off scene). She pulls her skirt up.

214 EXTERIOR RESTAURANT—GENERAL VIEW—STUDIO SHOT

Larry comes around the corner and walks toward the wide open entrance. THE CAMERA PANS WITH HIM. *He is again in profile when he reaches the entrance. He looks up at the sign, "Silver Slipper," above the door. Dandy looks expectantly toward the entrance. Larry steps forward to look inside. As he does so, a portly waitress moves between him and Dandy. The waitress puts one hand on the back of the chair and bends over, offering help. The applause from the television drowns out her voice. Larry scans the restaurant, turns away, and stands a moment in the doorway.*

215 CLOSER SHOT

Dandy's head appears from behind the waitress. She snaps her fingers in anger over the failure of her trick. Jonathan looks up at her. She assumes an expression of pain and closes her eyes. Jonathan looks toward the door.

216 REVERSE ANGLE—DOORWAY

Larry's back. He exits in the direction from which he came.

217 CLOSE-UP—JONATHAN

He smiles grimly and continues rubbing.

DISSOLVE TO

218 PAN SHOT—INTERIOR FLORIST'S SHOP

Donatello comes up from the cellar, closes the door, and turns, smiling, expecting to see Jonathan. The smile fades.

Donatello. Johnny!

He starts for the entrance door. The CAMERA PANS *with him.*

Donatello (*Continued*). Giovanni!

Donatello stops in the doorway as he is confronted by Larry, who steps in from the street.

Larry. Seen Dandy, Joe?

Donatello (*All smiles again*). Not since it's-a happen, you lucky boss man. *Con amore!* Congratulations!

Larry. Yeah. Where's Johnny Boone?

Donatello. You take-a the words right out of my mouth. He's-a vanish. You know what? My little Giovanni, he's-a gonna make a million dollars!

Larry. That Blue Ridge sapling?

Donatello. Yessiree, sir. That-a mountain billy and I—we got something *big*! Sit down!

He practically pushes Larry into a chair, closes the door, and pulls up another chair for himself.

DISSOLVE TO

219 MEDIUM SHOT—INTERIOR RESTAURANT AND BAR

(*Note: the following scene was designed for a definite song, to be shown on the television screen in the café. It is not given footage here because to describe a song is impossible. It has to be heard with the name singer who will present it.*) *The angle takes in Dandy and Jonathan and a part of the bar. Dandy's chair is nearer the bar. A song comes over the television. Jonathan is toying with the mustard.*

Jonathan (*Wise to her trick*). How's your ankle?

Dandy (*Smiling*). Good as new. What a technique, Dr. Boone!

Jonathan. Thank you.

Jonathan gestures toward her with his mustard paddle.

Jonathan (*Continued*). And I should like to remark—

Dandy (*Indicating the television, off scene*) Sh–sh! Listen!

Jonathan lowers the mustard paddle and studies Dandy critically.

Jonathan. Dandy Lyon, you're a flea.

Dandy (*Startled*). Wh—what?

Jonathan (*Sternly*). You'll always jump from one man to another, just like a flea.

Dandy (*Infuriated*). Why—why—you BOTANIST!

Jonathan (*Unmoved by her outburst*). You asked me to bring you here. That was an act—for Larry's benefit—a flea circus—starring Dandy Lyon.

Dandy (*Angry, but impressed*). Johnny!

Jonathan rises. The CAMERA PULLS BACK. *Jonathan offers his arm to Dandy.*

Jonathan. Suppose we watch a professional performance. You might learn something.

Dandy slowly rises and apprehensively takes his arm.

DISSOLVE TO

220 CLOSE SHOT—SIGN

The sign that says, FLOTOW'S FLEA CIRCUS. *The* CAMERA PULLS BACK *and reveals that Dandy and Jonathan, with several other people, are looking down at the flea circus that is performing on a shoulder-high table, with a fluorescent light shining down on it. The booth is partially hooded over with a shed-like wooden canopy. The fluorescent light is used during the day. Jonathan points a finger and calls Dandy's attention to the microscopic performer.*

Jonathan. You see?

221 VERY CLOSE SHOT—FLEA ARENA

A costume flea, with a tiny wire fastened around its neck, is making prodigious jumps and turns.

Jonathan's voice. Look at her! Look at her jump!

222 THREE-SHOT—DANDY, JONATHAN, AND TRAINER

Flotow, a bushy-eyebrowed gent with humorous eyes, gives Jonathan a dirty look.

Flotow. *Her,* indeed! That's Alfred!

Dandy (*To Jonathan*). There you are, genius. You're the flea, jumping at conclusions.

Jonathan. That's not very funny. (*To the trainer.*) Haven't you any lady performers?

Flotow. Of course I have. Juanita, from Mexico. She's next. Dances a beautiful jota. Look here.

Flotow picks up a pair of tweezers and opens a small mother-of-pearl casket, stuffed with cotton. His performers can be seen wiggling in the cotton. The trainer reaches out with the tweezers.

Flotow (*Continued*). Come, come, Juanita.

223 VERY CLOSE SHOT

The tweezers pick up a skirted, sombrero-hatted flea, and hold it by the wire collar as it struggles.

Flotow's voice. Easy does it, darling.

224 GROUP SHOUT

As Jonathan studies Juanita, Dandy leans close to him. This time he is so fascinated by the spectacle that when Dandy presses his hand, he squeezes back.

Jonathan. Beautiful!

As Jonathan gives Dandy a smile, then turns to examine Juanita again, Dandy glances in the opposite direction.

225 MEDIUM SHOT—FUN HOUSE

Larry Ellis comes into the scene from the direction of Donatello's and looks around. Scoop Kenton runs up to him, and the two men go into a heated discussion. Together, they start walking toward CAMERA.

226 GROUP SHOT—FLEA CIRCUS

Dandy thinks quickly, opens her shoulder-strap bag, and drops it.

227 CLOSE SHOT—THE GROUND

The bag falls into the shot. The contents spill out.

228 CLOSE SHOT—DANDY AND JONATHAN

Dandy makes a face.

Dandy. Butterfingers!

She starts to bend down to retrieve the bag. Her elbow hits the casket with the fleas in it. It, too, falls out of the shot.

229 CLOSE SHOT—THE GROUND

The contents of Dandy's bag shows in the shot. The casket hits the ground. The top flies open.

Flotow's voice (*Indignantly*). Please, Miss Dandy! My actors!

Dandy's voice. Oh, I'm *sorry!*

The trainer's hand comes into the shot, closes the casket, and takes it up out of the scene.

230 THREE-SHOT—DANDY, JONATHAN, AND FLOTOW

Flotow's head comes up into the scene. Dandy shoots a quick glance at the approaching Larry and Scoop (off scene).

Dandy. Maybe somebody escaped.

She jerks Jonathan out of the shot with her.

Flotow (*Looking at Dandy below*). My artists don't leave me. They love me. (*Pointing to his bare forearm.*) In fact, they eat me up.

He gives out with a prop laugh.

231 LONGER SHOT

The spectators join in the laugh. We can just make out Dandy and Jonathan below the table. They start picking up the contents of Dandy's bag. Larry and Scoop walk by in the foreground without seeing them.

232 GROUP SHOT

Dandy and Jonathan come up into the scene. Dandy shoots a quick look in the direction taken by Larry as she stuffs her lipstick, etc., back into the bag. Flotow has put Juanita to work and is replacing Alfred in the casket. Jonathan looks down into the arena.

Jonathan. I take it all back. Juanita isn't jumping.

Dandy's eyes widen, as she sees something off.

233 MEDIUM LONG SHOT—ROW OF CONCESSIONS

Larry and Scoop are questioning one of the proprietors. Larry takes Scoop by the arm, and they start forward.

234 MEDIUM SHOT—DANDY, JONATHAN, AND FLOTOW

Dandy reacts to the approaching menace.

Dandy (*Indicating her ankle*). I'd like to sit down a minute.

Jonathan gives her a skeptical eye, but she urges him quickly around the shed-like canopy out of the shot. A moment later, Scoop and Larry walk by again. Meanwhile, Juanita finishes her act. The spectators applaud. Flotow picks up Juanita by the neck wire and deposits her in the casket as the CAMERA DOLLIES TO A CLOSE SHOT. *Flotow decides to make assurance double sure. He starts counting the fleas in the casket, using the tweezers as a pointer.*

Flotow. Alfred—Juanita—Geronimo—Cleopatra—Horace—Helen—

He pauses and scrutinizes the casket closely. His tone changes to one of deep concern.

Flotow (*Continued*). Helen?

He turns to the customers fiercely.

Flotow (*Continued*). Who snatched Helen?

The spectators stare at one another accusingly.

235 MEDIUM SHOT—LAWN FACING SQUIRREL CAGE OF LOVE

Dandy and Jonathan enter. The concession known as the SQUIRREL CAGE OF LOVE *is in the background. It consists of a series of circular cages with seats in them. These revolve, turning the occupants upside down. Above the concession a big sign says:*

HEAD OVER HEELS IN

The Squirrel Cage of

LOVE

In the foreground, Dandy and Jonathan, who is peeling off his coat, study the sign.

Dandy. You see, Johnny, Juanita found the *right* Mr. Flea. That's why she wasn't jumping.

Jonathan (*Reminiscently*). And what beautiful brown eyes!

Dandy. They're blue, and I just couldn't take them off Alfred's biceps.

Jonathan (*Not a serious reproof*). I wasn't talking about your eyes.

Dandy takes a quick look at Jonathan's upper arm, then looks right back into his eyes.

Dandy. I wasn't really talking about Alfred.

Jonathan's resistance weakens. He is embarrassed but flattered. He drops his eyes and fidgets with his tie, giving the biceps a minor workout. Dandy reaches out and feels the muscle.

Dandy. Hmmm. So round, so firm, so fully packed.

Dandy sits down on a park bench facing the concession. Jonathan joins her, tossing his coat over the back of the bench. He stares at the concession sign.

236 CLOSE SHOT—THE SIGN

The shot features the word, LOVE.

237 REVERSE ANGLE CLOSE SHOT—DANDY AND JONATHAN

Jonathan wriggles and scratches his shoulder. Now we know where Helen is.

Jonathan (*Looking at the sign*). Scratch to itch and itch to scratch. That's what Socrates said it was.

Dandy (*Completely puzzled*). Was what?

Jonathan. Love.

Dandy. Socrates was a broken-down old cynic.

Jonathan (*Pedantically*). Platonist.

Dandy. So what? Spell 'em both backwards and what've you got? Nothing!
Jonathan (*Spelling to himself*). G–N–I–H–T. Nothing?
Dandy. Right. Platonic love is what a guy tells a girl he's got when he can't get *her*.
Jonathan (*Indignantly*). Now, *that's* cynical.
Dandy. It's a fact.

Dandy shimmies and scratches her shoulder. Jonathan reaches for it tentatively.

Jonathan (*Chivalrously*). May I?
Dandy. Help yourself.

Jonathan gently scratches the shoulder blade with the sensitive fingers of both hands. He does this so decorously that he might be playing a harp solo at Carnegie Hall. Dandy squirms and indicates her back. In attempting to cover both areas, and with considerable help from Dandy, the massage develops into a minor wrestling match. It winds up as a Rodin-esque embrace. Dandy's next shimmy is definitely seductio ad absurdum. *Apparently, Helen hops back to Jonathan. His next reaction suggests a slow rumba. Dandy sighs luxuriously.*

Dandy. If you try to tell me this is Platonic, I'll never speak to you again.
Jonathan (*Rapturously*). It's wonderful.

What is going on on the bench looks definitely like a rumba performed sitting down.

238 CLOSER SHOT

Jonathan disengages himself. He slaps his left hip and indulges in a minor anatomical earthquake.

Dandy (*With inconsistent female logic*). Stop flirting.

Jonathan blushes and moves a foot or two away from Dandy.

239 LONGER SHOT—DANDY AND JONATHAN

Dandy wriggles her shoulder.

Dandy. Scratch me.

Jonathan moves closer and scratches. Dandy indicates her right arm.

Dandy (*Continued*). Here.

Jonathan obeys.

Dandy (*Continued*). Now here.

She wriggles the other shoulder. Jonathan complies.

Dandy (*Continued*). Both at once.

Jonathan goes to work once more with the fingers of both hands. THE CAMERA DOLLIES IN CLOSE. *Dandy gives her face a rabbit-like quiver.*

Dandy (*Continued*). Here.

She points to her cheek dangerously close to the mouth. Jonathan disengages his left hand from her right shoulder. Dandy shakes her head.

Dandy (*Continued*). All at once.

Jonathan pauses. He is stumped.

Jonathan. I—I've only got two hands.

Dandy. Use your imagination.

She turns the cheek toward him. Jonathan brushes it with his lips. Suddenly, the cheek becomes the mouth. Jonathan does the inevitable. After a moment, his lips leave Dandy's just enough for him to feel the full magnetism of her eyes. The look holds. Her shoulders quiver. Jonathan makes an embarrassed apology.

Jonathan. I stopped scratching.

Dandy. M-m-m.

Jonathan. I'm sorry.

240 LONGER SHOT

Jonathan makes a fatal mistake. He swings Dandy around away from him and goes vigorously, but impersonally, to work on her shoulder blades from the rear.

Jonathan. I'm terribly sorry.

Dandy's mood is shattered. Her eyes blaze.

Dandy (*Viciously*). You should be.

She rises quickly.

241 MEDIUM CLOSE SHOT—THE TWO

Dandy rises into the scene. Jonathan comes up and stands behind her, breathing like a bassoon player.

Jonathan. I didn't mean to go so far. I—I—it's a terribly ticklish business.

He goes to work again on the small of her delightfully small back, but with an almost hysterical enthusiasm. Dandy squeals like a stuck pig, whirls in her tracks, and smacks Jonathan's face.

242 CLOSE-UP—JONATHAN

His stunned reaction gradually changes to anger.

243 CLOSE-UP—DANDY

Still madder than the proverbial wet hen.

244 MEDIUM CLOSE SHOT

Jonathan steps forward, grabs Dandy, and gives her a vengeful kiss. Then he shoves her away from him. They stand facing each other, breathing heavily like two fighters at the end of a tough round. The CAMERA WHIPS AWAY AND HOLDS ON LARRY AND SCOOP KENTON. *They have obviously arrived in time to see the last few seconds of the round. The two men move slowly forward. The* CAMERA SWINGS WITH THEM AND PULLS BACK *until it includes all four of them. Dandy turns and sees them.*

Larry. Tell her, Scoop.

245 CLOSE-UP—SCOOP

The press agent's face is an open book. And its pages are stamped with honesty.

    Scoop. The pictures were strictly my idea, Dandy. Larry told me he'd fire me if I took them, but I just couldn't resist.

246 CLOSE-UP—DANDY

She studies Scoop's face.

    Dandy. If you're lying—

247 CLOSE FOUR-SHOT FAVORING DANDY

    Scoop. It's the truth, Dandy.

    Dandy (*After a long look*). O.K., Scoop.

Scoop breathes a sigh of relief and leaves the scene. Larry comes closer.

    Larry. You never did give me a chance to give you this.

He hands Dandy the jewel case and walks away. The CAMERA LEAVES THE OTHERS AND FOLLOWS HIM. *When he has taken a dozen steps, Dandy's voice comes over the scene.*

    Dandy's voice. Larry!

Larry stops, turns, and looks back at Dandy.

248 CLOSE TWO-SHOT

Dandy has the case open. She takes out the gift.

249 VERY CLOSE SHOT

Dandy's hands hold a diamond pendant on a platinum chain. The workmanship is exquisite, the diamond is fabulous. The CAMERA TILTS UP TO DANDY'S FACE. *Her eyes leave the pendant and look mistily at Larry (off scene).*

    Dandy (*Whispering*). Larry.

250 CLOSE SHOT—LARRY

He moves forward as the CAMERA SWINGS WITH HIM AND PULLS BACK *until it includes the three.*

    Dandy. You're crazy, Larry.

Larry. Sure. I told you.

Now it is Jonathan's turn to walk away. CAMERA FOLLOWS HIM. *Dandy's voice comes over the scene.*

Dandy's voice. Come back here.

Jonathan stops, turns, and comes back as the CAMERA MOVEMENT FOLLOWS HIM, *and the scene becomes a two-shot of Jonathan and Dandy.*

Dandy (*Vengefully*). Have you ever seen anything so beautiful?

Jonathan clenches his teeth. He must be honest.

Jonathan. No.

He looks up from the pendant. His eyes find Dandy's. He corrects himself.

Jonathan. Yes—yes, I have.

251 CLOSE THREE-SHOT

Dandy is still too angry to accept Jonathan's belated attempt to reinstate himself. She hands Larry the case and tries to bring the platinum clasp together behind her neck. Her fingers fumble the job. She throws her next remark over her shoulder at Jonathan.

Dandy. You do it, Johnny.

Jonathan does the best he can with the fastening. Dandy takes a mirror-and-comb case from Larry's breast pocket. She makes it perfectly obvious that experience has taught her where to find it. She studies the effect in the glass. Jonathan completes his job and steps back. Dandy sees this in the mirror. Her hand goes to her forehead. She frowns, gives her head a little shake, and hands the mirror back to Larry. She puts her hand on his.

Dandy (*To Larry*). It's going to take me half my life to thank you.

252 CLOSE-UP—LARRY

He smiles.

Larry. Starting next Wednesday.

253 TWO-SHOT—DANDY AND LARRY

Dandy's head starts to bother her again.

Dandy. I—I want to see it with my costume on.

She presses both hands to her forehead.

Larry (*Concerned*). Hurts, hmm?

Dandy. It'll be all right.

Larry (*Taking her chin gently in his hands*). Hey, character. You wouldn't kid me?

Dandy. Don't worry about it.

254 CLOSE-UP—JONATHAN

He, too, is concerned. His eyes move from Dandy's face to Larry.

255 CLOSE TWO-SHOT—DANDY AND LARRY

Larry is looking at his wrist watch.

Larry. Next show's at four o'clock.

Dandy (*Frowning with pain*). I'll be there.

Larry. Sure you will, trouper—but I was thinking—why don't you let Marko give you his hypnotic treatment—

Dandy (*Her head is splitting*). No!

Despite the pain, she is instantly sorry for her brusqueness.

Dandy (*Continued*). Oh, I'm sorry, Larry. But he gives me the creeps.

Larry (*Nodding*). Yes, I know. Forget it.

Dandy. You're sweet.

She presses her eyes.

256 CLOSE SHOT—JONATHAN

He wants to do something to help but the situation leaves him tongue-tied.

257 TRUCKING SHOT—DANDY AND LARRY

Dandy takes her hands down from her eyes.

Dandy. I—Larry, could you cancel the afternoon show?

Larry. Of course, darling. Come along to your dressing room. You'd better lie down.

Dandy squeezes his hand. Her free hand digs into her temple as they start walking toward Dandy's dressing room. The CAMERA DOLLIES WITH THEM.

Larry (*Continued*). You know, Marko *has* cured some strange cases.

The implication stabs into Dandy's splitting head. She stops.

Dandy. Stop it! I'm not a strange case.

Larry (*Irritated, in spite of himself*). I didn't say that. Darling, please—if you're afraid—

Dandy. I'm not afraid.

Larry. All I meant was—

Dandy (*Peter Pain is killing her*). You meant I'm afraid. All right! ALL RIGHT! I'll let him try it.

She grabs her head and runs off. Larry stares after her. Jonathan walks into the scene, behind Larry.

Jonathan. You really think it is all right?

Larry turns sharply and stares at Jonathan.

Larry. Why not?

Jonathan (*Gravely*). She doesn't trust Marko.

Larry. Look. You need a drink. Come on. And stop worrying.

The two men start off.

258 CLOSE SHOT—BENCH

A French poodle is looking off in the direction taken by the two men. Suddenly the dog sits down and begins to scratch like mad. Helen (of Troy, no doubt) has gone to work on Paris.

259 MOVING CAMERA SHOT—INTERIOR MARKO'S DRESSING ROOM

Marko is seated at his dressing table. He has opened one of the drawers and taken out a tray that holds an assortment of the paste diamond rings he wears. He takes off the one he is wearing and looks over the half-dozen rings in the tray, muttering, "Eeny, meeny, pfiney—phony." The CAMERA PULLS BACK *and reveals the fact that Barton is leaning on the back of a chair, impatiently watching Marko. Between the two men, in the background, is a door leading to another room.*

Barton. Will you stop that and look at me?

Marko turns and regards the detective with a sardonic smile.

Marko. Like all flat-headed flatfeet, you make life so difficult. Well—?

Barton (*Whispering, and pointing toward the door*). It's about *him*.

Marko. Well?

Barton (*Still whispers*). I ran into Scoop Kenton. The boss just gave Dandy Lyon a wedding present. It's—

The door in the background opens, revealing Gerald Briggs. The stooge is carrying a platter on which is a decapitated wax head of John the Baptist. Briggs sees Barton. His expression changes to one of cold hatred. He retreats back into his workroom, slams the door, and turns the key in the lock. Barton reacts to the dirty look Briggs gives him and crosses to Marko. The CAMERA MOVES CLOSER.

Barton. That's what I mean. Larry's present was a chunk of ice as big as that. (*He touches the paste ring Marko has just put on.*) Only it's the real McCoy.

Marko. So—?

Barton (*Whispering, and pointing to the door*). His jail record—

Marko. Please! Briggs wanted to *copy* that emerald he took. For a statue he was modeling. He *borrowed* it.

Barton. The jury didn't think so.

Marko (*Puts up his hand*). Quiet, infidel! *I'm* telling the story. (*As though he were talking to a child.*) It's a funny story. Don't interrupt. You see—

There is a knock at the entrance door behind CAMERA. *Both men turn and look in that direction. Marko shrugs wearily.*

Marko (*Continued*). Come in, point killer.

260 MEDIUM SHOT—ENTRANCE DOOR

The door opens and Dandy comes in. One hand is pressing her eyes. As her fingers move down her cheek and finally rest on the pendant, the CAMERA DOLLIES IN FAST, *concentrating on the jewel.*

261 CLOSE SHOT—THE TWO MEN

They look at one another. Marko rises and walks out of the shot toward the door. Barton follows him.

262 MEDIUM SHOT—THE ENTRANCE DOOR

Marko comes into the scene. Dandy's fingers go back to her forehead. Barton comes into the shot and stands on the other side of Dandy, his back to the CAMERA.

Dandy (*In agony, to Marko*). You win. My head's splitting.

Marko (*To Barton*). Wait outside. This won't take long.

He takes Dandy's arm and leads her out of the shot. Barton stares after him for a moment, looks at his watch, starts to say something, thinks better of it, and goes on out.

263 REVERSE ANGLE MEDIUM SHOT

Marko is helping Dandy to sit down on the couch. She buries her head in her hands. Marko quickly steps to his dressing table and, with a magician's swift fingers, pours a glass of water and takes a box of tablets out of a drawer. He moves rapidly back to Dandy and offers her the glass and one of the tablets.

Marko. Empirin. It'll kill the pain while we're getting ready.

Dandy looks up at him. Her eyes are dull but they show her instinctive distrust of the hypnotist. The pain is killing her. She downs the tablet and drinks the water. Meanwhile, Marko is adjusting a baby spotlight near the couch.

264 MEDIUM SHOT—OUTSIDE MARKO'S DRESSING ROOM

Barton lights a cigarette and begins to pace up and down. A few House-of-Wonders customers pass by in the foreground.

265 CLOSE SHOT—INTERIOR MARKO'S DRESSING ROOM—DANDY AND MARKO

Dandy is lying on the couch. Marko is using his paste ring to reflect the rays of the spotlight into Dandy's eyes. The eyes close. Marko leans forward and begins to whisper in a soothing monotone.

    Marko. You're asleep. You're asleep and you're completely relaxed. Your hand is heavy. You can't raise it. Try to lift it.

Dandy tries. She can't get her hand off the couch.

    Marko (*Continued*). You see? You *are* asleep. Your headache's gone. It's never coming back. When you wake up, that's all you'll remember.

He reaches out and touches her neck.

    Marko (*Continued*). You can't feel my fingers. They're not really touching you.

He touches the pendant, throws a glance in the direction of Briggs's door, and gets up, still talking. The CAMERA FOLLOWS HIM AS HE MOVES TO THE DOOR *and quietly tries the handle.*

    Marko (*Continued*). You'll drift like a swallow when you're on the wire tonight. You'll be as sure of yourself as an eagle.

Marko has assured himself that Briggs's door is still locked. He moves to his dressing table and picks up a pair of eyebrow tweezers. He returns to Dandy and begins to work on the prongs that hold the diamond in the pendant.

    Marko (*Continued*). You feel nothing—absolutely nothing.

266 MEDIUM SHOT—OUTSIDE MARKO'S DRESSING ROOM

Barton stops pacing, tosses his cigarette on the floor, and grinds it out with his heel.

267 MEDIUM SHOT—INTERIOR MARKO'S DRESSING ROOM

We are shooting over Dandy in the foreground. Using the tweezers, Marko takes Dandy's diamond out of the setting and puts it in his pocket. He glances past CAMERA *toward Briggs's room and starts to pry open the prongs of his paste ring.*

268 CLOSE SHOT—INTERIOR BRIGGS'S WORKROOM

The key is in the lock. The CAMERA PULLS BACK AND PANS OVER *to Briggs. He is putting the finishing touches on the decapitated wax head. It is obvious that he is completely unaware of what is going on in the next room.*

269 CLOSE SHOT—INTERIOR RESTAURANT—JUKE BOX

It is playing the song Jonathan and Dandy heard on the television in the same restaurant.

DISSOLVE TO

270 CLOSE SHOT—JONATHAN AND LARRY

They are seated at the bar. No one else is near them. Jonathan is listening to the song. Larry is writing a check. Jonathan puts down his drink and leans close to Larry, who goes on writing.

Jonathan. I still think Dandy was right. I don't trust Marko either.

Larry tears the check out of his checkbook, puts the book in his pocket, and waves the check back and forth to dry it. During this by-play, Jonathan goes on talking.

Jonathan (*Continued*). At least you can telephone him, can't you?

Larry. Relax, Johnny. In a little while she'll be back in her dressing room. I'll give her ten minutes to rest. Then I'll join her. She'll tell me her headache's gone—that I was right.

Jonathan considers this and takes another drink.

Jonathan. I still don't like it.

Larry stops waving the check and rests his hand on the bar.

Larry. Maybe you'll like this. Joe Donatello told me about that plant restorer of yours. I'm interested.

Larry turns the check face up and shoves it along the bar under Jonathan's nose.

Larry (*Continued*). I'm *that* much interested.

Jonathan stares down at the check.

Larry (*Continued*). You're quite a man, Johnny. You're going places. I want to be your friend.

Jonathan (*Looking up from the check*). You can be my friend for less than five hundred dollars, Larry. We can be friends for nothing.

Larry takes a quick drink. The sound of his glass, as he bangs it on the bar, is an exclamation point.

Larry. Okay. Make it a straight business deal. You believe in your idea, don't you?

Jonathan nods and pushes the check back across the bar.

Jonathan. I still have to say, "No, thank you."

Larry slowly pockets the check.

271 CLOSE TWO-SHOT FAVORING LARRY

Larry faces Jonathan. He speaks with deep sincerity.

Larry. You're right, Johnny. I was trying to buy your friendship. I'm afraid of you.

Jonathan (*Puzzled*). Of me? In what way?

Larry (*Smiling wryly*). In a "Dandy" way.

272 CLOSE TWO-SHOT FAVORING JONATHAN

He stares down at his drink, then looks up at Larry.

    Jonathan. I don't believe that. You know I can't give her what you can.

273 CLOSE TWO-SHOT FAVORING LARRY

    Larry. That's right. You can't. And that's it. Suppose she should say yes to you. Either Dandy gives up her career and goes back with you to Boonesville, or you stay here—the guy who cleans up her dressing room while she's working.

274 CLOSE-UP—JONATHAN

He has been listening intently to Larry's picture of the future. At last, he frowns and speaks.

    Jonathan. But that isn't it. She's in love with you.

275 CLOSE-UP—LARRY

He answers quickly.

    Larry. Right again. Still—she does like you. That's what brought on that headache. Dandy's a *female* female, Johnny. She'd like to have you around—as sort of a spare tire—just in case. For a guy like you, that's murder. It's a long, slow suicide. I don't want you to get hurt, Johnny. I want you to make a clean break—now. I want you to leave the park.

276 CLOSE-UP—JONATHAN

Part of Larry's speech is played over the close-up. When Larry finishes, Jonathan moves back a little against the bar. His eyes leave Larry's. He is thinking hard.

277 OUTSIDE MARKO'S DRESSING ROOM

Dandy and Marko are coming out of the hypnotist's room. Barton walks up to them. A few people pass in front of them as the CAMERA DOLLIES IN TO A CLOSE SHOT OF THE THREE. *Dandy's eyes are bright. She turns to Marko and smiles.*

    Marko. Go ahead. Thank me.

    Dandy. What do you think I'm doing? I can hardly believe it. I'm going to do nip-ups and handsprings up there tonight.

    Marko. And every night. But take it easy for another twenty minutes. Lie down. Take a nap. And don't forget to tell Larry what I said about this.

He touches the pendant casually.

    Dandy. I won't—and I apologize.

    Marko. For what?

Dandy (*Smiling*). For being anti-hypnotist. I was wrong. They *are* people.

Marko. For that you should apologize.

Dandy stares at him.

Marko (*Continued*). People! B-r-r-r!

He shudders.

Dandy (*Still smiling*). You're hopeless.

She presses Marko's hand and walks briskly away. Marko eyes her departing back and turns to Barton.

Marko. I'll make the rest of the Briggs epic a *short* short story. I go on in ten minutes.

Barton leans against the door, ready to listen.

278 CLOSE TWO-SHOT—INTERIOR RESTAURANT

Larry and Jonathan are just about as we left them.

Jonathan (*Quietly*). All right, Larry. I'm going. But I can't leave till tomorrow. I won't know about my experiment for a couple of hours.

Larry nods. Jonathan goes on.

Jonathan (*Continued*). And I'll have to tell Ma and Pa that I'm leaving. I'll do that right now.

Larry. Take off whenever you like, Johnny. But, believe me, for your own good—the sooner, the quicker.

Jonathan gets up.

Jonathan. Dandy's ankle is still pretty weak, Larry. Marko hasn't cured *that*. She could still fall tonight.

Larry. She won't—I won't let her. She's going to be my wife, Johnny.

Jonathan nods slowly and goes. Gus, the bartender, comes into the scene. Larry glances at his wrist watch and edges his glass toward Gus.

Larry (*Continued*). Come again, Gus. But less soda.

Gus nods and picks up the glass.

279 MEDIUM SHOT—INTERIOR MARKO'S DRESSING ROOM

Marko is in the foreground at his dressing table. The entrance door is in the background. Marko is filling his meerschaum pipe from a tobacco tin. Suddenly an amusing idea strikes him. He puts down the tin and regards his pipe speculatively, still amused. He shifts the meerschaum into his left hand and puts his right into the coat pocket that holds Larry's diamond. Marko takes the diamond out of his pocket and puts it into the bowl of his pipe. He covers the jewel with a sprinkling of tobacco from the tin. He lights the pipe. The trick works. The bowl is large enough so that the pipe draws. Marko studies the effect in the mirror.

280 MEDIUM SHOT—EXTERIOR FLORIST SHOP AND HOUSE OF WONDERS
Jonathan comes into the scene on his way to see his mother at the House of Wonders. As he approaches the entrance, Donatello comes out of the florist shop next door and calls out to him.

Donatello. Giovanni!

He beckons to Jonathan. Jonathan doesn't want to face anybody.

Jonathan. I've got to talk to my mother.

Donatello comes toward Jonathan on the run.

Donatello. That's-a fine—

He holds out an envelope breathlessly. The CAMERA MOVES CLOSE.

Donatello (*Continued*). Talk to her about this.

Jonathan takes the envelope and looks at it without any real interest.

Donatello (*Continued*). Open it.

Jonathan does as he is told. As he is opening the envelope, Donatello keeps on talking.

Donatello (*Continued*). You gonna get big surprise.

Jonathan has the envelope opened. It is full of greenbacks and a slip of paper—a receipt.

Jonathan. Mr. Donatello!

Donatello (*An affectionate correction*). Joe.

Jonathan. Mr.—Joe. This is two hundred dollars!

Donatello. That's-a right. I get scared maybe boss man beat-a me to it. So I take my savings from the bank. Just-a sign on the spotted line. Then we are partners. Giuseppe and Giovanni. BUG JUICE!

Jonathan. I can't take this. I—I'll tell you why tomorrow morning.

Donatello. You take it and you sign—or I *sing*. I follow wherever you go and I sing.

And he does sing. And Pagliacci—*the real thing—and loud! Jonathan pockets the envelope and he signs. Donatello ad-libs, segueing from the Italian lyrics.*

> **Donatello** (*Continued*). And you get lawyers,
> And you get patent
> And we get rich-a
> On—with—the—show!

As when we first meet him, he sobs his little heart out as Jonathan disappears into the House of Wonders. Donatello wipes his eyes and goes back toward the store.

281 CLOSE SHOT—DANDY—INTERIOR DANDY'S DRESSING ROOM
Dandy is getting ready for the nap that Marko suggested. She is sitting in front of her mirror, tying the belt of her lounging robe. As she finishes with the belt and adjusts the pendant, she remembers something. She opens one of her dressing table drawers.

282 CLOSE SHOT—THE OPEN DRAWER
Jonathan's half-melted candy chrysanthemum is the only thing in the drawer. Dandy's hand comes into the scene and picks up the flower.

283 CLOSE SHOT—DANDY
She brings the chrysanthemum up into the shot and studies it. She smiles at its pathetic condition, then she holds it close to the pendant, as though she were comparing the two gifts. Someone knocks on the door.

Larry's voice. Holler if you're decent, character. The boss man cometh.

Dandy quickly slips Jonathan's flower back into the drawer and closes it.

Dandy. Come in, character. Meet the new woman.

She gets up. The CAMERA PULLS BACK as Larry comes into the scene, takes Dandy in his arms, and kisses her. Dandy makes it a quick one.

Dandy (*Continued*). I've got to collapse for ten minutes—Doctor Marko's orders.

Larry. He did the trick, hmm?

Dandy talks as she moves to the couch and sits on it. Larry and the CAMERA FOLLOW HER.

Dandy. Yes, *sir*. I fell like a million.

Larry, You look like a million. Go ahead and collapse. I'll be right back.

Dandy (*Touching the pendant*). Before you go—Marko thought you ought to keep this in your safe when I'm not wearing it. Barton's worried about Briggsy. Some corny story about an emerald.

Dandy starts to unfasten the pendant.

Larry. Oh, that. H-m-m-m. Maybe Marko's right. I'll take it along.

Dandy (*Handing him the pendant*). I'm going to be lost without it.

Larry (*Looking from the diamond to Dandy*). Johnny was right. You *are* more beautiful. And this isn't such bad competition.

He looks down again at the jewel. Suddenly he fingers it and holds it to the light. He frowns and monkeys with one of the prongs.

Dandy. Anything the matter?

Larry (*Nodding*). Looks like somebody's been fiddling with the setting. I'm going to check.

He moves over and picks up the telephone.

Larry (*Continued*). Dorothy? Mr. Ellis. Get me Plaza 3-9850. (*To Dandy.*) That's Freddy Blenheim—my jeweler. I'll get him right over here. (*Covering the mouthpiece.*) And you'd better hop into some clothes. You may have to dig up Barton for me if Dorothy can't find him.

Dandy nods, grabs some things, and starts to put on her shoes. Larry uncovers the mouthpiece and jiggles the phone.

Larry (*Continued*). What's happening with that number?

264 MEDIUM LONG SHOT—INTERIOR HOUSE OF WONDERS

Marko and Briggs are performing. As before, Marko is snapping his fingers in front of Briggs's eyes. (Note: this is actually a second take of Scene No. 177.)

285 MEDIUM SHOT—THE BOONES' BOOTH

As usual, the House of Wonders customers have deserted the Boones in favor of Marko. Jonathan, Ma, and Pa are grouped around the fence of the prop corral. Jonathan has just finished telling his mother that he is leaving the park in the morning and why. Ma picks up some sawdust from the floor and lets it trickle through her fingers. Pa Boone has acquired a new addition to his sartorial department—a plug hat. It is a half-size too large for him. Pa is stuffing strips of newspaper inside the hatband. As the scene goes on, he tries on the hat again. Still too large. He grunts and stuffs in some more paper. Ma Boone turns to Jonathan.

Ma. Stop frettin' about her, son. Those things happen. And stop worryin' about us. We'll git along fine.

Pa. That's right. We been sellin' photographs by the hundred. (*Gesturing toward Marko.*) Spite of Dracula.

Jonathan puts his hand on Ma's shoulders. His mouth tenses suddenly.

Jonathan. Every time I close my eyes, I see her falling from that wire.

Pa (*Trying on the oversized hat*). Quit thinkin' about her. She's gonna be Mrs. Larry Ellis. Let him do the worryin'.

286 CLOSE SHOT—MA

She turns to Pa with righteous indignation.

Ma. You didn't talk like that when you was courtin' me, Dawson Boone.

287 CLOSE-UP—PA

He yanks off the hat and shoves in more paper.

Pa. My head must-a shrunk.

288 TWO-SHOT—MA AND JONATHAN

Ma turns to Jonathan.

Ma. When you was a year old, a bull cornered me in a corral no bigger'n this. I'd been jumpin' in and out of it for practice. Pa picked up the fence rail I'd knocked off. He pasted that bull right a-tween the eyes. Laid him out cold. Pa didn't want *me* to get hurt.

289 CLOSE-UP—PA

He grins and looks toward his son.

Pa. Broke my heart to do it. Best bull I ever had.

He raps his forehead with the hat brim and puts it on at a cocky angle. It fits. Pa snaps his fingers.

Pa (*Continued*). Tell you what. If you don't want her to walk that wire tonight, git 'er drunk.

290 CLOSE SHOT—JONATHAN AND MA

The idea strikes them both as fantastic. Pa's voice comes over the shot.

Pa's voice. They won't let 'er get near that wire if she's pifflicated.

Ma and Jonathan look at one another. Pa's idea makes sense.

291 GROUP SHOT—THE THREE

Pa. Got nothin' to lose. All you're riskin' is eighty-seven cents, includin' tax, for a jug of hard cider.

Jonathan is sorely tempted. He reaches into his pocket to see how much money he's got. Ma Boone whips a five dollar bill from her stocking.

Ma. Hard cider for a city gal! (*To Jonathan.*) Here's five dollars. Git her the best.

Jonathan takes the money, kisses Ma on the cheek, and hurries out of the scene. Pa yells after him.

Pa (*Shouting*). Git 'er *good* and drunk!

Marko's customers applaud (off scene).

292 MEDIUM CLOSE SHOT—OUTSIDE DANDY'S DRESSING ROOM

Completely dressed now, Dandy is standing in the open doorway, her hand on the doorknob. Beyond her, Larry is talking on the telephone again.

Larry. O.K., Dorothy. Keep trying.

He hangs up and turns to Dandy.

Larry (*Continued*). Go ahead. She can't find him. He must be outside someplace.

Dandy. Consider him found. I'm part bloodhound.

She closes the door and walks out of the scene.

293 EXTERIOR ROW OF CONCESSIONS

Dandy comes into the scene. CAMERA TRUCKS WITH HER *as she walks along, looking from side to side. She bumps into Jonathan who is coming to the dressing room from the opposite direction. The* CAMERA HOLDS THEM IN A KNEE-FIGURE SHOT.

Dandy. Hello.

Jonathan (*Concerned*). You're all right?

Dandy. I'm terrific.

Jonathan. The ankle?

Dandy. What ankle?

Jonathan's eyes widen. Dandy is sorry that she kidded him. She smiles and rises on her toes.

Dandy (*Continued*). It's perfect. Just watch me tonight.

Jonathan's fear that she will be hurt makes him stumble for words.

Jonathan. I—I can't be there.

Dandy (*Worried about him*). Why not?

Jonathan. I'll be packing. I'm leaving the park tomorrow.

Dandy. Jonathan!

Jonathan. I'll tell you all about if—could we go someplace?

Dandy. I've got to—all right. Where shall we go?

Jonathan. Where we heard that song?

Dandy. All right, Johnny.

They walk out of the scene.

294 LONG SHOT—EXTERIOR CAFÉ—STUDIO SET

Jonathan and Dandy come into the scene. Jonathan holds open the door for Dandy. She goes in. Barton comes around the corner. He sees Jonathan and catches a glimpse of Dandy's back as Jonathan closes the door. Reilly, one of the park cops, comes into the scene behind Barton. He touches the detective on the shoulder. Barton turns toward him.

Reilly. The boss wants you in Miss Lyon's dressing room. He's been S.O.S.-ing you all over the joint.

Barton nods.

Barton. Better come with me.

The two men exit.

295 CLOSE SHOT—INTERIOR CAFÉ

Dandy and Jonathan are seated at the same table they used before. An instrumental version of their song is the background music. The waitress comes up to the table.

    Jonathan (*Pantomiming a tall drink*). Two.
    Waitress. Two what?
    Jonathan. Whiskies.

He repeats the gesture. The imaginary drink is even bigger.

    Jonathan (*Continued*). Whiskies.
    Dandy (*Smiling at the waitress*). Make mine—

With her thumb and forefinger, she pantomimes an infinitesimally small drink.

    Jonathan (*Seeing Pa's scheme going a-glimmering*). It's our farewell drink.
    Dandy (*Gently*). If I weren't—(*She repeats her pantomime.*) Even that would be too much. Usually I only drink D.D.T.
    Jonathan (*Really terrified*). D.D.T.? That's poison.
    Dandy. During Day Time.
    Jonathan. But it *is* daytime.
    Dandy (*Consulting her wrist watch*). Late daytime. Four hours and twenty minutes before I start bouncing.

By this time, the waitress is confused, annoyed, and ready to quit. When she speaks, her tone is bitter.

    Waitress. What's it gonna be?
    Jonathan. Whiskey.
    Waitress. Yeah, but which?

She does both pantomimes with her two hands, and Jonathan and Dandy repeat theirs. The waitress gives them a dirty look and exits.

296 CLOSER SHOT—JONATHAN AND DANDY

Dandy dismisses the incident and turns to Jonathan with puzzled interest.

    Dandy. Why are you leaving?
    Jonathan (*Trying to duck*). Personal reasons.
    Dandy. Larry?
    Jonathan (*Shaking his head*). Larry's my friend. He offered me five hundred dollars to back my experiment. Not only that—

Jonathan stops. He's afraid to reveal his emotions.

    Dandy. Yes?

Jonathan. He thought if I went away, I'd be happier about—everything.

Dandy (*Larry's maneuvering is suddenly clear to her*). Oh.

Jonathan (*Indicating the ankle*). Sure that's all right?

Dandy leans forward and touches Jonathan's hand.

Dandy. It's fine.

297 LONGER SHOT

The waitress comes into the scene and puts down her tray. On it are two highball glasses with ice in them, two bottles of soda which she has opened, a pint bottle of rye, a small jigger glass, and a large one. She pours a shot into the small jigger and one into the large one. She indicates Jonathan's jigger and repeats his big gesture.

Waitress. That's that, and—(*Repeating Dandy's little gesture.*) That's that. Pay at the bar.

She reaches for the whiskey bottle.

Jonathan. Leave it.

The waitress shrugs and goes out of the scene. The CAMERA DOLLIES CLOSER *as Jonathan hums Donatello's* Pagliacci *prologue and quickly pours the jiggers and the soda into the two glasses. He shoves his drink toward Dandy. She smiles.*

Dandy. That's yours.

Jonathan. It won't hurt you. Look.

He downs a huge gulp and smiles triumphantly. Dandy takes a tiny sip from her drink and watches him with affectionate amusement. Jonathan redoubles his efforts to get Dandy drunk. He indicates her highball.

Jonathan (*Continued*). Yours is practically empty.

He takes another swig from his glass, reducing the contents to almost nothing. He takes Dandy's glass and pours a shot into it from the bottle. Dandy reaches over, takes Jonathan's almost empty glass, and continues to sip. The double cross baffles Jonathan. He takes another drink from Dandy's glass, which he has just filled.

298 MEDIUM CLOSE SHOT—EXTERIOR DANDY'S DRESSING ROOM

Barton and Reilly enter the scene and knock on the door. Larry opens it. Blenheim, the jeweler, is adjusting his jeweler's eyepiece in the background.

Larry (*To Barton*). It's about time.

The two men step inside. Larry closes the door.

299 CLOSE SHOT—INTERIOR CAFÉ—DANDY AND JONATHAN

Jonathan is beginning to feel the drinks. Dandy eyes him as he shoots down another gulp.

Jonathan (*Craftily*). You're not drinking.

Dandy smiles and takes another sip.

Dandy. This is hard liquor.

Jonathan. How about some wine?

Dandy decides that, for Jonathan, this is the lesser of two evils.

Dandy. I'll split a glass with you.

Jonathan (*Enthusiastically*). A big glass.

He rises quickly—too quickly, and loses his balance slightly. He recovers himself with an amiable smile and exits from the scene toward the bar. Dandy looks after him. She fingers her plastic drink stirrer and doodles with it on the tablecloth as she thinks over what Jonathan told her about Larry.

300 MEDIUM CLOSE SHOT—GUS AT THE BAR

Jonathan comes into the scene and leans across the bar. The bartender has his back turned.

Jonathan. "Take a little wine for thy stomach's sake." His very words.

Gus turns and stares at him.

Gus. Whose words?

Jonathan (*Looking at the small amount of change*). St. Paul.

Gus. Butch St. Paul?

Jonathan (*Shaking his head*). SAINT St. Paul.

Gus. So?

Jonathan. So I want the best wine you've got.

Gus. Domestic?

Jonathan (*Looking down at his change*). Imported. Champagne!

Gus (*Pantomiming the size*). Fifth or magnum?

Jonathan. Wait a minute.

He reaches into his pocket and pulls out a dollar bill, some change, and Donatello's envelope. He fingers the money in the envelope. Gus sees this.

301 CLOSE-UP—REVERSE SHOT—JONATHAN OVER GUS'S SHOULDER

Jonathan closes his eyes.

DISSOLVE TO

302 LONG SHOT—DANDY ON THE SLACK WIRE—NIGHT

Dandy, close to the platform, tries to make a double turn on the wire. She slips and falls out of the shot.

DISSOLVE TO
303 CLOSE-UP—JONATHAN
He shudders, his eyes open, he stares at the bartender (off scene).
    Jonathan. Magnum!
304 TWO-SHOT—GUS AND JONATHAN
The angle is toward the bartender. He gives Jonathan a wise guy's smile.
    Gus. Mumm's?
Jonathan nods and puts his finger to his lips.
    Jonathan. —the word.
Jonathan turns and weaves his way out of the shot. The proprietor of the café enters the scene. He looks after Jonathan and turns to Gus.
    Proprietor. What's he think my place is—the Stork Club?
Gus beckons the proprietor and whispers.
    Gus (*Sotto voce*). He's got a fistful of folding money.
The café owner turns and looks off in the direction taken by Jonathan. He grins the grin reserved for suckers.
305 CLOSE SHOT—INTERIOR DANDY'S DRESSING ROOM
Blenheim has the jeweler's eyepiece in his eye. His fingers are twisting Marko's phony diamond. Larry's face and part of Barton's head and shoulders frame the shot.
DISSOLVE TO
306 CLOSE SHOT—INTERIOR CAFÉ—ENTRANCE DOOR
The door opens revealing Donatello. He looks around, his eyes widen suddenly.
307 MEDIUM SHOT—DANDY AND JONATHAN AT THE TABLE
The angle is from Donatello's point of view. A magnum of champagne is in an ice bucket close to the table. Dandy is tugging at Jonathan's sleeve. He has risen and is toasting the other occupants of the café as he sings Reginald de Koven's "Brown October Ale."
308 MEDIUM SHOT—DONATELLO IN THE DOORWAY
He smiles and moves forward as the CAMERA SWINGS WITH HIM.
    Donatello (*Joining in the chorus*). All my days, I'll sing the praise
                      Of Brown-a October Ale.
By now, Donatello has reached the table. He and Jonathan finish the song with their arms around each other's shoulders. Donatello picks up Dandy's glass and tastes the wine.
    Donatello (*Continued*). And it's champagne! (*To Dandy.*) So, my Yankee Doodlum Dandy, you give-a Giovanni big party to celembrate our-a partnership.

Dandy (*About to deny this*). Well—
Jonathan, thoroughly cockeyed, is still conscious enough to realize the coming catastrophe. He starts to say something but Donatello goes on.
Donatello (*To Dandy*). Don't-a apologize. What's about some more bubbles for the senior partner?
He signals to the bartender. Gus is already heaving a second magnum on to the bar as the proprietor smiles approvingly. They wave to Donatello and start around the bar with a second ice bucket. Donatello sits down. The CAMERA MOVES CLOSER *as Gus deposits a third glass on the table, sets down a new magnum, and exits.*
Jonathan (*Teetering back*). Before you partake—
Donatello. Don't-a bend backwards—
He reaches over and straightens Jonathan up in his chair.
Donatello (*Continued*) For Dandy—all this is just a drop in the buckle.
He fills his glass from the magnum.

309 MEDIUM SHOT—INTERIOR DANDY'S DRESSING ROOM
The three men are grouped around Blenheim. The jeweler takes the eyepiece out of his eye.
Blenheim. Not even a good imitation.
Barton moves to the door.
Barton. Let's nail Mister Briggs quick—before he swallows the real one.
Larry nods and joins Barton. Reilly follows him. Larry remembers something.
Larry (*To Barton*). What happened to Dandy?
Barton. She's at the Silver Slipper with Li'l Abner Boone.
Larry reacts and goes out the door. The others follow him, leaving Blenheim alone.

310 MEDIUM SHOT—INTERIOR CAFÉ
Donatello is testing the wine with a connoisseur's appreciation.
Donatello. Hottsa-tottsa! After a hard day's work, vino.
Gus returns and stands beside Jonathan.
Donatello (*Continued*). And after vino—
Gus (*To Jonathan*). The check.
Gus slides the check onto the table. Jonathan picks it up and stares at it stupidly for a moment. Donatello looks at him in astonishment. He expected Dandy to get the check. Jonathan tries to extract the florist's money from the envelope, under the table. Gus reaches down, takes the

envelope, and starts to count out the money. Donatello rises and stares at the evidence of Jonathan's treachery.

Donatello. Giovanni!

Donatello snatches the check from Jonathan. He is staggered by the amount. He turns on Jonathan with horror.

Donatello (*Continued*). You spend-a our money to get drunk.

Jonathan nods and tries to answer. Dandy gets up, grips Donatello's arm, ready to explain. The florist turns to the entrance door.

311 MEDIUM SHOT—ENTRANCE DOOR

Larry, Barton, and Reilly appear in the doorway. Larry's eyes find Jonathan's table and Dandy. He speaks over his shoulder to the others.

Larry. Pick up Briggs.

Larry walks out of the shot toward the table. Barton and Reilly turn and go out the door.

312 GROUP SHOT—AT TABLE

Jonathan sits down again and buries his head in his hands. Larry comes into the scene.

Larry (*To Dandy*). What is this?

Dandy. Johnny had a crazy idea my ankle was still bad. He was afraid I'd fall so he tried to get me high.

Larry (*Indicating the champagne*). Where'd he get the money?

Donatello. I gave it to him.

Larry (*To Donatello*). How much?

Donatello. I give-a him two hundred.

Gus hands Donatello the change from the bar bill and exits. Donatello looks down at the money.

Donatello (*Continued*). Here's-a what's left.

Larry reaches into his pocket and takes out the check he offered to Jonathan earlier. In his chair, Jonathan shakes his head like a punch-drunk fighter and looks up.

Larry. Here's five hundred—made out to cash. Pay me the difference later.

Jonathan staggers to his feet, snatches the check, and tears it up. He grabs the Italian's shoulder to steady himself.

Jonathan. Joe! *I'll* get the money. *I'll* pay you back. Today! I'm going to get the money, Joe.

Jonathan makes a desperate effort to get control of the himself, straightens up, and staggers out of the scene toward the entrance. Larry reaches for his checkbook again. Donatello stops him.

Donatello. No. If I take-a your money—I take-a also Johnny's self-respect. If all his life he's-a gonna have to say, "Thank-a you—and you—and you"—kiss people's feets—he's never gonna be real man. But if he does-a what he said, he's okay. He's-a work hard. Someday he's gonna be *great* man. No. No, thank you, boss. I take-a chance.

Larry and Dandy haven't moved.

313 CLOSE SHOT—ENTRANCE DOOR

Jonathan has stopped on the threshold to lean against the door jamb and get a whiff of air. He has heard Donatello. He takes a deep breath and goes out.

314 CLOSE SHOT—LARRY, DANDY, AND DONATELLO

None of them saw Jonathan's exit. Larry shrugs and takes Dandy's arm.

Larry. They've gone to pick up Briggs. He's got our diamond.

Larry urges Dandy to go. She doesn't move.

Dandy. I want to talk to Joe.

Larry eyes her coldly, releases her arm, and walks out of the shot. The CAMERA DOLLIES CLOSE. *Dandy turns to Donatello.*

Dandy (*Continued*). I suppose my money wouldn't be any good either.

Donatello takes her hand.

Donatello. That's-a right. But-a thank you. You find Johnny. You help-a him.

Dandy nods and runs out. Donatello smiles and moves out of the scene.

315 GROUP SHOT—INTERIOR MARKO'S DRESSING ROOM

Barton is whispering to Marko, indicating Briggs's door in the background. Marko takes his meerschaum out of his mouth. He gives a perfect imitation of shocked anger and hands the pipe to Barton.

Marko. Hold this.

He flings open Briggs's door. His stooge turns from the wax head of John the Baptist. Marko grabs Briggs by the shoulder.

Marko (*Continued*). You little sneak. You thief!

Before Briggs can answer the accusation, Marko crosses a vicious right to his chin. The stooge's head snaps back. He goes out like a snuffed candle and crashes to the floor, carrying the platter and the decapitated wax head with him. Barton steps past Marko, handing him the meerschaum en route, and kneels beside Briggs to search him. Reilly joins him. Larry Ellis bursts into the foreground with two more cops.

Larry (*To Marko*). Find it?

Marko. They're frisking him.

He indicates Briggs's room. Larry starts to go in. Marko stops him and gestures toward the two cops.

Marko (*Continued*). And search me.

Larry. What?

Marko. I'm ticklish—but I insist.

Larry (*Wearily*). All right. All right, boys.

Larry goes into Briggs's room. The cops begin to frisk Marko perfunctorily as he lights the pipe.

Marko (*To the cops*). Up to five bucks—finders keepers.

The coppers grin and continue their once-over-lightly.

316 MEDIUM SHOT—INTERIOR HOUSE OF WONDERS—BOONES' BOOTH

Ma and Pa are autographing pictures as usual, but it is obvious that their minds are not on their work. The drone of the talker's voice (he is off scene) comes over the shot. Dandy comes through a slit in the canvas backdrop with an empty bucket. She kneels down close to Ma and whispers as the autographing goes on.

Dandy (*Indicating the slit in the canvas*). He's coming round. The cold water did it.

Ma (*Also whispering*). Where's Johnny goin' to git the rest of the money? What Pa and I gave him is nothin'.

Dandy. He'll think of something.

Dandy smiles and moves away toward the slit in the backdrop.

317 MEDIUM CLOSE SHOT—BEHIND BACKDROP

In the foreground, Jonathan is seated on a bench, drying his face with a towel. One hand clutches the money Ma and Pa gave him. Dandy comes through the backdrop. She kneels on the bench beside Jonathan and massages the back of his neck. Jonathan is still groggy. He hands Dandy the money.

Jonathan. How much is that?

He goes to work again with the towel. Dandy makes a quick count. While Jonathan's face is covered, she manages to slip a bill from her purse into the kitty.

Dandy. Forty-four—forty-nine twenty-three.

Jonathan. That's all, hmm? I better take it to Joe.

Dandy. In a minute—

She steps behind him and works on his neck again.

318 CLOSE-UP—INTERIOR MARKO'S DRESSING ROOM

The meerschaum pipe and part of Marko's profile. The hypnotist's fingers remove the pipe from his mouth as he moves back, away from CAMERA. *At the same time, the* CAMERA PULLS BACK, *revealing the open door to Briggs's workroom. The cops are carrying out the still-unconscious stooge on an improvised stretcher. Marko has stepped back to let them pass as they exit close to* CAMERA. *Barton and Larry move into the foreground. The dressing room shows the effects of the ransacking that has been given it.*

Barton (*Calling after the cops*). Book him and make him talk. (*To Marko.*) What about the Waxworks?

Marko. We can look.

Barton. Through Joe's place.

They walk out of the shot. Larry turns to Reilly.

Larry. What about his make-up cream? His soap?

Reilly. Looked in everything.

Larry. Dig some more.

Reilly shoves back his cap, revealing a bald head, and goes to work. Larry joins in the search.

319 MEDIUM SHOT—INTERIOR FLORIST SHOP—BACK ENTRANCE DOOR

Donatello is peeking into the icebox to see if Julius is showing any results from the aloe extract. He takes the plant out. Marko and Barton come through the rear door. Its opening hides Donatello. Marko blows a healthy puff of smoke as he and Barton walk past Donatello out of the shot. The Italian closes the door, inhales the smoke, and points an accusing finger in the direction taken by the two men.

Donatello. That PIPE!

He stands angrily pointing.

320 REVERSE ANGLE—MARKO AND BARTON

The men's backs are to CAMERA. *Marko whirls. To him, Donatello's cry refers to the diamond. The pipe slips from his fingers and falls floorward.*

321 CLOSE SHOT—CEMENT FLOOR

The meerschaum falls into the shot. The stem breaks, ashes spill, but the diamond does not fall out of the pipe bowl.

322 CLOSE SHOT—MARKO AND BARTON

Marko recovers his poise, stoops down, and comes up with the pipe bowl and the stem.

323 CLOSE SHOT—DONATELLO

The Italian's rage subsides.

Donatello. Please, Mr. Marko. No smoke. My flowers! And-a dump out the ashes!

324 CLOSE-SHOT—MARKO AND BARTON

Marko smiles and looks around for an ashtray. Anxious to get going, Barton sees the flower pot in Donatello's hands (off scene). He walks forward. Marko follows.

325 MEDIUM CLOSE SHOT—NEAR ICEBOX

As the two enter, Donatello reaches for a broom. Barton takes Julius from the Italian's other hand.

Donatello. Careful with that. (*Indicating the icebox.*) In there.

Donatello goes out of the scene to clean up the ashes Marko left on the floor. Barton takes the saucer from beneath the flower pot and hands it to Marko for an ashtray. He replaces the flower pot in the icebox.

Barton (*To Donatello, off scene*). Hurry it up, Joe.

He picks up a dustpan and goes out of the scene toward Donatello. Marko watches the two men (off scene) and starts cautiously to dump the ashes into the saucer. The diamond roils out of the pipe bowl onto the saucer. Marko reaches quickly into the icebox, takes out Julius, and covers the saucer and the diamond with the parsnip's pot. The hole in the bottom of the pot makes a perfect hiding place. Marko starts for the backdoor carrying Julius. Donatello's voice comes over the scene.

Donatello's voice. Put-a that back where you found it!

THE CAMERA PULLS BACK *as Donatello reenters the scene and snatches Julius out of Marko's hand.*

Donatello. Do you think I let you walk off with million dollars maybe?

He puts Julius in the icebox and slams the door.

Donatello (*Continued*). Go away. You could-a spoil the whole experiment. (*He pronounces the word " experiment-ay."*)

Marko takes a good look at the icebox and the possibility of opening it later.

Marko. My humblest apologies.

Marko bows and exits from the shot.

326 MEDIUM CLOSE SHOT—BARTON

He is opening the door leading to the Chamber of Horrors. Marko comes into the scene. He and Barton exit. The door closes.

327 CLOSE SHOT—NEAR ICEBOX

Donatello bites his thumb and makes a broad gesture in the general direction of the departing hypnotist.

328 CLOSE SHOT—BACKSTAGE—BOONES' BOOTH
Jonathan is on his feet. He looks down at the money in his hand, turns to Dandy, steadies himself and exits.

329 CLOSE SHOT—INTERIOR FLORIST SHOP—AT ICEBOX
Donatello has his hat on. He plants a kiss on the icebox door and goes out of the scene toward the front entrance. The CAMERA SWINGS OVER *to the back entrance door. It opens and Jonathan weaves his way into the shop. Off scene, the front door slams shut. Jonathan looks up and moves a few steps forward.*

> **Jonathan.** Joe!

There is no answer. He is alone. He looks at the money in his hand. He stuffs it back into his pocket, stumbles to the icebox, and peers inside.

> **Jonathan** (*Continued, shaking his head*). Nothing. It's no good. Nothing's any good.

He feels sick and dizzy. The CAMERA FOLLOWS HIM *to the window. Jonathan throws it open and takes a deep breath. He leans on the sill and sticks his head out.*

330 CLOSE SHOT—REVERSE ANGLE SHOOTING INTO DONATELLO'S
Jonathan stares at the park.

331 LONG SHOT—THE PARK
The view begins to seesaw slowly up and down.

332 HEAD CLOSE-UP—JONATHAN
He closes his eyes to stop the dizziness. He opens them again.

333 LONG SHOT—THE PARK
The picture continues to teeter back and forth. Faster and faster. Finally, the park spins completely around like a pinwheel. The background music hits an eerie sustained discord.

334 CLOSE SHOT—JONATHAN—INTERIOR SHOP
He turns into the shop and puts his hands to his eyes. He is burning up and mutters, "Ice." The CAMERA PANS OVER *with him as he stumbles to the icebox. The angle breaks off. A harp chord comes over the shot. Jonathan shakes his head to clear it. Another harp chord is heard, and a coin drops to the floor in front of Jonathan. He looks at it, and several buds clink to the floor in front of him. They are falling out of the icebox. Jonathan reaches out of the shot and picks up a blossom. He unwraps it. He stares in amazement.*

335 INSERT—BUD IN HAND
As the fingers unwrap the bloom, we see a bright shiny coin.

336 CLOSE-UP—JONATHAN

He is now really speechless. He picks up other buds, and they all contain coins. He looks around for the source of his windfall, spies the icebox, and reaches for the handle.

337 CLOSE SHOT—THE ICEBOX

Jonathan's hand comes into the shot and pulls the door open. A Niagara of bills and coins come tumbling down to the strains of more harp music. Julius is plainly visible with shiny coins and bills all over him.

338 MEDIUM SHOT—JONATHAN

He stands ankle-deep in a pile of money. He bends down and grabs a fistful of bills. His face spreads into a wide grin of wonder. He takes out Julius.

339 CLOSE-UP—JULIUS HELD AT CHEST LEVEL

Bills and coins are falling from the plant (Special Effects Department).

340 CLOSE SHOT—JULIUS AND JONATHAN

Jonathan strokes Julius on his figurative head. CAMERA DOLLIES BACK *to include full figure. Jonathan is now standing knee-deep in bills.*
DISSOLVE TO

341 MEDIUM SHOT—OUTSIDE THE SHOP

Only one or two people pass by. The door opens slowly and Jonathan emerges. He looks from left to right, sees the coast is clear, and closes the door behind him. In one arm, he is carrying a wastebasket and, in the other, a large cardboard carton. Both are full to the brim with that green folding stuff. Jonathan starts to cross the street. As he approaches the CAMERA, IT DOLLIES BACK WITH HIM, *keeping him in a three-quarter shot.* TRUCK BACK FOR TEN FEET. *Jonathan is cautiously looking from side to side, when a gust of wind blows several bills out of the basket and into the street. He reaches to retrieve the bills and, as he does so, spills the waste basket headlong into the street. He looks around hurriedly and starts to stuff the money back.*

342 MEDIUM SHOT—MAN

He looks down at the ground, reaches out of the shot, and comes up with a twenty dollar bill in his hand. As he starts forward, the CAMERA PANS WITH HIM *until it reveals Jonathan alongside him.*

Man. Can I give you a hand there, buddy?

Jonathan (*Apprehensively*). I can manage, thank you!

He continues to pack away the dough.

343 LOW ANGLE SHOT—THE MAN

He regards Jonathan's actions with raised eyebrows. Three other men enter the shot and walk toward CAMERA. One of them pushes his way to the front, leans over, and looks down at Jonathan.

Second man. Where'd you get all the dough, fella?

344 HIGH ANGLE SHOT—JONATHAN

He finishes packing the bills, rises with his booty under his arms, and, without a word, walks out of the shot.

345 DOLLY SHOT—AHEAD OF JONATHAN WITH PEOPLE WALKING BEHIND

Jonathan looks apprehensively from side to side and to the rear. He picks up speed. The people in the rear can be heard over the shot.

Voices (*Overlapping*). Where did he get all that money? Looks suspicious to me. Sure does. Got a dishonest face, if you ask me. Must be a dangerous character. Somebody ought to call the cops.

Jonathan presses ahead of the DOLLY. CAMERA PANS so that we have him in a side shot. As he starts to break into a run, he bumps full force into a huge policeman, spilling his basket again.

346 LOW ANGLE SHOT—UP AT THE COP

He stands like a brick wall, with set jowls and uncompromising eyes.

347 GROUP SHOT—FAVORING JONATHAN AND COP

Jonathan is down at the cop's feet, retrieving his cabbage. Another cop enters the shot behind Jonathan.

First cop (*Slowly*). Where did you get the dough, boy?

Second cop (*Slowly*). Where you gonna go, boy?

Jonathan (*Rising*). I'm on my way to the bank, fellers, to settle up with the bank's—

He realizes he might be misunderstood—might sound like he was kidding the law. But he can't help it. He lamely finishes the sentence.

Jonathan (*Continued*).—tellers.

The cops raise their brows skeptically. A voice in the crowd pipes up.

Voice. I told you! I told you! He robbed the bank!

The cops exchange looks while the helpless Jonathan stands by. The crowd mills closer.

First cop. Let's check.

Second cop. Check!

They hoist the protesting Jonathan out of the shot.

DISSOLVE TO

348 EXTERIOR BANK SIGN

The name of the institution, THE BANKERS BANK AND TRUST COMPANY

DISSOLVE TO

349 THE BANK AND THE STEPS LEADING UP TO IT
A mob starts to mount the steps. Jonathan is at the point of the flying wedge. As the crowd storms into the building, we DOLLY IN TO THE WINDOW NEXT TO THE DOOR. *It reveals a sign setting forth the virtues of thrift. On it is printed:* MONEY DOESN'T GROW ON TREES.

350 GROUP SHOT—INTERIOR BANK
Mr. Asker, the bank manager, comes into the shot, as the incoming mob surrounds him. Asker is a genial middle-aged man with a professionally happy face. His immaculate suit sports a carnation. The first cop salutes and speaks.

    First cop. Here's the guy that robbed your bank, sir!
Mr. Asker smiles. The crowd mills close.
    Mr. Asker (*Indignantly*). I'll have you know there have been *no* robberies at any of the BANKERS BANK branches since 1886.
    Second cop. Year of the blizzard!

351 GROUP SHOT—FAVORING FIRST COP
He gives Cop Number Two a dirty look.
    First cop. Check it!
    Second cop (*He* knows *the year of the blizzard*). But I know—
    First Cop. Check it!
The Second cop walks out of the shot.
    Mr. Asker (*The salesman*). Now, while they're checking, could I interest you—

352 MEDIUM SHOT—ASKER'S DESK
Second cop lifts the phone on the desk.
    Second cop. Gimme headquarters—
He looks out of the scene.

353 GROUP SHOT—FAVORING JONATHAN
Jonathan is not too sure of himself.
    Jonathan. All I would like is a certified check for Mr. Donatello. Joe Donatello.
Asker pantomimes, "Of course."

354 MEDIUM SHOT—ASKER'S DESK
The cop gets his party.
    Second cop. Hello, O'Malley? This is O'Hare. I'm here with O'Reilly at the Bankers Bank and Trust Company. There's been a robbery. Well, check it.

355 GROUP SHOT—FAVORING ASKER
Asker is all smiles.

Mr. Asker. But the rest of the money? What about that?

Jonathan (*Hesitatingly*). Could—could I open a savings account?

Asker puts his arm around Jonathan and leads him out of the shot.

356 MEDIUM SHOT—ASKER'S DESK

O'Hare is desperate.

O'Hare. There *must* have been a robbery.

357 MEDIUM SHOT—CROWD WITH BANK DOOR IN BACKGROUND

Several reporters push their way through the crowd. Their upturned hats display press cards.

Reporters (*All speaking at once*). Mr. Boone, Mr. Boone! We want a story. I'm from the *Times-Dispatch*. I'm from the *Union-Herald*. How about a picture?

One of them grabs Jonathan's arm.

First reporter. We want the low-down on this dough. Rich uncle die?

Mr. Asker steps to the front.

Mr. Asker. Gentlemen. Gentlemen. One at a time.

358 MEDIUM SHOT—ASKER'S DESK

O'Hare is really sweating.

O'Hare. What! No robberies in the last fifteen days. (*Shaking his head.*) You sure, O'Kelly? Okay, O'Kelly. (*Disappointed.*) Oh, dear.

He rises and goes out of the shot.

359 CLOSE SHOT—GROUP FAVORING TELLER WINDOW AND JONATHAN

The money is being dumped out of the baskets onto the teller's counter. Asker is directing operations.

Mr. Asker. Hurry, please.

O'Hare enters the shot and takes Jonathan by the arm.

O'Hare. You can't deposit that. How do we know it's yours?

Jonathan (*Shaking himself free*). My good man! There is no law against having money. Yet!

First reporter pushes to the fore again.

First reporter. *Where* did you get all this cabbage?

Jonathan leans back on the sill.

Jonathan. Well, I'll tell you. I've been doing some experimenting.

Ma Boone's voice. Jonathan. Jonathan.

360 MEDIUM SHOT—GROUP WITH MA AND PA BOONE

Ma advances to the front.

Ma Boone. What have you done, boy?

361 CAMERA PANS PA AND MA INTO THE GROUP WITH JONATHAN

He puts his arm around his mother.
> **Jonathan.** It's all right, Ma. (*To the press.*) Now, as I was saying—
> **Reporters.** Yes? Yes?

Jonathan makes himself comfortable.
> **Jonathan.** I'm thinking of buying this park. Thinking of turning it into a giant experimental station.

362 MEDIUM SHOT—FAVORING MR. ASKER

A bank teller hands Mr. Asker a book.
> **Mr. Asker.** Here is your passbook, Mr. Boone. A nice little beginning. $568,932.20.

The crowd cannot restrain their "Ohs," and "Ahs."
> **Mr. Asker** (*Continued*). And here is Mr. Donatello's check.

Jonathan takes both the check and the passbook. With Ma and Pa, he turns and heads out of the door.

363 MEDIUM SHOT—EXTERIOR BANK

Several policemen are holding the crowd of noisy onlookers at bay. Jonathan comes out of the bank with the Boones and spies something.

364 MEDIUM LONG SHOT—THE LINCOLN CONVERTIBLE

The car stops in front of the bank. Dandy is driving. Larry is beside her.

365 CLOSE SHOT—JONATHAN ON TOP OF BANK STEPS

Jonathan waves tentatively at Dandy, wondering what her reaction will be.

366 MEDIUM CLOSE SHOT—CAR

Dandy gets out and smiles at Jonathan. Larry moves into Dandy's seat.

367 MEDIUM CLOSE SHOT—JONATHAN

He smiles back, reassured, and bounds down the steps.

368 MEDIUM SHOT—THE CAR

Jonathan runs into the shot.
> **Dandy.** I just heard.

She throws her arms around Jonathan's neck and kisses him. Larry burns. As they break, Dandy goes on.
> **Dandy** (*Continued*). What have you been up to? All this money—
> **Jonathan.** I—I cashed my bonus check.

369 MEDIUM SHOT—THE CAR

As Dandy shows her skepticism, Jonathan turns to Larry.
> **Jonathan.** Donatello's, James—er—Lawrence—er—Larry.

Jonathan helps Dandy into the back seat. The car pulls away.
DISSOLVE TO

370 MEDIUM SHOT—OUTSIDE DONATELLO'S

The car enters the shot. A happy and excited Donatello rushes out to greet them.

Donatello (*To Jonathan*). It's-a work, bambino. It's-a work. I know. I know—

Jonathan tries to quiet him, indicating the gathering crowd.

Jonathan. Yes—but they don't. Here's your check, Mr. D.

Donatello effusively mutters, "Grazie!" Jonathan pushes his way through the door, the crowd behind him.

371 MEDIUM SHOT—REVERSE ANGLE—INTERIOR DONATELLO'S

Jonathan opens the door and the crowd fills in behind him. They stop dead in their tracks and hold it for a second. Jonathan indicates Julius (off scene).

372 CLOSE SHOT—JULIUS

The plant is now three feet tall and covered with money. Julius has shed it all over the floor. The plant straightens up proudly and holds out his leaves to Jonathan in welcome.

373 REVERSE ANGLE—SHOOTING AT CROWD AND JONATHAN

Jonathan points with pride.

Jonathan. Well, friends. There he is. Julius! I taught him all he knows.

Jonathan moves forward.

374 MEDIUM LONG SHOT

Julius is in the foreground. Jonathan and Donatello come close to the plant. The crowd gathers around them. Dandy and Larry edge up to Jonathan. Julius drops a few measly twenties. Two reporters push to the front muttering.

Reporters. Gee whiz! Gee whiz! Gee whiz!

375 MEDIUM CLOSE SHOT—JONATHAN, DANDY, AND LARRY

Jonathan is thoroughly enjoying the commotion he has caused. Dandy is at his side with love-light in her eyes—Larry, uncomfortable beside her. Donatello is overjoyed.

Jonathan (*To a reporter*). You may quote me as saying that this is only one of several experiments. I'm working on a formula to convert the Atlantic Ocean into milk—

The crowd emits a sigh of wonderment.

Jonathan (*Continued*). The Pacific into buttermilk!

The crowd is overwhelmed. Jonathan looks longingly at Dandy. She returns his burning gaze. Larry tries to share the enthusiasm, but his

heart isn't in it. Jonathan is about to continue expounding his plans when he is interrupted by voices from the doorway.
> **Voices.** Mademoiselle Dandy!

375A MEDIUM SHOT—ENTRANCE DOOR

Three male modistes are standing in the doorway. Two of them are tall—one is short. They are all in cutaways, and their arms are laden with material and tailor's equipment. Dandy's voice comes over the shot.
> **Dandy's voice.** Antoine!

The first tall modiste bows.
> **Dandy's voice** (*Continued*). Gaston!

The second tall modiste bows.
> **Dandy's voice** (*Continued*). Butch!

The third (short)modiste bows. All three smile and start out of the shot.

376 GROUP SHOT—JONATHAN AND THE CROWD

The male modistes rush into the scene. Without a word, they toss their equipment aside and start measuring Jonathan, Ma, Pa, and Dandy. Pa resists. The scene becomes a madhouse of measuring, the three couturiers screaming measurements in French. Dandy manages to shout a word of explanation.
> **Dandy** (*To Jonathan*). You're a great man, Johnny. You've got to look like a million!

The three musketeers scream instructions and go on with their work. Bedlam!

DISSOLVE TO

376A MEDIUM CLOSE SHOT—EXTERIOR DONATELLO'S

The door flings open. Jonathan, arrayed in a resplendent cutaway, complete with boutonniere and topper, comes out, followed by Dandy in an equally resplendent new outfit. Larry comes alongside. He is laden with most of Jonathan's old clothes. Jonathan tosses his suspendered old pants over Larry's arm and moves out of the shot with Dandy. Through the door come Pa and Ma Boone. Ma is in a beautiful sequined evening gown with a train. She is pulling along a pair of mechanical rabbits. Pa, in full evening dress, is dragging along a cart stuffed with greenbacks. He tips his topper to the crowd and puts it on. It slips down over his ears. He stops and yanks it off, reaches into the cart, stuffs the hatband with bills, and offers his arm to Ma. They stride on out of the shot, followed by the "ah"-ing crowd.

DISSOLVE TO

377 LONG SHOT—AT CORNER OF BANK

A procession is coming down the street bearing placards. A truck rolls by with a banner on its side: BOOM WITH BOONE. *Others read:* BOONE FOR PRESIDENT, BOONE FOR PRESIDENT OF THE U.N. *The music of a band comes over the scene, building it to a pitch of excitement. Two girls in skin-tight briefs, wielding drum-major batons, head another group. They carry a smaller banner reading:* BOONE FOR SECRETARY OF AGRICULTURE. *The crowd mills around, and Jonathan accepts their applause.*

378 MEDIUM GROUP SHOT—FAVORING BANK DOOR

Mr. Asker comes out of the bank, smiling from ear to ear. He indicates the busy interior of the bank.

Mr. Asker. Welcome, Mr. Boone. We have put on eight additional men just to service your account.

The eight men appear and take Pa's cart inside, as Mr. Asker continues.

Mr. Asker (*Continued*). You may wait for your passbook here if you like, sir.

Jonathan's eyes do a tired Noel Coward.

Jonathan. Send it!

Asker bows.

379 MEDIUM SHOT—OVER CROWD TOWARD THE GROUP

The band is playing. The mob cheers college fashion, ending with three "Hoorays." Megaphones are evident in the crowd. The group with a gay Dandy and a tired Larry, laden down with props, return the accolade of the people. Pa waves with his topper. They are all a bit bored with it.

380 CLOSE SHOT—JONATHAN'S SHOULDER—CROWD BEYOND

Jonathan's shoulder blocks out much of the mob. His arm is raised in greeting when a strong hand heavily falls on his shoulder. Jonathan turns.

381 CLOSE SHOT—REVERSE ANGLE—ASKER

Asker's hand is still on Jonathan's shoulder, his eyes, cold and hard.

Mr. Asker. Where did you get that money?

382 CLOSE TWO-SHOT—ASKER AND JONATHAN

Jonathan resents Mr. Asker's tone. He answers with a superior air.

Jonathan. I told you where I got it. It's my—invention!

Mr. Asker. Exactly. The money is counterfeit!

The onlookers gasp their unbelief.

383 CLOSE-UP—JONATHAN

He gulps unbelievingly and starts to stammer.

Jonathan. But that's impossible. (*To the crowd.*) You—you all saw it—on Julius—

384 MEDIUM GROUP SHOT—FAVORING JONATHAN

O'Hare and O'Toole and the other cops are in the scene.

O'Hare (*Menacingly*). We want to see "Julius"—*again*!

Jonathan is yanked out of the scene by the police as the crowd mills about and voices its disappointment.

DISSOLVE TO

385 INTERIOR DONATELLO'S

Julius is standing in the corner, six feet tall, and loaded down with bills. Police and bank officials are wading through the tons of money. They mutter, "Counterfeit," every time they pick up a bill. This makes a chorus under the scene and increases in intensity as it progresses. Mr. Asker comes to the front of the shot. He addresses himself to O'Hare.

Mr. Asker. Every last one of them is counterfeit.

CAMERA PANS WITH O'HARE *as he crosses to Jonathan.*

O'Hare. You're under arrest, Boone.

He starts to take Jonathan by the arm, but Jonathan protests.

Jonathan. Please, sir! Julius may be a skunk parsnip, but he's not a counterfeiter. Please!

O'Hare nods, "O.K." Jonathan turns out of the shot.

386 CLOSE SHOT—JULIUS

Jonathan enters and looks up and down at Julius's new stalks.

Jonathan. Julius! How could you do this to me?

He looks down into Julius's little pot.

387 INSERT—JULIUS'S FLOWER POT

At the base of the stalk, on which the leaves seem to form a skirt, is another little stalk.

388 CLOSE TWO-SHOT—JONATHAN AND JULIUS

Jonathan's eyes pop. He looks amazed.

Jonathan. Why—why didn't you tell me you were going to be a mother!

Julius turns away to one side.

389 CLOSE-UP—DANDY

She is deeply hurt at what she is learning.

390 CLOSE TWO-SHOT—JONATHAN AND JULIUS

Jonathan turns back from looking at Dandy.

Jonathan. I didn't know. You were *jealous*! That's why you made them counterfeit.

391 CLOSE SHOT—MA AND PA

Tears are coming into their eyes. It's a sad thing they behold. Ma wipes her nose on her sequin gown. In the presence of motherhood, Pa removes his hat.

392 CLOSE SHOT—JONATHAN AND JULIUS

    Jonathan. Can you ever forgive me? Juli—*Julia!*

Julia moves further away to one side.

393 CLOSE SHOT—MR. ASKER AND THE TWO COPS

They too are moved. They remove their hats and sniffle.

394 CLOSE TWO-SHOT—JONATHAN AND JULIA

Jonathan has his arm around the stalk.

    Jonathan. Please try to forgive me. Try. On my bended knees, I beg forgiveness, Julia, my hope and inspiration.

395 MEDIUM SHOT—DANDY AND LARRY

Larry laughs derisively, not believing Jonathan's plea. He also becomes aware that he still is carrying Jonathan's clothing. He flings the clothes angrily to the floor. Dandy turns to him.

    Dandy. Take me away, Larry. Away from that Romeo and his Juliet!

She buries her head in Larry's shoulder.

396 MEDIUM SHOT—THE GROUP

They are all crying except Jonathan. He is too moved to cry. O'Hare comes up to him in the foreground.

    O'Hare (*Full of tears*). C—come along now. It's t—time.

They go for the door. The CAMERA PANS WITH THEM. *Jonathan stops for one final look. He sees something.*

397 CLOSE TWO-SHOT—LARRY AND DANDY

We see what Jonathan sees. Dandy and Larry are in a tight embrace.

398 CLOSE SHOT—JONATHAN AT DOOR

Jonathan's eyes are green with jealousy. O'Hare yanks him through the door.

DISSOLVE TO

399 CORNER OF COURT ROOM

Jonathan sits on a wooden bench. His cutaway is a wrinkled mess. There is a spotlight focused on him. He is getting the third and fourth degrees. The men surrounding him wear long flowing coats. Their collars are higher than normal and their string ties, stringier. This scene will be shot silent with cut-in flashes of the faces surrounding Jonathan.

The CAMERA SHOOTS AT OFF ANGLES, *and the chant of "Counterfeit," which was set up in scene 385, comes to a peak here.*
DISSOLVE TO

400 MEDIUM SHOT—JUDGE ON BENCH

The angle is from below. The bench seems very high and the two lamps at either end are at crazy angles. The judge pounds for silence. A hush falls.

Judge. You, Jonathan Boone, stand before this tribunal accused of grave and heinous crimes. Forgery. Counterfeiting. Arson. Misrepresentation. Disorderly conduct. And spitting in the subway. How do you plead?

401 HIGH ANGLE—SHOOTING DOWN AT JONATHAN

Jonathan is kneeling on the floor. His hands are tied by ropes and he is wearing Franciscan robes.

Jonathan. Innocent, your honor.

402 MEDIUM SHOT—JUDGE ON BENCH

The judge laughs.

Judge. Innocent, eh? Ladies and gentlemen of the jury, how find you the defendant?

He turns off scene.

403 MEDIUM SHOT—JURY BOX

The jury is in long flowing robes, leaning forward on their left elbows. The first row shows Marko, Barton, Briggs, Donatello, Flotow, and Larry. The second row shows O'Hare, O'Toole, Mr. Asker, and Dandy. Dandy is dressed in her ballet tutu. As the judge's voice (echo chamber) dies out, the jury raises their right hands in the Roman fashion and turns thumbs down.

404 CLOSE SHOT—JONATHAN

He is stunned. He starts to tear madly at his bindings.

405 MEDIUM SHOT—THE JUDGE

The judge points his finger down at Jonathan.

Judge. You have been found guilty as charged and are hereby sentenced to be—guillotined—until you are dead.

The off-scene crowd roars its approval.
DISSOLVE TO

406 MEDIUM SHOT—THE STREET

The mob is going wild. Many wear caps reminiscent of the French revolution. Pikes and staves are in evidence. Jonathan comes along, riding in an oxcart. CAMERA DOLLIES *along with the crowd until it* brings the guillotine used in Marko's act into view. Jonathan is taken out of the cart and hoisted up the steps.

407 CLOSE SHOT—THE EXECUTIONER
Through the slits of the mask we can see it is Marko.

408 CLOSE SHOT—THE BLOCK
Jonathan's head s being put in place. He sees something.

409 VERY CLOSE SHOT—DANDY AND LARRY
They are at the side of the steps. Smoke steams up from their clinch.

410 CLOSE SHOT—THE SUSPENDED BLADE
The crowd roars. The blade teeters. It falls down, out of the shot.

411 MEDIUM SHOT—INTERIOR FLORIST SHOP WINDOW FROM OUTSIDE
Jonathan's arms are on the window sill. His head is on his hands. His eyes are closed. The window frame falls on his neck. The dream music comes to a crashing finale, then holds in a drawn out discord, as Jonathan's eyes open and he stares straight ahead in terror.

412 LONG SHOT—PARK
The vista is teetering as before. It stops teetering. Silence. The music stops.

413 MEDIUM SHOT—INTERIOR FLORIST SHOP
Jonathan raises the window until it catches. He shakes his head, still not sure where he is. The CAMERA PANS OVER *as he comes to, hurries to the icebox, and opens it.*

414 CLOSE SHOT—JONATHAN
He takes Julius out of the icebox. There is no money on the parsnip, but its leaves have stopped drooping, and there are three buds on the plant. Jonathan smiles slowly, then grins with joy.

    Jonathan. It worked! This isn't a dream.

He moves out of the scene with Julius and the jar of aloe extract.

415 MEDIUM SHOT—NEAR DOOR TO CHAMBER OF HORRORS
Jonathan comes into the shot and sets Julius down on a low, glass-topped table. It has a second round shelf—a mirror—beneath the circular glass tabletop. He sinks into a chair and starts to open the aloe jar. Suddenly his eyes widen.

416 CLOSE-UP—MIRRORED TABLE SHELF
Reflected in the mirror, Dandy's diamond sparkles in the bottom of the flower pot.

417 CLOSE SHOT—JONATHAN
He picks up the flower pot and turns it carefully upside down. He reaches out and touches the diamond.

Marko's voice. So you're the thief!
Jonathan reacts and looks off scene.
418 CLOSE SHOT—MARKO
The hypnotist is standing in the doorway leading to the Chamber of Horrors. He is alone. He closes the door behind him and moves toward Jonathan. The CAMERA SWINGS WITH HIM UNTIL IT INCLUDES JONATHAN. *Jonathan's eyes are question marks.*
    Marko. That's Dandy's diamond—
He holds out his hand and moves forward. Jonathan gets up and backs away. Marko's suavity is gone.
    Jonathan. I didn't even know. *You* stole it! You hid it here. You—
Marko clips Jonathan on the chin. He goes down. The flower pot rolls out of the shot. Marko starts after it. Jonathan dives after him.
419 MEDIUM SHOT—FLORIST SHOP
Jonathan tackles Marko around the knees as he picks up Julius. Both men stagger to their feet. Jonathan socks Marko. The hypnotist staggers back against the wall, holding the flower pot.
420 CLOSE SHOT—MARKO
His head bounces back from the wall. He sneaks a look down at the floor.
421 CLOSE SHOT—FLOOR
The diamond is lying in a scattering of dirt that spilled out of the pot.
422 CLOSE SHOT—MARKO
His eyes come up to Jonathan's.
423 CLOSE SHOT—JONATHAN (FLASH)
He hasn't seen the diamond. He stares at Marko.
424 CLOSE SHOT—MARKO
He smiles and dashes out of the scene toward Jonathan, still carrying Julius.
425 MEDIUM SHOT—FLORIST SHOP
Marko comes into the scene and slugs Jonathan. As they fight, Marko lets Jonathan get the flower pot. Then he slugs Jonathan hard. Jonathan's knees buckle. He supports himself against the wall. His head turns away from his assailant. Marko quickly picks up the diamond. Barton comes through the door leading to the Chamber of Horrors. Marko sticks the diamond in his pocket.
426 MEDIUM SHOT—REAR ENTRANCE DOOR
Larry, Reilly, and another cop come through the door and walk forward out of the shot.

427 CLOSE SHOT—ENTRANCE DOOR

Donatello enters and stands, amazed at what he sees.

428 GENERAL VIEW

Larry, the second cop, and Reilly, his hat in his hand, come into the scene. Jonathan, Marko, and Barton are about as we last saw them.

Marko (*Indicating Jonathan*). There's your thief. The diamond's in that flower pot.

Jonathan is clutching the pot. He thinks the diamond is in it. Confronted by two cops, he hesitates before answering. Donatello comes in from the entrance door.

Donatello (*To Marko*). You must-a be crazy.

Reilly takes a step forward. Jonathan moves back.

Marko. He's going to run. Slug him!

Reilly reaches for his hip pocket. Jonathan snatches the aloe jar from the table and crowns Reilly on his bald pate. Reilly crumples to the floor. The second cop starts for Jonathan. He runs out toward the entrance door. Donatello blocks Larry and the second cop as they go for Jonathan. They throw him aside and run after the fugitive. Marko starts for the door leading to the Chamber of Horrors as though to head Jonathan off. Barton grabs Marko's arm. The hypnotist has no choice. He runs for the front door with Barton. Dandy, with Ma and Pa in tow, comes into the scene from the direction of the rear entrance door. Dandy grabs Donatello and swings him around to ask him what happened.

429 MEDIUM SHOT—EXTERIOR FLORIST SHOP

The entrance door is open. Larry and the second cop are looking up and down the street for Jonathan. Barton and Marko are with them.

Larry. He's vanished.

Marko pretends that he thinks Jonathan may have gone into the House of Wonders next door. To get away from the others, he crosses and goes in. But the rest follow him—Larry last. As they go, Dandy comes out of the florist shop, swinging the door closed. Jonathan is behind it. He grabs Dandy's hand and they hotfoot out of the scene. Larry turns and sees them. He yells inside to the others.

Larry (*Continued*). Out here!

Barton and the second cop, with Marko between them, reappear from the House of Wonders.

Barton. Stop, thief!

The four men hightail after Jonathan and Dandy. Several of the passersby follow them.

430 MEDIUM LONG SHOT—EXTERIOR ROLLER COASTER

Jonathan and Dandy come running in. A car is unloading passengers at the end of a ride. Jonathan starts to explain to Dandy what happened. The voices of the pursuers come over the shot.

    Voices. Stop, thief! STOP, THIEF!

Jonathan looks off, then grabs Dandy's arm.

    Jonathan. Got to hide a minute.

Jonathan takes advantage of the screen formed by the people leaving the ride and pulls Dandy into the front seat of the stationary car.

431 CLOSE SHOT—JONATHAN AND DANDY

As they sit down in the car seat.

    Jonathan (*Talking fast*). They think I stole your diamond—
    Dandy. Joe told me.
    Jonathan. I didn't but—(*Turning Julius upside down.*) But I've got it. Marko put it in here.

He stares down at the inverted pot. The hole is empty.

    Jonathan. It's gone. Must have dropped it.

They bend over and begin to search frantically on the car floor.

432 LONGER SHOT

A few passengers, getting into the car, hide Dandy and Jonathan as they look on the floor. Larry, Barton, Marko, the second cop, and the small crowd that followed them run into the shot as the roller coaster attendant reaches for the lever that starts the car.

    Barton (*To the attendant*). Where is he?
    Attendant (*Shoving the lever*). Where's who?

The car jerks forward. Jonathan and Dandy straighten up. Barton sees them. He dives for the car, shoving Marko into one of the rear seats. Larry and the cop dive into the car after them, just in time. The car rolls out of the shot.

    Attendant. Will somebody please tell me—

The crowd starts to jabber.

433 GENERAL VIEW—ROLLER COASTER*

(*Note: * indicates second unit shots with doubles.*)

The car is coming to the summit of its uphill climb. Barton and the cops are crawling forward over people to reach Jonathan. The car goes over the hump and starts down the incline.

434 TIED-OFF EYEMO SHOT WITH PRINCIPALS

The descent throws Barton and the cop off balance. They save themselves from falling and scramble around with the occupants of the car, two seats behind Jonathan and Dandy. The car is traveling a mile a minute. The girl occupants scream.

435 ANGLE SHOT*

The car whips around a curve like a catapult and slows down slightly as it starts up a second rise.

436 EYEMO SHOT WITH PRINCIPALS

Barton and the cop start forward again. Larry yells encouragement from behind them. Marko is looking about him, trying to figure a way out when the ride is over.

437 PAN SHOT—LONG FOCUS LENS*

The car goes over a second hump and starts down again. This time, Barton and the cop are almost thrown out of the car. As the car whirls around another curve, the cop yanks Barton back into the car.

438 GROUP SHOT—CROWD

They are looking up at the roller coaster. Their eyes follow the whizzing car (off scene). A woman screams and covers her face.

439 PAN SHOT—LONG FOCUS LENS*

The car hurtles downhill again. The cop starts for Jonathan. The others are a tangle of arms and legs.

440 EYEMO SHOT—JONATHAN, DANDY, AND COP

Jonathan and Dandy tear the cop's hand off Jonathan's shoulder and shove him back into the seat behind them.

441 ANGLE SHOT*

The car is hurtling along as it nears the end of the ride. Barton and the cop get ready to make the pinch. Barton loses his balance once again. He and the cop fall backwards onto Larry.

442 MEDIUM SHOT—HIGH ANGLE—EXTERIOR ROLLER COASTER

The car rolls to a stop—the finish of the ride. The crowd mills around the car. Barton staggers forward and grabs Jonathan. Marko eases himself out of the scene.

    Barton. You're under arrest.
    Dandy. No!
    Jonathan (*Pointing off*). He's got it! Look!

443 MEDIUM SHOT—EXTERIOR PARK GROUNDS

Marko, trying to lose himself in the crowd, turns, sees Jonathan pointing, and runs out of the scene.

444 MEDIUM CLOSE SHOT—ROLLER COASTER

Jonathan wrenches himself free from Barton and dashes after Marko. The others hesitate.

Dandy. Don't stand there!

Dandy, Barton, Larry, and the cop spring out of the scene.

445 MEDIUM LONG SHOT—EXTERIOR FLORIST SHOP

Marko runs in, looks back, and darts into the shop.

446 GENERAL VIEW—INTERIOR FLORIST SHOP

We are shooting toward the entrance door in the background. Donatello, Ma, and Pa are grouped around the fallen Reilly whose head is hidden by the glass-topped table. Marko comes in through the entrance door and runs over to the door leading to the Chamber of Horrors, stumbling over the prostrate Reilly en route. Marko gets back on his feet. Jonathan bursts into the shop, just as Marko disappears into the passageway. Jonathan follows him. We hear them fighting. Reilly staggers to his feet and weaves toward the mirror by the entrance door.

447 GENERAL VIEW—INTERIOR PASSAGEWAY

Marko slugs Jonathan. As Jonathan staggers back and goes down to his knees, Marko runs out of the scene toward the Chamber of Horrors.

448 CLOSE SHOT—INTERIOR FLORIST SHOP

Reilly is staring at himself in the mirror. His bald head is covered with something like the fuzz on a peach. Reilly runs his hand over the fuzz.

Reilly. Hair!

He turns and looks off toward Donatello.

449 GROUP SHOT—DONATELLO, MA, AND PA

Donatello bends down quickly and comes up with the broken bottom of the aloe extract jar. He looks from the jar to Reilly.

Donatello. Abso-positively!

450 GENERAL VIEW

Barton, Larry, the second cop, and Dandy come through the entrance door. A small crowd fills the doorway behind them. Dandy turns to Donatello as the rest look around the shop.

Dandy. Johnny get him?

Donatello (*Indicating the door*). Through there.

Dandy dashes into the passageway. The rest start to follow her. Donatello stops Barton.

Donatello (*Continued*). Go around outside.

Barton. What for?

Donatello. Back door. Marko could get away.

Larry. Joe's right. I'll show you.

The three men run out the front entrance. Reilly takes another pleased look at himself in the mirror and follows them. Donatello, Ma, and Pa exit through the door to the Chamber of Horrors.

451 INTERIOR CHAMBER OF HORRORS—REAR EXIT

The exit door is marked FIRE EXIT. *A few discarded wax dummies and a big piece of scenery lean against the wall—the scenic piece, two or three feet from the wall at its base. Marko comes running in and tries the exit door handle. The door sticks. Marko puts his foot against the wall and yanks on the handle. After a couple of hard tugs, the door pulls open. Marko starts through it. The Hudson River, Grant's Tomb, and a big cathedral spire can be seen on the New York side. Barton, Larry, Reilly, and the second cop run into the scene just outside the door. Marko slams the door in their faces and locks it. He pockets the key as he hears Dandy's voice behind him.*

Dandy's voice. Johnny! Where are you?

Marko listens intently.

Jonathan's voice. Over here. He got away from me.

Marko thinks fast and decides that his only out is back through the florist shop. Barton and the rest start pounding on the locked door. Marko ducks behind the leaning scenery. Jonathan and Dandy run in, look about them, hear the voices outside, and try to open the locked door.

Dandy (*Yelling*). It's locked. Go back the other way.

The men outside shout a muffled answer. Something falls behind Dandy and Jonathan. They turn and exit in the direction of the sound.

452 CLOSE SHOT—CHAMBER OF HORRORS

Marko picks up the prop he knocked over and tiptoes out of the scene. Dandy and Jonathan come running in a moment later. Jonathan goes off in the direction taken by Marko.

453 INTERIOR CHAMBER OF HORRORS—NEAR DU BARRY GROUP

Marko's miniature guillotine is in the foreground of the shadowy area. Jonathan comes in past the guillotine. As his back goes away from us, the CAMERA PANS, *disclosing the motionless figure of Marko beside the instrument of death. The guillotine's prop blade falls. Jonathan turns, sees Marko's figure, steps forward, and clips the hypnotist on the chin. The figure goes over backwards toward* CAMERA.

454 CLOSE SHOT—FLOOR

As Marko's head and upper body land and shatter into a dozen wax pieces.

455 CLOSE SHOT—JONATHAN

He reacts to the breaking of the wax dummy. The real Marko appears behind him and raises a heavy iron cudgel.

456 CLOSE-UP—DANDY

She screams and runs forward.

457 MEDIUM CLOSE SHOT—JONATHAN AND MARKO

The weapon descends, and Jonathan ducks. The iron crashes against the guillotine. Jonathan straightens up and lands a haymaker on Marko's jaw. The hypnotist staggers back.

458 GENERAL VIEW—JONATHAN AND MARKO

Marko hurtles to the floor—out cold. Jonathan bends over him and starts to search Marko for the diamond.

459 MEDIUM CLOSE SHOT—DU BARRY GROUP

Dandy comes running into the scene but is stymied behind the chaise longue in her effort to get to Jonathan. As she steps over the couch, Jonathan enters the scene and hands her the diamond.

460 CLOSE SHOT—CHAMBER OF HORRORS

Donatello, with Ma and Pa Boone, comes into the scene between some stalagmites and stops. The three look off past CAMERA. *Dandy's voice comes over the scene.*

    Dandy's voice (*Meaning, "What is this new look!"*). Jonathan!

461 CLOSE SHOT—DANDY AND JONATHAN

Jonathan's expression is definitely Rhett Butler-ish. He seizes Dandy in his arms. The CAMERA TILTS DOWN WITH THEM *as they stumble onto the chaise longue, knocking Du Barry off the couch, out of the shot.*

462 CLOSE SHOT—DU BARRY

The wax figure lands on the floor and teeters back toward the end of the couch where Jonathan and Dandy are, so that Du Barry is facing them (off scene). The figure continues to teeter around, so that it faces the CAMERA WHICH DOLLIES IN TO A HEAD CLOSE-UP. *One of the mechanical eyes winks slowly and knowingly.*

FADE OUT

Falling Star

Original Story Idea and Screenplay
by
Frank Tuttle

FADE IN
1   "Falling Star" and remaining credit titles.
DISSOLVE TO
2   CLOSE OVER-SHOULDER SHOT—ANDREW AND FRANCES
Frances's back is to CAMERA. *Facing her is Andrew, a coldly handsome man of fifty in a dinner jacket. He is frowning.*

    Andrew. What's happened to you? You're not the woman I married. You don't even look like her. What became of that woman?
    Frances (*Quietly*). You killed her.
Andrew glances down at Frances's hand (not visible).
    Andrew. Give me that!
Frances whirls away from him so that she, too, is facing CAMERA. *She is holding a highball glass, which is half full.*
    Frances. Fat chance! It's my only friend.
    Andrew. I just can't understand it. When I married you, you were sweet, talented.
    Frances (*Sloshing the glass's contents*). That's right.
    Andrew. What did this to you?
    Frances. You did! (*Drinking quickly and turning back to him.*) You and your I-own-you attitude. You had to marry someone like me so you could point me out to your friends and say, "Look!" (*Turning toward* CAMERA *and gesturing with her glass.*) "Look at my prize possession—my wife! Sing for them, darling! Dance for them! Act for them! I bought you. I own you. Perform!" So I performed—
She walks past him to a table. As he turns to watch her, she pours a stiff shot into her glass and twists toward him again. Once again, she faces CAMERA.
    Frances (*Continued*). But if one of them liked what I did just a little too much—if he liked me for myself—why, then—Yi, yi!

Those scenes! In front of everybody—even the servants you hired to spy on me. It made me cringe. And after every stupid, insane jealous outburst, you'd end up sobbing and screaming how much you loved me!

Andrew. Frances, I did love you. I still do!

Frances. Ho–ho! There's one for the mocking birds! You loved you—*you*! No one but you! Look at me. Look what that love did to me—a psychopath! A drunk!

Andrew. You said that! I didn't. Remember that!

Frances. But you're the one who made me a lush. You remember that! Old song! (*Raising her glass.*) You made me what I am tonight, I hope you're satisfied. (*She drinks.*) Let me tell you something, Andy-Pandy. When those nurses drive up to cart me away to the ga-ga hatch, I'll welcome them. I'll sing out loud and clear at the top of my lungs: "Come in, ladies in white! Pin a rose on my straight jacket! It's a pleasure to go with your smiling faces, away from this—(*Pointing at Andrew.*) this cold, selfish, dried up PIG! Yes, ladies, that's what he is and that's why I'm this—(*Tapping her breast.*) a broken down, miserable, useless *freak*!"

She bursts into sobs, sits down, and leans on the table. It collapses. Frances is flabbergasted.

3   REVERSE CLOSE SHOT—CAMERA CREW

The shot reveals that what we have just seen is a sequence being photographed in a motion picture studio. The director jumps up and runs toward the fallen actress.

4   MEDIUM CLOSE SHOT—AT BROKEN CHAIR

George Harrington, the actor who was playing Andrew, is helping up Lola Murray, the actress who was playing Frances. She is doing her best to be a good sport about the accident. The director runs in.

Director. You all right, Lola?

Lola. I—I think so. Just a bit shook up.

Director. The take was sensational. You won't have to do the whole thing over again. We can print it and move in for a close shot of the finish—just the last line. And that'll be it.

Lola (*Wry smile*). Oh, no, Lester. That was it! We'll finish it tomorrow. I'm going to have a little talk with the head man.

Director. You know what Henry Meizner will say. "Stop work? At four o'clock—with two more hours shooting time!"

Lola frowns at the director.

Lola. He's better not say that to Lola Murray!

Harrington. Particularly after that performance. You were superb, my sweet. Had me all choked up. Shall I take you to Henry's office?

Lola (*Patting his cheek*). No, thank you. You just keep on being handsome Harrington, George.

She walks off. CAMERA MOVES CLOSER *as the director grins at Harrington.*

Director. Of course you know what'll happen. Svengali will give her the old butter-up routine, and she'll be right back and finish the sequence. (*To the electricians.*) Save 'em!

The lights begin to dim out.

5   CLOSE SHOT—INTERIOR HENRY MEIZNER'S OFFICE—LOLA AND MEIZNER

The angle favors Meizner, who looks like a well-to-do, tired businessman, which is exactly what he is. It is obvious that Lola has just told him about the mishap, and he has commiserated. She emphasizes her point.

Lola. But Henry, that was the third goof today.

Meizner. So it'll be the last one. They always go in threes.

Lola. No—it's me. For Pyramid I'm a female Jonah. You should let Mercury buy my contract. I tell you, I'm just no good for you.

6   CLOSE SHOT—MEIZNER

He appears to be deeply hurt.

Meizner. No good for us? My dear Lola, that's treason. You're the greatest star Pyramid ever had!

7   CLOSE SHOT—LOLA

She is not totally unmoved by his flattery, but she is too honest to swallow the whole bit.

Lola. Perhaps I was once, but now I'm afraid I'm kind of a falling star.

8   CLOSE-UP—MEIZNER

Now he is shocked.

Meizner. Don't say such a thing—even as a joke. Let me tell you something, and remember I'm like your older brother—

9   CLOSE-UP—LOLA

A glint shines in her eye, which her intimate friends have learned is a definite warming.

Lola. Last time you sold me something you were like my father.

10 CLOSE-UP—MEIZNER
This startles him.
> **Meizner.** Wh–what? But I'm not selling you anything. It's just that I've been watching the rushes on this picture with particular care. They're the best thing you've ever done in your whole career. Absolutely superb. Why, that scene yesterday—I was crying!

11 CLOSE-UP—LOLA
She can't resist the temptation.
> **Lola.** Shouldn't you wait until you check the box office before you do that, Henry?

12 TWO-SHOT—FAVORING MEIZNER
He is just a bit slow getting her jibe. He frowns.
> **Meizner.** That's enough of that, young lady. If you finish this sequence tonight, you'll clean up everything by tomorrow. And if you do that, I'm going to give you three weeks off.
> **Lola.** Fair enough. I'll do it.
> **Meizner.** Good. Good. Oh—er—
> **Lola** (*Rising*). Yes?

CAMERA MOVES SLOWLY CLOSER
> **Meizner.** How do you like George Harrington to work with?
> **Lola.** Fine. Good actor.
> **Meizner.** You've been seeing quite a lot of him, haven't you?
> **Lola.** Not even often enough to make the gossip columns. What is this—the FBI?
> **Meizner.** Good heavens, no. Just curious.
> **Lola.** Don't worry. You know the way I feel about actresses getting married, after booting my one try at it.
> **Meizner.** I never agreed with you that that was your fault. Well, I mustn't keep you from getting back on the set—showing those know-it-all youngsters the way a real trouper troupes!
> **Lola.** Aren't you the one—

She gives her employer a little pat on the head and leaves as we FADE OUT.

FADE IN

13 MOVING SHOT—EXTERIOR SWIMMING POOL—DAY
After holding for several feet on a full shot of Lola Murray's two-story Colonial house, which is partially reflected in her swimming pool, CAMERA SWINGS AND MOVES CLOSE *to Lola and Meizner who are seated at the edge of the pool, quite close together at a small garden*

table. *The angle favors Lola who is wearing a garden frock and a picture hat. Meizner's hands support his face, which is partially hidden by them as he listens.*

    Lola. Come on, now, Henry. We finished a day ahead of schedule—due largely to me. So how about letting your hard-working hired help make just one picture a year *not* on your beautiful lot? Is that so much to ask?

    Meizner. Yes, Lola. Yes it is. In fact, my board of directors would never permit it.

    Lola. They would if you insisted. Don't be modest, Henry. Matter of fact, you *are* Pyramid's board of directors.

14 OVER-SHOULDER SHOT—FAVORING MEIZNER

He lowers the supporting hands, disclosing that he is almost on the point of tears. He hasn't been watching and bargaining with actors for twenty years for nothing.

    Meizner. But why? I mean, why should you ask me to do such a thing?

15 CLOSE SHOT—LOLA

Still the gracious lady.

    Lola. Because once in a while, there's a part I want to play at some other studio—and sometimes they'll pay me three times what you do!

16 CLOSE SHOT—MEIZNER

Switching quickly to the sharp horse trader.

    Meizner. Most of which would go to the government?

17 CLOSE-UP—LOLA

Still the charmer.

    Lola. But it would look so pretty in print—in *Variety*.

18 CLOSE-UP—MEIZNER

Ready for tears if called for.

    Meizner. My dear! For more than ten years Lola Murray has been my star. I made her!

    Lola's voice. Really, Henry! I think I had a little to do with that—

    Meizner. Granted. But you must know that I'll always find you the greatest stories, the greatest supporting casts, the greatest directors!

19 CLOSE-UP—LOLA

More and more annoyed.

    Lola. But always at Pyramid.

Meizner's voice. Where we all love you.

Lola. Then let me do just one lousy picture off the lot.

20 CLOSE TWO-SHOT—MEIZNER AND LOLA

Meizner smirks.

Meizner. Without me, that's what it would be—lousy! NO!

Lola. Suppose I quit?

Meizner. I'll sue you.

Lola. In that case, goodbye—EGOMANIAC!

She shoves back her chair.

21 LONGER SHOT

Lola rises with the mocking laugh that won her an Academy Award, sweeps off her picture hat, bows low, and speaks.

Lola. Goodbye forever!

She flicks Meizner's nose with the hat brim. He snatches the fifty-dollar chapeau and scales it into the pool. CAMERA TILTS DOWN *as the hat hits the water. The sound of a motor which gets louder and louder comes over.*

22 FULL SHOT

Lola grabs a carton of cigarettes from the table and smacks the offending hand. Meizner yelps and backs away. At this moment, like a visitor from outer space, a young man, seated in a strange contraption shaped like an eight-foot-high vertical cigar with wings whirling above the man's head, bounces down upon Lola's lawn in the foreground of the shot. Simultaneously, in the background, the terrified Pyramid executive trips and falls. The enraged star stumbles over him and flops into the pool. Meizner makes a quick getaway.

23 CLOSE SHOT—THE CONTRAPTION

The young man, in his late twenties, sees what has happened and whips off his seat belt. He shuts off his motor and runs out of the scene.

24 MEDIUM CLOSE SHOT—LOLA—SHOOTING DOWN AT POOL

She comes up blinded with rage and water, grabs the pool's ladder, clambers up and takes a swing at the flier before he can utter a word. He ducks and shoves her back into the pool—hard. She comes up again, wipes the water from her eyes and takes a good look.

25 CLOSE SHOT—THE YOUNG MAN

He is grinning down at her.

26 CLOSE-UP—LOLA

She likes what she sees. She grins back.

Lola. I'm sorry. I'm an idiot. I thought you were one of Meizner's yes-men.

She puts out her hand. CAMERA PULLS BACK *as he takes it and helps her come ashore. She wrings out a corner of her skirt and starts walking toward the pool dressing rooms. He goes with her,* CAMERA PULLING BACK *in front of them.*

The young man. I was trying out my machine there—the Larry Hunt Coptoglider—

TRUCKING SHOT. *Lola scarcely glances at the copter (off).*

Lola. Hello, Larry Hunt. I'm Lola Murray.

The young man gives her an appreciating look.

The young man. Who else? But I'm not Larry Hunt. He's the inventor. I'm John Pierpont.

Lola is puzzled.

Lola. You can't be. He must be fifty.

Johnny. That's my father. I'm John, the Third.

They are close to the dressing rooms. She stops and smiles at Johnny.

Lola. Oh. Well, if you'll excuse me, John, the Third, I'll change.

Johnny (*Quickly*). No, don't. Please—

Lola. Hmm?

Johnny. (*With a complimentary gesture*). I mean, in general, don't.

Lola gives him her most enchanting smile.

Lola. You just keep talking like that while I'm doing it—

She vanishes inside the dressing room. Her voice continues.

Lola's voice. Are the Pierpont zillions backing that copter thingamy?

CAMERA MOVES WITH JOHNNY *as he walks toward the copter.*

Johnny. I'm just demonstrating it for Larry. We were classmates. (*He stops close to the machine and calls off.*) Hey, Larry! I'm over here!

27 CLOSE SHOT—AT HEDGE

There is a gap in the hedge. An answering voice comes from several feet beyond the opening.

Larry's voice. Coming up!

A moment later, he walks through the hedge gap. He wears glasses and a sports outfit. CAMERA PANS HIM OVER TO JOHNNY *who is examining the copter.*

Larry. What happened, skipper?

Johnny. Nothing—I mean, nothing important.

Lola's voice comes over the scene.

Lola's voice. Well! I guess that puts me in my place.

28 CLOSE SHOT—AT DRESSING ROOMS—LOLA

She is wearing a terry cloth robe over her bikini as she comes forward smiling, and the CAMERA PANS HER *to the two men. Johnny's voice starts speaking before she gets there.*

Johnny's voice. Miss Lola Murray, may I present Mr. Larry Astronaut Hunt.

Lola and Harry. Hello. How are you. Great to know you.

Larry (*Unlimbering a Rolleiflex*). The monster will be on the market pretty soon. I wonder if—

He gestures toward the copter.

Lola. I'd be delighted.

Johnny takes off the robe and sits beside her in the machine as Larry takes the shot and we DISSOLVE.

29 INSERT—STILL PHOTOGRAPH

Lola and Johnny in the copter seat. They are looking at one another with obvious approval. A man's voice comes over the INSERT.

Man's voice. Who took this?

Johnny's voice. Larry Hunt, the guy who invented the coptoglider—

30 CLOSE GROUP SHOT—INTERIOR PAPKE BILLIARD ROOM—DAY

Three men are with Johnny. The man holding the snapshot is their host at the Cucamonga residence, Havana Papke—a one-time Prohibition beer baron, now in his sixties. The one who asked about the picture is a cocky Irish American in his thirties, Jimmy Duffy. Milo, the third man, is a cheap-looking Latin type. Johnny continues.

Johnny. When I got out here last week, Havana insisted I go to work for some upright citizen, so I'm Larry Hunt's demonstrator.

Havana. I figured it looks better your boss is respectable. Just like them income tax snoopers can take a good look out there—

He gestures. The others look.

31 FULL SHOT—WINDOW

*The view beyond shows acre after acre of vineyards. (*NOTE: *The interior and the window will be taken to a location in Cucamonga.)*

Havana's voice.—at all them acres of my beautiful grapes. Strictly legit!

32 CLOSE GROUP SHOT—THE FOUR MEN

Now Havana taps the picture.

Havana. Looks like Lady Lola kinda goes for you.

Johnny. Perhaps—in time—

Havana gives Johnny a shrewd look.

Havana. No rush.

He exits from the shot, followed by Jimmy Duffy.

33 MEDIUM CLOSE SHOT—WINDOW AND CUE BACK

We see that the window with the vineyards beyond it is in a corner of the room next to the billiard cue rack. Havana speaks as he enters and picks out a cue, followed by Jimmy.

Havana (*Continued*). Long as Jimmy here goes to work 4th of July weekend.

Johnny enters the shot.

Johnny. Why then?

Jimmy. Well, you see, Mr. Pierpont—

Johnny. Johnny!

Jimmy. Johnny—Lotta stores close up shop during that four-day holiday. So I'll ease in next to some sucker's phone that's got a number we'll use—

Johnny (*Selecting a cue and turning to Havana*). Oh, one thing. This Lola Murray is a good pal. No chance she'll get stuck personally, is there? I mean, you're sure she's covered?

Havana. Like a tent—by International Insurance.

Johnny. That's funny.

Havana. Why? It's the biggest.

Johnny. I know. My old man owns it.

He walks out of the shot.

34 MEDIUM CLOSE SHOT

Milo is leaning against the pool table as Johnny comes into the shot and starts chalking his cue.

Milo. If you're a genuine Pierpont and all, how come you're a shill for Havana Papke?

Johnny (*Sizing up an obvious envier*). You see, I haven't taken my first false step—yet.

Havana and Jimmy enter the scene.

Johnny (*Continued*). Perhaps Havana better tell you how we started going steady.

As Havana starts to explain and to rack up the balls, Johnny moves out of the shot.

Havana. It started the winter Johnny got kicked out of Ha-a-a-vud. He was spillin' trunkfuls of Pierpont pennies around my Deuces Wild Club in Miami. Pretty soon Johnny owes me a couple grand more than I permit bein' carried on my books—Ivy League or no Ivy League.

35 CLOSE-UP—MILO

He is puzzled.

    Milo. Who's she?
    Havana's voice. Who's who?
    Milo. Ivy Lee.

36 TIGHT TWO-SHOT—HAVANA AND DUFFY

Havana's face freezes. He twists toward Jimmy Duffy.

    Havana. You bring this meathead?
    Jimmy. Milo's okay.
    Havana. Okay? He thinks Ivy League is a broad!

37 CLOSE THREE SHOT

Milo starts to protest, but Havana cuts in.

    Havana (*Continued*). Shut up! So I tell Johnny I give him a week to pay up or—

Havana brings an imaginary gun to the back of his head and pulls the imaginary trigger, at the same time banging two pool balls together with his left hand.

38 CLOSE-UP—JOHNNY

He winces.

39 LONGER SHOT

Havana finishes racking up as he goes on.

    Havana (*Continued*). So Johnny wires his old man and next day he gets an answer saying no, sonny boy, and you and my money are parted forever and ever, amen. Best Johnny can do is start payin' off by introducing me to his rich friends and so forth and so fifth, until now—six years later—it looks like his old man's insurance company will roundabout pay Johnny twice what he originally asked for!

Havana's cue ball smacks the triangle of balls with a mighty cur-rash kerbang! DISSOLVE TO

40 FULL SHOT—EXTERIOR LOLA MURRAY'S RESIDENCE—DAY

Johnny whirls up the driveway and stops next to another car—a convertible—gets out and bangs the knocker.

41 CLOSE SHOT—ENTRANCE DOOR

Winton, Lola's butler, opens the door.

Winton. Yes, sir?

Johnny. Miss Murray's expecting me—Mr. Pierpont.

Winton (*Gesturing*). She's at the pool with Mr. Harrington.

Johnny. Who?

Winton. Mr. George Harrington—the actor.

Johnny. Fine. I mean, some of my best friends are actors.

He makes a gesture and walks off in the direction Winton indicated. Alone, Winton smiles at Johnny's little joke as he closes the door.

42   MEDIUM CLOSE SHOT—AT SWIMMING POOL

Lola is stretched out on a wicker chaise longue, listening to Harrington who is reading, with a slight touch of a commercial voiceover for Swift, Armour, etc. He is in trunks.

Harrington. "From morn to noon he fell,
  From noon to dewy eve,
  A summer's day; and with the setting sun
  Dropp'd from the Zenith, like a falling star."
(*Closing the book.*) Why don't they write lines like that today, instead of the tripe I'll have to mouth in Mexico next week?

Lola. Now, George, you can't expect Hollywood to make a picture of *Paradise Lost*—I mean, don't let's be naïve.

Harrington. Of course, you're right.

During this, Johnny has walked into the scene. Lola sits up.

Lola. Hello, Johnny.

Johnny. Hi, princess.

Lola. This is George Harrington—John Pierpont, the Third.

Johnny and Harrington. How d'y'do? How are you?

Johnny. Say, you really read that—

Harrington (*Agreeing completely*), Thank you.

Johnny grins.

Johnny. Although to level with you, I must admit I prefer some of his lighter things, like—
  "Haste thee, Nymph, and bring with thee
  Jest and youthful Jollity!"

Harrington. Great Scott! You know Milton!

Johnny. Not really. Just a couple of those bits they make you memorize at school.

Harrington. Still unusual—

Johnny. No. They stick in your head somehow. I must apologize for crashing this party. (*Turning to Lola.*) But I did want to ask Miss Murray if she'd be free this evening.
Lola. Oh, Johnny, I'm sorry—I mean—
Harrington. She means she just accepted my invitation—
Johnny. My fault. Should have hollered sooner.
Lola. But you will ask me again—the minute George takes off for Mexico—right after the 4th.
Johnny. That's a date. (*To Harrington.*) You flying down, sir?
Harrington. That's right—on the 5th.
Johnny. Hey! You should fly yourself down—Larry Hunt's coptoglider—
Harrington. What's *that*? I haven't flown anything for nearly a year.

Johnny warms to his work.

Johnny. You've got to let me show it to you. You'll really flip. Could you possibly spare this handsome guy for the rest of the afternoon, Miss Murray? I mean, you know what it's like and you *will* be together tonight?
Lola. You should see it, George. It's an amazing contraption. I've never seen anything like it.
Johnny. I'll call Larry and have him get it up for us in about an hour. I'll meet you in the Hop Off Café, right at the edge of the Burbank field. 'Bye for now!

And he is gone before Harrington can protest or say another word.
DISSOLVE TO

43 CLOSE SHOT—INTERIOR TELEPHONE BOOTH
Johnny has called his number. Someone answers.

Johnny. Hi, Larry. Now, get this. What I'm cooking up isn't going to sell your copter, but it is going to move up my chances of a date with Lola Murray. Need I say more? You will? Oh, Buster! Now, here's the way we'll work it.
DISSOLVE TO

44 MEDIUM CLOSE SHOT—INTERIOR HOP OFF CAFÉ
Johnny, Harrington, and Larry are drinking three beers at a table close to CAMERA. *Larry's stein is just about empty and so is Harrington's. Johnny has scarcely touched his, but he hides this from Harrington by keeping his left elbow in front of the stein. Larry is talking.*

Larry. If you'll look out there, you'll see what I mean—

Harrington turns and looks off. His back is now toward Larry and Johnny, who quickly hands his full stein to Larry, who gives him his almost empty one and goes right on talking.

> **Larry** (*Continued*). Just keep your eye on that plane taking off—
> **Harrington.** Yes—I'm watching it.
> **Larry.** See how much speed you need before you dare leave the ground?
> **Harrington.** Of course, but—

He turns back to Larry. Johnny takes the ball.

> **Johnny.** You don't have to tell him that! (*Draining Larry's empty stein.*) He was a flier.
> **Larry.** Forgive me. But, on the other hand, let's consider my coptoglider. It goes straight up right now—the minute you want it to. No delay—no fiddling around. But why talk about it? Let's go out there and have Johnny demonstrate it. It speaks for itself. Another beer?
> **Harrington.** Good Lord, no! This is my third.
> **Larry.** Well, go ahead. I'll take care of the check.

CAMERA PULLS BACK *as Larry motions to the waiter and Johnny and Harrington move out of the shot.*

DISSOLVE TO

45   CLOSE SHOT—THE COPTOGLIDER

Harrington, full of what made Milwaukee famous, is already strapped into the seat beside Johnny, who is monkeying with his seat belt as Larry steps into the shot.

> **Larry.** Good luck. You have no idea, Mr. Harrington, absolutely no idea what the sensation is when—

Johnny starts his motor which completely drowns out Larry's sales talk, Johnny motions Larry to back away. He does so.

46   LONG SHOT—COPTOGLIDER

(NOTE: *Actually a real helicopter is above our constructed one and can take it wherever it wants to with wires. The two men in the coptoglider are stunt men.*)

With a roar, Larry's invention goes straight up, as Larry, on the ground, continues to step back from the machine. Now the contraption heads back for the field, which it hits with a bump, goes up several feet, bounces down again and makes a series of shorter and shorter hops.

47   PROCESS CLOSE-UP—JOHNNY AND HARRINGTON

The background should be trees and sky, so that we can bump the copter seat up and down as violently as the real actors can take it.

Johnny. Never get mobility—like this—in any other aircraft—huh?

Harrington. A bit too much mo–mo–mobility for me.

Johnny (*Shouting*). You get used to it. Like rising to the trot. These bumps don't mean a thing—like a roller coaster.

Harrington. Sorry you said that!

Johnny. Me too. Should have said BRONCO BUSTING!

Harrington. Said nothing—would be better! Ugh! That BEER!

Johnny. Up she comes again! Way up! Bee-yup!

Harrington is holding down the beer with difficulty.

48 LONG SHOT—MINIATURE—CLOUD BACKING

There is the flat field and several trees in the bottom of the picture. The coptoglider goes straight up against a background of clouds.

49 CLOSE SHOT—JOHNNY AND HARRINGTON—CLOUD BACKING

The desire to upchuck is assailing George Harrington with a frightful urgency.

Harrington. I don't believe— ugh! I—I'm afraid I'm going to—uh!

Johnny (*Cheerfully*). Go right ahead.

Harrington stuffs a handkerchief into his mouth.

Johnny. I'll swing her around into the wind!

The copter revolves until the backs of the two men are toward CAMERA. *Harrington leaps forward and his shoulders heave.*

50 LONG SHOT—MINIATURE—CLOUD BACKING

The copter trembles slightly—then spins back to its original position.

51 PROCESS CLOSE SHOT—JOHNNY AND HARRINGTON—CLOUD BACKING

The copter twists till it faces CAMERA. *Harrington leans back, exhausted.*

Johnny. Going down! Next stop, main floor. Tranquilizers, hypnotizers, night-all-izers.

He reaches for his controls.

52 LONG SHOT—MINIATURE—CLOUD BACKING

The coptoglider descends to the ground, bounces a couple of times, and settles down.

53 CLOSE SHOT—JOHNNY AND HARRINGTON

As they make their final bounce, Harrington groans.

Johnny. Good old terra firma. How you feel?

Harrington shudders.
>**Harrington.** Don't ask. Tell you tomorrow—
>**Johnny.** Bad as that, hmm?

Larry runs into the shot.
>**Larry.** What went wrong?
>**Harrington.** Beer. Went up instead of down!

Johnny is unfastening the seat belts.
>**Johnny.** We'll drive him home—put him to bed. Call a doctor. Then I make one more call about tonight—personal!

They support Harrington, practically out on his feet, and move away from the copter.
Dissolve to

54   Interior Murray Residence Den—Nite

Winton is coming down the stairs which show through an archway, as John, the Third, glances casually at the back of Lola Murray's TV set. He takes out an envelope and a pencil.
>**Winton.** Miss Murray will be a few minutes, sir. Would you care for a drink?
>**Johnny.** No, thank you, Winton, but Mr. Larry Hunt wanted me to ask you if you could recommend a good TV repair man.
>**Winton** (*Enthusiastically*). We use a George Gateson. Name's in the Beverly Hills book. Excellent—and very reasonable.

Johnny notes down the name.
>**Johnny.** Thank you, Winton. Er—you and Mrs. Winton really take care of this establishment alone?
>**Winton.** It's not too difficult, sir. Once a month, a cleaning woman comes in; and, of course, Miss Murray has a personal maid.

Johnny makes a quizzical sound as Winton leaves. As John turns back to the TV, Lola comes down the stairway. She looks particularly lovely.
>**Lola.** I'm late, and I'm sorry.
>**Johnny.** The difference when *you* say that is you're worth waiting for.

Lola makes a little bow as they move toward the door.
Dissolve to

55   Full Shot—Japanese Garden Restaurant

The spot is in the Hollywood Hills. It features a full moon and the conventional lanterns.
Dissolve to

56 CLOSE TWO-SHOT—AT TABLE
Johnny is doing a fine job of buttering up without overdoing it.
>**Johnny.** I've been a sucker for ninety-nine and forty-four hundredths percent of Lola Murray pictures, but the one that really clobbered me was *Still Waters*.
>
>**Lola.** I liked that one—but hey! You must have been about twelve when you saw it.
>
>**Johnny.** I *have* aged a bit since then—but you haven't—

57 CLOSE-UP—LOLA
She shakes her head a little ruefully.
>**Lola.** I don't like polite lies, Johnny. I've finally learned that the truth is beautiful—even when it hurts.

58 CLOSE-UP—JOHNNY
He makes a valiant effort. He is on thin ice and he knows it.
>**Johnny.** *You're* beautiful! And that's the truth—

59 CLOSE TWO-SHOT
It takes Lola a moment to answer.
>**Lola.** At least you *think* it's true—I think.

She puts her hand in his.
>**Lola** (*Continued*). I like you, Johnny. Don't ever do anything to spoil that.

Johnny's throat is dry when he answers. He has an ugly feeling he is betraying her.
>**Johnny.** I won't.... Let's get out of here.

He tosses a bill on the table as we
DISSOLVE TO

60 CLOSE SHOT—JOHNNY'S CAR
They are settling back in the seat. Lola smiles up at Johnny.
>**Lola.** Where to?

He kisses her.
>**Lola** (*Continued*). Mmm. That place I liked.

Johnny kisses her again as we
DISSOLVE TO

61 CLOSE SHOT—INTERIOR PUBLIC TELEPHONE BOOTH
Johnny is dialing a number.

62 MEDIUM SHOT—INTERIOR LOLA MURRAY'S DEN—DAY
Winton, his arms full of packages, comes through one door to answer the ringing telephone, as Mrs. Winton, a nice-looking woman in her

forties, comes through a second door. As Winton starts to put down the bundles, his wife picks up the receiver.

Mrs. Winton. Who?

63 HEAD CLOSE-UP—JOHNNY

He speaks like a man with a terrible cold.

Johnny. Hello, Bissus Winton. This is George Gateson. I'b goig to the desert to kill this dab co'd. If you need eddythig—call Terrence TV, good friend of bine. Fine workban. Here's the dumber—

64 ANGLE SHOT—LOLA'S DEN

Mrs. Winton, in the foreground, signals her husband to write down what she'll say.

Mrs. Winton. Good. I'll give it to my husband. Terrence TV—Crestview 4-4080. Thank you. You get well now.

She hangs up.

65 CLOSE SHOT—JOHNNY

He hangs up and dials a second number.

66 EXTERIOR BEVERLY HILLS STATIONERS—INSERT

The door is lettered "Griggs Stationery." CAMERA TILTS DOWN to sign. "Closed July 1ˢᵗ to July 5ᵗʰ."

DISSOLVE TO

67 CLOSE SHOT—INTERIOR STATIONERS

Jimmy Duffy picks up the receiver.

Jimmy. Terrence TV.

68 CLOSE-UP—JOHNNY

He recognizes the voice.

Johnny. Hi, Jimmy. This is Jonathan. Is that sign on your truck all set? Good. Those people will be having a little trouble on their TV set tomorrow night. You can expect them to call—

69 CLOSE-UP—JIMMY

He smiles and nods.

Jimmy. I'll be here. So long, pal.

He hangs up.

70 ANGLE SHOT—HOLLYWOOD COUNTER RESTAURANT

Shooting from behind the counter. Larry Hunt is seated on the foreground stool. The one next to it is empty. The phone booth is in the background. Johnny comes out of it and sits next to Larry, who is finishing his lunch. Johnny picks up his coffee cup.

Larry. So tomorrow's the big night, huh?

Johnny nearly spills his coffee.
> **Johnny.** Wha—!
> **Larry.** I mean your date with Lola—
> **Johnny.** Oh, yeah. Hmmm. You know, her butler told me she hasn't dated the same guy twice in one week for two years.
> **Larry.** Don't make me have to shrink your head. You'd never have met her but for my copter!
> **Johnny.** Tonto grateful. Man, I haven't felt like this since I took Miss America of '54 to the Junior Prom. . . . No kidding. I've got Lola fever. (*Grabbing the checks.*) I'm buyin' 'em!

DISSOLVE TO

71 MEDIUM CLOSE SHOT—INTERIOR MURRAY DEN—NITE
In a dinner jacket, Johnny tamps out his cigarette and moves behind Lola's TV set. As he starts to remove the back piece, he hears something and ducks down behind the set.

72 MEDIUM SHOT—ENTRANCE HALL AND DEN
Lola Murray's maid, Frances, carrying a sewing basket, comes across the hall and starts upstairs as Johnny finishes ducking down. He can be seen through the open door leading to the den. CAMERA MOVES CLOSE *as Frances disappears and Johnny straightens up and removes the back piece. He quickly does something—we cannot see what—to the horizontal controls, replaces the back piece, picks up a New Yorker magazine, and moves into the hall area. He turns to the stairway.*

73 TRUCKING SHOT—LOLA
In an elegant formal, Lola is coming down the stairs. She is radiantly beautiful.

74 CLOSE SHOT—JOHNNY
He watches, enchanted. When Lola enters the shot, he shakes his head.
> **Johnny.** I'm speechless—I can't even whistle.
> **Lola.** Oh, come on now—
> **Johnny.** That I'll be delighted to do.

He holds out his arm. As Lola takes it, Frances runs into the shot.
> **Frances.** You've got the wrong compact, Miss Murray—
> **Lola.** Oh, no!

She opens her evening bag and takes out the compact.
> **Lola** (*Continued*). I might have known. Frances is always right.

They exchange compacts. Johnny thinks quickly and pulls one out of the air.

Johnny. Of course, you know what Frances will be doing at nine this evening!

Lola. Of course, I don't—and if *you* do—

Johnny. I'm psychic. Frances and Mrs. Winton will be talking her husband into dialing that Fashion Show on Channel Two.

Lola. Honestly! These men!

Johnny (*To Frances*). Happy Hattie Carnegie!

He puts Lola's arm through his and they move toward the entrance door.

DISSOLVE TO

75   TIGHT TWO-SHOT—DANCE FLOOR TABLE

Lola is smiling as Johnny whispers something endearing into her ear, but if he were shouting we wouldn't hear him, the orchestra's brass section is so loud. Behind them are the well-groomed torsos of tightly jammed couples dancing by. John's whisper becomes a kiss.

DISSOLVE TO

76   CLOSE GROUP SHOT—INTERIOR LOLA'S DEN

The back of the TV set is angled toward us. Winton is half hidden behind it as he fiddles with the dials. In the background, Mrs. Winton and Frances are getting edgy.

Mrs. Winton. No, dear. Everything you try makes it worse. I'll call that number Gateson gave us.

Frances. Yes, please!

Winton. I guess you'd better.

Mrs. Winton is already halfway to the telephone.

DISSOLVE TO

77   MEDIUM SHOT—MULHOLLAND DRIVE

CAMERA IS HIGH, *shooting down at the Hollywood lights below. Johnny's car drives into the shot and onto a promontory overlooking the lights.*

(NOTE: *This should be shot at dusk so that a certain amount of daylight will give the shot all the depth possible and, at the same time, the lights will have been turned on in Hollywood. When a couple of satisfactory takes have been made, the process crew should make the plates of the rest of the scenes in this sequence.*)

78   PROCESS—TWO-SHOT—LOLA AND JOHNNY

CAMERA *is behind Lola and Johnny, who is at the wheel, with Lola beside him. Unless a special mock-up is constructed for this sequence, the car Johnny uses throughout the picture would be chosen for this scene. In other words, it should be the type of car in which the front seat is in two sections which can be moved forward and backward. If this kind of car is used,* CAMERA *can get a fifty-fifty two shot of the actors, and the windshield should be removable. Johnny's radio is playing a tango. He turns down the sound.*

Johnny. After that blasting brass, this is nice and peaceful, hmm?
Lola. It's beautiful—
Johnny. By now, I suppose, you know that Hollywood is going to wink its applause at you every night?

79 OVER-SHOULDER SHOT—LOLA
She smiles and shakes her head.
Lola. No. Applause always astonishes me. And I'm not being coy. What I mean is that I do my job and hope they'll like me. But there are so many funny little ifs in what we're trying to do, that you just can't be sure.

80 OVER-SHOULDER SHOT—JOHNNY
He considers this.
Johnny. Mmm. Of course, today, with that big firecracker on the world's shopping list, who's sure of anything? Except, perhaps, my old man.

81 CLOSE-UP—LOLA
The sudden introduction of Johnny's father intrigues her.
Lola. He's pretty positive, hmm?
Johnny smiles grimly.
Johnny. He's *positively* positive. Which is natural, when you figure how the cards are all stacked in his favor, just as they were in his father's favor—

83 CLOSE-UP—LOLA
She nods.
Lola. And will be in yours—?

84 CLOSE-UP—JOHNNY
He cuts her short.
Johnny. No. No. You see, I don't want things to be sure. That gets to be pretty dull. I pick my friends from outer space, sort of. I'm bored stiff by those "solid" people John, the Second, insists on having around to kiss his astronomical pronouncements. They are super-squares. I kind of go for kooks and excitement—

85 CLOSE TWO-SHOT
Lola is delighted with all of this.

Lola. So, I'm a kook?

Johnny. Don't know yet. Could be. And you certainly qualify in the excitement department.

Lola (*Preening herself*). Well—thank you, sir.

86 OVER-SHOULDER SHOT—JOHNNY

Johnny gives Lola's remark the mental brush.

Johnny. I tell you what I don't like—knowing exactly what every minute of every day is going to be like—every meal, every move—every person I'll see. All arranged for and all stuffy-stupid. I like *this*. All of a sudden we come here. I may never see you again—though I hope and pray with all my heart I will—

87 OVER-SHOULDER SHOT—LOLA

She is captivated and wants him to know it.

Lola. I hope you will—

88 CLOSE TWO-SHOT

He smiles warmly.

Johnny. One wonderful surprise after another—

Lola. Enumerate, please.

Johnny. Uh-uh. I refuse to go into a male version of that Elizabeth Barrett Browning bit—"How do I love you? Let me count the ways." Not for me. I mean, as soon as you start counting something—whftt! It's gone. You? You're you. What more can a man say?

89 CLOSE-UP—LOLA

She is pleased.

Lola. You're very sweet.

90 CLOSE-UP—JOHNNY

He is equally delighted.

Johnny. Just talkative—and all about me. Tell me. Why didn't you ever get married again? Unless you hate talking about it—

91 CLOSE-UP—LOLA

To his surprise, she likes the switch.

Lola. No. Matter of fact, I like to talk about it—give you a chance to know a little more about me. I guess my husband was quite a lot like your father. He was very definite, possessive—obstinate—

92 CLOSE-UP—JOHNNY

Interrupting.

Johnny. That has a couple of angles. At least it has with father. He's so sure of himself, he makes a virtue out of stepping on some competitor's neck. Not me. I can always see the other fellow's side of the scrap.

93 CLOSE-UP—LOLA
She is really looking deep inside herself.
    Lola. Me too. It's ridiculous.

94 CLOSE-UP—JOHNNY
Making a new point.
    Johnny. It's worse than that. It's weak. If there's a real war on.

95 CLOSE TWO-SHOT
Lola reacts from her stomach.
    Lola. Don't let's even think about that!
    Johnny. If someone doesn't think about it, we could have one—
    Lola. Please—
    Johnny. Sure. I know. But if it's here you've got to stop it—Mr. Bernard Shaw's way.
Puzzled, Lola wants the answer.
    Lola. What's that?
    Johnny. Very simple. The soldiers on both sides shoot their generals and go home.
    Lola. I'll buy that. And my only child's a girl.
    Johnny. It's not a bad idea—but I didn't mean to get you off the subject. Your husband—

96 CLOSE-UP—LOLA
She frowns.
    Lola. Oh, yes. If I did something he didn't like, he said so in a loud voice. If I did it twice, he'd stop talking to me for a week.

97 CLOSE-UP—JOHNNY
He smiles.
    Johnny. That's a punishment I'll bet you sort of liked—

98 CLOSE TWO-SHOT
She smiles back.
    Lola. The point is I'm a bit stubborn myself.
    Johnny. You mean you stood up to him and fought back?
    Lola. Yes, I did—unless I thought changing to what he wanted was right and good for us both. Of course, there were some things he used to bawl me out for—like always being late.
Johnny makes a "well-now-after-all" face.
    Johnny. Yeah—that does drive most men nuts. But as I told you, the night I pinch-hitted for the Duke of Harrington, waiting for

you is worth it. And another thing. We men have all got to adjust ourselves to the idea that, when a woman takes all that trouble to look her loveliest to please *us*, we should be flattered and tell her so!

Lola. Well, well! What a grown-up young man.

Johnny. Not really. And I'm not so young, either. Here I am, teetering on the corner of thirtieth street, and I haven't yet made up my mind what I really want to do—except—

He leans close and kisses her. A moment later, Lola is able to put in a word.

Lola. You're going to be awfully difficult to argue with. I like you. I like you a lot, and that needn't worry you one bit.

99 OVER-SHOULDER SHOT—JOHNNY

He is puzzled.

Johnny. I don't understand. Why should it?

100 OVER-SHOULDER SHOT—LOLA

She touches his cheek.

Lola. I mean, in case you should ever get serious about us, just remember that my marriage did go kaput and my career did the opposite. So I decided that a good actress would be even better if she really devoted herself to being one—to getting the best parts possible and working like a dog to give a good account of herself when she got them.

101 OVER-SHOULDER SHOT—JOHNNY

He is secretly pleased, but he wants to make sure.

Johnny. Here, here! But suppose some day he comes along—

102 OVER-SHOULDER SHOT—LOLA

She smiles and sings the rest of it.

Lola. "The man I love!" No. No supposing. I'm like you. I'll face that when it happens. After all, a lady can retire.

103 CLOSE-UP—JOHNNY

An imp appears in his eyes.

Johnny. Alone? How very dull!

104 CLOSE-UP—LOLA

A matching imp materializes in her eyes.

Lola. Young man! In my mother's day, I'd have slapped your face for that remark, but it just so happens that this is my day—

105 CLOSE TWO-SHOT

She moves toward him. They kiss.

DISSOLVE TO

106 LOLA MURRAY'S DRIVEWAY—NITE

A truck with a large sign on it—Ted Terrence TV—*is parked in the driveway.*

DISSOLVE TO

107 CLOSE GROUP SHOT—INTERIOR LOLA'S DEN

The angle is just about what it was before, but this time, the Wintons and Frances are in the background, watching, and Jimmy Duffy is in the foreground, twisting the horizontal controls. He moves around beside the others to watch the result of his efforts. The sound of the program comes over.

Jimmy. What do you think?

The trio. Great, Mr. Terrence! Just perfect. You have no idea. Tremendously grateful.

Jimmy. Glad to help. (*To Winton.*) If you'd sign here.

He presents the butler with a receipt book, which Winton signs. As he is doing this, Jimmy turns on his most winning smile.

Jimmy (*Continued*). George Gateson's brother-in-law told me Miss Murray has a set upstairs. Guess I'd better have a look at it.

Winton. Good idea. I'll show you where it is.

Jimmy. Yeah. Thanks.

He picks up a large case, after tossing the tools he was using into it, and goes up the stairs behind Winton.

DISSOLVE TO

108 SEMI-REVERSE ANGLE—SHOOTING ACROSS BOTTOM STAIR-RAIL

Winton comes down the stairs and calls out to his wife.

Winton. Is there some hot coffee, Angela? Mr. Terrence would—er—

Mrs. Winton. Of course. Why didn't I think of that? It'll only take a few minutes. He certainly deserves it—

She hurries off toward the kitchen.

109 MOVING CAMERA—INTERIOR LOLA'S BEDROOM

Jimmy Duffy is filling his big case with a mink coat, muttering as he works.

Jimmy. Pretty pussy cat! Nice pussy!

CAMERA FOLLOWS HIM *as he tiptoes quickly to a jewel case and makes a quick choice of several rings, bracelets, earrings, etc.*

Jimmy. Lady, when you got it, you got it. Only now, Jimmy's got it. Button, button—!

He goes on "working."

110 SEMI-REVERSE ANGLE—BEYOND STAIR-RAIL

Mrs. Winton appears with a tray and the coffee.

Mrs. Winton. Shall I take it up?

Winton (*Kindly smile*). You watch that show.

Mrs. Winton. You see, Frances? That's the kind of husband you should get.

Frances. Or train *after* I get him.

Winton takes the tray and starts for the stairway, but Jimmy appears with his case.

Jimmy. Well, how about that?

Frances steps forward.

Frances (*A bit coyly*). You asked for it.

Jimmy puts down his case, sits on it, and takes the coffee cup from Winton.

Jimmy. I know, but—(*A bit sip.*) Sure hits the spot. (*Glancing at his watch.*) Doggone, I'm late for one last job—won't possibly be as good as this one—

Winton. Good having *you*.

Jimmy. Thanks. Thanks for everything—coffee—the greatest.

Jimmy picks up his case.

Jimmy (*Continued*). Too bad I won't see you again—

Frances. Oh?

Jimmy. Well, I mean—Gateson'll be back.

Frances. Of course. I forgot.

Jimmy. I won't forget you. Believe me. Nighty-night!

He goes. We hear the entrance door close. CAMERA MOVES CLOSE TO THE TRIO. *Mrs. Winton sighs.*

Mrs. Winton. What a nice young man!

The other two join in the chorus.

DISSOLVE TO

111 INSERT—CLOCK—JOHNNY'S CAR—NITE

It is 2:19. The car radio is now playing a Viennese waltz.

112 PAN SHOT—JOHNNY'S CAR

As it swings up the driveway and stops in front of the entrance doors, Johnny helps Lola out, kisses her good night. She goes inside. Johnny vaults back into the driver's seat.

113 CLOSER PAN SHOT—THE CAR

Johnny drives slowly along the side of the house, then stops and looks up.

114 MEDIUM SHOT—BALCONY OUTSIDE LOLA'S BEDROOM

A light goes on inside the bedroom. CAMERA MOVES CLOSER. *We can see Lola vaguely as she prepares for bed.*

115 CLOSE SHOT—JOHNNY

He twists the radio dial. The music gets louder.

116 CLOSE SHOT—FRENCH WINDOW—LOLA'S BEDROOM

She pauses, arranging her peignoir, turns as she hears the music and comes forward. CAMERA DOLLIES BACK *as she comes out onto the balcony, looks down, and leans on the rail.*

Lola. Wherefore art thou, Romeo?

117 BOOM SHOT—JOHNNY

CAMERA STAYS CLOSE *as Johnny does a Douglas Fairbanks up the trellis, over the balcony rail, and stops a few feet away from Lola who is now in the shot too.*

Johnny. It seems she hangs upon the cheek of night. Like a rich jewel in an Ethiop's ear. Beauty too rich for use, for earth, too dear.

118 CLOSE-UP—LOLA

Her eyes widen.

Lola. Why—why you read that beautifully!

119 CLOSE-UP—JOHNNY—MOVING CAMERA

Johnny is intensely serious.

Johnny. It's a beautiful speech. You just can't forget it.

He comes slowly forward until both heads are in the shot.

Johnny (*Continued*). And I meant it—

They kiss.

DISSOLVE TO

120 CARPET AND SIDE OF LOLA'S BED

A pool of light illuminates the white carpet as Lola moves close to the bed, The peignoir drops to the carpet. The legs wriggle into bed.

121 VERY CLOSE SHOT—BASE OF BED LAMP

Lola's fingers enter and turn out the bed lamp which takes the place of a
FADE OUT.

FADE IN

122 CLOSE SHOT—JOHNNY—INTERIOR HOTEL ROOM—DAY

This is a single-room apartment in a modest Hollywood hotel. A small table TV is in the foreground. Johnny is seated looking at and listening to the noon newscast. *At the same time, he is fumbling with the cuff links of the formal shirt he wore the night before. He is in a bathrobe.*

Newscaster's voice. Our State Department feels that this action will have a favorable effect in the Middle East—

123 HEAD CLOSE-UP—JOHNNY

His eyes leave the TV screen and look down at his shirt cuff.

124 CLOSE INSERT—CUFFS

These are the type of cuff links that are joined by a snap, but one side of the cuff is empty.

125 HEAD CLOSE-UP—JOHNNY

His eyes come back to the screen as the newscaster shifts to a new subject.

Newscaster's voice. Locally, a daring burglar made off with thousands of dollars worth of jewelry and furs belonging to Pyramid Pictures star, Lola Murray.

126 LONGER SHOT—ACROSS TV SET

Still listening, Johnny begins to search the floor and move the furniture, looking for the missing half of his cuff link.

Newscaster's voice. The Beverly Hills police are reported to be searching for a truck bearing the following identification: Terrence TV. Tomorrow's weather will be cloudy until noon—

Johnny shuts off the TV but continues with his search. The telephone rings. Johnny crosses to it as CAMERA DOLLIES CLOSE.

Johnny. Hello? I know. I just heard it on TV. How in the hell do you suppose—I'm sick about it. Uh-huh. I'd like to talk to him. I'm on my way—

He hangs up and starts to change.

DISSOLVE TO

127 MEDIUM SHOT—INTERIOR LOLA'S DEN—DAY

Detective Sergeant Joseph Stout is talking to Mrs. Winton. She is seated as are Lola and Frances. Winton is standing.

Sergeant Stout. But you see, Mrs. Winton, Gateson didn't really call you. He hasn't got a cold, he never left town—and, what's more, he never heard of Terrence TV. In fact, there is no such animal.

Mrs. Winton. Well then, how on earth—

Lola. It's pretty obvious, isn't it, sergeant? I mean, it was that "charming" young repair man, making out he had a cold.

Mrs. Winton is dreadfully upset.

Mrs. Winton. Oh, dear me!
Sergeant Stout. I know, but could be.
Winton. There's one thing I can't fathom at all, sir—
Sergeant Stout. And what's that?

The entrance door knocker sounds. Frances gets up.

Frances. I'll answer that.

She goes. Winton turns to the sergeant, who nods for him to continue.

Winton. I mean, how could whoever it was know that our set was going to develop those wavy lines on that particular evening?
Sergeant Stout. You've certainly got a point there. Someone must have monkeyed with your TV yesterday sometime—

Frances comes into the scene with Johnny, who moves to Lola.

Johnny. I really stepped on it.
Lola. I'm sure. Thank you. This is Sergeant Stout, Mr. Pierpont.
Both. Hiya, Sergeant. How d'y'do, sir.
Lola. I explained where we were last night and the sergeant asked me to call you.
Johnny. Glad he did. I heard what you said. Of course, anyone of us could have jimmied up the set—and another of course—a little more likely, I think, sergeant. Someone could have heard one of us yakking about being out for the evening.

Sergeant Stout smiles.

Sergeant Stout. Best guess yet, if you ask me, sir. And by tomorrow, I'm sure we'll be doing a little more than guessing. (*To the Wintons and Frances.*) You people can go on with your work, if you like.

They ad lib good nights and go. CAMERA MOVES CLOSER *to the three.*

Johnny (*Almost a whisper*). You told the sergeant what swell people they all are, hmm?
Lola. Naturally—and he knows it instinctively.
Johnny. Sorry I put it that way. Oh, you're insured, aren't you?
Lola. Yes, praise be! Oh, dear—one or two of those clips and things—well, they just can't be replaced.
Johnny. I know how you feel, but that's sort of covered by a fine American saying of my father's.
Lola. Oh?
Johnny. Uh-huh. He says, "It's not so much the sentimental value—it's the money!"
Lola. You and your old man.

Sergeant Stout. On my salary I got to go along with him! And I just plain got to go along—turn in my report. I'll call when there's something. Nice to have seen you, Mr. Pierpont.

Lola and Johnny. Good night. And thank you.

He exits from the shot. They move toward the den.

128 TRUCKING SHOT—LOLA AND JOHNNY

As they pass the TV set, Johnny sneaks a quick look at the floor.

Lola. You know what's awful about a thing like this? You start thinking suspicious thoughts about people you love, like Frances—

Johnny. Hey, now—

He drops behind her and starts really looking at the floor.

Lola. But you do. What are you doing?

Johnny. Oh, I was just wondering if that phony TV guy left any kind of a clue?

Lola. We thought of that. We looked. Nothing!

Johnny. You know, I like that Sergeant Stout. He's bright.

Lola. I like someone else. He's an idiot. He likes me.

Johnny. Yes—yes—

He takes her in his arms.

DISSOLVE TO

129 CLOSE-UP—JOHNNY—PROCESS SHOT

He is driving along the highway. The car is not the one he usually drives.

130 PAN SHOT—EXTERIOR HAVANA'S CUCAMONGA HOUSE

Johnny drives up to the door, parks, gets out, walks to the doorway, and rings the bell.

131 CLOSE SHOT—AT DOORWAY

Havana, in Bermuda shorts, opens the door. He is not glad to see Johnny, but he glances beyond his visitor, then motions him to come in. Johnny goes inside.

132 CLOSE SHOT—INTERIOR HAVANA'S ENTRANCE HALL—DAY

Havana closes the door behind Johnny.

Havana. Too soon, Johnny. You should've waited at least a week. The cops—!

Johnny. I rented that car and nobody tailed me. I just had to see you.

Havana (*Gesturing*). The patio.

They wait.

133 TRUCKING SHOT—HAVANA'S PATIO.
   As they sit down at a white-iron table, CAMERA MOVES CLOSE.
   Johnny. I lost part of one of my gold cuff links.
   Havana (*Astonished at this nothing*). So I'll give you a pair of mine—I got dozens of 'em.
   Johnny. Not with "J.P." on 'em. I'll be quick. Lola called me and I went out there. The cop in charge treated me great. I think I put on a pretty good act.
   Havana grins and pantomimes applause.
   Johnny (*Continued*). After he left, I took a quick peek at the floor—no cuff link—and nobody had mentioned finding it.
   Havana. So it's somewheres in your hotel room.
   Johnny. No, sir. There I really looked. And the maid hadn't found it.

134 CLOSE-UP—HAVANA
   He lights a panatela.
   Havana. Keep your chemise on, boy. Your links'll show. Oh, I got a long-distance call. Our young Irish friend did better than I'd hoped. The ice is already bein' pried loose in Tijuana by experts. Your cut will be pretty bulky, looks like.

135 CLOSE-UP—JOHNNY
   A worried look is on his face.
   Johnny. As long as it will pay you off—but the works, so I can kiss this business goodbye.
   Havana's voice. You didn't like it?
   Johnny. That's just it. I loved it. That's why I've got to quit before it gets to be like a habit.

136 CLOSE-UP—HAVANA
   He is sizing up Oliver Twist à la Fagin. He smiles.
   Havana. But you won't get sick from it—you'll get rich.

137 CLOSE-UP—JOHNNY
   He leans forward.
   Johnny. Look. I've been giving myself that sales talk and, boy, am I buying it! You see, I'm lousy at those nine-to-five-thirty jobs—and if you'd ever watched the way my old man works, the throats he cuts, you'd know what I think about the ethics of the "Million-Dollar-Deal" boys. Same as yours, believe me!

138 CLOSE-UP—HAVANA
   He shrugs.

Havana. Except they had a much bigger stack than mine when they started.

139 CLOSE TWO-SHOT—SLIGHTLY FAVORING JOHNNY

Johnny nods in agreement.

>**Johnny.** Check. And I agree with Mr. Proudhon. He was the Frenchman who said, "Property is theft."
>**Havana.** How's that?
>**Johnny.** What he meant was that way, way back, the land and the gold and the oil was grabbed off—stolen. It's only lately that the great grandsons of the ones who heisted it got to be so respectable—but on the other hand, there's a bunch of people like Larry Hunt—and doctors, scientists, teachers—and them nobody can buy. For some crazy reason, those crazy people I like—I want to join their club—before it's too late.
>**Havana.** About that I can't argue with you. It's like religion or politics.
>**Johnny.** You're right. And I was glad to help on this one—if it was only to meet one of the greatest—Lola Murray.
>**Milo's voice.** Bah! She's a rube from Iowa!

The two men look off.

140 CLOSE SHOT—MILO

He is leaning against the patio wall.

141 MEDIUM SHOT—THE THREE MEN—FAVORING MILO

Havana is indignant.

>**Havana.** Listen, you. Don't you never come out here without phoning—understand?

Milo indicates Johnny.

>**Milo.** Did he phone?

Havana spits out a piece of his cigar.

>**Havana.** You get the hell out of here!

Milo straightens up.

>**Milo.** Okay, Mr. Papke. But stop treatin' me like I was an L7!
>**Havana.** You *are* a square—so how else can I treat you?
>**Milo.** Man, I know chicks got four times what Murray's got—in all departments. She's strictly a has-been from Hicksville!
>**Johnny** (*Getting up*). Watch your mouth!
>**Milo.** Oh! A boy scout!

Johnny crosses quickly to him. Milo turns to Havana.

>**Milo** (*Continued*). Look who's got ants for that broken-down bag!

Johnny clips him. Milo goes down. Havana steps between them.

Havana. Go on home, Johnny. I want to talk to this meathead.

Johnny goes. Havana picks up a table lighter and lights his cigar, as Milo gets up and brushes himself off.

DISSOLVE TO

142 MEDIUM CLOSE SHOT—INTERIOR LOLA'S DEN—DAY

The angle is three-quarters toward the TV set, behind which Johnny is prying off the back of the instrument. He is wearing gloves. CAMERA MOVES GRADUALLY TO A POINT *where we are behind Johnny. During this, Johnny finds the lost half cuff link. It had obviously fallen behind the TV's innards when he twisted the horizontal control rod. He slips the link into his coat pocket, reaches down, and picks up the instrument's back. As he starts to replace it, Lola appears over his shoulder, her arms full of packages. He sees her. He is caught, but he goes right on with the job of replacing the back piece.*

Johnny. Hi!

Lola. What are you doing?

Johnny. One second—I'm going to call Sergeant Whosis—

Lola. Stout.

Johnny. Had an inspiration. Whoever twisted the control rod to put this thing on the blink maybe left fingerprints. So I just took a look—wearing these of course. There. Now, put down our packages, while I make the call.

Lola does what he says, but she is not quite satisfied with his explanation. Johnny finishes dialing and pockets the gloves.

Johnny (*Continued*). Police department? Sergeant Stout, please. Thank you.

He leans over and kisses Lola. She responds happily. Someone speaks on the phone.

Johnny (*Continued*). Hello, sergeant. This is Johnny Pierpont. I just took a squint at Miss Murray's TV and I was wondering if you shouldn't check its control rod for fingerprints. Oh, you did. Oh. Miss Murray was out so I just did one of those dumb amateur things while I was waiting for her. Okay. Nothing else yet, huh? Right. Bye.

He turns to Lola, after hanging up.

Johnny (*Continued*). My bright idea wasn't so bright.

Lola straightens his tie.

Lola. No. It wasn't. In fact, that whole complicated yarn you cooked up would make anyone who's ever seen a TV mystery pick John, the Third, as the main suspect—which, by the way, is pronounced "sus*pect*." I know, because I worked with Bill Powell in one of those Philo Vance things. Yes, sir! When I finish unpacking these beautiful packages, I'm going to call that handsome sergeant and tell him to stick you in the cooler. You *stole* my STOLE!

Johnny (*Barely managing to clown*). Please, lady! I did it for my crippled sister.

CAMERA FOLLOWS *as Lola picks up the packages and starts up the stairs.*

Lola. I'll cripple you, you CROOK!

She disappears. Johnny wipes his forehead, moves to the telephone, and dials a number. CAMERA MOVES CLOSE.

Johnny. Hello. Look. I'd like to buy you a drink. But this is important. How about the Turk and Tankard in an hour? Right.

He hangs up, takes the cuff link from his coat pocket and shoves it into a trouser pocket.

DISSOLVE TO

143 CLOSE SHOT—SIGN

The sign is over a small tavern off the main thoroughfare. It reads, TURK AND TANKARD.

DISSOLVE TO

144 MOVING CAMERA—INTERIOR TURK AND TANKARD

CAMERA SWINGS *from a very few people at the bar to a compartment occupied by two men. The one facing us is Johnny.* CAMERA COMES CLOSE TO HIM. *Johnny is finishing a long recital.*

Johnny. So the point is, do you think she'll call the law if she finds out it was me who loused up the TV set?

145 CLOSE SHOT—HAVANA

He is wearing a hat, tilted over his eyes, and is drinking a glass of milk.

Havana. I useta have lotsa expensive mouthpieces which I useta listen to very careful. Now, all them Clarence Darrelicts kept hammerin' into my noggin that a wife can't testify versus her husband, see what I mean? You marry this broad—and quick, before she talks you and me into San Quentin where the air conditioning is lousy!

145A CLOSE-UP—JOHNNY

He thinks hard, muttering something unintelligible.

145B CLOSE-UP—HAVANA

Havana. Whatsa matter? All of a sudden you don't like that beautiful kisser?

146 CLOSE-UP—JOHNNY

Deeply sincere.

Johnny. Like her? *I'm nuts about her.* I never felt like this about anyone before. But she's got some kind of a traumatic block against marriage for actresses. You see, her own was a flop.

147 CLOSE-UP—HAVANA

He puts up a finger.

Havana. Not all flop. I mean Milo tells me she's got a very pretty kid at school or something. And mentioning Mr. Meathead, I would hate to encourage him to maybe stick an ice pick into you—but you got to protect us, on account it's a rule of free enterprise that you ain't free to enterprise if you're in the large house. So make her say, "Yes," when you say, "Will you?" Now blow!

148 LONGER SHOT—THE TWO MEN IN BOOTH

Johnny smacks the table and gets up. Havana follows suit. They shake hands.

Johnny. Will do!

He hurries out of the scene as Havana raises his glass in, if you'll pardon the bad joke, a milk toast.

DISSOLVE TO

149 CLOSE SHOT—LOLA AND JOHNNY—EXTERIOR POOL—DAY

Lola is seated at the table where we first met her in another terry cloth robe. Johnny is close to her—leaning on the table.

Johnny. So you think an actress shouldn't marry?
Lola. Definitely.
Johnny. All right. I've got a little surprise for you. You're not an actress!
Lola. What? Why, I—
Johnny. Just a minute. As I understand it, unless Meizner gives you what you want, you refuse to work for him.
Lola. That is correct.
Johnny. Fine. Except your contract still has four years to go. Right?
Lola. Y–yes.

Johnny. Then—for the next four years—where's the actress going to act?

150 CLOSE-UP—LOLA

She wrestles with the disturbing thought.

    Lola. Why—OH! Oh, yes, of course.

151 CLOSE-UP—JOHNNY

As the words come out, he means them.

    Johnny. And, my sweet, for you and me, I don't believe in long engagements—not that long!

152 CLOSE TWO-SHOT

She has to agree.

    Lola. Of course not. Neither do I.

    Johnny. All right, then. For the 97th time—marry me!

Lola gets up, takes a step or two, and turns back to him.

    Lola. Here's what I'll do. The only lawyer in the world I trust is in New York—Fred Davis. I'll fly back tomorrow and have him check my contract. I'll give you my answer before the week's up.

She throws her arms around him.

    Lola (*Continued*). I'll make a reservation and pack my things. Come up and splash around while I'm gone. And miss me! Please miss me!

    Johnny. Are you kidding! Anything I can do?

    Lola. Without me? No.

She kisses him goodbye and hurries toward her cabana. Johnny heads for the driveway where his car is.

DISSOLVE TO

153 LOLA'S DRIVEWAY

As Johnny gets into his car, a police car drives up. Sergeant Stout gets out and crosses to Johnny.

154 CLOSE SHOT—JOHNNY AND STOUT

As they shake hands.

    Sergeant Stout. Boy, am I lucky! I was going to ask Miss Murray for your number.

    Johnny. You have some news?

    Sergeant Stout. Not really. Our kind of routine goes on forever. But once in a while—like last night, one of my boys overheard a punk in some Venice beatnik joint talking about how he knew you.

    Johnny. Oh?

Sergeant Stout. Probably one of those name-droppers—heard someone mention you were in town. Doubt if he really knows you. Name's Fernandez—Ramon Fernandez.

155 CLOSE-UP—JOHNNY

He had expected the name to be Milo. He does a good job of covering up his relief.

Johnny. Doesn't ring any bell. I've only been out here a couple of weeks. He could have seen me at Larry Hunt's—where I work. What's he look like?

156 TWO-SHOT

Stout's manner is casual.

Sergeant Stout. A bit on the Latin-lover side. Cocky.

Johnny. No. Definitely no.

Sergeant Stout. It figures. But we have to check. You see, Fernandez is wanted in San Francisco for pushing dope.

Johnny. That's not exactly nice, is it? But it was nice running into you, Sergeant. Oh, you can reach me at the Clinton Arms. So long.

157 LONGER SHOT

Johnny drives off. The Sergeant moves toward the police car.

DISSOLVE TO

158 LONG SHOT—JET PLANE

The background is a bank of clouds.

DISSOLVE TO

159 PROCESS SHOT—INTERIOR PLANE

Wearing a smart suit, Lola is studying a copy of her contract.

DISSOLVE TO

160 INSERT OFFICE DOOR

Printed on the glass is:

    FREDERICK DAVIS
    ATTORNEY AND COUNSELOR AT LAW

DISSOLVE TO

161 MEDIUM CLOSE SHOT—INTERIOR DAVIS'S NEW YORK OFFICE

This is a modern office, with a huge window through which can be seen a vista of skyscrapers. Seated at his desk, Davis, white-haired and vital, taps the contract Lola was re-reading on the plane. Lola is seated close beside him.

Davis. I've really given this the fine-toothed comb, Lola, and they've got you over the well-known barrel. Pretty though they are, you haven't got a leg to stand on. So now then—let's talk about something pleasant. What can I give you for a wedding present?

Lola. Thank you, Fred, but Johnny is present enough.

Davis. Good to hear you say that—but I'll pay no attention. I hate to see you leave so quickly. Goodbye, dear.

Lola gives him a warm smile and gets up. He rises too.

Lola. Next time I'll bring Johnny with me.

Davis. You do that. Goodbye, dear.

He kisses her cheek. She gives him a big hug.

Lola. 'Bye, Fred. Thank you for trying.

She walks out of the scene, right to left.

162 MEDIUM SHOT—DAVIS'S OUTER OFFICE

This is a small reception room. A secretary, Miss Frazer, gets up from her desk in the background as she sees Lola coming from Davis's office. Thinking of getting back to Johnny, Lola is all smiles.

Lola. 'Bye, Miss Frazer.

Miss Frazer. Goodbye, Miss Murray. Don't make it so long before we see you again.

Lola. I won't. Word of honor.

Miss Frazer goes into Davis's office. CAMERA PANS *with Lola as she moves forward and reaches for the handle of the corridor door. Just before she gets to it, the door opens, disclosing a nice-looking woman with the usual middle-aged spread. She stops in her tracks and stares at Lola.*

The woman. Lola Murray!

Lola stares back, but she is not quite sure. Then she knows.

Lola. Gladys! Well, for heaven's sake. What on earth are you doing here?

Gladys (*Hugging her, then holding her at arm's length*). Now that's a pretty goofy question. Fred Davis has been my lawyer for—but you know that. Now I'll ask you one. Haven't they got any lawyers in Hollywood, or do your pals get all those divorces just by making eyes at the judge? Don't answer that. Sit down over there, while I tell Miss Frazer to tell Mr. Davis I'm out here with you.

CAMERA SWINGS *with her as she hurries to the office door, and Lola moves to a couch with magazines on it. Gladys returns from Miss Frazer and sits down beside her, talking as she does so.* CAMERA DOLLIES CLOSE.

Gladys. She says he says he'll give me five minutes. Now then—golly! Of course, Wally and I and the kids (*She holds up four fingers.*) see all your pictures and love them, but you know something?

Lola. Nothing—absolutely nothing.

Gladys. In real life, you look prettier and, what's even worse, younger!

Lola. Don't overdo it, Gladys.

Gladys. But you do. And I'm two years younger than you.

Lola. And look it!

Gladys. Ho–ho! It is to laugh!

Lola. But you do. Ask anybody.

Gladys. I'm calling you. MISS FRAZER!

Lola. Now wait—

Miss Frazer appears from the Davis office as CAMERA PULLS BACK.

Miss Frazer. Yes, Mrs. Driscoll?

Gladys glares at Miss Frazer.

Gladys. Will you kindly cross your heart and hope to die?

Actually a bit frightened, Miss Frazer crosses her heart.

Gladys (*Continued*). Who looks younger—Miss Murray or me?

163 CLOSE-UP—MISS FRAZER

She is in an impossible spot and knows it. She tries to stall.

Miss Frazer. Well! I—er—I mean that's pretty difficult to say—

164 CLOSE-UP—GLADYS

Triumphantly she smiles.

Gladys. The eyes just said it. You're excused.

165 CLOSE-UP—LOLA

Outraged.

Lola. Why you—that's nonsense!

166 MEDIUM SHOT

Miss Frazer is on her way back to the office. Gladys is still triumphant. CAMERA MOVES CLOSE.

Gladys. No, it isn't—but when you've got an overworked husband and four children with over-active thyroids, what's to do about my overstuffed seat?

Lola. Just a minute. There is such a thing as massage.

Gladys. Of course. And such a thing as a Cadillac. But who's got the time or the money—present company excepted?

Lola is indignant.

Lola. Now that's a nasty crack!

Gladys. It was. Plain envy. You just keep right on doing whatever you're doing.

Lola. I have to, darling. This (*Indicating her face.*) is part of what they pay me for. And I don't do so much to it—(*Pantomiming as only Lola can.*) A little of this—little of that. And watching my food.

167 CLOSE-UP—GLADYS

A broad grin of approval.

Gladys. More power to you. You'll still look the same five years from now—mmm, well, four anyway.

168 CLOSE-UP—LOLA

That one hurt.

Lola. Hey! Quiet, please. I'll look like this for at least—well—for quite a while.

169 CLOSE-UP—GLADYS

Fascinated.

Gladys. You mean you're gonna have it lifted?

170 CLOSE-UP—LOLA

This scares her.

Lola. Lifted? Not till I'm eighty—and stop counting.

DISSOLVE TO

171 CLOSE SHOT—INTERIOR ELEVATOR

Lola is in the foreground of the shot. CAMERA MOVES CLOSER *to two teenagers who recognize Lola, nudge one another, and whisper. One of them takes an envelope and a pencil from her handbag. She holds them out to the star and smiles hopefully.*

Teenager. Would you, Miss Murray?

Lola. Of course. Er—what's your name?

Teenager. Edythe—with a "y."

Second teenager. Mine's Charlotte.

Lola (*As she writes*). Mmm. What pretty names!

172 MOVING CAMERA—AT GROUND FLOOR ELEVATOR DOOR

As Lola steps from the elevator, with other occupants of the car crowding around her and jabbering as they present various slips of paper for her to autograph, Lola, doing her best to be gracious, moves slowly—but with determination—toward the entrance door. CAMERA SWINGS *so that it is photographing her back as she makes a sudden dash and goes out the door. The crowd hurries after her.*

173 MEDIUM SHOT—EXTERIOR NEW YORK OFFICE BUILDING

A parked taxi is in the foreground of the shot. Lola hurries from the office building entrance in the background. The taxi driver is elderly with a white moustache. He is reading a book.

    Lola. You free?

    Driver. Where to, lady?

    Lola. Anywhere. 'Round the park.

    Driver. One of those, huh?

As Lola jumps in and he slams the door, the pursuing autograph hunters run up. The cab whirls away.

174 CLOSE PROCESS SHOT—THREE-QUARTERS BACK

Lola is sitting forward on the edge of her seat. The driver is in the left corner of the shot.

    Driver. You clobber somebody back there?

    Lola (*Almost haughtily*). Certainly not! I'm Lola Murray.

    Driver. So? I'm Thaddeus Rodakiewicz. I mean, should I have heard of you?

    Lola. You might have seen me in a few moving pictures.

    Driver. Not me, lady. Save my glad money for opera tickets. Lots of people love pitchers. I'm queer. Opera!

    Lola. Then I'm queer. *I* love opera.

175 PROCESS CLOSE-UP—THADDEUS

Thaddeus is skeptical.

    Thaddeus. Do, huh? What, for instance?

176 PROCESS CLOSE-UP—LOLA

Knits her brows.

    Lola, Oh—*Tannhäuser. Tristan.* Most of Wagner.

177 PROCESS CLOSE-UP—THADDEUS

He grins.

    Thaddeus. Well, what do you know? Say, would you mind chinning with an old man for a minute? I mean, you say Wagner to most New Yorkers, they think you're talkin' about the mayor.

178 PROCESS CLOSE-UP—LOLA

She smiles back at him.

    Lola. Love to. Why don't you stop along here someplace. We could sit on one of those park benches.

    Thaddeus's voice. Yes, ma'am!

179 FULL SHOT—EXTERIOR CENTRAL PARK

The cab pulls up. Thaddeus hops down and opens the door. Lola gets out. They cross to a bench and sit.

180 CLOSE SHOT—LOLA AND THADDEUS

They settle back.

    Thaddeus. I turned off the meter.
    Lola. That was very thoughtful.
    Thaddeus. No. It was pretty stupid. You with all that Hollywood loot. But I'll tell you something. Since my wife died, you're the first lady I seen I felt I'd like to jabber with.
    Lola. Now, that's even more thoughtful.

181 CLOSE-UP—THADDEUS

His expression changes as he studies Lola's face.

182 CLOSE-UP—LOLA

She is looking off at the sky and trees.

183 CLOSE-UP—THADDEUS

A look of recognition blooms.

    Thaddeus. Say—I did see you in the movies. Yes, sir! On one of those "Late, Late Shows."

184 CLOSE-UP—LOLA

Snapping out of her daydream.

    Lola. Well?

185 CLOSE TWO-SHOT

Thaddeus continues to stare.

    Thaddeus. Sure I did. Say, you're good. Real good!
    Lola. Thank you.
    Thaddeus. You're very welcome. And you know something? You haven't changed a mite—not a mite.
    Lola (*Reprovingly*). Oh—oh!
    Thaddeus. I wouldn't lie to you.
    Lola. I hope not. Funny. The first time I had a date with the man back home I'm going to marry, I made him promise never to lie to me—even if it hurt.
    Thaddeus. Well, of course. My wife and I had the same agreement—an' I never broke it.

186 CLOSE TWO-SHOT

Lola watches him almost affectionately.

    Lola. How long ago did you lose her?

187 CLOSE-UP—THADDEUS

His emotion is real beyond any doubt.

Thaddeus. Seven years. What a woman. Beautiful. Inside and out. Not like these fliberty-gibbets you see around nowadays—tryin' to act like they was teenagers. My wife was nearly ten years older'n me—but nobody'd believe it. Know her secret?
Lola's voice. Tell me.
Thaddeus. She thought young.

188 CLOSE-UP—LOLA

She searches his face eagerly.

Lola. Then you honestly don't believe that it handicaps the chances of a marriage succeeding if the woman is older?

189 CLOSE TWO-SHOT

The question puzzles Thaddeus.

Thaddeus. I just told you. Why should it? But what *is* important is that you both got to like people. Not make-believe like, but really like. Yes, ma'am. All the trouble that's ever been in this world was cooked up by people who hated people. Listen. My old man was a Pole and Poles love two things—no three. Freedom, and music, and people. Kosciusko—Paderewski. You like people?
Lola. Yes.

He watches searchingly.

Thaddeus. And your guy?
Lola. He loves 'em.
Thaddeus. Then you can love him and never worry about a thing.
Lola. Yes. I believe that too. Thank you for helping me to say that I do out loud. Well—
Thaddeus. You got to be going?
Lola. I really should—yes. This was wonderful.
Thaddeus. Kind of enjoyed it myself. What's that name again?
Lola. Lola. Lola Murray.
Thaddeus. Nice meeting you, Lola. I'm going to tell my daughter about it. She's just about your age I'll bet. She's—
Lola. Don't tell me.

They move to the cab, CAMERA PANNING WITH THEM.

Lola (*Continued*). That's one thing about a woman you should never tell anyone.
Thaddeus (*Helping her back into the cab*). By golly, guess you're right about that. Yes, sir. Amy wouldn't like that at all!

He slams the door, gets in, and drives off.

DISSOLVE TO

190 CLOSE-UP TELEPHONE—INTERIOR JOHNNY'S HOTEL ROOM—DAY

The telephone rings. Johnny's hand enters the scene and picks up the receiver. CAMERA TILTS UP *as receiver reaches Johnny's ear, and we see that he is wearing an open-at-the-throat sport shirt.*

Johnny. Hello. Oh, hi. You kidding? Who else talks like that?

191 CLOSE-UP—HAVANA—IN HIS BILLIARD ROOM

He looks unhappy.

Havana. Get out here right away, will you? I got a visitor. He's got something. He'll show it to you. Park down the road a ways. Yeah. And step on it.

He hangs up.

192 CLOSE-UP—JOHNNY

He also hangs up, stands a moment, shrugs, and walks out of the scene.

DISSOLVE TO

193 MOVING CAMERA—EXTERIOR HAVANA'S HOUSE

Johnny drives under the shade of a pepper tree in the background of the shot, glances around, then moves quickly to Havana's entrance door in the foreground, and rings the bell. As Johnny lights a cigarette, Havana opens the door. Johnny goes inside.

194 CLOSE SHOT—INTERIOR HAVANA'S HALLWAY

As Havana closes the door, he jerks his head toward the interior.

Havana. Billiard room.

He leads the way out of the shot. We hear the billiard balls (off) as someone makes a shot.

195 CLOSE SHOT—ENTRANCE TO BILLIARD ROOM

Johnny and Havana enter and stare off.

196 CLOSE SHOT—POOL PLAYER'S BACK

He is still bent over, watching the result of his shot. He straightens up, turns toward CAMERA, *and smiles as he sits on the edge of his table. It is Tony Milo.*

Milo. Well, glad you could come, Mr. P.

197 CLOSE SHOT—HAVANA AND JOHNNY

Havana obviously wants to get down to business.

Havana. Show him.

198 REVERSE THREE-SHOT

A few feet away, Milo is framed between Havana and Johnny. As he slides down from the table and comes forward, he reaches into his pocket and brings out a small square of paper which he hands to Johnny, who scrutinizes it.

199 VERY CLOSE INSERT

This is an extremely sharp snapshot of Havana and Johnny shaking hands in the compartment where they discussed how to keep Lola from testifying against Johnny.

200 CLOSE REVERSE THREE-SHOT

Johnny's eyes flick a look at Havana whose face reveals nothing, then stares at Milo's smiling face.

    Johnny. How'd you get this?
    Milo. Little idea I dreamed up, so a friend of mine took it with a telephoto lens. He's got the negative—and he's harmless. Knows from nothing. I told him it's a gag.
    Havana. Negative's for sale—to us, or the cops.
    Milo. Tell you, Mr. Pierpont. Understand it's no malarkey that you're pretty broke.
    Johnny. Flat.

Milo nods and goes on.

    Milo. And Havana here I'd always like to keep as a friend—if you know what I mean—
    Johnny (*Dryly*). I know precisely what you mean.
    Milo. And me bein' a little short myself, I said I'd be satisfied with a grand.
    Johnny. He's crazy.

201 CLOSE-UP—HAVANA

His tone is placating.

    Havana. I wouldn't go that far. You see, unless we show up at Meathead's pal's place today with the lettuce, he'll take that negative to your buddy, Sergeant Stout. . . . And one important however—I did get him down to five hundred cash, which I'll donate when that negative is negative—if you know what *I* mean.

202 CLOSE-UP—JOHNNY

While he is amused at Havana's shrewdness, he also appreciates what he is doing for him.

    Johnny. I'll contribute to that—I'll borrow it from Larry.
    Havana. That we'll talk about after we pay a visit to Ling How's camera shop in Chinatown. And we'll all go separate.

DISSOLVE TO

203 LONG SHOT—EXTERIOR HAVANA'S HOUSE

Johnny steps into his car (parked under the tree) and flips the starter. Havana's closed car backs out of the garage and takes off, followed by Johnny. Now a scooter, with Milo on the first of its two seats, appears from behind a clump of bushes and whips out of the shot behind the two cars.
DISSOLVE TO
204 MEDIUM ANGLE SHOT—EXTERIOR LING HOW'S CAMERA STORE
Johnny's car pulls up in front of the store that bears this lettering: LING HOW—CAMERA SUPPLIES. *Looking in the window, which he is using as a mirror, Havana sees Johnny's entrance and looks down the street beyond Johnny's car.*
205 MOVING CAMERA SHOT—MILO'S SCOOTER
The machine stops about half a block behind Johnny's car. Milo dismounts and strolls to the entrance of an alley that is just beyond the shop. The CAMERA HAS SWUNG WITH MILO, *so that we can now see Johnny and Havana. Milo pauses just long enough to make sure the two men see what he is doing, then disappears down the alley. Havana strolls after him. Johnny hops out of his car and follows Havana's slow walk with rapid steps.*
206 MEDIUM CLOSE SHOT—LING HOW'S ALLEY DOOR
Milo approaches the door and knocks as Havana and Johnny join him. CAMERA *moves closer as an elderly Chinese opens the door. Milo talks the dialect ignorant Americans use with foreigners.*

Milo. I friend Ling How. He here?

Chinese (*No accent*). Ling How is in San Francisco.

Milo. When'll he be back?

Chinese. Not for two weeks—perhaps longer.

Milo. There's something of mine in the safe. You know the combination?

Chinese. No. I'm sorry. Do you know Ling's sister?

Milo. Mary How? Sure. She still work at that restaurant 'round the corner?

Chinese. Yes, she does. And she has the combination.

Milo. Aiee! Thanks, grampa. We'll be back.

The Chinese bows and goes inside. Milo signals the others to follow him
DISSOLVE TO
206A MEDIUM CLOSE SHOT—INTERIOR CHINESE RESTAURANT—CASHIER'S DESK

Mary How, the cashier, is a honey, extremely pretty and with lovely manners. One of those ever cheerful little men, with a large sourpuss for a wife, is paying his check. Milo comes into the shot at an angle behind Mary and wiggles his fingers at her.

Milo. Hi, Mary.

Mary (*Polite, but unenthusiastic*). Hello.

Milo wriggles in behind the couple who are paying their lunch check.

Mary (*Continued, to the customer*). Hope you had a nice lunch.

Customer. Sure did.

Mary hands him his change.

Customer (*Continued*). Great place, great food, great cashier!

His wife. Come, Harold!

Mary. Thank you both.

Milo is next in line. He speaks quickly.

Milo. Look, Mary, you gotta get away for about ten minutes. There's something of mine in Ling's safe—

Mary. Goodness. We're pretty busy.

Milo. Is Yen around?

Mary. He was. Yes. There he is.

207 ANOTHER ANGLE—PROPRIETOR IN FOREGROUND

The cashier's desk is in the background and Johnny and Havana are on one side of the shot. Milo hurries up to the proprietor, Yen. CAMERA MOVES CLOSE.

Yen is checking a slip one of the waitresses has just handed him.

Milo. Hiya, Yen. Say, could you fix it for some other dame to handle that cashier bit for fifteen minutes maybe? You see, Ling's in Frisco and Mary's the only character knows the combo to his safe—

Yen. Well, let's see now. I think Jenny here has handled the job before.

Jenny. Yes, sir. I have.

Yen. Okay, then. You're all set. Come with me, Jenny.

He goes toward the desk. CAMERA PULLS BACK TO ALLOW *Johnny and Havana to come into the setup.*

Milo. A real break, men. You can't go wrong when you travel with Tony Milo.

Mary How comes into the scene. Milo does the honors.

Milo (*Continued*). Couple of friends of mine, Mary. Mary How, men. Let's travel, huh?

They move toward the door.
DISSOLVE TO

208 BACK ROOM—LING HOW'S CAMERA STORE

The angle shows Mary working the safe combination as the four men watch. She makes the last twist which is followed by a click; she opens the door, takes out a small envelope, checks the name on it, and hands it to Milo.

    Milo. Thank you, baby. Look, lemme—
    Mary. Oh, no, sir.
    Havana. Tell me—is there an empty room someplace?
    Mary. Right through there.

They exit.

209 MEDIUM CLOSE SHOT—LING HOW'S STOREROOM

The room is filled with all sorts of boxes containing camera supplies. Havana snaps on the light switch as the three men come in. A swinging cone-covered bulb lights up, disclosing a table, packed shelves, and a second door to the right. Havana takes out a roll of bills and turns to Milo.

    Havana. Give it to Johnny to check.
    Milo. What a character!

He hands the envelope to Johnny, who takes out the negative and holds it up to the light.

    Johnny. This is it.
    Havana. Burn it.

Johnny sets fire to the negative. It burns quickly.

    Havana (*Continued*). Okay, Meathead.

He starts to count out the bills. Someone knocks. Havana puts his hand over the money, the other hand moving to where his holster should be.

    Havana (*Continued*). Come in.

Mary How steps into the storeroom and addresses Milo.

    Mary. I'm sorry. They just told me there *is* a five dollar charge for using Ling's safe.
    Milo. I thought there would be. That's why I—here.

He tosses a bill on the table.

    Mary. It was my fault, Mr. Fernandez.
    Johnny (*As if he'd grabbed a hot poker*). Ramon Fernandez?
    Mary. Of course—

Milo grabs Havana's billfold and shoves him—hard! Havana's hand automatically goes for his gun, but the rough push cracks his head against the door jamb. He slides to the floor. Johnny grabs Milo, but Milo gives him his knee in the groin. Johnny doubles up with a groan as Milo runs to the second door. It is locked. Johnny manages to straighten up and gasp.

> **Johnny.** Not Milo. He's Fernandez—he's wanted in San Francisco for pushing dope!

Milo twists the key back and forth till it opens the door and he dashes out. Johnny staggers after him as Mary helps Havana to his feet. He shakes his head and does his best to hurry after Johnny.

210 FULL SHOT—ALLEY

This alley actually exists in Chinatown, as do all the exteriors described here. On the left side of screen there is a flight of wooden stairs which were painted red some time ago. About ten feet up, a second flight of stairs goes off profile to the left. Milo has come into the alley from the door he ran out of at the rear of the narrow passage. Now he turns and starts up the red stairs, two at a time, but a Chinese comes down the second flight. It is obvious they will collide. Milo backs down as Johnny appears from the rear of the alley. Johnny bumps into the Chinese, shoves him aside, and continues after Milo. Havana trots down the alleyway and follows the others off.

211 FULL SHOT—CHINATOWN STREET

This angle shows part of the Hong Kong Restaurant in the right background and a store, bearing the strange name, SINCERE IMPORTING, *in the left background. Milo runs through this setup, right to left,* CAMERA SWINGING WITH HIM. *Johnny is not far behind him. Havana comes along as fast as he can make it.*

212 FULL SHOT—SECOND ALLEY

This alley is opposite MOYTEL [sic] *at 946 Yale Street. Chinese children are playing in this alley. They flatten against the wall as the three men run past them, right to left. Milo manages to push a small cart so that it blocks the alley. Johnny shoves it out of the way as Havana joins him, and they hurry after Milo.*

213 ANGLE SHOT—EXTERIOR CHINATOWN—SHOOTING TOWARD BROADWAY

In the left foreground is one of those booths bearing a sign, TAKE YOUR OWN PHOTO. *Its curtain is drawn and the feet of the man, taking his own picture, show beneath it. A few passersby can be seen in the background, and in the right foreground stands a Chinese wearing one* of those huge straw hats. His back is to us as Johnny comes running up (entering right to left) and accosts him, CAMERA MOVING close.

Johnny. Did you see a man running—

214 REVERSE OVER-SHOULDER SHOT—CHINESE WITH HAT

He holds up a cup and some pencils. The sign, PLEASE HELP . . . I AM BLIND is hardly necessary.

Johnny. I'm sorry. I didn't—

He comes up with a bill and shoves it into the cup.

215 LONGER SHOT

Johnny turns away quickly, bumping into Havana who makes no comment. Johnny is embarrassed and confused.

Johnny. We were right behind him. Now he's vanished.

Havana nods and moves over to the photo booth. Johnny runs up to a white woman trundling a baby carriage and questions her, but they are far enough away so that we cannot hear what they say. Finally, Johnny tips his hat and looks toward Havana with a helpless shrug. Havana beckons to him with a broad gesture. Johnny hurries to him. CAMERA MOVES CLOSE. Havana indicates the booth.

Havana. Whoever's in there's gotta be a Narcissy—already ten minutes at least.

Johnny agrees; still, what of it? Havana points down.

Havana (*Continued*). Take a gander at those pedals—

Johnny looks down.

216 VERY CLOSE SHOT—BOTTOM CLOSED CURTAIN

The feet of the man in the booth are in the air a foot from the ground. Apparently he thinks they don't show.

217 CLOSE SHOT—BOOTH AND TWO MEN

Havana whips open the curtain. Milo, scrunched up, his feet dangling, is revealed. Havana reaches for his gun as he sits beside the thoroughly scared Milo and yanks his wallet from the latter's pocket. Next he whips the curtain closed again.

Milo's voice (*Terrified*). Don't. DON'T.

There is a silence of several seconds.

Havana's voice. I'm itchy, but maybe I won't. Be better if Johnny's high-toned copper sent you north for a nice long crate in the coop. But maybe I say no—even to that. Maybe—

Milo's voice. I'll do anything—

Havana's voice. Then fade—and never open that big yap of yours about anything. Get the picture?

Milo's voice. Sure. Sure, I got it.

Havana whips open the curtain and stows his gun. Milo practically runs, CAMERA FOLLOWING HIM. *He stops and turns back, just managing a touch of his old cockiness.*

Milo. And my name's not Fernandez neither!

He turns and runs.

218 CLOSE SHOT AT BOOTH

Havana rises and turns to Johnny.

Havana. He ain't kiddin'—it's *dirt*!

As they walk away, Johnny shudders.

Johnny. Water's goin' to feel real good!

219 TRUCKING SHOT—AT LOLA'S POOL—DAY

In a sport shirt and Bermuda shorts, Johnny is walking along toward the men's dressing rooms. Suddenly, he stops and looks down. CAMERA TILTS DOWN *to the torso of a girl. She is lying on her unfastened bra. She twists her head around and looks up. She is an eighteen-year-old replica of Lola, and equally attractive.*

The girl. Hi, John, the Third. I'm Diane. Mother said you'd show up. If you go inside and put on your whatevers, I'll put on mine.

220 CLOSE-UP—JOHNNY

With all his sophistication, it takes him a moment to answer.

Johnny. You know, somehow I have a feeling I'm on the short end of that!

221 LONGER SHOT

The prone figure of Diane is in the background as Johnny walks into the men's department of the dressing rooms. Her back to us, she sits up after fastening her bra.

DISSOLVE TO

222 MEDIUM CLOSE SHOT

Diane is standing in the shallow end of the pool, mixing herself a gin and tonic from the assorted ingredients on a tray in front of her. She looks up as Johnny walks by in his trunks.

Diane. Name it.

Johnny. Later.

CAMERA FOLLOWS *as he moves around to the springboard, makes a perfect swan dive, swims a few strokes underwater, reappears, does a crawl back to Diane, pulls himself up, and twists into a sitting position close to her.* CAMERA IS NOW CLOSE *on the couple. She smacks her lips, pleased with the drink and what she has seen.*

Diane. Mama mia! If you were any younger, I'd have to throw you back, but if you think I'm going to you're cr–r–razy!

Johnny shakes his head like a fighter clearing his head.

Johnny. I'll have that drink.

He mixes it, thinking, "Man, she's got to be kidding, but she isn't." As Johnny stirs his drink, Diane watches him like a French gourmet savoring a wine.

Diane. You going steady with anyone?

Johnny. Uh-huh.

Diane. Is it steady–steady, or just two on the seesaw—to coin a phrase?

Johnny. Steady. I've asked her to marry me.

Diane. How *do* you do! That's really steady. Look. Why don't you bring her up here so I can decide whether or not I'll permit this. But if I don't like her—

Johnny. You'll like her—but she's in New York.

223 CLOSE-UP—DIANE

She thinks this over and smiles.

Diane. Well! At least that gives me a little time.

224 CLOSE-UP—JOHNNY

He gulps his drink.

Johnny. Forget it. I told you this is steady-steady. Behave yourself!

225 CLOSE-UP—DIANE

She looks him over.

Diane. But you have such a nice mouth!

226 CLOSE TWO-SHOT

Johnny puts down his drink.

Johnny. I'm warning you.

Diane. Really nice.

Her arms go around his neck, his go around her waist. He lifts her up as if to kiss her, but just as their lips meet, he twists her across his knees and wallops her buttocks hard. She yelps.

Diane. Hey! That hurt!

Johnny. Which you probably enjoyed. But I didn't, and I don't. I don't like any part of this ridiculous game—this *seductio ad absurdum*.

Diane (*Wriggling around and sitting up*). Now he makes with the puns in Latin, already yet! An intellectual sadist!

Johnny. For the last time, lay off! Or I'll really whale the tar out of you!

Diane. You know, I think you would.

Johnny. Just try something.

Diane. You're really mean!

They stare at one another. The pool telephone rings. Diane reaches out of the shot and grabs it.

Diane (*Continued*). Hello? This is she. Oh, hello. Nice to talk to you. When? Why I—I guess in about an hour. Sure. That would be fine. See you.

She hangs up and turns to Johnny.

Diane (*Continued*). That was Marv Grafton—he directs at Pyramid. There's a bit in his new picture I might be right for. Wants me to come flyin'. Would you drive me there?

Johnny. Of course. Glad to.

And he is. It will definitely put a stop to Diane's sexy maneuverings. He jumps up and holds out his hand to Diane.

DISSOLVE TO

227 MEDIUM SHOT—INTERIOR GRAFTON'S OFFICE

The office is tastefully decorated. Grafton, a bright-looking man in his forties, is talking to Johnny in the foreground of the shot. Both he and Diane have finished reading the scripts he has given them.

Grafton. Sorry I have to ask you to read this with Diane, Mr. Pierpont, but all our contract boys are working out at Chatsworth.

Johnny (*Smiling*). Glad to help—unless it turns out not to be—

Grafton. Don't worry about it. This guy's just a guy—like yourself.

Johnny. Okay—if *you* can take it.

Grafton. Fine. (*To Diane.*) Let's see now, Diane. Er—start here. I'll watch from back there.

He moves quickly to his chair behind the desk in the background.

228 CLOSE SHOT—GRAFTON

As he sits down.

Grafton. Whenever you're ready—

229 MEDIUM CLOSE REVERSE SHOT—DIANE AND JOHNNY

They both glance at one another. Johnny nods. Diane starts to read.

Diane. Man! What crazy music. Get that cool beat!

Johnny. It's all right.

Diane. All right? Get you. Name something better!

Johnny is going great guns.

    Johnny. Hmm—er—*Boris.*

    Diane. Boris who?

    Johnny. *Boris Godonov*—the opera.

    Diane. Please! Those fat sopranos dying of consumption—consumption of candy bars! You can have Boris Whatsis.

    Johnny. Thanks. But I've got it. The whole album—with Chaliapin. That mad scene sends chills up and down my back. What a great artist!

230 CLOSE-UP—GRAFTON

He is listening to Johnny with real interest. Diane's voice comes over the close-up.

    Diane's voice. Man, you really are a long-haired iggy.

231 CLOSE SHOT—DIANE AND JOHNNY

Johnny smiles.

    Johnny. I'll get a haircut.

    Diane. You're cute. A little on the square side—but definitely cute. In fact, between you and me and the bedpost—you send me. Shall we neck?

    Johnny. Now, once in a while, you talk sense.

They kiss.

232 CLOSE SHOT—GRAFTON—THEN TRUCKING

Grafton gets up and CAMERA FOLLOWS HIM *as he moves around the deck and joins Diane and Johnny, speaking as he walks.*

    Grafton. Good, Diane—very good indeed. Tell you what. Bone up on that scene on page 68—same two characters. I'll be right back.

He exits from the shot. Diane turns to Johnny.

    Diane. Hey! You're good.

    Johnny. Cut it. But you heard what the man said about you.

    Diane. And what does this man say?

    Johnny. Let's study that scene.

    Diane. What a one-track mind!

    Johnny. Read it. Go ahead.

Diane finds the place.

    Diane. Okay, slave driver—top of 68. (*Reading from the script.*) I just don't dig this kind of an arty party, Billy. Who reads poetry?

    Johnny. Mr. Carl Sandburg does—his own—and it's beautiful.

    Diane. Never heard of him.

Johnny. I thought maybe you'd seen him on TV—with Gene Kelly.

233 CLOSE SHOT—OFFICE DOOR

Grafton is standing there with Henry Meizner.

    Diane's voice. When he dances—it's music!

Meizner's eyebrows go up and his eyes shift to Johnny.

234 CLOSE SHOT—DIANE AND JOHNNY

Johnny is really "in" the scene.

    Johnny. Yes, it is—which goes for Mr. Sandburg's poetry too. The greatest. Even I know some of it. Listen to this:

        "Man is a long time coming.

        Man will yet win.

        Brother may yet line up with brother:

        This old anvil laughs at

        Many broken hammers.

        There are men who can't be bought—"

Applause comes over the scene. The two look off.

235 CLOSE SHOT—AT OFFICE DOOR

The two men continue applauding as they move to Diane and Johnny, who gets up as CAMERA BRINGS THEM CLOSE.

    Grafton. Well! Diane, this is Mr. Meizner. And Henry, shake hands with John Pierpont, the Fourth.

    The trio. Happy to meet you. Glad to know you. How d'you do.

    Grafton. You can see what Mr. Meizner thinks. Right, Henry?

    Meizner. Quite so. You've got a lot of your mother's looks and talent. And, Marvin, you certainly can pick them. (*Turning to Johnny.*) And where have you been all our lives?

    Johnny. What?

    Meizner. I'm offering you that part you just read and our option on a seven-year contract—starting at a hundred a week.

Johnny is quite honestly bowled over.

    Johnny. But I've never acted—

    Grafton. I'll grant you this is a one in a million shot, but David Niven hit it the first time he tried—and so did Burt Lancaster.

    Meizner. And don't forget Fred MacMurray.

    Johnny. No, really. I'm flattered, but no.

    Meizner. A hundred and fifty.

    Johnny. Besides, I've got a job. Demonstrating for Larry Hunt—the coptoglider man.

Meizner. Two hundred!

Johnny. Sorry.

Meizner (*Putting his hand on Johnny's shoulder*). If you do this for me, I'll okay this young lady's mother making that outside picture she's been bugging me to let her do.

Johnny. She's in New York—talking to her attorney there. And it would still be no. Thank you again. Come along Diane.

They move toward the door.

DISSOLVE TO

236 CLOSE-UP—JOHNNY—INTERIOR TELEPHONE BOOTH

He is controlling his exuberance.

Johnny. Can you imagine my cutting my own throat and letting her off that marriage deal—I mean, if she says yes.

237 CLOSE-UP—HAVANA

He, too, is smiling.

Havana. Glad tidings! You really pulled a Houdini! Oh, I put like adhesive tape on the Meathead's mouth. He's talking now like he's got Lola Murray's chick kid interested in him.

238 CLOSE-UP—JOHNNY

Johnny makes a face.

Johnny. With that one—it could happen. Four-leaf clovers to us, "Mahster"!

He hangs up.

DISSOLVE TO

239 MEDIUM CLOSE SHOT—INTERIOR BAR

Johnny and Larry Hunt are looking at the TV screen which is tipped into one corner of the shot. Johnny looks at his wrist watch.

Johnny. I caught this Late Show last night. The close-up I mean goes on at exactly 12:10. Watch now. There. Isn't that beautiful?

240 CLOSE SHOT—TV SCREEN

A long, silent shot of Lola Murray. She is ravishing.

Johnny's voice. How about that?

241 CLOSE SHOT—JOHNNY AND LARRY

Johnny is really gone.

Johnny. Ever see anything so lovely?

Larry watches his friend almost with alarm.

Larry. That must be seven years old. Man, you've really gone overboard.

Johnny keeps on looking. He hasn't heard a word.

DISSOLVE TO

242 PANNING SHOT—INTERIOR JOHNNY'S HOTEL—NITE

CAMERA SWINGS *with Johnny as he comes through the entrance door and goes to the desk. The night clerk, a smart aleck, hands Johnny his key with a wink.*

Johnny. What's the wink for?

Clerk. For instance. I mean *good* night, sir. But really good!

Johnny shrugs.

Johnny. You've been drinking the ink, Otis.

He turns and walks out of the shot toward the elevator (off).

DISSOLVE TO

243 INTERIOR JOHNNY'S ROOM

The key turns in the lock, the door opens, and Johnny snaps on the light. Johnny stares at something off scene.

Johnny. Hmm. Reason for wink. For instance.

244 CLOSE SHOT—JOHNNY'S BED.

Diane, wearing a check sport shirt of Johnny's, is asleep in his bed. She moves slowly in a manner which does interesting things to the unbuttoned shirt.

245 CLOSE-UP—JOHNNY

He hustles forward.

246 CLOSE SHOT—DIANE IN BED

Johnny pulls the shirt together and buttons it up, starting at the bottom. Diane opens one eye. Johnny addresses her severely.

Johnny. How did you get in here?

Diane (*Smiling*). Human cupidity. Otis likes ten buckaroos.

Johnny. That Otis! I'll bet he gives courses in juvenile delinquency.

Diane sticks out her lower lip.

Diane. Otis adores me. I give him instant erotic reaction. Which is more than I do to you. Or is it?

She pats the bed. Johnny is figuring what he's up against. This one is perfectly capable of screaming for help if he's too unfriendly. As casually as possible, he sits down beside her. She kisses him.

Diane (*Continued*). That's better. Except—well—aren't you a trifle overdressed?

Johnny. I just got here.

He rises and moves quickly to the nearest closet, CAMERA FOLLOWING, *shedding his coat and tie as he goes, hanging them up on a hanger on* the door, which he uses to block Diane's view of him. (She is no longer in the shot.)

    Johnny (*Continued, talking a blue streak*). You know, you make one minor mistake in your approach to the "Sex Problem"—

247 CLOSE-UP—DIANE

Trying to see him around the closet door jamb.

    Diane. Who thinks that's a *problem*?

248 CLOSE SHOT—JOHNNY

He slips on a dressing gown as he talks, finds a muffler which might make a good gag, and shoves it into a pocket of the robe.

    Johnny. Only the approach, Cleopatra. A tactful young dazzler should befuddle the male she's after into thinking—even though you and I and Bernard Shaw know the opposite is true—that the man is the pursuer. It flatters the idiot!

He looks around the door to see how he's doing.

249 CLOSE-UP—DIANE'S LEG AND FOOT

The toes wiggle at Johnny, then CAMERA MOVES TO *her head and shoulders as she answers him.*

    Diane. Of course Shaw's right. Naturally woman's the pursuer. Good old Life Force! It made us that way. Can't help it. But before you let my old lady sign you on the spotted line, you might at least treat the "younger degeneration" with more—Oh, come here!

She reaches out and yanks him into the scene. He lands partly on the floor.

    Diane (*Continued*). Listen to me, Artful Dodger. Before Lolita the Great took off, I gave her a hot tip. I told her to go see your old man, dress the part, tell him she doesn't need his money. And she agreed.

Johnny crawls to his knees.

    Johnny. She agreed to what?

    Diane. To have a heart-to-heart with Pompous Pierpont.

    Johnny. You know what'll happen if he tells her—that I—oh, YOU!

He moves quickly to the telephone, CAMERA FOLLOWING *and holding him in a* HEAD CLOSE-UP.

    Johnny (*Continued*). Get me the Hotel Pierre in New York. That's right. A person-to-person call to Lola Murray.

He lowers the phone. He mumbles to himself.

    Johnny (*Continued*). Got to tell her the truth—all of it—before she talks to him.

His eyes light on Diane. They gleam murderously.
Johnny (*Continued*). You and your ideas! You're going to look very pretty—DEAD!

250 CLOSE-UP—DIANE
She realizes that something terrible may happen.
Diane. Why? What have I done?

251 CLOSE-UP—JOHNNY
He whips out the muffler and waves it.
Johnny. I'll strangle you!
The operator's voice mutters something.
Johnny (*Continued*). No—not you. She's what? Checked out? Oh, no. That's the end!
He hangs up, turns to Diane—who is out of the shot.
Johnny (*Continued*). Go get your clothes on!
Still wearing Johnny's shirt, Diane walks through the shot on her way to the chair where her clothes are. The moment she is out of the scene, Johnny's shirt comes sailing into his arms. He looks straight at her without seeing her—the crowning insult.
Johnny (*Continued*). Listen to me. I've done the most dreadful thing. You see, if Lola's lawyer back there has told her Pyramid can keep her from working, she'll marry me. But what she doesn't know is that it's quite possible that if she doesn't marry me, I'll go to jail because—oh, it's too complicated to explain, except that I love her. But if her talk with my old man has let a very black cat out of the bag, Lola won't believe that I do.
Almost dressed, Diane re-enters the scene as CAMERA PULLS BACK.
Diane. Why would she doubt you?
Johnny. Never mind. When I get you home, you stay there till Lola calls or wires and then buzz me here. And don't you dare to get out of earshot of that telephone, or I *will* strangle you.
Diane. Hmm. If she doesn't call before the middle of the afternoon, I won't be there. I've got a date with a character who's so loathsome he fascinates me.
Johnny snaps his muffler threateningly.
Johnny. You'll be there!
Diane gives him a nasty look, steps into her shoes, and they head for the door.
DISSOLVE TO

252 CLOSE SHOT—JOHNNY—INTERIOR HOTEL ROOM

He has finished breakfast and is sipping a second cup of coffee, dressed in gray trousers and a sport shirt. The telephone rings. He snatches the receiver.

Johnny. Hello. My darling! Am I glad to hear you!

253 CLOSE SHOT—LOLA—AT STUDY TELEPHONE

She is wearing a suit. She smiles.

Lola. You sound very nice yourself. How soon can you get here?

254 CLOSE-UP—JOHNNY

Relieved at her warm tone of voice.

Johnny. So fast you'll think I came by Larry's coptoglider.

255 CLOSE-UP—LOLA

Still smiling.

Lola. Slow down, astronaut. I'm going to change into something cooler—

256 CLOSE-UP—JOHNNY

Johnny laughs.

Johnny. Make it fast, my love—er, what did you think of my old man?

257 CLOSE-UP—LOLA

She takes off her hat and pats her hair.

Lola. I didn't bother to see him. I wanted to get back to his son. I'll meet *him* at the wedding.

258 CLOSE SHOT—JOHNNY

Now everything seems wonderful.

Johnny. Coming, ready or not!

He takes one last swallow of coffee, jumps up, grabs a sports jacket, starts to put it on, then thinks of something, moves to the telephone, and picks up the receiver.

Johnny (*Continued*). This is Mr. Pierpont. Would you get me Mr. Henry Meizner at the Pyramid Studio, please. Yeah. Thanks.

He hangs up and finishes putting on the sports jacket. The telephone rings.

Johnny (*Continued*). Pierpont talking. Hello. How are you, Mr. Meizner? I've been thinking about that acting contract. Yes. I'll tell you what I'll do. If you'll send Miss Murray a letter giving her the right to make one picture a year not on the Pyramid lot—I'll be delighted to sign your option—at the last figure you mentioned. That's right. That was it. Thank you, sir.

He hangs up and dashes out of the room.

DISSOLVE TO

259 PANNING SHOT—EXTERIOR LOLA'S DRIVEWAY—DAY

As Johnny whirls up the driveway, a motor scooter, doing over thirty-five comes down it. The driver of the scooter lowers his head as he approaches. His passenger is Diane. As he nears the house, Johnny stops, twisting around to get a second look.

260 POV SHOT

The scooter disappears down the driveway.

261 CLOSE SHOT—JOHNNY

He still isn't sure who the man was. He gets out of his car, crosses to the entrance door, and bangs with the knocker. CAMERA DOLLIES CLOSE. *Winton opens the door.*

262 CLOSE SHOT—INTERIOR HALLWAY

His back to CAMERA, *Winton finishes opening the door.*

 Winton. How d'y'do, sir?

Johnny answers as he enters and Winton closes the door behind him.

 Johnny. Fine, thank you. Who was that man on the scooter?

 Winton. I never saw him before. Miss Diane let him in herself.

 Johnny. Oh. I believe Miss Murray's expecting me—

 Winton. Yes, sir. She asked me to tell you to wait in the den. She'll be right down.

 Johnny. Right.

He walks out of the shot.

263 MEDIUM SHOT—INTERIOR DEN

Johnny comes in and moves to a table as Winton crosses in the background. Johnny picks up a fan magazine with Lola's picture on the cover. He thumbs through the pages, then turns as he sense Lola approaching.

264 MEDIUM SHOT ENDING AS A CLOSE SHOT

Lola is coming down the last steps of the stairway. As she moves closer, we can see that there has been a drastic change in her since she talked to Johnny on the telephone. She stops walking. She is now close to CAMERA. *Her eyes look at him accusingly.*

265 CLOSE-UP—JOHNNY

His smile of greeting fades away as he confronts her.

 Johnny. What's the matter? What happened?

266 CLOSE-UP—LOLA

The accusing eyes stare at him

 Lola. She's told me.

267 CLOSE-UP—JOHNNY
He thinks hard and fast.
   Johnny. You mean Diane has?
268 CLOSE-UP—LOLA
She nods.
   Lola. Everything.
269 CLOSE SHOT—JOHNNY
CAMERA SWINGS *with him as he moves close to her so that she, too, is in the shot. He speaks as he moves.*
   Johnny. There isn't any everything. There isn't any anything.
   Lola. You promised me once that you'd never lie to me—
   Johnny. And I won't, but if you'll tell me what she said about me—I—I—what was it?
   Lola. It was true.
   Johnny. But what exactly did she say?
270 CLOSE-UP—LOLA
What Diane told hers till hurts and her whole attitude shows it.
   Lola. That you had told her that all you wanted from me was money—to get yourself out of some horrible mess you're in.
271 CLOSE-UP—JOHNNY
Furious.
   Johnny. She was lying—although it's true I am in a mess.
272 HEAD CLOSE-UP—LOLA
Sick at heart.
   Lola. And you said I must be an idiot if I thought you wanted anything else from a broken-down has-been!
273 HEAD CLOSE-UP—JOHNNY
Cold with anger.
   Johnny. What a horrible lie! Total! I'll kill that little tramp! Let me tell you what's behind this. The first minute she laid eyes on me she made a play—just for kicks. And I paddled her bottom. To get even with me, I guess, she dreamed up this rubbish. Sure. That's it. The woman scorned angle. But she's no woman—she's a cheap little nympho!
274 HEAD CLOSE-UP—LOLA
Shocked.
   Lola. Johnny!
275 CLOSE TWO-SHOT
Johnny has a sudden idea.

Johnny. Where did she go with that date of hers?
Lola. I've no idea—
Johnny. Try to think—so I can find her and bring her here and wallop the truth out of her.
Lola. That *was* the truth.
Johnny. You don't believe that. You can't! Wait a minute. Before I left my hotel, I called Henry Meizner at Pyramid. He finally promised me he'd send you a letter—yes—you'll have it tomorrow—stating that you *do* have the right to make one picture a year off the Pyramid lot. You're an actress again. If I wanted your money, would I have done that?

For the first time, Lola begins to feel the truth from Johnny. She moves to a chair and sits down.

276 CLOSE-UP—LOLA

She presses her fingers to her forehead.

Johnny's voice. I couldn't lie to you. I love you!

Lola gestures that she wants to think. The telephone rings. Lola reaches out of the shot and picks up the receiver.

Lola. What? Who is this?

Her face tenses.

Lola (*Continued*). Where? Say that again—slowly. Yes. Yes, I'll bring it. I understand. Let me talk to her.

277 CLOSE-UP—JOHNNY

Watching and listening.

278 HEAD CLOSE-UP—LOLA

As she waits.

Lola. Diane! Are you all right? Yes. Yes. No, I won't. Of course. It shouldn't take more than an hour. I'll hurry, my darling.

Lola hangs up, with a deep release of her breath.

279 MOVING CLOSE-UP—JOHNNY

He walks quickly to Lola and kneels beside her as he speaks.

Johnny. Where is she?
Lola. Someone's kidnapped her. He said if I called the police, he'd—he has a knife.
Johnny. He'd use it too. Don't call 'em. What did he tell you to do?

Lola does a good job of controlling herself.

Lola. I'm to get $50,000 in cash from the bank and drive with it—of course, I must be alone and no one must follow me—to the entrance of the Griffith Park Observatory—

Johnny. Smart. Public place, but very few people around outside.

Lola. He said there's one ashcan under a street light there that's yellow. I'm supposed to bring the bills wrapped in the pages of a newspaper and toss them into that ashcan. He'll watch me drive off and pick them up when I'm way down the hill someplace.

Johnny. Hmm. Will the bank let you have that much without asking any questions?

Lola. I'm sure Mr. Gaddis will.

Johnny. Good luck, then. Do exactly what he told you to do—except when you drive down the hill, turn around at the first crossroad and drive up again slowly. Just leave the rest to me—understand?

Lola. Yes, my darling. I must go now—

Johnny. Just one second. I've got to tell you the whole truth about that mess I'm in—

Lola. All right. But quickly!

Johnny. Okay. Here's what it's all about—

He starts to explain.

DISSOLVE TO

280 PROCESS SHOT—UPHILL—GRIFFITH PARK

The angle is three-quarters right to left. Lola's face is tense as she hurries to deliver the money.

281 FULL SHOT—SHOOTING DOWNHILL FROM CREST NEAR OBSERVATORY

Lola's long car goes by CAMERA, right to left.

282 REVERSE LONG SHOT

Lola's car enters right to left and parks close to the street light where the yellow ashcan is. Beyond, we see the impressive façade of the Observatory. Lola gets out of the car, the newspaper-wrapped package under her arm.

283 MEDIUM SHOT—STILL TOWARD OBSERVATORY

The kidnapper is partly hidden by the foliage of a tree on the left side of the shot. Behind him is the Observatory.

283A MEDIUM CLOSE SHOT—REVERSE

Lola comes close to the ashcan, but a couple walks by in the direction away from the Observatory. Lola hesitates, pretending to notice something in the newspaper.

284 CLOSE SHOT—CLUMP OF TREES—JOHNNY

The copter is behind him. We can hear its motor. Johnny raises a pair of field glasses and looks off.

285 CLOSE SHOT—THE KIDNAPPER

As he watches Lola, we get a good look at him. It is Tony Milo.

286 REVERSE CLOSE SHOT—LOLA

She raises the lid of the ashcan, tosses in the money, and moves off toward her car.

287 CLOSE SHOT—JOHNNY AND COPTER

The copter rises up out of the shot.

288 LONG SHOT (PROBABLY MINIATURE)—COPTER

As it comes up above a clump of fir trees and sails out of the shot.

289 CLOSE-UP—MILO

A small smile as he watches Lola.

290 FULL SHOT TOWARD OBSERVATORY

Lola crosses to her car in the foreground, gets in, and drives away. The road curves around to the left and starts downhill. Driving at normal speed, Lola makes this turn.

291 REVERSE ANGLE—AND CLOSER

Lola makes the turn and goes down the hill.

292 CLOSE SHOT—MILO

He watches Lola go, then glances at his wrist watch.

293 SKY SHOT AGAINST CLOUDS (PROBABLY MINIATURE)

The coptoglider moves across screen, left to right, and begins to drop slowly toward the ground.

294 GRIFFITH PARK ROADWAY UPHILL

A crossroad branches into this main, uphill road, joining it from the right. Lola's car enters the shot from the crossroad, turns left into the uphill road, and passes CAMERA, *right to left.*

295 CLOSE-UP—MILO

He glances again at his watch and moves out of the shot.

296 MEDIUM LONG SHOT

The yellow ashcan is in the extreme foreground. Milo walks with assumed casualness. As he comes near the ashcan, a couple of kids run up to it, throw an old book of comics into it, replace the cover, which Lola had leaned against its side, and run off. Milo passes the can and walks by it, left to right.

297 TRUCKING SHOT

We repeat the action of the last scene, but now Milo is in a waist figure so that we clearly see all his reactions. CAMERA STOPS TRUCKING *as Milo comes abreast of his motor scooter, which is parked correctly, facing the Observatory. Milo mounts the scooter and revs it. Then he dismounts. As he starts back toward the ashcan, a teenager, cigarette in mouth and patting his pocket, stops him.*

Teenager. Got a match, dad?

Milo fishes for a package, finds one, and hands it to the youth.

Milo. Keep 'em.

Teenager. Thanks, dad.

He exits.

298 LONG SHOT—SHOOTING TOWARD OBSERVATORY

Milo is in the foreground, still some distance from the ashcan. The teenager comes toward us and walks out of the shot. Milo turns toward CAMERA *to watch him go. At this moment, Johnny's coptoglider lands on the broad expanse of lawn in front of the Observatory. Milo starts to turn.*

299 REVERSE CLOSE-UP—MILO

As he turns and stares, startled, at the apparition.

300 CLOSE SHOT—JOHNNY

He unfastens his belt and runs forward.

301 REVERSE CLOSE SHOT—MILO

As he runs to the ashcan, CAMERA SWINGS WITH HIM. *He gets there a step or two ahead of Johnny, snatches off the ashcan cover, and grabs the money. Johnny sprints into the scene, calling out.*

Johnny. Drop that!

Milo. Make me!

As though it came from nowhere, he brandishes a switchblade. Johnny moves back a step, bends quickly, and picks up the ashcan cover. They circle one another.

302 LONG SHOT

Except for a couple of children, the entire area is deserted.

303 MEDIUM CLOSE SHOT—JOHNNY AND MILO

Milo makes a vicious swipe at Johnny with the knife. Johnny clips Milo's wrist with the edge of the cover. The knife drops. Johnny kicks it.

304 CLOSE SHOT—THE KNIFE

It goes over the edge of the steep declivity.

305 MEDIUM CLOSE TRUCKING SHOT

Milo clasps the money and starts for the scooter. Johnny scales the cover at his legs. Milo goes down. CAMERA MOVES CLOSE. *Johnny twists Milo's free arm behind his back. He puts on the pressure.*

306 CLOSE SHOT—BOTH MEN ON THE SIDEWALK

Milo grits his teeth.

  Johnny. Where is she?
  Milo. Go—!
Johnny really bends the arm.
  Johnny. Where?
  Milo. Schoolhouse—next crest over.
Johnny grabs the money and lets Milo get up.

307 LONGER SHOT

Milo grunts and moans as though he were in agony. He goes down on one knee, grabs the ashcan cover, swings it at Johnny, who turns away just enough to escape the full impact of the blow, but he goes down. Milo grabs the money and rushes to the scooter. Johnny is just able to call out.

  Johnny. Sergeant!

307A CLOSE SHOT—NEAR OBSERVATORY—SERGEANT STOUT AND TWO OTHER PLAINCLOTHESMEN

As arranged with Johnny, they have been waiting for him to holler. Now they run forward with drawn guns.

308 MEDIUM SHOT

Lola's car coming up the hill, just as it did at the beginning of the sequence.

309 FULL SHOT

As Milo runs to the scooter and hops aboard, Lola's car passes him and Johnny, who is staggering to his feet. She comes to a stop so that the length of her car, which is exactly across the middle of the curve, prevents Milo from going downhill the way she did. He makes a quick turn to the left and hurtles down a narrow roadway, which turns off into a dirt road close to a small telescope beside the Observatory. As CAMERA SWINGS WITH THE SCOOTER, *the three cops appear in the background.*

310 REVERSE LONG SHOT

The Observatory is out of the shot behind CAMERA. *Sergeant Stout and his two men are in the extreme foreground. Milo is coming straight at them. In the extreme background, Lola is joining Johnny. Stout calls out to Milo.*

  Stout. Stop—or we'll shoot!

But Milo doesn't stop. As he comes close to CAMERA, *he turns sharply to the left and hurtles out of the shot.*

311 FULL SHOT—DIRT ROAD, TREES, AND EMBANKMENT

The scooter and Milo (a reasonable facsimile) shoot off the dirt road and down the embankment.

312 REVERSE SHOT

CAMERA *is at the base of a high, steep embankment. The scooter and its rider come hurtling down. An explosion. Flames.*

313 CLOSE SHOT—STOUT AND THE TWO MEN

They are looking down and feeling a bit sick.

One cop. Hardly any sense going down there, I guess.

Stout. I don't know about that. There's $50,000 of Miss Murray's that says you're wrong. Let's take a look.

The other two nod and move away.

314 CLOSE SHOT—LOLA AND JOHNNY

Johnny is pointing off.

Johnny. She's up there—in that schoolhouse. I'll go by copter. Couple of things I'd like to tell the young lady while I'm untying her, before you get there and weep over her.

He leans forward and kisses her, then limps off toward the copter.

DISSOLVE TO

315 CLOSE SHOT—INTERIOR SCHOOLHOUSE

Milo has tied Diane to the teacher's chair. Otherwise—it being the month of July—the room is empty. Johnny has already unfastened the rope that was around Diane's legs and arms. Now he unties the gag and frees her mouth.

Diane. That cheap louse! I'll kill him!

Johnny. It won't be necessary. He's dead.

Diane. What?

Johnny. He went off a cliff in that scooter.

Diane. Oh! How horrible for me to have said that!

Johnny. Not as horrible as some of the things you said (*Tapping his chest.*) about *this* louse.

Diane gets up as CAMERA PULLS BACK. *She rubs her ankle where the rope cut in.*

Diane. Oh, Johnny! I'm just no good.

Johnny. That's right. But maybe you've learned something.

Diane. I hope. I hope.

She looks off.

316 CLOSE SHOT—LOLA

She is standing in the doorway.

Lola. It's my fault, suppose. I guess I've spoiled you.

CAMERA SWINGS *as she joins them and puts her arms around Diane.*
317 INTERIOR SCHOOLHOUSE
Diane begins to sniffle.

    Diane. Don't be nice to me. I got exactly what I deserved—only not nearly enough. I should be whipped for those dreadful lies I told you.

    Johnny. Look ladies, if you don't mind: two actresses emoting—I just can't take it. Give the little darling your car keys, mother, so you and I can coptoglide home together.

He gestures toward the door and they go through it, Lola giving Diane the keys as they go.

318 MEDIUM SHOT—MOVING CAMERA
Diane hops into Lola's car. Lola kisses her and she drives off. CAMERA SWINGS *with Lola as she joins Johnny at the copter. He has started the motor and they get in. He fastens the seat belt.*

    Lola (*Smiling*). You know, I was just thinking that if this were a picture and the handsome sergeant ever found out what you told me, you'd have to do a nice long stretch.

    Johnny. Don't try to get rid of me, sweet. This is for real!

He kisses her. The copter rises.

319 LONG SHOT (MINIATURE)
Against the best clouds the special effects department can produce, the Larry Hunt Coptoglider sails heavenward.

FADE OUT

www.ingramcontent.com/pod-product-compliance
Lightning Source LLC
Chambersburg PA
CBHW021833220426
43663CB00005B/229